WHAT EVERY PROGRAMMER SHOULD KNOW ABOUT OBJECT-ORIENTED DESIGN

WHAT EVERY PROGRAMMER SHOULD KNOW ABOUT OBJECT-ORIENTED DESIGN

MEILIR PAGE-JONES

Dorset House Publishing
353 West 12th Street
New York, New York 10014

Library of Congress Cataloging-in-Publication Data

Page-Jones, Meilir.
What every programmer should know about object-oriented design / Meilir Page-Jones.
p. cm.
Includes bibliographical references and index.
ISBN 0-932633-31-5
1. Object-oriented programming (Computer science) I. Title.
QA76.64.P34 1995
005.1'2--dc20 95-22067
CIP

Cover Design and Illustration: Conrad Cooper
Cover Author Photo: Eric J. Lurch

Distributed in the United Kingdom, Ireland, Europe, and Africa by John Wiley & Sons Ltd., Chichester, Sussex, England.

Distributed in the English language in Singapore, the Philippines, and Southeast Asia by Toppan Co., Ltd., Singapore and in the English language in Japan by Toppan Co., Ltd., Tokyo, Japan.

Printed in the United States of America
Library of Congress Catalog Number: 95-22067

ISBN: 0-932633-31-5 12 11 10 9 8 7 6 5 4 3 2

To Sandy

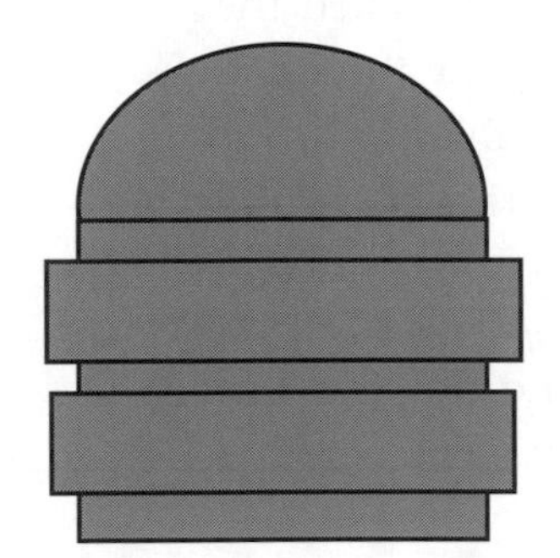

Acknowledgments

If I were explicitly to acknowledge all the people that I should, the credits would still be rolling on page 94. So, instead, I offer a blanket "thank you" to the large group of folks who've inspired me, taught me, and set me straight over the years. But some special people deserve particular thanks:

- The team who reviewed my manuscript in its early, less coherent form: Bob Binder, Tom Bragg, Tom Bruce, Mike Frankel, David McClintock, Jim Odell, David Ruble, Ben Sano, and Becky Winant.

- Steve Weiss, who (along with Walter Beck) convinced me to branch out into object orientation, long before object orientation was fashionable. Without Steve, I would never have embarked on this book.

- Larry Constantine, who hit the first homerun in software-design principles.

- Ed Yourdon and Tim Lister, for their faith in me.

- Bertrand Meyer, who has been a continual source of inspiration.

- Paul Becker, for his encouragement over the years.

- Roland Racko, for sharing his many insights.

- The sixty-two authors of the object-oriented works that sit, partially read, on my bookshelf.

- Steve McConnell, author of *Code Complete,* who said that he liked the technical parts of my previous books, but didn't find their intended humor very funny. (Steve, you'll be happy to hear that I followed your advice and kept the jokes, anecdotes, and word-plays in this book to a minimum.)

- The staff of Dorset House, high-quality prosemasters and bibliophiles, who work with great diligence and the latest technology. Their taking the not inconsiderable trouble to completely remove syllepses, litotes, split infinitives, obscure words, unwieldy sentences beginning with gerunds that run on far too long, gratuitous self-references (such as this one), parenthetical and tangential (even distracting) digressions, inconsistent tenses, and superfluous adjectives that weren't needed created a professional work from an inchoate manuscript.

- Readers of my other books who took the time to write to me. I appreciate your comments immensely.

- My e-mail correspondents, whose erudite and witty messages have educated and diverted me for (far too) many hours.

- Clients and students around the world, who shared their experiences with me and did their best to keep me honest.

- My family, who have retained their patience while living with a book-scribbling troglodyte.

Finally, no acknowledgment can be complete without a recognition of the legendary Professor Sid Dijkstra, whose contribution to software engineering is impossible to measure.

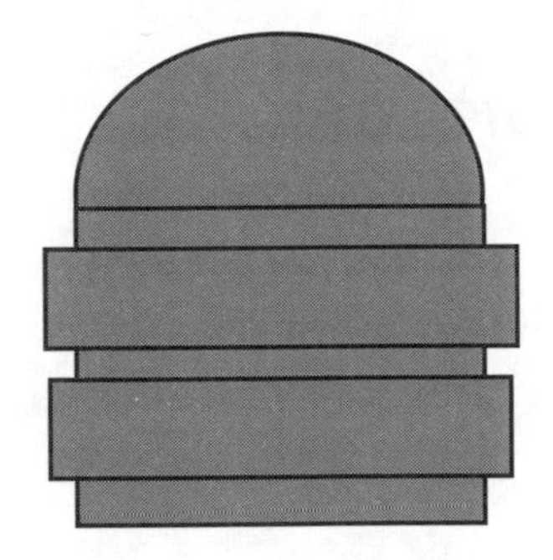

Contents

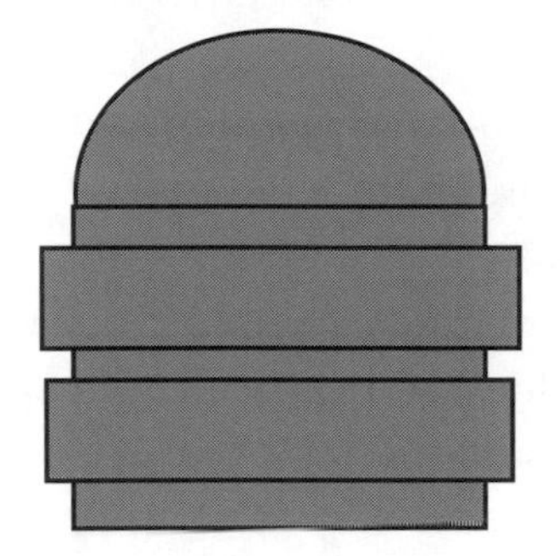

Foreword

The appearance of another book on object orientation is the sort of publishing event that can draw deep yawns from battle-scarred programming veterans and blank stares from bleary-eyed reviewers. This book, however, is a book on the object-oriented paradigm by Meilir Page-Jones, one of the most consistently lucid thinkers and readable authors in software development today. And that makes this book worthwhile reading for anyone interested in truly understanding what object orientation is about, including those reviewers and programmers who think they already have it figured out.

What Every Programmer Should Know About Object-Oriented Design may not be the first book on object orientation, but the time it has taken to write it has paid off in the wealth of experience that it incorporates. The book is filled with fresh insights on object-oriented development, from the uses and abuses of inheritance, to how to model dog owners and panda bears in software. It is vintage Page-Jones, meaning up-to-the-minute and unflaggingly intelligent.

I first met Meilir because he had done a paperback popularization of the book on structured design I wrote with Ed Yourdon. Meilir's book, titled *Practical Guide to Structured Systems Design* (Yourdon Press/Prentice Hall, 1980), was an immense success, outselling my book severalfold for the simple reason that it was much better written and a whole lot easier to understand. When, in 1989, I learned that both of us would be speaking at the same conference, I was eager to meet this author who had so effectively taken the substance of structured design and turned it into something more useful to practicing programmers. He, as it turned out, was somewhat apprehensive about meeting me, at least until I made clear to him how much I had enjoyed his book and how glad I was that he had carried the message of structured design to so many more people. We've been collaborating and challenging each other ever since. As he wrote the Foreword to my *Constantine on Peopleware* (Prentice Hall, 1995), I now have the opportunity to get even.

The truth is, Meilir is a gifted teacher who has a knack for taking complex and often misunderstood ideas and casting a conceptual light on them that makes them stand out in sharp relief from the confusing shadows. He can take a barrow-load of problems and wrap them up in a single archetypal example that makes it all seem so obvious that the rest of us are left wondering how we could ever have failed to see. What do you do when milking time arrives in the object-oriented dairy application? Do you send a message to the COW object to milk itself or a message to the MILK to un-cow itself? A moment's reflection and the need for an event manager to coordinate the milking becomes crystal clear. His clarifying examples, such as this one from a conference panel or the "PERSON OWNS DOG" conundrum found in this book, have become part of the essential folklore of object orientation.

Indeed, this book demonstrates how the long-established principles of sound design already used by practicing professionals can carry over into and be adapted for developing object-oriented systems. This book is not about broad principles, however, or small practical details, for that matter—it is about both. It maintains a relentlessly pragmatic focus based on real-world experience while distilling the essence of that experience into compact examples to guide the developer, whether novice or old hand, toward better object-oriented software solutions.

Meilir draws on extensive experience with object-oriented development, as a consultant, as a teacher, and as a methodologist. He was codeveloper of the Synthesis method, an early approach to object-oriented analysis and design, and was a collaborator on the creation of the influential Uniform Object Notation, whose features can be found today reflected in and incorporated into numerous object-oriented methods and notations, from OODL to MOSES. The latest revision of this versatile modeling medium, now called OODN, is used to illustrate and clarify examples throughout the book.

Not only are the basic techniques for designing and building with objects explained here with exceptional clarity, but they are illustrated with abundant examples, elaborated with discussions of the do's and don'ts of good object-oriented systems, and even followed by exercises and questions. Who could ask for more?

June 1995
Sydney, Australia

Larry L. Constantine
Professor of Computing Sciences
University of Technology, Sydney

Preface

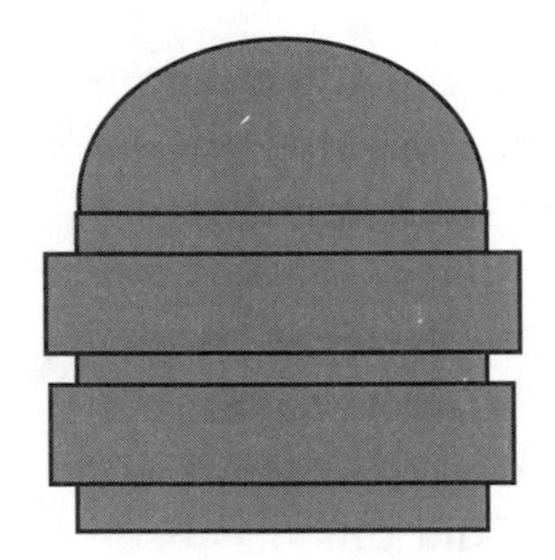

"All feel an habitual gratitude, and something of an honourable bigotry, for the objects which have long continued to please them."

—William Wordsworth, *Lyrical Ballads*

People who reviewed this book in its draft form had several questions for me, questions that perhaps you share. Let me address some of them.

Why does the title say every programmer? *Surely you exaggerate.*

I believe there are two kinds of programmers: those writing object-oriented code right now and those who'll be writing object-oriented code soon. Everyone who writes code also *designs* code—either well or badly, either consciously or unconsciously. My goal in writing this book is to encourage people to create good object-oriented designs consciously and prior to coding. To this end, I introduce notation, principles, and terminology that you and your colleagues can use to evaluate your designs and to discuss them meaningfully with each other.

Will this book teach me an object-oriented programming language?

No. Although I occasionally swoop down close to code, this isn't a book on object-oriented programming.

But if I'm learning an object-oriented language, will this book help?

Yes, it will. If you don't currently know an object-oriented programming language, you can begin your object-oriented knowledge with Chapter 1. Knowing the key concepts of object orientation will speed your learning an object-oriented language and, I hope, boost your morale as you move into unfamiliar territory. The later chapters of the book, on sound design, will also help you in getting your early programs to work successfully.

On the other hand, if you're already an experienced object-oriented programmer, you can use Parts II and III of the book to enhance the design skills that are vital to your being a rounded, professional software designer or programmer.

Why aren't the code examples in this book in C++?

I've written the code in this book in a language of my own devising, which is a blend of three popular languages: C++, Eiffel, and Smalltalk. I did this because—guess what!—there are two kinds of programmers: those who are fluent in C++ and those who aren't. If you're a C++ aficionado, then you'll find the code a breeze to translate into C++. If you're not familiar with C++, then you might have found that language's arcane syntax getting in the way of the examples. I'd like you to feel welcome in this book whatever your programming language might be.

Why isn't this book devoted to the design of windows, icons, and menus?

There are two reasons: First, I don't believe that object orientation is useful only for the design of graphical user interfaces. Second, there are many books on the market devoted solely to the topic of object-oriented window design. I want this book to cover topics that are not well covered by other object-oriented books.

Is this book about a methodology?

No. As you know, a development methodology contains much more than design. For example, there's requirements analysis, library management, and so on. Also, a true methodology needs to explain how the various development activities fit together. A lot of stuff!

So, instead of turning out a book as diffuse as many other books on object orientation, I decided to focus on a single topic: object-oriented design.

You've said a lot about what this book isn't about. What is it about?

It's about the fundamental ideas, notation, terminology, criteria, and principles of object-oriented software design. Object-oriented software is software that comprises objects and the classes to which they belong. An object is a component in which methods (which are like functions or procedures) are organized around a set of variables (which are like data). A class implements a type defining the group of objects that belong to that class.

The above modest sentences hold some surprising implications for software designers and programmers, implications that arise from the design concepts of inheritance, polymorphism, and second-order design. But, since you asked a specific question, let me give you a specific answer.

Part I of the book (Chapters 1-2) provides an introduction to object orientation. Chapter 1 summarizes the key concepts and demystifies "polymorphism," "genericity," and all the other O.O. jargon. Chapter 2 sets object orientation into the framework of previous developments in software. If you're already familiar with object orientation (perhaps by having programmed in an object-oriented language), then you can skip or skim Part I.

Part II (Chapters 3-7) covers object-oriented design notation and, in passing, illustrates many of the structures that you find in object-oriented systems. Chapter 3 introduces notation for depicting classes, along with their external and internal designs. Chapter 4 covers notation for hierarchies of subclasses and superclasses and notation for aggregate objects. Chapter 5 sets out notation for messages (both synchronous and asynchronous), while Chapter 6 discusses object-oriented modifications to traditional state-transition diagrams. Chapter 7 ties up loose ends, by covering notation for object persistence, system architecture, and the windows that form a human interface.

Part III (Chapters 8-12) covers object-oriented design principles in some depth. Chapter 8 sets the scene with the crucial notions of connascence and level-2 encapsulation. Chapter 9 explores the various domains that "classes come from" and describes different degrees of class cohesion. Chapter 10, the central pillar of Part III, uses the concepts of state-space and behavior to assess when a class hierarchy is both sound and extendable.

Chapter 11 offers some light relief, as it examines designs taken from real projects, including both the subtle and the absurd. (Chapter 11 is really about the dangers of abusing inheritance and polymorphism.) Chapter 12 rounds off the book by taking a stab at the old question, What makes a *good* class? In answering this question, Chapter 12 describes the various kinds of class interface—ranging from the seemly to the horrid—and explains design techniques such as mix-in classes and method rings, that you can use to make your classes as robust and as maintainable as possible.

Although I've added plenty of examples, diagrams, and exercises to reinforce what I say in the main text, I must admit that the material in Part III gets tough at times. Nevertheless, I decided not to trivialize or dilute important issues. Some aspects of object-oriented design *are* difficult and to suggest otherwise would be to patronize you. Anyway, I know you can take it!

Does this book cover **everything** *in object-oriented design?*

I very much doubt it. Each day, I learn more about object orientation—and I'm sure you do, too. Indeed, it would be a dull world if a single book could tell us everything about object-oriented design and leave us with nothing more to learn. And not everything in this book may be completely true! I certainly changed my mind about one or two things after I wrote my previous books, as I became older and wiser—well, older, anyway.

So, although I think that I've covered many important design principles in this book, if you're serious about object orientation you should continue to read as much as you can and always challenge what you read. And, please, do your best to refine the ideas that I've presented here.

Bottom-line, as they say: Is this book for me?

What kind of question is that? You expect me to say, "No!"? But seriously, folks, this book's for you if you are—or are about to become—a programmer, designer, systems engineer, or technical manager on a project using object-oriented techniques. Even if you're a beginner to object orientation, you can glean a lot from this book by reading Part I, practicing some object-oriented programming, and then returning to Parts II and III.

You should also read this book if you're a university student or professional programmer who has mastered the techniques of standard procedural programming and is looking for wider horizons. Much of the book's material is suitable for a final-year computer-science or software-engineering course in object orientation.

But, whatever your role in life, I hope that you enjoy this book and find it useful. Good luck!

April 1995 Meilir Page-Jones
Bellevue, Washington
CompuServe 76334,1247

WHAT EVERY PROGRAMMER SHOULD KNOW ABOUT OBJECT-ORIENTED DESIGN

Part I: Introduction

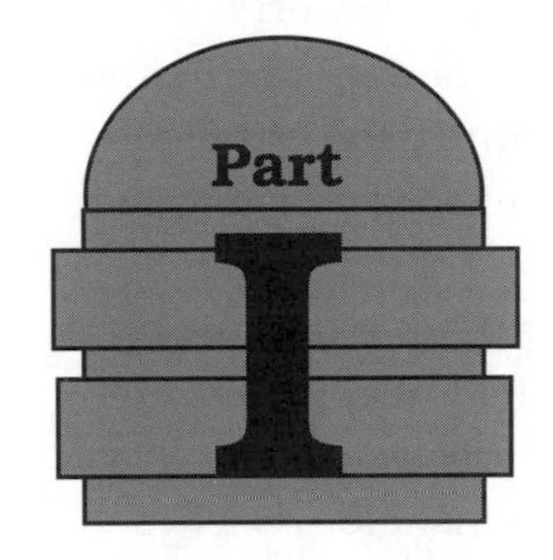

"Life is a struggle with objects to maintain itself among them. Concepts are the strategic plan we form in answer to the attack."

—Jose Ortega y Gasset, *The Revolt of the Masses*

The term "object oriented" is intrinsically meaningless. "Object" is about the most general word in the English language. Look it up in a dictionary and you'll find a definition such as

> *Object*: A thing presented to or capable of being presented to the senses.

In other words, an object is just about anything!

The word "oriented" isn't of much help either. Defined as "directed toward," it usually plays the role of casting the term "object oriented" into an adjective. Thus, we have

> *Object oriented*: Directed toward just about anything you can think of.

No wonder the software industry has failed to alight upon an agreeable definition of "object oriented." And no wonder that this lack of clarity has allowed any peddler of soft wares to claim that his shrink-wrapped miracles are "object oriented."

A few years ago, I decided to settle the matter once and for all. I grabbed a dozen doyens of the object-oriented world and locked them in a room without food or water. I told them that they'd be allowed out only when they'd agreed on a definition of object orientation that I could publish to a yearning software world.

An hour of screaming and banging within the room was followed by silence. Fearing the worst, I gingerly unlocked the door and peered in at the potentially gory sight. The gurus were alive, but sitting apart and no longer speaking to one another.

Apparently, each guru began the session by trying to establish a definition of object orientation by the time-honored scientific practice of loud and repeated assertion. When that led nowhere, each of them agreed to list the properties of an object-oriented environment that he or she considered indispensable. Each one created a list of about six-to-ten vital properties.

At this point, they presumably had two options: They could create one long list, being the union of their individual lists; or, they could create a short list that was the intersection of their lists. They chose the latter option and produced a short list of the properties that were on all the individual lists.

The list was very short indeed. It was the word "encapsulation."

So the large-number-of-gurus-in-a-brawl approach to defining object orientation didn't yield much fruit. The problem is that the term "object oriented" is devoid of inherent meaning, and so its definition is totally arbitrary.

My view is that a language (or environment) is object oriented if it possesses most of the following properties: encapsulation, information/implementation hiding, state retention, object identity, messages, classes, inheritance, polymorphism, and genericity. These also happen to be the nine most popular properties selected by the gurus in the room. I cover each of these properties in detail in Chapter 1.

In Chapter 2, I identify the originators of the object-oriented abstractions covered in Chapter 1. Following that, I analyze some current attitudes toward object orientation and discuss object orientation from an engineering point of view. I conclude Chapter 2 with a discussion of the benefits of object orientation to the various people in a software shop during each phase of software development.

What Does It Mean to Be Object Oriented, Anyway?

Although there may never be agreement among object-oriented gurus about which abstractions deserve to be on the "object-oriented list," I believe that the nine important properties of object orientation are

Encapsulation
Information/implementation hiding
State retention
Object identity
Messages
Classes
Inheritance
Polymorphism
Genericity

The best way to illuminate the meaning behind these terms is to use a small example of object-oriented code. As I discuss this code during the chapter, you'll discover that the polysyllabic jargon of object orientation is less fierce in meaning than in appearance. Indeed, you're probably already familiar with many object-oriented concepts—albeit under different names—from your previous software experience.[1]

---

[1] If you're curious about how object-oriented terminology varies from programming language to programming language, please take a look at the Blitz Guide to Object-Oriented Terminology at the end of the book.

Three notes are in order before we begin. First, the code that I present is a portion of a very simple object-oriented application. The application is a display of a miniature hominoid moving around a grid on a screen (the kind of thing that you might see in a video game). Although object orientation is certainly not limited to screen applications, such an application provides an excellent opening example.

Second, since I don't dwell much on the code's syntax or semantics, don't worry if the code doesn't make perfect sense at first. As I explain object-oriented terminology, I'll also explain the details of the code itself. I wrote the code in a made-up language, the syntax of which is an average of the syntax of several mainstream object-oriented languages. (Incidentally, the **repeat** . . . **until** . . . **endrepeat** construct has nothing to do with object orientation. It's pure structured programming—a loop with the test in the middle.)

Third, although the two classes are not perfectly designed, they're good enough for our purposes in this chapter. But if you have any complaints about, say, the class HOMINOID, stay tuned until Chapter 9, in which I cover its design deficiency. (The deficiency is called "mixed-domain cohesion.")

Now, let's look at the application by dropping in on a memo from the software-team manager to the team itself.

MEMORANDUM

From: **Alinah Koad, Software-Development Manager**

To: **The Hominoid Software Team**

Subject: **Hominoid-Controlling Software (V1.0)**

I just got word from on high that the moguls in the oak offices want a demo of our hominoid-controlling software on Monday.

In Version 1 of the software, the hominoid will simply have to navigate a bent linear path like the one shown below. You can think of it as consisting of square blocks placed in such a way as to yield a path one block wide, running from a START square to a FINISH square. Each turn along the path will be a right angle. (See Fig 1.1.)

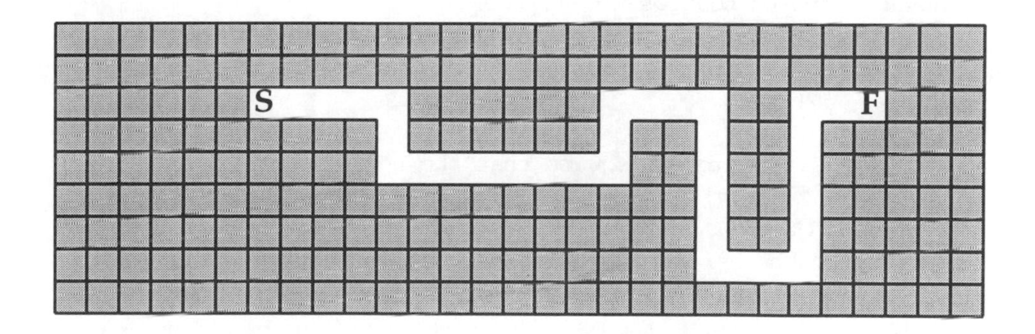

Fig. 1.1: A path through the hominoid's grid.

A single advancement by the hominoid carries it exactly one square forward (in the direction of its nose). It's important that the hominoid visit every square on the path from START to FINISH. It's even more important that the hominoid does not hit a wall, because then we'll look stupid and they won't let us install the software in the actual hardware hominoid.

Fortunately, we already have two classes written and stored in our object-oriented library. These are GRID and HOMINOID itself. So, all you have to do by Monday is write the object-oriented code that uses the methods of these classes.

If you have any more questions, you can contact me at my usual cabin in the Julius Marx Country Club. Have a nice weekend!

P.S. I enclose brief specifications for the two classes (HOMINOID and GRID) that we have in the library.

```
CLASS EXTERNAL-INTERFACE SPECIFICATIONS
        (of the classes in the library)

HOMINOID

    New: HOMINOID
    // creates and returns a new instance of HOMINOID

    set-in-grid (grid:GRID, location:SQUARE;): BOOL
    // places the hominoid in the specified grid at the
    // specified location and returns whether successful

    turn-left
    // turns the hominoid counterclockwise by 90°

    turn-right
    // turns the hominoid clockwise by 90°

    advance (no-of-squares:INT;): BOOL
    // moves the hominoid a certain number of squares along the
    // direction that it's facing and returns whether successful

    location: SQUARE
    // returns the current square that the hominoid is on

    facing-wall: BOOL
    // returns whether hominoid is at a wall of the grid

    display
    // shows the hominoid as an icon on the screen

GRID

    New: GRID
    // creates and returns a new instance of GRID with a random pattern

    start: SQUARE
    // returns the square that is the designated start of the grid

    finish: SQUARE
    // returns the square that is the designated finish of the grid

    display
    // shows the grid as a pattern on the screen
```

Key to Code:

advance	Words set in lowercase denote methods and variables
HOMINOID	Words set in all-uppercase denote classes

set-in-grid (grid:GRID, start-square:SQUARE; set-ok:BOOL);
Denotes a method that takes an object of class GRID and an object of class SQUARE, and returns an object of class BOOL

:=	Assignment operator, which means "now points to"
var set-ok	Denotes a variable named **set-ok**
;	Input and output lists are separated (in this programming notation) by a semicolon.

(Note that where I quote fragments of code in the body of the book's text, I often use a bold, helvetica font. I use this font simply to make the code stand out, rather than to convey any deep technical meaning.)

After their lost weekend, the team turned in the following object-oriented code. In the remainder of this chapter, I often refer back to this code to provide examples of the object-oriented abstractions that I describe.

```
var grid:GRID := GRID.new;               // creates new instances of GRID . . .
var hom1:HOMINOID := HOMINOID.new;       // . . . and HOMINOID
                                         // (The new instance of HOMINOID
                                         // will be pointed to by hom1)

var set-ok: BOOL;
var start-square: SQUARE;
const one-square = 1;

start-square := grid.start;
hom1.set-in-grid (grid, start-square; set-ok);

if not set-ok
then abort everything!;
endif;

// set the hominoid in the right direction:
repeat 4 times max or until not hom1.facing-wall
  hom1.turn-left;
endrepeat;

grid.display;
hom1.display;

repeat until hom1.location = grid.finish

  if hom1.facing-wall
  then hom1.turn-left;
      if hom1.facing-wall
      then hom1.turn-right; hom1.turn-right;
      endif;
  endif;

  hom1.advance(one-square;);
  hom1.display;

endrepeat

// hominoid is at finish—success !
```

Let's turn again to the nine properties of object orientation using the hominoid code to illustrate them. I begin with the property on all the gurus' lists—encapsulation.

1.1 Encapsulation

Encapsulation is a concept that's almost as old as software itself. As early as the 1940s, programmers noticed that similar patterns of instructions would appear several times within the same program. People (such as Maurice Wilkes and his colleagues at Cambridge University) realized that such a repeating pattern could be hived away to a corner of the program and invoked by a single name from several different points in the main program.[2]

> *Encapsulation* is the grouping of related ideas into one unit, which can thenceforth be referred to by a single name.

Thus was born the subroutine, as this encapsulation of instructions was termed. The subroutine was clearly a good way to save computer memory—a very precious commodity in those days. However, people subsequently realized that the subroutine also saved human memory: It represented a conceptual chunk that a person could (at one level, at least) consider and manipulate as a single idea. See Fig. 1.2.

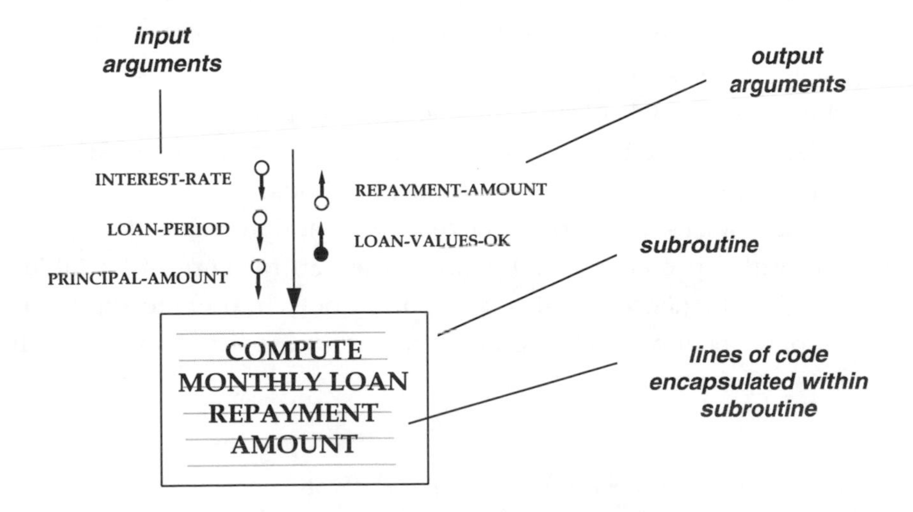

Fig. 1.2: A subroutine.

[2] See [Wilkes et al., 1951].

Encapsulation in object orientation has a purpose similar to that of the subroutine. But it is structurally more sophisticated.

> *Object-oriented encapsulation* is the grouping of procedures around data.[3]

An object consists of a set of methods and a set of variables, as shown in Fig. 1.3. For example, an object such as the one pointed to by **hom1** has methods **turn-left**, **facing-wall**, and so on. Each method is a procedure that's publicly visible, which means that it can be called upon by other objects.

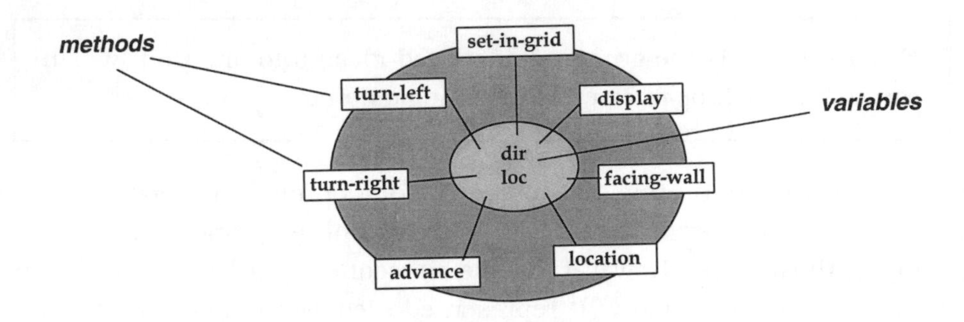

Fig. 1.3: The methods and variables of a hominoid object.

Variables are used internally by an object to remember information.[4] For example, the object **hom1** may have within it variables such as **direction**, **location**, and so on. Variables are accessed and updated by an object's methods. Each variable is private to the object, which means that no other object can access the variable directly. Another object needing information held by that variable can access the information only by appeal to one of the object's methods.

Since only the object's methods may read and update the object's variables, these methods form a protective ring around the central core of variables. For example, the method **location** provides "us"—other objects outside the hominoid—with the hominoid's location. We cannot directly access any variable within the object to get this information.

---

[3] Actually, to be a little more precise in terminology, it's the encapsulation of state within the procedural mechanisms for accessing and modifying that state.

[4] You can think of these variables as containing data. However, as we'll see later, variables usually point to other objects.

An object's structure resembles a medieval European city. (See Fig. 1.4.) Around a typical city was a protective wall. Well-defined and well-guarded gates through the wall regulated ingress to and egress from the city.

Fig. 1.4: A walled city.

The norm was that honest citizens would enter the city only via one of the gates. They would buy their pig in the marketplace and then leave through the gate. Only rogues and blackguards would try to climb over the wall, steal a pig, and get out again over the wall.

In the interest of accuracy, I should point out that many object-oriented languages allow a programmer to designate each method of an object to be a *public method* (visible to other objects) or a *private method* (visible only within the object). Unless I state otherwise, I use *method* to mean the typical method, a public method.

You may also designate each variable of an object to be a *public variable* (visible to other objects—not necessarily a good idea, as we'll see) or a *private variable* (visible only within the object). Unless I state otherwise, I use *variable* to mean the typical variable, a private variable.

1.2 Information/Implementation Hiding

You may view an encapsulated unit from the outside (the "public view") or from the inside (the "private view"). The payoff of good encapsulation is the suppression in the public view of the myriad details to be seen in the private view. This suppression takes two forms: information hiding and implementation hiding. The term "information hiding" implies that information within the unit cannot be perceived outside the unit. The term "implementation hiding" implies that implementation details within the unit cannot be perceived from outside.

> *Information/implementation hiding* is the use of encapsulation to restrict from external visibility certain information or implementation decisions that are internal to the encapsulation structure.

The hominoid object exemplifies the property of information hiding in that it contains some private information that's inaccessible from outside. An example is the direction in which the hominoid is pointing. From outside the object we can change this information (through **turn-left**, perhaps), but we cannot find its value—except, I suppose, by getting the hominoid to display itself and checking which way its nose points.

However, the term "information hiding" addresses only part of what a good encapsulation may hide. Encapsulation often reveals information, but hides implementation. For example, although the hominoid object will tell us what its location is (via the method **location**), we don't know how the object stores its location internally. It could be as (**x-coord**, **y-coord**) or (**y-coord**, **x-coord**) or polar coordinates or some magnificent scheme that its designer dreamed up at 1 a.m. So long as the object exports its location to us in a standard way, we don't care *how* it remembers its location.

Hominoid's **direction** is an example not only of information hiding, but also of implementation hiding. For example, we don't know whether the information is held within the object as a single character (with values of **N**, **E**, **S**, and **W**) or as a numerical angle (with values of 0–359 degrees).

Again, even if in a future design a method were to export direction, we still wouldn't know whether the implementation of the private information within the object was the same as that of the public information. For example, the object could hold **direction** privately as a character and—by converting it—export it publicly as an angle.

Information/implementation hiding is a powerful technique for taming software complexity. It means that an object appears as a black box to an external observer. In other words, the external observer has full knowledge of *what* the object can do, but has knowledge neither of *how* the object may do it nor of *how* the object is constructed internally. I show this schematically in Fig. 1.5.

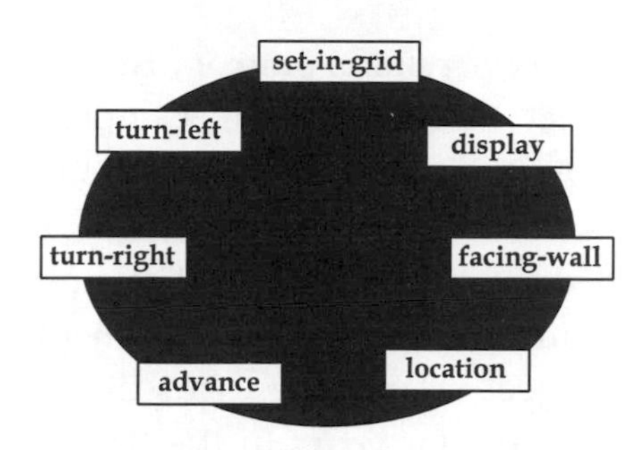

Fig. 1.5: The hominoid object seen as a black box.

Information/implementation hiding has two major benefits:

1. It localizes design decisions. Private design decisions (those within an object) have little or no impact on the rest of the system. Therefore, such local decisions can be made and changed with minimal impact upon the system as a whole. This limits the "ripple of change" effect.

2. It decouples the content of information from its form of representation. Thus, no user of information who is external to an object can become tied to any particular internal information format. This prevents external users of an object from meddling within it. It also prevents people from introducing connections to an object that depend on tricks and accidents of format and are therefore unstable.

1.3 State Retention

The third abstraction of object orientation pertains to an object's ability to retain state. When a traditional procedural module (function, subprogram, procedure, and so on) returns to its caller, the module dies, leaving only its result as its legacy. When the same module is called on again, it's as if it were born again for the first time. The module has no memory of anything that happened in its previous lives; indeed, like humans, it has no idea that it even had a previous existence.

But an object, such as the hominoid, *is* aware of its past. It retains information inside itself for an indefinite length of time. For example, a "caller" of an object may give it a piece of information and that caller—or another one—may later ask the object to offer up that information again. In other words, an object doesn't die when it's finished executing: It stands by, ready to leap into action again.

Technically speaking, an object retains state.[5] (State means, in effect, the set of values that an object holds. More on this in Chapter 10.) For example, the hominoid retains indefinitely its knowledge of the square that it's on and the direction that it's facing. As we saw in Sections 1.1 and 1.2, however, *how* the object chooses to retain that knowledge is its own internal business.

Object-oriented encapsulation, information/implementation hiding, and state retention are at the core of object orientation. But they're not new ideas. Computer scientists have studied them for years in the field of the *abstract data-type* (ADT).[6] However, object orientation goes well beyond the ADT, as the following six properties of object orientation reveal.

1.4 Object Identity

A crucial property of object orientation, which transcends the concept of the ADT, is that each object has its own identity.

> *Object identity* is the property by which each object (regardless of its class or current state) can be identified and treated as a distinct software entity.

There's something unique about a given object that distinguishes it from all its fellow objects. This "something unique" is provided by the object-handle mechanism, which I'll explain through a dissection of one line of the hominoid code:

var hom1:HOMINOID := HOMINOID.new;

The right-hand side of this line creates a new object (of class HOMINOID), which I show in Fig. 1.6. Notice the object's handle, which for the object in the figure is

---

[5] If you're familiar with structured design, you may recognize this concept as *state memory*, as exemplified by an *information cluster*. See [Page-Jones, 1980], for example.

[6] An ADT is a data-type that provides a set of values and a set of interrelated operations whose external definition (as seen by outside users of that data-type) is independent of their internal representation or implementation. See [Liskov et al., 1981], for example.

the number 102237. The handle is an identifier attached to an object when it's created.

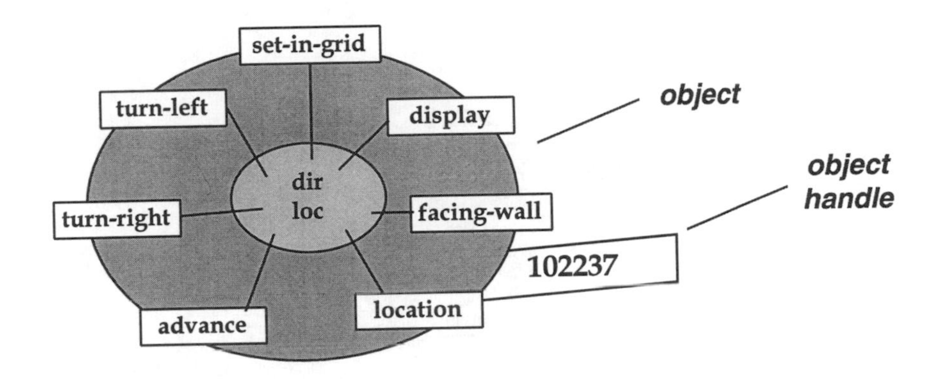

Fig. 1.6: An object with its handle.

Two rules apply to handles:

1. The same handle remains with the object for its entire life, regardless of what may befall the object during that time.

2. No two objects can have the same handle. Whenever the system creates a new object at run-time, the system assigns to the object a handle that's different from all other—past, present, or future—handles.[7] Therefore, you can always tell two objects apart, even if they're identical in structure and in the information they hold. They will have different handles.

The left-hand side of the line of code is the declaration **var hom1:HOMINOID**. This is a normal program declaration that gives a programmer-meaningful name (in this case, **hom1**) to, say, a word of memory that can hold a value. The term HOMINOID here is the name of hom1's class, a topic that I discuss in Section 1.6.

As you may have guessed, the assignment (**:=**, which you read as "now points to" or "now refers to") causes the variable **hom1** to hold the handle of the object created on the right-hand side of the assignment statement.[8]

[7] The handle is known formally as the Object Identifier (OID). Most—but not all—object-oriented environments create this unique OID automatically.

[8] I use "points to" (and, later on, "pointer") in a general sense. Under the umbrella term "pointer," I include C++ *pointers*, C++ *references*, Eiffel *entities*, Smalltalk *variables*, and so on.

No one (programmer, user, anyone) will ever actually *see* the handle (102237) of the new object. Instead, the programmer will access the object via the variable **hom1**. As shown in Fig. 1.7, **hom1** points to the object whose handle is 102237.

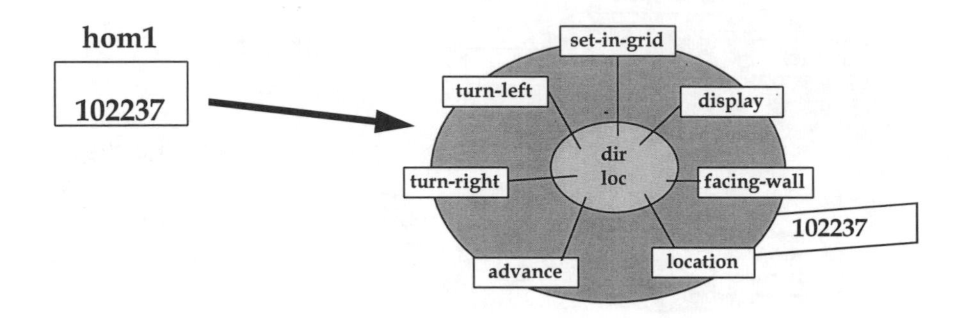

Fig. 1.7: **hom1** *points at the object whose handle is 102237.*

Some object-oriented environments use the physical memory address of the object as its handle. This is simple, but it can turn ugly if the object is moved in memory or gets swapped out to disk. It's better for a handle to be a meaningless, random, but unique number (though, of course, as object-oriented programmers and not compiler designers, we have no control over how handle values are conjured up).

Let's say that we were now to execute another, similar, line of code:

```
var hom2:HOMINOID := HOMINOID.new;
```

This will create another object (also of class HOMINOID) with a handle of, say, 142857, and will store that handle in the variable **hom2**. (See Fig. 1.8.)

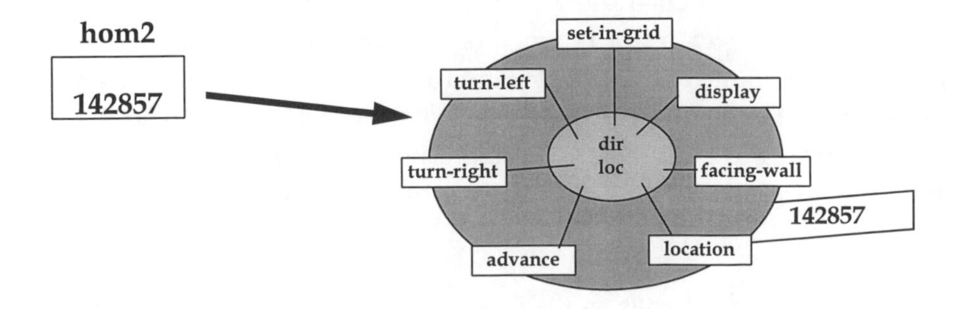

Fig. 1.8: **hom2** *points to the object whose handle is 142857.*

To make a point, I'll write another assignment statement:

hom2 := hom1

Now the variables **hom1** and **hom2** both point to the same object (the first one we created, the instance of HOMINOID with the handle 102237). Having two variables pointing to the same object is not typically useful. But worse, we now have no way to reach the second object (the one whose handle is 142857). Effectively, therefore, that object has disappeared—just as if it had fallen down a black hole! See Fig. 1.9. In practice, it disappears too. Most object-oriented environments would summon a garbage collector at this juncture to remove the object from memory.

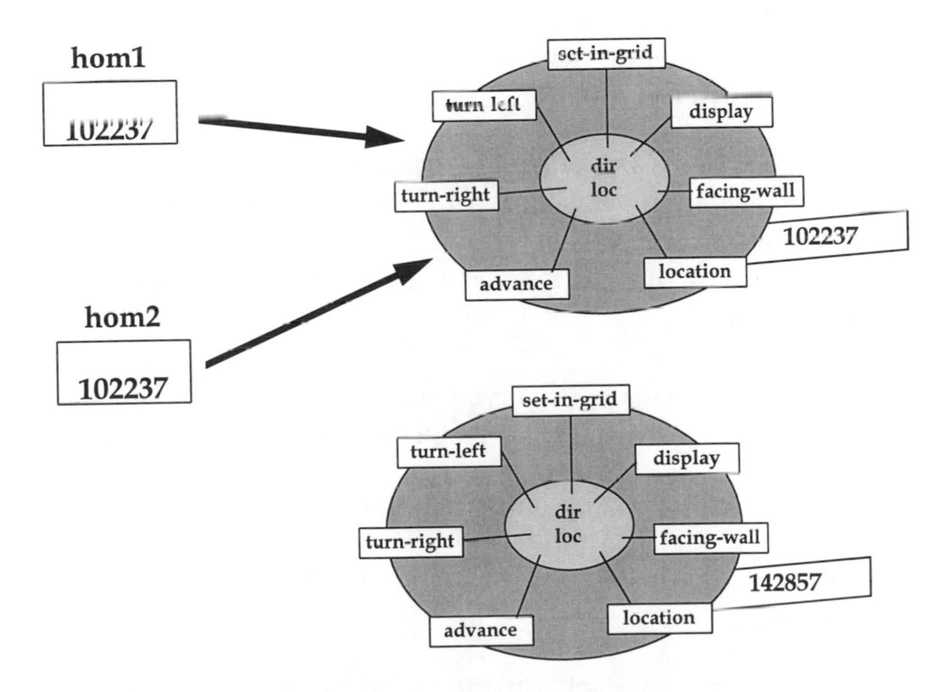

Fig. 1.9: Now both **hom1** *and* **hom2** *point to the same object and the other object is no longer reachable.*

The idea of giving every object its own identity by means of a handle seems innocuous in the extreme. Surprisingly, however, this simple idea causes a profound change in the way that we design and build object-oriented software. And that change is coming up in the next section. Stay tuned!

1.5 Messages

An object requests another object to carry out an activity via a message. A typical message also conveys some information from one object to another.

> A *message* is the way in which a sender object **ob1** conveys to a target object **ob2** a demand for object **ob2** to apply one of its methods.[9]

In this section, I describe the anatomy of a message, the characteristics of message arguments, the roles of the object sending a message and the object receiving a message, and the three types of message.

1.5.1 Message structure

A message comprises several syntactic parts, each of which is important in its own right in object-oriented design. Indeed, we'll return to each component of a message many times throughout the book.

In order for object **ob1** to send a sensible message to object **ob2**, object **ob1** must know three things:

1. The handle of **ob2**. (Obviously, when you send a message you should know to whom it's going.) **ob1** will normally keep **ob2**'s handle in one of its variables.

2. The name of the method of **ob2** that **ob1** wishes to execute.

3. Any supplementary information (*arguments*) that **ob2** will require in the execution of its method.

The object sending the message (**ob1** in the above) is called the *sender*, and the object receiving the message (**ob2**) is called the *target*.

The hominoid software offers several examples of messages.[10] One is this:

```
hom1.turn-left;
```

---

[9] Object **ob1** and object **ob2** may be the same object. Hence, as I discuss in Chapter 5, an object may send a message to itself.

[10] The code in the example earlier in this chapter is code within a sender object that I didn't specify.

Here, **hom1** points to (contains the handle of) the target object of the message. (If you recall, the handle was assigned to **hom1** by the assignment **var hom1 := HOMINOID.new.**) **turn-left** is the name of the method (belonging to the target object) that's to be executed. (This message doesn't need any arguments.)

The sending of a message is like the traditional calling of a function or procedure. For instance, in a traditional language we might have said,

call turn-left (hom1);

But notice the inversion. With traditional techniques, we appeal to a procedural unit and supply it with the object upon which to act; in object orientation, we appeal to an object, which then executes one of its procedural units.

At this stage of the book, such a distinction seems only syntactic—or at best philosophical. However, when I discuss polymorphism, overloading, and dynamic binding in Section 1.8, we'll see that the inversion creates an important practical difference between object-oriented structure and traditional structure. This is because different classes of objects may use the same method name for methods that accomplish different or class-specific behaviors.

1.5.2 Message arguments

Like the old-fashioned subroutine, most messages pass arguments back and forth. For instance, if we made the method named **advance** return a flag holding the outcome of the advancement, then we'd have

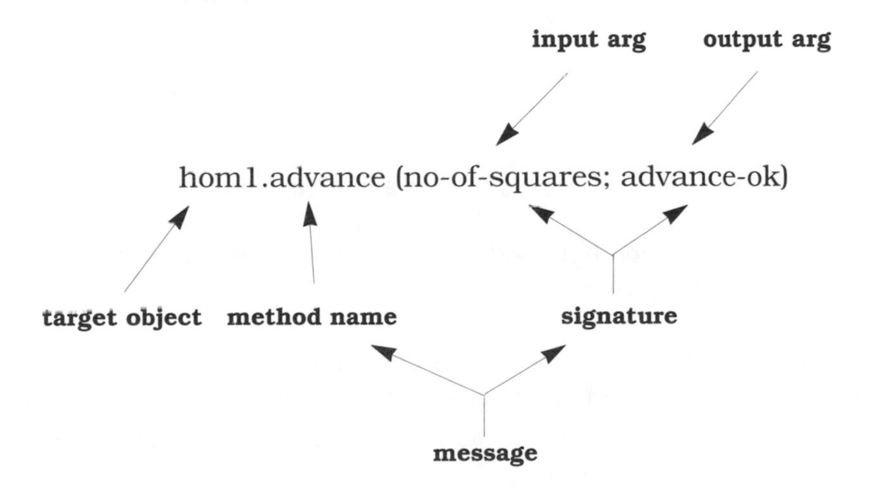

Thus, a message to a target object consists of two parts: the method name and the signature.

> The *signature* is a list of input arguments (to the target object) followed by a list of output arguments (from the target object).

The input and output lists are separated (in this programming notation) by a semicolon. Either list may be empty. Also, the same argument may appear in both lists.[11]

The arguments of a message reflect another fundamental contrast between object-oriented software and traditional software. In a pure object-oriented environment (such as Smalltalk's), message arguments are not data; they're handles of objects. Message arguments are therefore like objects on the hoof!

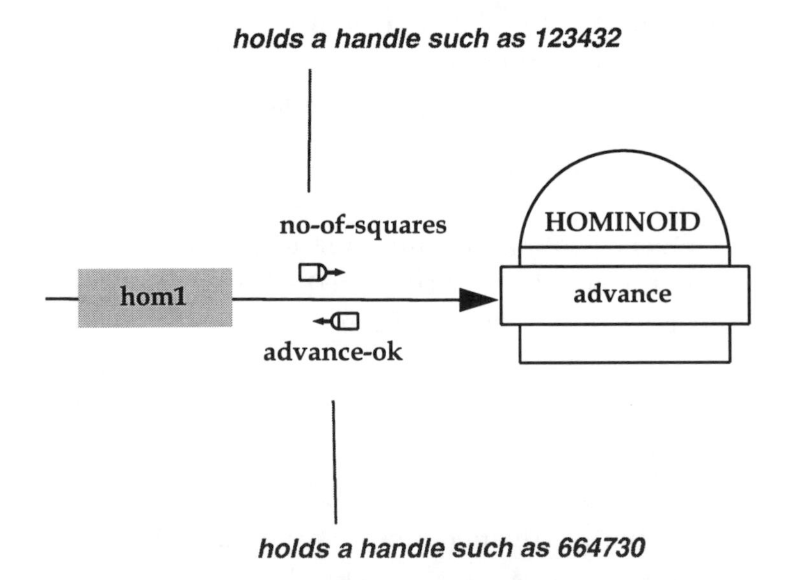

Fig. 1.10: The message **hom1.advance (no-of-squares; advance-ok)** *in graphic form.*

To illustrate this point, in Fig. 1.10 I show in graphic notation one message—**hom1.advance (no-of-squares; advance-ok)**—of the hominoid program being executed. If we were to snapshot the running hominoid program while it was execut-

---

[11] This is rare in pure object orientation. See Exercise 3 at the end of this chapter.

ing this message and dump out the values of the message's arguments, we would find something unexpected. We might find, for instance:

no-of-squares	set to 123432
advance-ok	set to 664730

Why these strange numbers? Because 123432 might be the handle of the object (of class INT) that we normally think of as the integer 2, and 664730 might be the handle of the object (of class BOOL) that we normally think of as the logical value **true**.

As another example, if we were executing an object-oriented personnel system and did the same thing, we might find the argument **emp-of-month** set to 441523. 441523 would perhaps be the handle of the object (of class EMPLOYEE) that represents Mr. Jim Spriggs.

1.5.3 The roles of objects in messages

In this section, I review the four roles that we've seen objects play in an object-oriented system. An object may be

- the sender of a message
- the target of a message
- pointed to by a variable within another object (as we saw in Section 1.4)
- pointed to by an argument passed back or forth in a message

A given object may play any one of these roles at some time in its life. In Fig. 1.11, we can see all these roles choreographed together.

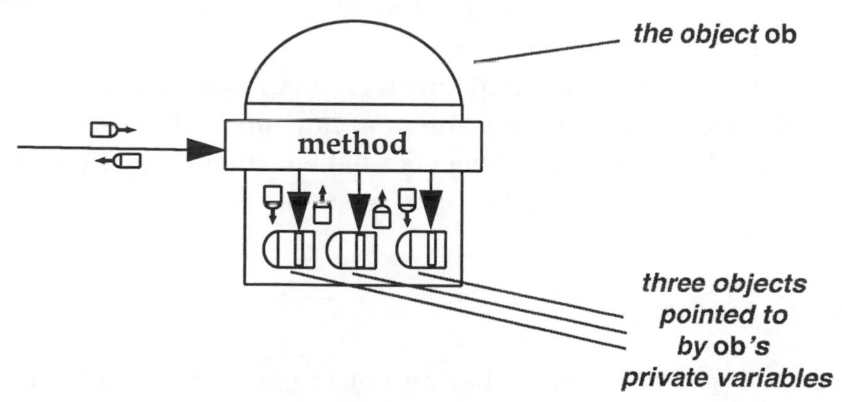

Fig. 1.11: A method of an object sending messages to the three objects pointed to by private variables.

In the figure, we see a method of an object (let's call it **ob**) sending messages to the objects pointed to by each of **ob**'s three private variables. The first message has an input and an output argument; the second has only an output argument; the third has only an input argument. Each of these arguments is itself a pointer to an object. This structure is very, very typical of how an object's methods interact with an object's variables.

Some authors suggest that each object is a "born sender" or a "born target." This isn't so, as Fig. 1.12 illustrates.

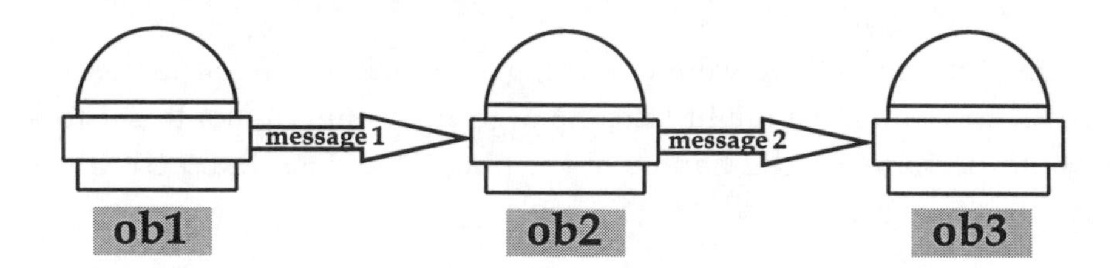

Fig. 1.12: Two messages between pairs of objects.

For **message1**, **ob1** is the sender and **ob2** is the target. For **message2**, **ob2** is the sender and **ob3** is the target. So we see that, at different times, the same object can play the part of sender or target. The terms "sender" and "target" are therefore relative to a given message. They aren't fixed properties of the objects themselves.

Above, we saw objects playing several different roles. A pure object-oriented environment contains only objects, each of which play one or more of these roles. In pure object orientation, there is no need for data, because objects can do all of data's necessary software jobs. And in Smalltalk (a very pure object-oriented language), there really *isn't* any data! At run-time, there are only objects pointing to other objects (via variables) and communicating to other objects by passing back and forth handles of yet other objects.

However, in C++ (which is a mixed language—both data/function-oriented and object-oriented), arguments can be pointers to anything. If your C++ code is as pure as Smalltalk, then all your arguments will be pointers to objects. But if you mix objects and data in your program, then some of your arguments may be simple data (or pointers to data).[12]

1.5.4 Types of message

There are three types of message that an object may receive: informative messages, interrogative messages, and imperative messages. In this section, I briefly

[12] See Exercise 4 at the end of this chapter for more on the distinction between objects and data values.

define and give an example of each kind of message, using the hominoid once more.

> An *informative message* is a message to an object that provides it with information to update itself. (It is also known as an *update, forward,* or *push* message.) It is a "past-oriented" message, in that it usually informs the object of what has already taken place elsewhere.

An example of an informative message is **hom1.set-in-grid (grid, start-square; set-ok)**. This message tells the hominoid object the start square on which it's been placed. In general, an informative message tells an object something that's happened in the part of the real world represented by that object.

> An *interrogative message* is a message to an object requesting it to reveal some information about itself. (It is also known as a *read, backward,* or *pull* message.) It is a "present-oriented" method, in that it asks the object for some current information.

An example of an interrogative message is **hom1.location**, which asks the hominoid to tell us which square it's currently on. This kind of message doesn't change anything; instead, it's usually a query about the piece of the world that the target object represents.

> An *imperative message* is a message to an object that requests the object to take some action on itself, another object, or even the environment around the system. (It is also known as a *force* or *action* message.) It is a "future-oriented" message, in that it asks the object to carry out some action in the immediate future.

An example of an imperative message is **hom1.advance**, which causes the hominoid to move forward. This kind of message often results in the target object's executing some significant algorithm in order to work out what to do. Imagine, for example, that we could send to a hominoid an imperative message **hom1.gotolocation (square:SQUARE; feasible:BOOL)**, which would take the hominoid to a particular square, so long as that was feasible. The calculation that the hominoid would have to carry out would be immense.

Real-time object-oriented systems, in which objects control pieces of hardware, often contain many imperative messages. These systems clearly illustrate the future-action spirit of an imperative message.

We'll return to these message types at the very end of the book, in Chapter 12, when we examine different design options for communicating objects. But now, on to classes of objects.

1.6 Classes

Recall that in the hominoid software we created an object (to represent a hominoid) by saying **HOMINOID.new**. HOMINOID, which is an example of a *class*, served as a model from which we created hominoid objects (such as the one with the handle 102237). Whenever we execute the statement **HOMINOID.new**, we instantiate an object that is structurally identical to every other object created by the statement **HOMINOID.new**. By "structurally identical," I mean that each hominoid object has the same methods and variables as the others—specifically, the methods and variables that the programmer coded when he wrote the class HOMINOID.[13] See Fig. 1.13.

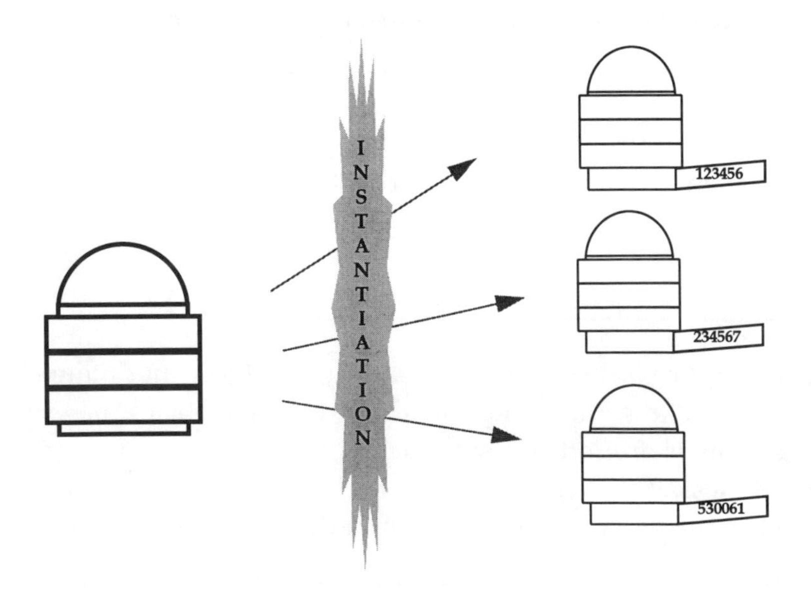

Fig. 1.13: Three objects instantiated from the same class.

[13] By the way, throughout this book, I intend an indefinite "he" to mean "he or she." In other words, as they say in British Civil Service documents, it is to be understood in the following that "he" embraces "she."

A *class* is the stencil from which objects are created (instantiated). Each object has the same structure and behavior as the class from which it is instantiated.

If object **ob** belongs to class C, we say "**ob** is an *instance* of C."

There are two differences between objects of the same class: Each object has a different handle and, at any particular time, each object will probably have a different state (which means different "values" stored in its variables).

At first you may be confused about the distinction between a class and an object. The simple way to remember the distinction is this:

- a class is what you design and program;
- objects are what you create (from a class) at run-time.[14]

Popular software packages provide a close analogy to classes and objects. Let's say that you buy a spreadsheet package called Visigoth 5.0 from the Wallisoft Corp. The package itself would be the analogue of the class. The actual spreadsheets that you create from it would be similar to objects. Each spreadsheet has all the "spreadsheet machinery" available to it as an instance of the Visigoth class.

At run-time, a class such as HOMINOID may spawn 3, 300, or 3,000 objects (that is, instances of HOMINOID). A class therefore resembles a stencil. You may design a shape and then cut it out from a piece of plastic. You do this just once. Thenceforth, you can draw the shape thousands of times on a piece of paper. All of the drawings will be identical to one another and, of course, to the shape of the original stencil.

To clarify this further, let's look more closely at the population of objects generated from a single class. As we've seen, all of the objects have the same structure. In particular, their methods are identical and so are the variables that they use. Each object (instance) of a class has its own copy of the set of methods and set of variables that it needs. There are at a given time, in principle, as many copies (0, 3, 300, ...) as there are instantiated objects at that time. See Fig. 1.14.

[14] So *object-oriented programming* should really be termed *class-structured programming*. However, I don't expect this term to catch on!

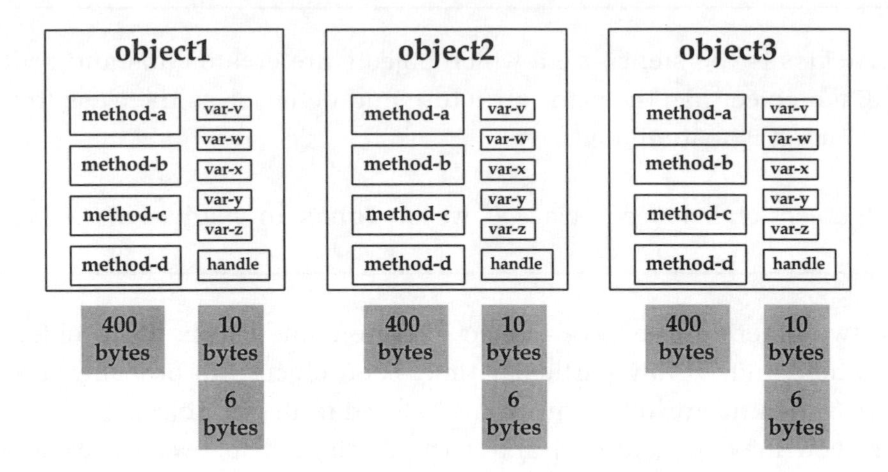

Fig. 1.14: The methods, variables, and handles of three objects of the same class, together with the objects' memory requirements.

For a moment, if you don't mind, I'll descend deep into computer implementation in order to explain further the real structure of a bunch of objects of the same class, C. Let's assume that every method of Fig. 1.14 occupies 100 bytes, every variable occupies 2 bytes, and every handle occupies 6 bytes. Therefore, **object1** will occupy 416 bytes of memory (that is, 4 * 100 + 5 * 2 + 6). The three objects together will therefore occupy 1,248 bytes (that is, 3 * 416). Fifteen such objects would occupy 6,240 bytes (that is, 15 * 416).

But this approach to allocating memory to objects is very wasteful, because each of the 15 sets of methods of the 15 objects is identical. And, since each set of methods is purely procedural code, a single set can be shared by all the objects. So, in principle each object has its own set of methods, but in practice (to save space) they all share the same physical copy.

On the other hand, although the handles and the variables of each object are identical in structure from object to object, they *cannot* be shared among objects. The reason, of course, is that they must contain different values at run-time.

So if C's objects all share the same set of methods, the total memory consumed by C's 15 objects will actually be only 640 bytes (400 bytes for the single set of methods, 150 bytes for the 15 sets of variables, and 90 bytes for the 15 handles). This 640 bytes is much better than 6,240 bytes and it's the normal way that an object-oriented environment allocates memory to objects. See Fig. 1.15.

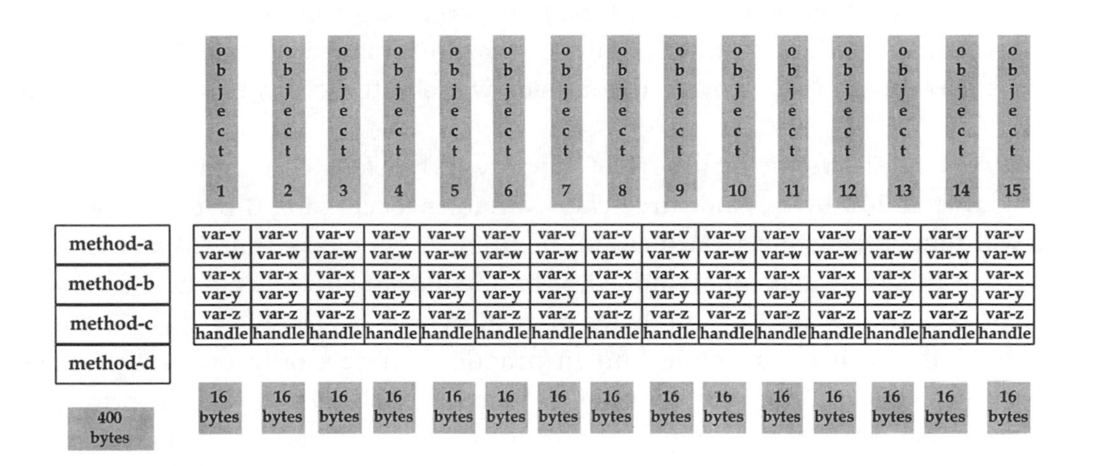

Fig. 1.15: Schematic depiction of the actual memory (640 bytes) used by 15 objects of the same class.

Almost all of the methods and variables that we've looked at in this chapter belong to individual objects. They're called *object instance methods* and *object instance variables*, or *instance methods* and *instance variables* for short. However, there are also *class methods* and *class variables*. By definition, there's exactly one set of class methods and class variables for a given class at all times—regardless of how many objects of that class may have been instantiated.

Class methods and class variables are needed to handle situations that cannot be the responsibility of any individual object. The most famous example of a class method is **new**, which instantiates a new object of a given class.

The message **new** could never be sent to an individual object. Say, for example, that we had three objects of class BANK-CUSTOMER, representing actual bank customers (let's refer to these objects as **bob**, **carol**, and **ted**) and we wanted to instantiate a new BANK-CUSTOMER object (say, **alice**). To which object would we send the message **new**? There would be no particular reason to send it to **bob**, as opposed to **carol** or **ted**. Worse still, we could never have instantiated the first bank customer, because initially there wouldn't have been any object of class BANK-CUSTOMER to which to send the **new** message.

So **new** is a message that must be sent to a class, rather than to an individual object. The example from the hominoid game was **HOMINOID.new**. This was a class message to the class HOMINOID to execute its class method **new** and thus create a fresh object, a fresh instance of the class HOMINOID.

An example of a class variable might be **no-of-hominoids-created: INT**. This would be incremented by **new** each time **new** executed. However many hominoid objects there were, there would be only one copy of this class variable. You may design a class method to provide the outside world with access to this class variable.

Figure 1.16 shows the structure of memory if the class C has two class methods (occupying 200 bytes) and three class variables (occupying 6 bytes). This 206 bytes will remain constant regardless of the number of objects that C has instantiated. With this class machinery added, C and its flock of 15 objects now consume a total of 846 (that is, 206 + 640) bytes of memory.

Note that—both in principle and in practice—there's only one set of class methods per class. This is in contrast to instance methods, where, in principle, each object has its own set. (Only to save memory do we make objects share the same set.) The distinction between class variables and instance variables is more clear: Each class has only one set of class variables, whereas there *really is* one set of instance variables for each object of that class.

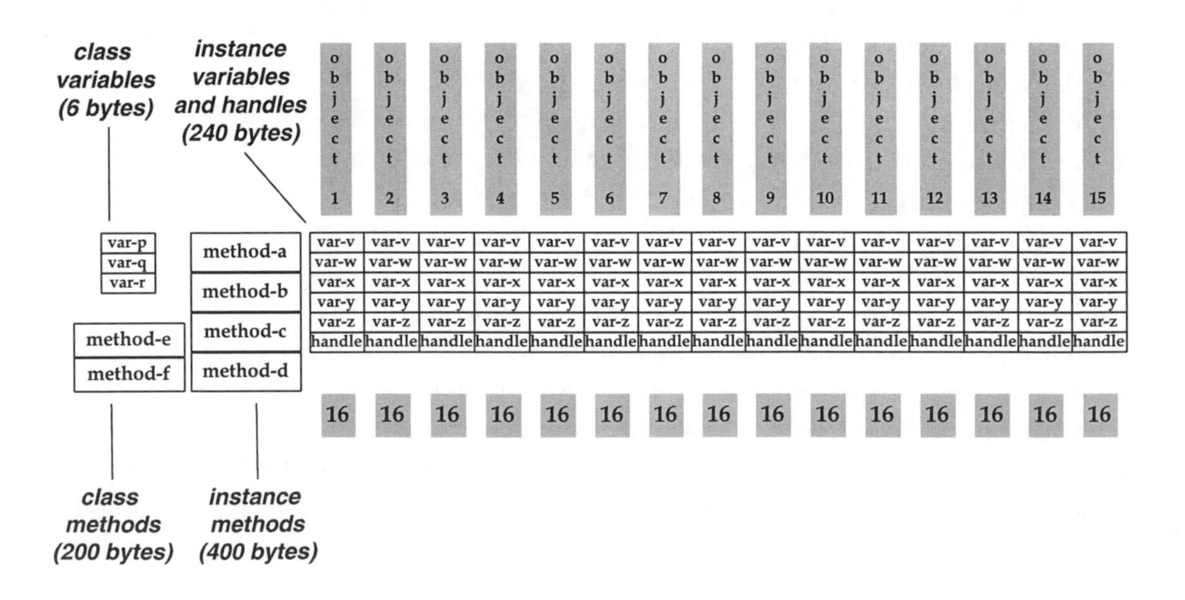

Fig. 1.16: Schematic depiction of the actual memory (846 bytes) used by 15 objects and the "class machinery."

If you've studied abstract data-types (ADTs)—perhaps at university—you may wonder what the difference is between a class and an ADT. The answer is that an

ADT describes an interface; it's a facade that declares what will be provided for users of that ADT, but says nothing about how the ADT will be implemented.

A class is a thing of flesh and blood—or at least of internal design and code—that implements an ADT. Indeed, for a given ADT you could design and build several different classes. For example, one such class could yield objects that run very efficiently; another class for the same ADT could yield objects that take up little memory.

I have much more to say about abstract data-types and classes in Part III of the book. For now, however, let's move on to the important concept of inheritance.

1.7 Inheritance

What would you do if you wrote a class C and then later discovered a class D that was almost identical to C except that it had a few extra methods? One solution would be simply to duplicate all the methods of C and put them in D. But not only would this be extra work for you, the duplication would also make maintenance a nuisance. A better solution would be to have the class D somehow "ask to use the methods" of the class C. This solution is called inheritance.

> *Inheritance* (by D from C) is the facility by which objects of a class D may use a method or variable that would otherwise be available only to objects of class C, as if that method or variable had been defined upon D.
>
> C is termed a *superclass* of D. D is a *subclass* of C.

Inheritance represents another major way in which object orientation departs from traditional systems approaches. It effectively allows you to build software incrementally in this way: First, build classes to cope with the most straightforward (or general) case. Then, in order to deal with special cases, add more specialized classes that inherit from the first class. These new classes will be entitled to use all the methods and variables (both class and instance methods and variables) of the original class.

As usual, an example will help to illustrate the principle. Let's say that we have a class AIRCRAFT in an aviation application. AIRCRAFT may have defined on it an instance method named **turn** and within it an instance variable named **course**.

The class AIRCRAFT deals with activity or information pertinent to any kind of flying craft. However, there are special kinds of aircraft that carry out special activities and require special pieces of information. For example, a glider carries out special activities (for example, releasing its towline) and may need to record special information (for example, whether it is attached to a towline).

Thus we may define another class—GLIDER—that inherits from AIRCRAFT. GLIDER will have an instance method named **release-towline** and an instance variable named **whether-attached**. This will give us the structure shown in Fig. 1.17, in which the broad, solid arrow denotes inheritance.

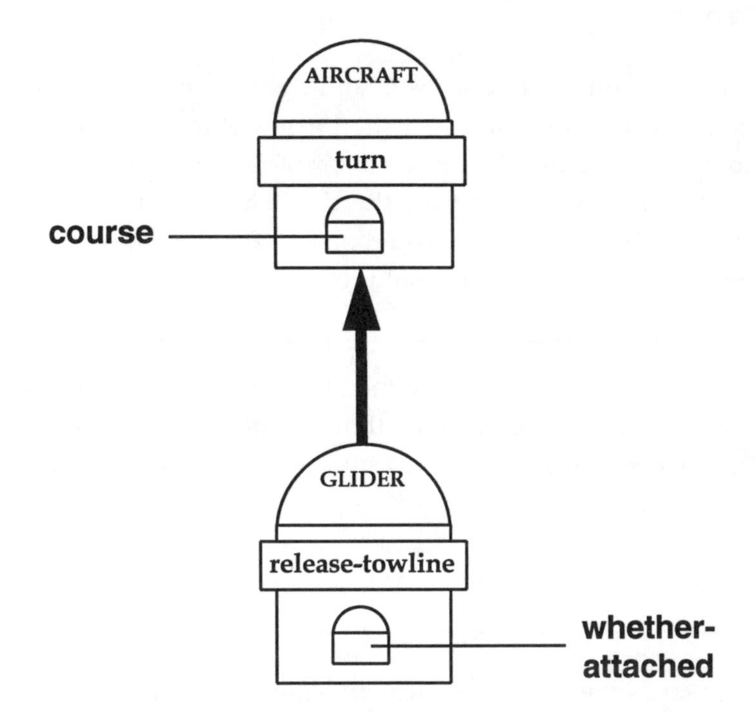

Fig. 1.17: GLIDER is a subclass that inherits from its superclass, AIRCRAFT.

Now we'll look at the mechanics of inheritance by imagining some object-oriented code that first spawns objects from the classes AIRCRAFT and GLIDER and then sends messages to those objects. The code is followed by a discussion of the four statements tagged (1) through (4).

```
var ac:AIRCRAFT := AIRCRAFT.new;
var gl:GLIDER  := GLIDER.new;
...
ac.turn (new-course; turn-ok);   (1)
gl.release-towline;              (2)
gl.turn (new-course; turn-ok);   (3)
ac.release-towline;              (4)
...
```

(1) The object pointed to by **ac** receives the message **turn (new-course; turn-ok)**, which causes it to apply the method **turn** (with the appropriate arguments). Since **ac** is an instance of AIRCRAFT, **ac** will simply use the method **turn** that has been defined on the class AIRCRAFT.

(2) The object pointed to by **gl** receives the message **release-towline**, which causes it to apply the method **release-towline** (which needs no arguments). Since **gl** is an instance of GLIDER, **gl** will simply use the method **release-towline** that has been defined on the class GLIDER.

(3) The object pointed to by **gl** receives the message **turn (new-course; turn-ok)**, which causes it to apply the method **turn** (with the appropriate arguments). Without inheritance, this message would cause a run-time error (such as "UNDEFINED METHOD **turn**") because **gl** is an instance of GLIDER, which has no method named **turn**.

However, since AIRCRAFT is a superclass of GLIDER, the object **gl** is also entitled to use any method of AIRCRAFT. (If AIRCRAFT had a superclass FLY-ING-THING, **gl** would also be entitled to use any method of FLYING-THING.) Therefore, the line of code marked (3) will work successfully, and the method **turn**, as defined on AIRCRAFT, will be executed.

(4) This will not work! **ac** refers to an instance of AIRCRAFT, which has no method named **release-towline**. Inheritance is no help here, since GLIDER is the only class that has **release-towline** defined on it, and GLIDER is a *sub*class of AIR-CRAFT. Inheritance doesn't work in this direction, and the system will stop with a run-time error. This makes sense, since **ac** may point to a big jet plane, for which **release-towline** would have no meaning.

In Section 1.6, we saw the distinction between class and object. Now we see that there's also a subtle distinction between object and instance. Although up to now we've used "object" and "instance" almost synonymously, we see that inheritance in a sense permits a single object to be simultaneously an instance of more than one class.

This corresponds well to the real world. If you own a glider, you own exactly one object with one identification (handle) on its tail. Yet this glider is (obviously!) an example of a glider and, at the same time, an example of an aircraft. Conceptually then, the object representing the thing that you own is an instance of GLIDER *and* an instance of AIRCRAFT.

Indeed, the above example demonstrates a telling test for the valid use of inheritance: It's called the *is a* test. If you can say: "a D *is a* C," then D almost certainly should be a subclass of C. Thus, because "a glider *is an* aircraft," the class GLIDER should be a subclass of AIRCRAFT.[15]

Let's explore this topic further by taking a behind-the-scenes look at inheritance. The object referred to by **gl** will be represented at run-time by an amalgamation of two parts. One part will be the instance methods and instance variables defined for GLIDER; the other part will be the instance methods and instance variables defined for AIRCRAFT, as shown in Fig. 1.18.[16]

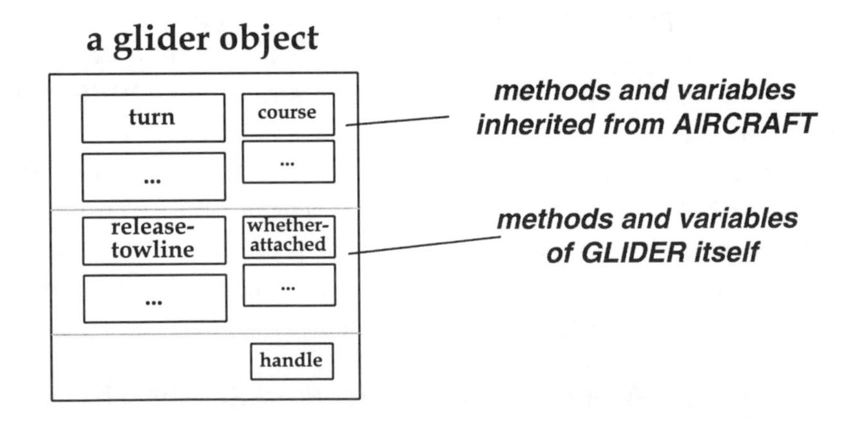

Fig. 1.18: The instance methods and instance variables available to an object of class GLIDER.

[15] I go much further into the *is a* topic and the correct uses of inheritance in Chapters 10 and 11.

[16] In fact, a *class-flattener*—a tool built into environments such as Eiffel—provides exactly this view.

The actual code to implement inheritance in good object-oriented languages is straightforward. You simply state the superclass in the class definition of each subclass that is to inherit from the superclass. For example,

class GLIDER **inherits from** AIRCRAFT;

...

The example of inheritance in this section is one of *single inheritance*, which means that each class has at most one direct superclass. *Multiple inheritance* is also possible. With multiple inheritance each class may have an arbitrary number of direct superclasses.

Multiple inheritance converts the inheritance tree of single inheritance into an inheritance lattice. See Fig. 1.19.

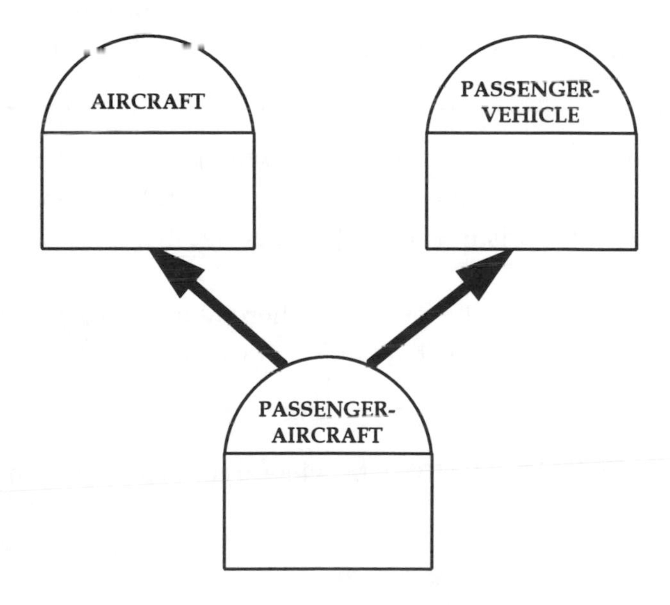

Fig. 1.19: Multiple inheritance—a subclass with two or more superclasses.

Multiple inheritance introduces some difficult design issues, including the possibility of a subclass inheriting clashing methods (or variables) from its multiple ancestors. (Clashing methods have the same name and the inheriting subclass cannot easily tell which one to inherit.)

Difficulties such as the name-clash problem have given multiple inheritance a bad reputation and in recent years both the condemnation and defense of multiple inheritance have reached a fever pitch. I should reveal that I'm in favor of multiple inheritance because the real world frequently calls for multiply inheriting subclasses. For example, the class PASSENGER-AIRCRAFT could inherit from both AIRCRAFT and, say, PASSENGER-VEHICLE.

Nevertheless, since multiple inheritance may create complex and incomprehensible structures, you should use multiple inheritance judiciously—even more judiciously than single inheritance.[17]

1.8 Polymorphism

The word "polymorphism" comes from two Greek words that mean, respectively, "many" and "form." Something that's polymorphic therefore has the ability to take on many forms.

Object-oriented textbooks contain two definitions of polymorphism. In the definition box below, I've marked them (A) and (B). Both definitions are valid and both properties of polymorphism work hand in hand to bring a great deal of power to object orientation. In this section, I explain both definitions together.

> (A) *Polymorphism* is the facility by which a single method name may be defined upon more than one class and may take on different implementations in each of those classes.
>
> (B) *Polymorphism* is the property whereby a variable may point to (hold the handle of) objects of different classes at different times.

Assume that we have a class POLYGON, which represents the kind of 2-D shape that Fig. 1.20 exemplifies.

[17] I return to the issue of multiple inheritance several times in the book, especially in Chapters 11 and 12. You may also want to look at [Meyer, 1992] for a discussion of multiple inheritance and its less-useful cousin, repeated inheritance (whereby a class inherits features from the same superclass more than once).

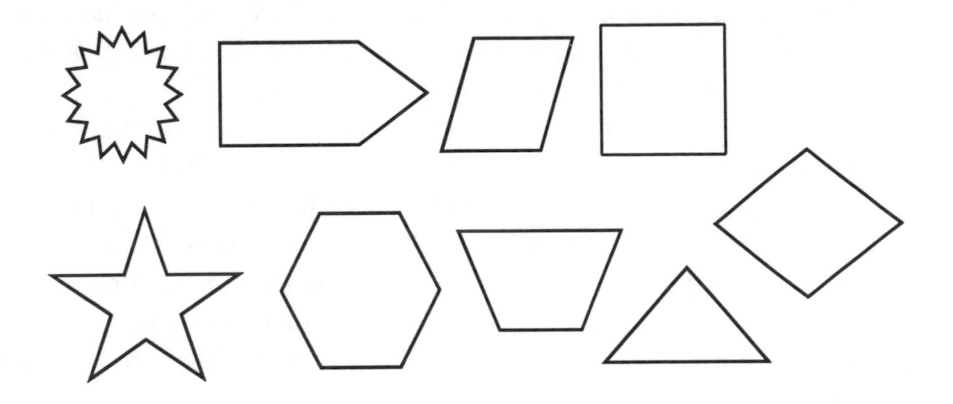

Fig. 1.20: Some plane polygons.

We may define a method on POLYGON named **area**. This method would need a fairly sophisticated algorithm because it would have to take care of any of the oddly shaped polygons of Fig. 1.20. Now let's add some more classes—say TRIANGLE, RECTANGLE, and HEXAGON—which are subclasses of (and thus inherit from) POLYGON. This makes sense, because a triangle *is a* polygon; a rectangle *is a* polygon; and so on. See Fig. 1.21.

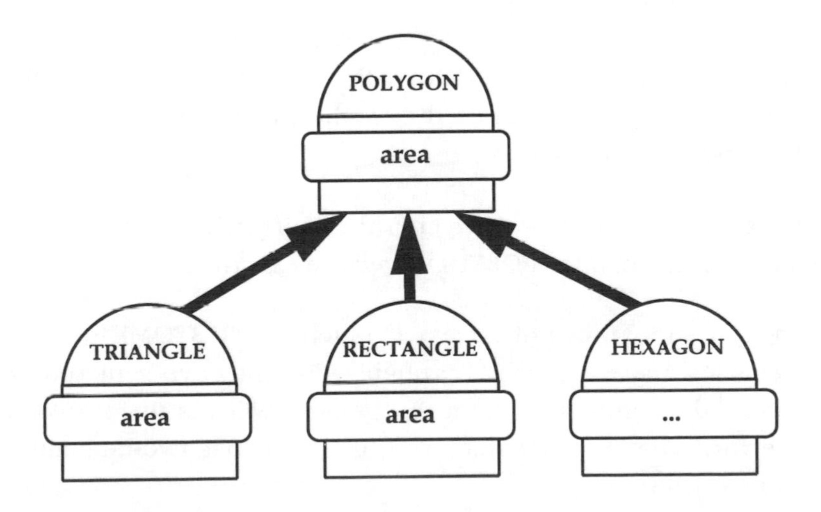

Fig. 1.21: POLYGON and its three subclasses.

Notice that in Fig. 1.21 the classes TRIANGLE and RECTANGLE also have methods named **area**. These methods accomplish the same job as POLYGON's **area**—namely, to compute the total surface area bounded by the shape.

However, the designer/programmer of **area** for RECTANGLE would write the code for this method very differently from the code of **area** for POLYGON. Why? Because the area of a rectangle is simply **length * breadth**; the code for RECTANGLE's method **area** is consequently simple and efficient. However, since the algorithm to compute the area of an arbitrary complex polygon is complicated and less efficient, we wouldn't want to use it to calculate the area of a rectangle.

So, if we write some code that sends the following message to an object referred to by **two-d-shape**:

```
two-d-shape.area
```

we may not know which algorithm for computing area will be executed. The reason is that we may not know exactly to which class **two-d-shape** belongs. There are five possibilities:

1. **two-d-shape** is an instance of TRIANGLE. The method **area**, as defined for TRIANGLE, will be executed.

2. **two-d-shape** is an instance of RECTANGLE. The method **area**, as defined for RECTANGLE, will be executed.

3. **two-d-shape** is an instance of HEXAGON. Since HEXAGON lacks a method named **area**, through inheritance the method **area**, as defined for POLYGON, will be executed.

4. **two-d-shape** is an instance of a general, arbitrarily shaped POLYGON. The method **area**, as defined for POLYGON, will be executed.

5. **two-d-shape** is an instance of a class C (such as CUSTOMER) that isn't any of the four classes above. Since C probably doesn't have a method named **area** defined on it, the sending of the message **area** will result in a compile-time or run-time error. That's reasonable, of course, because **two-d-shape** shouldn't be pointing to a customer.

You may think it odd that an object may not know the exact class of the target object to which it's sending a message. However, that situation is quite common. For example, in the final line of code below, at compile-time we can't tell to what class of object **p** will point at run-time. The actual object pointed to will be determined by a last-minute user choice (in the **if** statement).

```
var p: POLYGON;
var t: TRIANGLE := TRIANGLE.new;
var h: HEXAGON := HEXAGON.new;
...
if     user says OK
then p := t
else  p := h
endif;
...
p.area;                    // here p may refer to a triangle or a hexagon
...
```

Notice that in the above piece of object-oriented code, we don't need a test around **p.area** to determine which version of **area** to execute. This is an example of very convenient implementation hiding. It allows us to add a new subclass of POLYGON (say, OCTAGON) without changing the above code in any way. The metaphor is: The target object "knows how to give its area," and so the sender doesn't need to worry.

Notice too the declaration **var p: POLYGON**. This is a safety restriction on the polymorphism of the variable, **p**. It means that **p** is permitted to point only to objects of class POLYGON (or to objects of one of POLYGON's subclasses). If **p** were ever assigned the handle of a CUSTOMER object or a HORSE object, then the program would stop with a run-time error.

The method **area**, being defined on several classes, provides a good example of polymorphism, as defined under (A). The variable **p**, being capable of pointing to objects of several different classes (for example, TRIANGLE and HEXAGON), is a good example of definition (B). The whole example shows how the two aspects of polymorphism work together to simplify programming.

An object-oriented environment implements polymorphism through *dynamic binding*. The environment inspects the actual class of the target object of a message at the last possible moment—at run-time, when the message is sent.

> *Dynamic binding* (or *run-time binding* or *late binding*) is the technique by which the exact piece of code to be executed is assessed only at run-time (as opposed to compile-time).

The above example, in which the method **area** is defined on POLYGON and TRIANGLE, also demonstrates the concept of *overriding.*

> *Overriding* is the redefinition of a method defined on a class C in one of C's subclasses.

The method **area**, which was originally defined on POLYGON, is overridden in TRIANGLE. TRIANGLE's method has the same name, but a different algorithm. You may occasionally use the technique of overriding to *cancel* a method defined on a class C in one of C's subclasses. You may cancel a method by redefining it simply to return an error.[18]

Related to polymorphism is the concept of *overloading*—not to be confused with overriding.

> *Overloading* of a name or symbol occurs when several methods (or operators) defined on the same class have that name or symbol. We say that the name or symbol is *overloaded.*

Both polymorphism and overloading often require that the specific method to be executed be picked out at run-time. As we saw in the small sample of code above, the reason is that the exact class of a target object—and thus the specific implementation of the method to be executed—may not be known until run-time.

The distinction between polymorphism and overloading is that polymorphism allows the same method name to be defined differently across different classes, while overloading allows the same method name to be defined differently several times in the same class.

Which polymorphic method is selected depends only on the class of the target object to which the message is addressed. But, with an overloaded method, how is

[18] If you rely heavily on cancellation, however, it's probably because you've begun with a shaky superclass/subclass hierarchy.

the correct piece of code bound to the method name at run-time? The answer is, by the signature—the number and/or class of the arguments—of the message. Here are two examples:

```
1a.    product1.mark-down
1b.    product1.mark-down (huge-percentage;)
2a.    matrix1 * i
2b.    matrix1 * matrix2
```

In the first example, the price of a product is reduced by the method **mark-down**. If **mark-down** is invoked with zero arguments (as in 1a), then the method uses a standard discount percentage; if **mark-down** is invoked with one argument (as in 1b)—a percentage—then the method applies the actual percentage supplied.

In the second example, the operator * is overloaded. If the second operand is an integer (as in 2a), then the operator * is scalar multiplication. If the second operand is another matrix (as in 2b), then the operator * is matrix multiplication.

1.9 Genericity

> *Genericity* is the construction of a class C so that one or more of the classes that it uses internally is supplied only at run-time (at the time that an object of class C is instantiated).

The best way to illustrate the concept of genericity is by means of a story from the thrilling days of yesteryear. When I was a university student, I took a course called Data Structures 101. One semester, Professor Rossini gave us an assignment to design and program a sorted, balanced, binary tree of integers. (See Fig. 1.22.) The main feature of a balanced tree is that all its leaves "bottom out" at the same level (give or take one level).

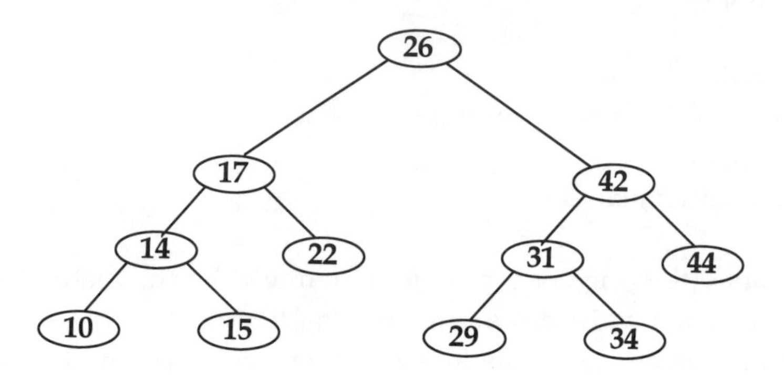

Fig. 1.22: A balanced binary tree of sorted integers.

That's all very simple—until you have to insert another integer into the tree (say 5, in Fig. 1.23). Then, the tree may become unbalanced, and you have to execute some painful node-twisting until the tree regains its balance.

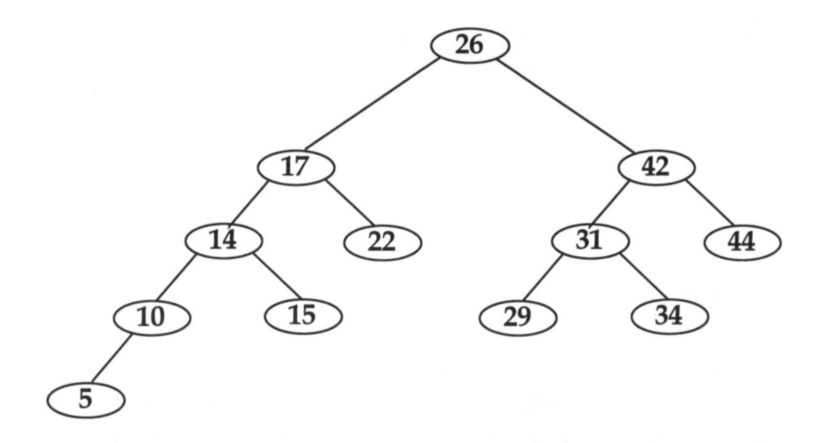

Fig. 1.23: A tree that's just become unbalanced.

After various amounts of desktop design and on-line debugging, most of us got our algorithms to work. With self-satisfied smiles, we turned in our programs, went on vacation, and forgot all about sorted, balanced, binary trees.

However, Professor Rossini's balanced-tree exercise was but an overture to a much bigger assignment. As part of an application during the next semester—maybe it was in Business Applications 101—we needed to keep sorted lists of customers and products. We smart alecks from Data Structures 101 simply dragged out our old code and copied it twice. In one copy, we replaced **integer** with **customer-id**; in the other, we replaced **integer** with **product-id**.

This cloning of old code greatly increased our productivity. However, this approach is not a silver bullet, because there's significant clone danger. The danger comes from the fact that we now have to maintain three copies of almost identical code.

Thus, if we found a better balanced-tree algorithm, we'd have to revise three pieces of code. Not only would this be extra work, but managing the three versions would also be complicated (unless we could come up with an automated clone changer—and pronto). What we needed was a way to write the basic structure of the balanced-tree algorithm only once and then (without merely cloning) to be able to apply it as many times as we wished to integers, customers, products, or whatever else.

At this point, genericity comes galloping up to rescue us. If we define BALANCED-TREE to be a generic class, it means that at least one of the classes used within BALANCED-TREE needn't be assigned until run-time. That would presumably be the class of the items to be stored in the nodes of the particular balanced-tree object that we instantiate.

I could therefore write the class BALANCED-TREE as follows:

```
class BALANCED-TREE [CLASS-OF-NODE-ITEM];
...
var current-node: CLASS-OF-NODE-ITEM := CLASS-OF-NODE-ITEM.new;
...
current-node.print;
...
```

Notice the generic class argument CLASS-OF-NODE-ITEM. This is a formal argument, whose actual "value" will be supplied only at run-time. For example, when we instantiate a new object of class BALANCED-TREE, we will supply a real class name as an argument, as follows:

```
...
var cust-tree:BALANCED-TREE := BALANCED-TREE.new [CUSTOMER];
var prod-tree:BALANCED-TREE := BALANCED-TREE.new [PRODUCT];
...
```

Thus, **cust-tree** now points to an object (an instance of BALANCED-TREE) that keeps instances of class CUSTOMER in its nodes, as shown in Fig. 1.24. (Similarly for **prod-tree**, of course.)

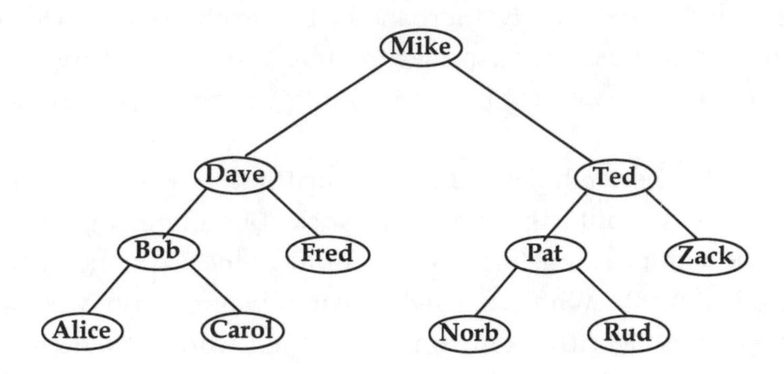

Fig. 1.24: A balanced binary tree of CUSTOMER objects. (I represent the customers held at the nodes by their first names.) This tree is the object to which the variable **cust-tree** *points.*

It's as if we'd cloned the first piece of code twice (once for CUSTOMER, once for PRODUCT) to read

```
class BALANCED-CUSTOMER-TREE;
    ...
    var current-node:CUSTOMER := CUSTOMER.new;
    ...
    current-node.print;
    ...
class BALANCED-PRODUCT-TREE;
    ...
    var current-node:PRODUCT := PRODUCT.new;
    ...
    current-node.print;
    ...
```

Finally, notice the statement **current-node.print**. This is a fine piece of polymorphism, because when we write that statement in the generic class BALANCED-TREE, we don't know what **current-node**'s class might be. Thus, anyone who instantiates a BALANCED-TREE had better take care that the method **print** actually is defined upon any class that is used to instantiate a particular tree.

As another example, if you design a generic class HASH-TABLE [C], you should point out that any class (such as SYMBOL) provided as the actual argument to C must have the method **hash** defined on it. (I cover this possible peril of genericity in detail in Chapter 11.)

You may have realized that there's a way to write BALANCED-TREE without genericity and without cloning. We could let the nodes of a balanced tree accept an object of the very topmost class in the superclass/subclass hierarchy. If we name this top class OBJECT, then the code would be

```
class BALANCED-TREE;
    ...
    var current-node:OBJECT := OBJECT.new;
    ...
    current-node.print;
    ...
```

Now each node of a balanced tree would accept the insertion of absolutely *any* kind of object. In particular, we could mix customers, integers, products, polygons, and horses in the very same tree. This would almost certainly be nonsense. Worse still, it would be very unlikely that all these different classes of objects would understand the message **print**.

Both BALANCED-TREE and HASH-TABLE are examples of *container classes.* A container class serves to hold objects in some—often sophisticated—structure. Genericity is often used in object orientation to design such container classes. Although genericity isn't strictly necessary to write reusable code for container classes, it's certainly superior to cloned code or to a fragile design where arbitrary classes are mixed within the same container-class structure.

1.10 Summary

Since "object orientation" lacks an *a priori* English meaning, there's been little historical consensus on the set of properties that define it. I consider the following properties to be central to object orientation: encapsulation, information/implementation hiding, state retention, object identity, messages, classes, inheritance, polymorphism, and genericity.

Object-oriented encapsulation yields a software structure (an "object") that comprises a ring of procedural methods around variables that retain the state of the object. Such encapsulation ensures that all external access to the variables is via the object's methods.

Information/implementation hiding is the payoff for good encapsulation. Good encapsulation allows information local to an object and design decisions about the internal implementation of the object to be protected from the gaze and meddling of outsiders.

State retention is the property by which an object can retain information indefinitely, including during the intervals between activation of its methods.

Object identity gives every object a unique identity that's independent of its current state. The object handle is the usual mechanism for assigning an identity to an object.

The handle of an object must be known to any objects that wish to send messages to that object. A message consists of the name of a method defined for the target object, together with any arguments to be passed to or from the method. Arguments may be data or pointers to data. However, in a pure object-oriented environment, arguments refer or point only to objects.

Objects derived from the same class share the same structure and behavior. A class is a stencil that is designed and programmed to be the pattern from which instances of the class—objects—are "manufactured" at run-time. A class may have a set of class methods and class variables. Each object has its own set of instance methods and instance variables. Objects of the same class save memory usage by sharing the same copy of each of their instance methods.

Classes may form inheritance hierarchies—or, more properly, lattices—of superclasses and subclasses. Inheritance allows objects of one class to use the facilities of any of the superclasses of that class. Selectively, methods of a class may be redefined ("overridden") in a subclass.

Polymorphism is the facility by which a single method name may be defined upon many different classes and may take on different implementations in each of those classes. Alternatively, polymorphism is the property whereby a variable is permitted to point to (hold the handle of) objects of different classes at different times.

Polymorphism adds a new twist to implementation hiding and gives object orientation much of its power. For example, a sender object may send a message without knowing the exact class of the target object. So long as all possible classes have access to an appropriate method, the selection of the particular method can be left to the run-time environment.

Overloading is a concept similar to polymorphism in which one of a number of different implementations of a method is chosen at run-time by inspecting the number and/or classes of the arguments of a message. Both polymorphism and overloading typically call for dynamic (or run-time) binding.

Genericity allows a generic class to take a class as an argument whenever an object is instantiated. This allows for the easy creation of "generic" container classes, which serve as skeletal classes on which the specific flesh can be added at run-time. Generic classes offer the advantages of cloned code without the overhead of replicated maintenance.

1.11 Exercises

1. Rewrite the hominoid-navigation algorithm to make it more robust. (One suggestion: Suppose someone forgot to mark the finish square in the grid. How should the algorithm cope with that?)

2. Does an object know its own handle? If so, how does an object refer to its handle?

3. Why would it be rare for the same argument name to appear both as an input argument and an output argument in the signature of a message? (Assume that the argument points to—that is, holds the handle of—an object.)

4. In Section 1.5, I said that "in object orientation there is no data." In other words, everything is an object (an encapsulation of methods around variables, which themselves point to objects). But surely there must be data "at the bottom of it all," or wouldn't we spiral down into an infinite recursive descent? So, can everything *really* be an object?

   And what about integers and reals, of which there are millions of instances? How do they get created?

5. An instance method may directly access a class variable (or it may send a class message to obtain information about that class variable). However, in a truly object-oriented environment, a class method cannot directly access an instance variable. Why not?

6. When we executed **GLIDER.new**—see Section 1.7—how many objects did we create?

7. Come up with an example of a class/subclass (*is a*) hierarchy. Hint: I found some old textbooks with rich examples from biological taxonomy.

8. How does an object-oriented program get started?

9. What happens to all your objects when you turn the computer off?

10. What happens to all your classes when you turn the computer off?

11. Can you think of a simple way to circumvent object orientation's robust encapsulation mechanism in a language such as C++?

12. Peter Wegner, in a *tour de force* paper, categorized environments as being *object-structured, object-based, class-based,* or *object-oriented.* The first has only encapsulation and state retention; the second adds object identity; the third adds the concept of the class; and the last adds inheritance and the other properties in this chapter.[19] Decide which of these four terms is most appropriate for the language that you're currently using.

13. Consider a piece of software that you (or your company) have purchased, which, its vendor claims, is "object oriented." What characteristics of the software did the vendor identify as being "object oriented"? Do you believe that the vendor's claims were justified? What benefits, if any, did you derive from the touted object-oriented characteristics of the product?

[19] I've modified Wegner's definitions somewhat. The original definitions are in [Wegner, 1990].

1.12 Answers

1. You're on your own!

2. Yes. An object has a variable that you don't need to declare, which holds its own handle. The variable is named **self**, **this**, or **Current** (in Smalltalk, C++, or Eiffel, respectively).

3. It would imply that the target of the message had changed the handle in one of the arguments, which is a nasty design practice. A sender of a message has the right to assume that its variables hold the same handles after it sends a message as they did before.

4. In a dyed-in-the-wool object-oriented language such as Smalltalk, everything *is* an object, and Smalltalk has unwaveringly adopted the position that "there is no data." For example, in Smalltalk the following act of addition

```
x <- 5 + 7
```

is interpreted as "send the message **plus** to the object **5** with the object **7** as the argument." The handle of the object **12** is then placed in the variable **x**.

Not all object-oriented languages, however, are as austere as Smalltalk. In a language such as Eiffel, there are still data-types (such as **int**, **real**, **char**, **bool**, and so on). However, any grander structures are classes that create object instances—not data instances—at run-time. Eiffel compromises the principle that "everything is an object" for a pragmatic reason: Treating integers, characters, and so forth as data-types allows interface compatibility with C code. In C++, standard C code with standard data-types may be arbitrarily mixed with C++ code. So in C++, all bets are off!

But when I tell people that pure object orientation has no data, they often hurl assorted legumes at me. The most popular examples that people counter me with are INT and DATE. How can these be classes, rather than old-fashioned data-types? Do we have to say **INT.new** before we can use the number 5, and **DATE.new** before we can use 25th September 1066?

No, that would be hopelessly unwieldy. Classes such as INT or DATE are known as *literal classes*. The objects that belong to them are known as *literal objects*. A literal object is simply what its value is. (Most literal objects are also *immutable*: They never change value. But there are exceptions. In Smalltalk, for example, a string is a literal object that *can* change its value.)

Although each object-oriented language has its own treatment of literal classes, most languages make the assumption that all instances of literal classes are predefined (or are created *in situ* by converting text strings like "15th March"). Other languages treat such "classes" as standard data-types, in which the instances are indeed old-fashioned data values rather than objects. In either case, instantiations from literal classes are unnecessary and illegal:

```
INT.new;          // illegal code!
DATE.new;         // illegal code!
```

5. The difficulty is, "instance variable of which object?" Remember that for a given class there may be thousands of objects of that class around at run-time. The only way for the class to "get at" the intended object is for the class to have the handle of that object and send a message to it. The object may then graciously return information from the variable requested to the class that sent the message.

6. One. (Whenever we execute the class method **new**, we always create exactly one object with, of course, one handle.) However, this object, which we named **gl**, is an instance of GLIDER and—via inheritance—also an instance of AIRCRAFT.

7. This is the class hierarchy that I came up with for LIVING-ANTHROPOID:

LIVING-ANTHROPOID
- 1. OLD-WORLD-PRIMATE
  - 1.1 OLD-WORLD-MONKEY
    - 1.1.1 CERCOPITH
      - BABOON, GUENON, MACAQUE
    - 1.1.2 COLOBIN
      - GUEREZA, LANGUR
  - 1.2 APE-HUMAN
    - 1.2.1 LESSER-APE
      - GIBBON
    - 1.2.2 GREAT-APE
      - GORILLA, ORANGUTAN, CHIMPANZEE
    - 1.2.3 HUMAN
      - HOMO SAPIENS
- 2. NEW-WORLD-PRIMATE

2.1 NEW-WORLD-MONKEY
    2.1.1 CEBID
        BEARDED-SAKI
    2.1.2 MARMOSET
        COMMON-MARMOSET

8. The initiation of an object-oriented program depends both on the language and operating system that you use. However, there are three popular ways in which an operating system may transfer control to your application program.

   The first is to begin execution at a main function, which, as in a regular procedural language, gains control at program start-up. The second is automatically to instantiate an object of a programmer-defined ROOT class, which, on its initiation, begins the execution of the entire program. The third is to bring up an object-oriented browsing environment, usually with a graphical interface. The user/programmer may then interactively send a message to an appropriate class (or object) to get things going.

9. When you turn the computer off, you lose all your objects in volatile memory, together with the information that they contain. If that's a problem, then you must store that information on disk before your object-oriented program terminates. With an object-oriented database-management system (ODBMS), you can store your objects more or less directly. But if you're using, say, a relational database, you'll have to "unpack" the objects' information into normalized, tabular form before you store them. (I discuss object persistence further in Chapter 7.)

10. When you turn the computer off, nothing happens to your classes (in most environments, anyway). Your classes are code that you've compiled and stored on your permanent disk. This illustrates again the difference between classes, which are permanent stencils, and objects, which are mercurial, everchanging, run-time units.

11. In some languages, a naughty designer can set up ways for outsiders to "climb over an object's walls" and mess with its variables directly. One way is through C++'s friend function. Like most other design sins, this one is usually perpetrated in the name of the great god Efficiency. (I discuss the friend function again in Chapter 5, Exercise 5, as well as in Section 8.2.)

12. Now that you've described your current language, consider which of its object-oriented properties (if any) you find most valuable. If your language isn't fully object oriented, which of the properties that I've outlined in this chapter do you most wish that your language had? Why?

Object Orientation— Who Ordered *That*?

Now that we've examined the intrinsic properties of object orientation, let's look at how object orientation fits into the wider landscape of software development. I begin this chapter by listing some of the people who "ordered" it.[1] I next set object orientation in a social context by discussing the attitudes toward object orientation—some of them extreme—that have arisen. Then, I set object orientation in an engineering context by making a parallel between object orientation and electronics. Finally, I indicate what object orientation might actually be good for, with respect to the programmers, analysts, and managers who make up your shop.

2.1 Where Did Object Orientation Come From?

Unlike many developments in human discovery, object orientation did not spring forth at a single moment. Rather than being the "Eureka!" inspiration of a single person in a bathtub, it's the amalgamation of the work of many people in many bathtubs over many years. The concepts of object orientation, which we covered in Chapter 1, are like several tributaries that have flowed together almost by historical accident to form the river of object orientation.

---

[1] The title of this chapter derives from a famous quote by Professor Isidor I. Rabi, who upon hearing Professor Wolfgang Pauli's proposal of the mu-meson retorted, "Who ordered *that*?"

So—with my apologies if I've left out your favorite software researcher—here (in approximate chronological order) are some of the folks who, I believe, have made significant theoretical or practical additions to the object-oriented flood:

2.1.1 Larry Constantine

Since no catalog of software contributors would be complete without him, let's start with Larry Constantine. Although in the 1960s Constantine did nothing under the heading "object orientation," he did research extensively into the fundamental criteria for good software design [Constantine, 1968]. Indeed, he was one of the first people even to suggest that software *could* be designed before it was programmed. Many of Constantine's notions have proven relevant to today's world of object orientation. In Chapter 8, I cover connascence, a concept based firmly on Constantine's durable concepts of coupling and cohesion.

2.1.2 O.-J. Dahl and K. Nygaard

Dahl and Nygaard introduced several ideas that are now considered object oriented. The best example is the idea of the class, which first appeared in the language Simula [Dahl and Nygaard, 1966].

2.1.3 Alan Kay, Adele Goldberg, and others

Kay, Goldberg, and their colleagues introduced the first incarnations of the Smalltalk language at the Xerox Palo Alto Research Center in the years around 1970 [Kay, 1969]. This research gave us many of the concepts that we now consider central to object orientation (such as messages and inheritance). Many people still consider the Smalltalk language and environment (now best known as Smalltalk-80 [Goldberg and Robson, 1989]) to be the purest implementation of object orientation in existence today.

2.1.4 Edsger Dijkstra

Dijkstra, the Conscience of Software Correctness, has been causing us perpetual guilt for more than thirty years. In his early work, he proposed the ideas of building software in layers of abstraction with strict semantic separation between successive layers. This represents a strong form of encapsulation, which is central to object orientation.

2.1.5 Barbara Liskov

Liskov made significant progress in the 1970s on the theory and implementation of the abstract data-type (ADT), which forms the foundation of object orientation. One of the most salient results of Liskov's work was the CLU language, in which the notion of hidden internal data representations is solidly supported.

2.1.6 David Parnas

In a landmark paper, Parnas wrote about the principles of good modular software construction [Parnas, 1972]. Although the constructs of object orientation transcend traditional procedural modules, many of Parnas' basic tenets of information hiding are still applicable in object-oriented systems.

2.1.7 Jean Ichbiah and others

Ichbiah and his group developed the "Green" Programming Language, which the U.S. Department of Defense adopted as the language Ada (now known as Ada-83).[2] Two of Ada-83's constructs (genericity and the package) are at the very heart of object orientation. A later version of the language, Ada-95, supports full object orientation.

2.1.8 Bjarne Stroustrup

The language C++ has an interesting genealogy. Once upon a time, there was Martin Richards' BCPL language [Richards and Whitby-Strevens, 1980]. This begat a language B, which was an abbreviation (!) for BCPL. B begat C, and C (through the work of Stroustrup) begat the object-oriented language C++.

As Stroustrup describes it [Stroustrup, 1991, p. 4], the "begetting of C++" sounds a tad fortuitous:

> C++ was primarily designed so that the author and his friends would not have to program in assembler, C, or various modern high-level languages. Its main purpose is to make writing good programs easier and more pleasant for the individual programmer. There never was a C++ paper design; design, documentation and implementation went on simultaneously.

---

[2] Ada® is a registered trademark of the United States government.

Since the object orientation of C++ was grafted upon earlier, non-object-oriented and fairly low-level languages, its syntax is not always clean. Nevertheless, C++ is currently the most widely used object-oriented language. Its C ancestry has given it portability across many machines and operating systems and has therefore vastly increased the popularity of object-oriented programming. In that respect, Stroustrup's contribution to the field has been huge.

2.1.9 Bertrand Meyer

Meyer's strength is the melding of the best ideas of computer science with the best ideas of object orientation. The result: a language and environment called Eiffel. Eiffel is a rarity in the software world, for it appeals simultaneously to academics, to software engineers, and to those folks in the trenches who need robust code. Whatever the chosen object-oriented language of your shop, you should definitely learn the concepts behind Eiffel if you want to become a real object-oriented professional.[3] In Chapter 10, I address class invariants, preconditions, and postconditions, the foundation of Meyer's "design by contract."

2.2 Object Orientation in a Social Context

This section describes how the software industry has reacted to the advent of object orientation. I begin by discussing the history of our industry, which has established an arena for the current strife over object orientation.[4]

2.2.1 The history of the mainstream

There's an old saw in biology: *Ontogeny recapitulates phylogeny.* This mouthful means that the development of an individual embryo often mimics the evolutionary development of its species as a whole. (An example would be the transient development of gills in the human embryo.) Of course, there's an enormous difference in time scale. Ontogeny takes months, whereas phylogeny takes eons.

There's a new saw in software engineering: *The history of object-oriented software engineering recapitulates the history of traditional software engineering.* Of course, there's an enormous difference in time scale. It took us decades to get our act together (sort of!) in procedural and database constructs; we're getting to grips with object-oriented software in a matter of years.

---

[3] An excellent book for learning Eiffel is [Wiener, 1995].

[4] Portions of the following sections were excerpted in *The Dorset House Quarterly*, Vol. 4, No. 4 (November 1994). Reprinted by permission.

Software development began simply with programming. As system size and human experience both grew, people realized that merely writing code for an application in a torrent of consciousness wasn't good enough. Even if such an application miraculously worked, its code would be so disorganized that any changes to it would be nigh impossible to make.

Enter design. Designing software made it possible to lay out a plan for a rational organization of code before a single line was actually chiseled into the coding pad. This radical idea even allowed people to assess potential maintenance problems at the paper-tiger stage.

So far, so good. Now we were capable of turning out exquisitely crafted software. However, some astute individuals noticed that much of this exquisite software didn't meet the users' needs. To satisfy the users' quirky passion for useful software, orderly and more rigorous analysis was ushered in.

Finally, we were blessed with Computer-Aided Software-Engineering (CASE) tools, which, though at first very rickety, later became only somewhat rickety. These CASE tools attempted to help us with the disciplines of analyzing requirements, designing software, and building software. They also attempted to make software development and maintenance more manageable.

During the entire history of software, people have attempted to achieve reusability. Unfortunately, most procedural units of code aren't self-contained enough to be reused independently. But now, with object orientation, we have another chance to gain the paradise of reuse.

However, object orientation guarantees no miracles. If object classes are not designed carefully along guidelines such as those that I set out in this book, object orientation will also fail to provide reusability. And then, as management expectations fall from grace once more, we *will* be able to reuse tales of managers' woe.

2.2.2 To the barricades: the object-oriented revolutionaries

As we saw in the previous section, object orientation's history paralleled that of the software mainstream. However, with object orientation, the progression from implementation toward abstraction has occurred at an extraordinary pace. Object-oriented programming first attained popularity in the 1980s. That same decade saw the introduction of both object-oriented design and object-oriented analysis. Object-oriented database-management systems (ODBMSs) and object-oriented CASE tools began to creep in around 1990.

The rapid arrival of these object-oriented fields led to a strange amnesia. Some of the people undergoing object-oriented ontogenesis suddenly forgot their mainstream phylogenesis. Their slogan became: "Anything known before 1980 isn't worth knowing!" They were the hot-blooded, take-no-prisoners, die-hard, object-oriented *revolutionaries*.

2.2.3 Forward to the past: the object-oriented reactionaries

Then came the rebuff as the object-oriented *reactionaries* lumbered out to be heard. Their slogan was: "Nothing significant in software has happened since the Sixties!"

And so began the strife. The reactionaries shook their heads and muttered at the revolutionaries: "All this object-oriented malarkey is just the same old stuff that we've always done, but with a few fancy name changes."

The revolutionaries decried the reactionaries as being coelacanths, primitive creatures lurking in the industry's depths and refusing to die out. They accused the reactionaries of holding back progress to preserve their own Paleozoic hides.

2.2.4 Enter the evolutionists (stage middle)

I'm an evolutionist. I take the position that both the reactionaries and the revolutionaries are dangerous extremists. I believe that progress in software is cumulative and not a series of nihilist revolutions. I have two powerful allies in this position, albeit allies by analogy.

First, when Nature comes up with a new species, it doesn't throw out millions of years of genetic rehearsal and start completely afresh. Nature tends to keep around what the new species will need and discard what it won't need. So, as humans, we get to keep the durable construct of the leg, whereas the gill idea gets thrown out.

Second, progress in science has been evolutionary. Even the so-called scientific revolutions [Kuhn, 1970] have really been evolutions built upon an abiding base. For example, you can see a typical evolutionary sequence of scientific thinking in the physical theories of Ptolemy, Copernicus, Kepler, Newton, and Einstein: Ptolemy modeled the earth as the center of the universe; Copernicus modeled the sun as the center of the solar system; Kepler derived planetary laws from Copernicus' model; Newton generalized Kepler's laws into a universal law of gravitation; Einstein generalized Newton's laws to accommodate relativistic effects.

Therefore, I contend that the object-oriented revolutionaries are wrong to take the position that object orientation is so new and different that nothing we knew before 1980 could possibly be relevant to this brave new world. I think that they may soon regret their disdainfully tossing out the principles of software development that we've discovered—often the hard way—since the dawn of software.

I also believe that the reactionaries are wrong in their position that nothing new has occurred since 1969. It would be wonderful if nothing ever changed in the world of software—at least long enough for us to master what we're trying to do at the moment. Unfortunately, our software world doesn't work like that. To see why, let's compare software development to the manufacturing process.

A manufacturing process has input (raw material) and output (product). At the most fundamental level, software manufacture consumes human thought as raw material and yields ones and zeros as product. See Fig. 2.1.

Fig. 2.1: Manufacturing software—a minimalist perspective.

Software manufacturing has some parallels with other kinds of manufacturing. For example, if the manufacturer didn't put enough raw material into your coffee mug, it would probably fall apart when you tried to drink from it. Similarly, if a software developer doesn't put enough human thought into software development, then the software may well fall apart when you try to use it.

So what's changed in software manufacturing over the last few decades? The most obvious and basic answer is, system size. In the 1950s, mammoth, million-dollar machines were so computationally feeble that there simply wasn't much software that you *could* fit into a given system. Approaches in those days were very concerned with harsh implementation constraints and had to emphasize ways of stuffing a quart of software into a pint of processor.

By about 1970, machines had become large enough for a given system to encompass quite a few ones and zeros. The trick then became to marshal the ones and zeros into an organization that would allow programmers to retain whatever sanity they possessed. By then, editors and compilers—the forerunners of contemporary CASE tools—were available to help with the job.

By 1980, as systems had grown even more gigantic, it became clear that another problem was looming, this time at the other end of the manufacturing process. Delivery of the raw material itself—human thoughts about requirements—was getting out of hand. While hardware systems had been simple and weak, human thoughts about software had necessarily been limited; it took no great talent to capture them and write them down. However, corralling many unruly, vague, and conflicting ideas now became the number-one priority for software approaches.

Figure 2.2 shows the three major parts of software manufacturing:

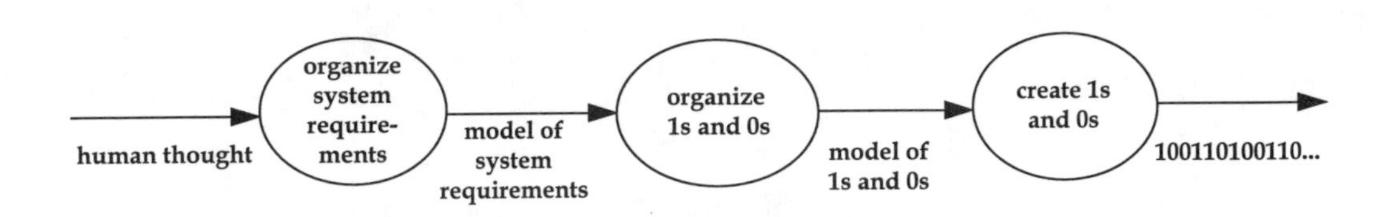

Fig. 2.2: Manufacturing software—the major activities.

Notice that nowadays we have to cope with size (tantamount to complexity) at both the human-thought end and at the ones-and-zeros end. Moreover, we have to deal with the bridge between the two ends, which is formed by the translation of the human-thought model into a system-structure model, the high-level model of the ones and zeros of the software.

Structured analysis was one of the first front-end approaches for manufacturing software. It teamed up with structured design, which was an approach to the large-scale organization of ones and zeros. Although structured analysis and structured design worked well in their respective domains, the bridge between them was awkward to traverse.

As systems grew, the abstractions provided by structured analysis and design became less adequate. For example, structured analysis and design don't offer the encapsulation of object-oriented approaches. Furthermore, there's a better match between analysis and design if each uses object-oriented abstractions.

Advances in hardware show no sign of relenting their incredible pace and, since system size is ultimately driven by hardware power, our software approaches are driven ever forward by innovation in—of all things—hardware design.

One day no doubt, as systems continue to grow, even object-oriented approaches will no longer be up to the job of system abstraction. Then, we'll see other approaches (subject-oriented systems, perhaps?) that contain object-oriented approaches as a subset within them.

2.3 Object Orientation As an Engineering Discipline

In 1986, Brad Cox observed that a software object in some ways resembles the hardware integrated circuit (IC) upon which so much of today's life depends [Cox, 1986]. I recalled this appealing analogy recently as archaeologists from the University of Washington were digging through the strata of paper in my office. They unearthed a book called *Introduction to Radar Systems* by Merrill Skolnik, in which Mr. Skolnik makes the observation that

> Electronic engineering may be categorized according to: (1) components, (2) techniques and (3) systems. Components are the basic building blocks that are combined, using proper techniques, to yield a system.

If we make a small substitution in Mr. Skolnik's prose, replacing "electronic" with "software" and "components" with "classes," we have

> Software engineering may be categorized according to: (1) classes, (2) techniques and (3) systems. Classes are the basic building blocks that are combined, using proper techniques, to yield a system.

Although this image is alluring, we shouldn't forget that the choice of worthwhile circuits to encapsulate on a chip depends on engineers' ability to identify useful abstractions. People will rush out to buy ICs for operational amplifiers, audio amplifiers, timers, line-drivers, and so on. But no one would even toddle out to buy an ultra-large-scale IC of random transistors, inductors, and resistors. Before the first useful IC was built, engineers had had decades to discover the useful patterns that crop up in system after electronic system.

In software, by analogy, we must make sure that the classes that we develop are based on sound, robust, handy abstractions. Classes such as CUSTOMER and the lovable, furry old STACK are likely to receive standing ovations; classes such as EGABRAGRETTU are more likely to be dumped at the edge of town.

Mr. Skolnik's second point is about techniques. Since ICs that couldn't be combined would be almost useless, it's fortunate that electronic engineers have at their disposal printed-circuit boards (PCBs) to serve to hook ICs together.

Similarly, in developing object-oriented software, we must also attend to the "macro" level of design. This level deals with the ways that classes (and the objects that classes generate at run-time) are interconnected. Clearly, there'll be a strong correlation between what we design at the intra-class level and what we design at this higher, inter-class level. That's to be expected of course, since the layout of a PCB certainly depends to some extent on the design of the ICs that sit on it.[5]

There can be good and bad object-oriented designs at both the intra-class level and the inter-class level. Thus, good object-oriented systems, like good electronic systems, depend not only upon high-quality abstractions but also upon high-quality techniques for building with those abstractions. Parts II and III of this book deal with these issues. But first, we must ask a basic question: What is object orientation good for?

2.4 What's Object Orientation Good For?

The title of this section is an invitation to cynics and fanatics. Some reactionaries would say that object orientation is good for nothing; it's merely a religious cult, or a global conspiracy based somewhere on the West Coast. Some revolutionaries will say that object orientation is the first and only miracle solution to all our software woes. Not only will it do windows, but it will also slice and dice vegetables, wax floors, and top off desserts.

Once again, I dwell at neither of these extremes. I believe that object orientation *is* useful, that it's *not* a miracle, that it's not even perfect, and that its specific utility depends upon how you put it to use in your software-development process.

No respectable software-engineering approach should be treated as a "Fad of the Year." A Fad of the Year is an approach that becomes all the rage for a few months or a year.[6] Its adherents espouse it hysterically as the solution to every roaming software problem. Skeptics are dragged aboard its bandwagon by the forces of fanaticism. Later, after the approach has been used and abused indiscriminately to mediocre effect, its adherents abandon it *en masse* and swarm forth to next year's Fad. If your shop "surfs on technology," moving rapidly from fad to fad, you're likely to benefit little from object orientation.

Neither is object orientation a mindless solution to the problems besieging your shop. Instead, as we'll see in this book, object orientation is a powerful—but challenging—approach to developing software. A mature, professional shop does not play with object orientation with all brains in the OFF position; it works hard at the object-oriented approach and integrates object orientation into its long-term plans for developing professional software.

---

[5] If you've studied standard structured design (see [Page-Jones, 1980], for example), you'll remember a similar principle: The coupling among a set of modules largely depends on the cohesion of each module in the set.

[6] See [Page-Jones, 1991] for more details on "Fad of the Year."

In the rest of this section, I discuss object orientation's potential effects on six of a shop's typical software activities.

2.4.1 Analyzing users' requirements

Structured techniques have never converged peaceably to a consensus over where the boundary between procedural and data analysis should be. The procedural world of the dataflow diagram has always coexisted uneasily with the data world of the entity-relationship diagram. Procedural and data analysis became clashing tectonic plates, meeting in some places, subducting each other seismically in other places, and missing each other altogether in others. The clash was especially noticeable in real-time system modeling, where (for example) the correspondence between the control process and the data model was often unclear.

An object-oriented approach to analysis melds procedural and data investigation early in the lifecycle. Although (as mentioned in Footnote 3 of Chapter 1) we can't really say "procedural and data analysis" when we talk about object orientation—"dynamic and static analysis" would be better—the up-front use of object-oriented concepts brings sweeter harmony to these two aspects of analysis. Although I find their comparison extravagant, some people have likened object orientation's blending of procedure and data to Einstein's fusing of space and time in his theories of relativity.

2.4.2 Designing software

In design, object orientation is both a boon and a bane. Object orientation is a boon because it allows a designer to hide behind the scenic walls of encapsulation such software eyesores as: convoluted data structures, complex combinatorial logic, elaborate relationships between procedure and data, sophisticated algorithms, and ugly device drivers.

Object orientation is a bane because the structures that it employs (such as encapsulation and inheritance) may themselves become complex. In object orientation, it's all too easy to create a Gordian hammock of inextricable interconnections that either is unbuildable or will result in a system that runs like a horse in a sack race.

The purpose of this book is to neutralize object orientation's bane. In the next part of the book, I provide a notation for depicting and exploring design decisions. In Part III, I offer several design principles and criteria by which you can judge a design. Using these design principles and criteria, you can create object-oriented constructs that will cooperate when you construct systems from them, and yet will be independently maintainable. Although object-oriented design will sometimes demand exceptionally diligent work, it's work that, when well done, will reward you with the taming of larger units of complexity than you could attain via other design techniques.

2.4.3 Constructing software

The qualities that are most frequently touted for systems built in an object-oriented way are reusability, reliability, robustness, and extensibility.

Reusability

Object orientation enhances reusability because it promotes reuse of code at the class level rather than at the level of the individual subroutine. By developing and tending a library of classes for *your* applications in *your* shop, you are, in effect, creating a new, very-high-level language tailored specifically to your needs.

It appears empirically that the object class is a sophisticated-enough organism to be able to migrate from application to application across your company as a self-contained unit of software.

Reliability

Reliable code is code that works repeatedly and consistently. Your code will attain these qualities only if you can verify its correctness in some way. Object-oriented code lends itself to verification through the use of certain assertions called *class invariants*. A class invariant is a condition that every object of a given class must satisfy. (For example, an invariant of class PERSON may be **date-of-birth <= todays-date**.)

Class invariants (and other assertions that I also cover in Chapter 10) make it possible to verify code very thoroughly. In a walkthrough or inspection, you can check that a design or its resulting code meets the intended invariants. Although—even using object orientation—you can never prove code *absolutely* correct, object orientation does make it easier to check that the code will do what you think it should.[7]

Robustness

Robustness in software is its ability to recover gracefully whenever a failure occurs. (Typical failures are assertion violations, external-device errors, and arith-

[7] The ultimate reason is that the concept of correctness is not an absolute one that's fixed for all observers, but one that's relative to the frame of reference of a particular observer. In other words, correctness is ultimately subjective.

metic overflows.) Software becomes robust when it can trap such an unexpected failure (usually termed an *exception*) and can execute a routine (usually termed an *exception handler* or *rescue clause*) to recover from the failure.

Many modern object-oriented languages and environments support exception detection and handling and thus encourage the development of robust software. An excellent way to achieve robustness of object-oriented code is to combine the idea of assertions and invariants with that of exception handlers. In some object-oriented environments, you can monitor class invariants and other assertions at run-time and also have your software deftly recover if (Heaven forfend!) an assertion should be violated.

The alternatives to exception handling are (1) merely to let the software crash when an exception occurs, or (2) not to bother ever to detect exceptions. Neither alternative represents robustness, of course.

Extensibility

Easy extensibility of software depends technically on what's called a "homomorphism between the domain of specification and the domain of implementation." Ouch! In less formal words, it means that you should make the shape of the solution fit the shape of the problem. By doing this, you ensure that a small user change will not become a major system nightmare. Because object orientation builds units of software with higher-level, more true-to-life abstractions, object orientation comes closer to this "homomorphism" than traditional techniques did.

Extensibility and inheritance often go hand in hand. Users often want to extend a system by adding variations to an already stated theme. (For example: "Instead of just *customers*, we now want to have *domestic and foreign customers*."[8]) Using object orientation, you can make such extensions incrementally by adding inheriting subclasses under an already implemented superclass.

2.4.4 Maintaining software

The qualities of reusability, reliability, robustness, and extensibility are the four pillars of maintainability. (Maintenance, of course, is what many shops spend most of their money on.)

Because reusability cuts down the amount of new code that has to be written for a system—especially after your first one or two object-oriented projects—reusability also reduces the overall body of code that your shop must maintain.

[8] However, this is a glib example. As we'll see in Chapters 10, 11, and 12, most real-life examples aren't so neat and easy.

Reliability in software diminishes users' winces of discontent and their pained cries for fixes. Robustness ensures that software being maintained won't fall completely to pieces on the operating table. Extensibility takes advantage of the users' natural tendency to ask for "base-displacement" kinds of modifications to their systems, whereby they continually ask for many, comparatively minor, modifications to existing software.

2.4.5 Using software

Graphical applications have always been a popular choice for object orientation. In particular, modern graphical user interfaces (GUIs) are often implemented by means of object orientation. There are two reasons for this: The first is conceptual; the second, implementational.

Conceptually, the metaphor of object orientation fits well with the typical window/mouse/icon interface. Let's say that you have an icon on a screen. This icon may be a visible representation of an object, say a customer. Click on the icon with a mouse to select that customer. Then, bring up a menu. The options on the menu may correspond closely to methods that apply to a customer. For example, there may be an option to **change-address**, another to **reassess-credit-limit**, and so on. A domestic customer could have a different menu from an export customer, based on which business actions apply to each kind of customer support.

Even polymorphism—the ability for a method to take on different meanings or implementations with respect to different classes—may appear at the user interface. Let's say you have one icon on the screen representing a spreadsheet object and another representing a document object. When you click on the **Open** menu item, you will attach either the spreadsheet program or the text-processing program to the object, depending on which of the two icons was highlighted. In other words, the particular version of the **open** method that's executed depends on whether the class of the highlighted object was SPREADSHEET or DOCUMENT.

Implementationally, many commercially available libraries of components that let you build window/mouse/icon interfaces are written in an object-oriented language. Since a window naturally has many properties of an object, most development tools for windowing interfaces also have a seam of object orientation running through them.

So, while it's not quite true to say that object orientation *per se* makes software more usable, it is true that a good graphical user interface makes software more usable and that object orientation may be the best approach to building software libraries to support graphical user interfaces.

2.4.6 Managing software projects

So far, I've directed almost everything that I've introduced in this book toward technical people. But what of the poor manager? Is object orientation another technical innovation that must be borne in silent suffering until its advocates wither away or join another shop? Or worse, is object orientation merely another silver bullet with which a manager can shoot himself in the foot?

No. Object orientation isn't just for nerds. Object orientation's technical advantages are advantages for managers too. For example, a technique that reduces maintenance clearly frees up a manager's resources to attack the pressing application backlogs. But, for managers, object orientation goes further than the mere technical. Object orientation deals change both to a shop's organization and to managers' jobs.

For many reasons, a shop's organization will change when it adopts object orientation. Reuse of classes will require a class library and a class librarian. Each programmer will migrate into one of two groups: the group designing and coding new classes or the group using classes to create new applications. With less emphasis on programming (reusability implies less new code), requirements analysis will become relatively more important.

As a manager whose shop is moving into object orientation, you should be aware of such organizational changes. You will need to train your staff for their new roles. You will need to manage people in these roles. You will need to encourage reusing, rather than recoding. You will need to give people time to think through their class designs so that the classes they construct are fit for reuse. In short, you will need to run project teams that are suddenly using different terminology, different tools, and a different lifecycle, and—at the same time—aiming at goals that are new, or at least have found a new significance.

Object orientation works well only if managers treat it as a means, rather than an end. Object orientation is the means to—pick one that interests you—maintainability, extensibility, robustness, reduced delivery time, and so on. As a manager, you should focus on your goal at all times and use object orientation as a technology to achieve that goal. As one manager put it to me: "When I buy soap, I always remember that I'm really after clean hands."

If you don't keep your goal in mind, then object orientation with all its transitional costs (financial, organizational, social, and emotional) will seem like an expensive boondoggle. But if you know not only what you're doing, but also *why* you're doing it, then you'll derive the stamina to score the object-oriented goal you're seeking.

2.5 Summary

Part of the appeal of object orientation is the analogy between object-oriented software components and electronic integrated circuits. At last, we in software have the opportunity to build systems in a way similar to that of modern electronic engineers by connecting prefabricated components that implement powerful abstractions. But, to take advantage of this, we must first identify sound software abstractions and have ways to link them constructively.

Techniques for achieving these "software integrated circuits" fall broadly under the rubric of object orientation. "Object orientation" is a term that gathers together the ideas of many software researchers from the 1960s to the present day. However, not everyone would agree with this point of view. Some people (object-oriented revolutionaries) would say that object orientation represents a complete break with the past. Others (reactionaries) take the opposite position: Object orientation is, at most, a veneer of jargon over the "same old stuff."

My experience is that object orientation is neither the same old stuff nor a complete break from everything we ever learned about software. Instead, it's a welcome evolutionary step that goes far toward meeting the challenge of developing ever-more-complex software.

Object orientation also addresses two problems of structured techniques. The first is the rift between procedure and data and the mismatch between the requirements-analysis model and the software-design model. The second is the gap between so-called information and real-time systems-development approaches. In my opinion, a good object-oriented approach spans both categories of system.

Object orientation makes itself felt in all phases of software development. In analysis, it demands a deep investigation of the abstractions within the users' dominions—at least if true reusability is to be achieved. In design, it calls for the sound organization of software components, many of which are more sophisticated than those found in traditional structured design.

Constructing reliable and robust object-oriented software requires establishing various assertions, such as class invariants, that can be monitored for exceptions at run-time. Software maintenance is improved not only because reusability yields "less code to maintain" but also because the software is built on sounder abstractions.

Although object orientation isn't just for graphics anymore, it's still valuable for building graphical user interfaces. For this reason, the object-oriented abstractions fit well with the friendly, natural interfaces that many users have come to expect.

Finally, object-oriented software development will be successful only if it is managed intelligently. Managers should introduce object orientation smoothly and then manage its demands (such as software-engineering discipline) and results (such as reusability) carefully.

2.6 Exercises

1. Most analogies break down somewhere. As you read through the chapters of this book, consider the flaws in the analogy between a software object class and an electronic integrated circuit.

2. From what you know of object orientation, where would you place yourself in the spectrum *reactionary . . . evolutionist . . . revolutionary*? Justify your position by comparing developments in object orientation with those in the traditional mainstream of software development.

3. In your opinion, is it necessary for a shop to choose a language (or operating environment) that has *all* of the object-oriented properties that I described in Chapter 1? In other words, do you concur with some object-oriented revolutionaries, who tend to sneer at shops that choose something less than full object orientation?

4. Consider the Object-Oriented Hall of Fame of Section 2.1. Whom, in your opinion, have I left out? What contribution did he or she make to the theme of object orientation?

5. I mentioned some advantages of object orientation in Section 2.4. Did I leave out any applications of object orientation that you consider important? In particular, are there any tools that you've used that exploit object orientation in a practical way?

2.7 Answers

1. One flaw in the analogy stems from the way that software ICs are wired together in most current object-oriented languages. Electronic ICs remain symmetrically anonymous to one another. Wiring goes from one IC socket to another IC socket and at no time does an IC "know" to which other ICs it's connected; it "knows" only its own pins and not the pins of other ICs.

   Not so with classes and objects. Classes are connected to other classes by explicit name. For example, if CLASS-A inherits from CLASS-B, then CLASS-A will contain a line of code such as **inherits from CLASS-B**. Objects send messages by naming a method of another object. This is like connecting an IC to another by soldering a lead from the inside of one to a pin of the other.

   Peter Wegner discusses this concept further in Section 6.1.3 of his paper [Wegner, 1990]. (In the remainder of this book, I also cover the connections among classes in more detail.)

2. If you're an object-oriented reactionary, then look back at the key abstractions of object orientation that I covered in Chapter 1. Check each one carefully to see whether you can find reference to a similar abstraction in some pre-object-oriented publication. If you're an object-oriented revolutionary, read for example Yourdon and Constantine's book on structured design [Yourdon and Constantine, 1975]. Can you make a case that the major concepts of this work (such as coupling and cohesion) are irrelevant to our brave, new, object-oriented world?

3. In my opinion, the debate over whether I Am More Object Oriented Than Thou is a religious, moot point having little to do with engineering. The engineering issue is, Which benefits of object orientation are most important to us in achieving our shop's goals? A partially object-oriented environment has *some* of the software-engineering advantages of object orientation and lacks others. Therefore, a shop that understands its needs and chooses an environment that satisfies those needs is exercising good judgment.

4. As grist for your answer, you may want to consider, for example, the developers of the languages, tools, and methodologies that you use in your shop.

5. Although this is clearly an open-ended question, let me suggest two kinds of tool for your list. The first is an application-development tool that allows you to develop applications to run on multiple, distributed computers, without your having to write screeds of code to handle the communication between

pieces of the application that run on the various machines. A common point among such tools is that you build your application in an object-oriented way and the tool mediates the messages among your run-time objects. This means that, although objects may reside on different machines, this distribution is transparent to you, as the application designer and programmer. Thus, you can write messages in the usual, single-processor way and let the message mediator (or "broker") provided by the tool handle inter-machine communication.

A second kind of tool that exploits object orientation is an object-oriented database-management system (ODBMS). An ODBMS is useful if you're building any object-oriented application, and is especially useful if your application manipulates sound or graphics, neither of which is easily held in a standard relational, tabular form. An ODBMS will hold objects of arbitrary classes (not only STRING, REAL, INT, and DATE) and provides object-oriented encapsulation, inheritance, polymorphism, and so on. Most ODBMSs come with a query language (such as object-query language, OQL), which replaces the structured-query language (SQL) of relational DBMSs.

Part II: Object-Oriented Design Notation

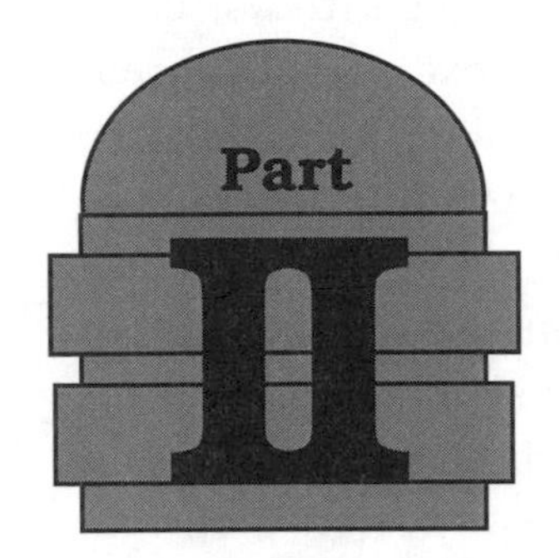

"When I behold, upon the night's starr'd face,
Huge cloudy symbols of a high romance."

—John Keats, *Sonnet*, "When I Have Fears"

Part I explored object orientation through its key abstractions and its context in software engineering. Part II—Chapters 3 through 7—presents object-oriented software structure more pictorially, as we examine a graphic notation for representing design constructs.

In 1990, Larry Constantine, Steve Weiss, and I developed a prototype object-oriented design notation.[1] It was called Uniform Object Notation (or UON), meaning that it could be used "uniformly" to depict systems built by means of structured techniques, object-oriented techniques, or a mixture of both. However, UON addressed only some of the constructs found in object-oriented systems.

Later, Brian Henderson-Sellers and Julian Edwards developed UON beyond its primitive beginnings into a notation that became part of their MOSES methodology.[2] Working partly with Henderson-Sellers and Edwards and partly alone, I extended UON further, into a notation called Object-Oriented Design Notation (or OODN).

Like UON, OODN is a notation for expressing the structure of object-oriented code at a level above that of individual lines of code. But, unlike its simpler forebear, OODN contains diagrams that span the gamut of constructs that appear in typical object-oriented systems. These diagrams include, for

[1] See [Page-Jones, Constantine, Weiss, 1990] for the previous work on UON.

[2] See [Henderson-Sellers and Edwards, 1994] for the MOSES notation.

instance, the object-aggregation diagram, the state-transition diagram, and the window-navigation diagram.

I believe that a good design notation should show overall system structure graphically, but leave detailed semantic definitions (such as algorithms, class invariants, and method preconditions and postconditions) to text. For that reason, OODN doesn't try to replace textual definitions of classes and their methods. Instead, the notation provides a graphic framework for organizing design components and then defining each component via appropriate text.

Each of the five chapters in Part II introduces diagrams and symbols that cover a particular group of object-oriented design constructs. Chapter 3 introduces the class-external-interface (or pin-out) diagram, which shows a class and the formal signatures of its methods, and the class-internal-design diagram, which shows the interaction of methods with other internal components of a class.

Chapter 4 covers the class-inheritance diagram, which shows a hierarchy of singly or multiply inheriting classes, and the object-aggregation diagram, which shows the pointers to other objects contained in an object's private variables. The object-aggregation diagram is chiefly used to show the component objects of which an aggregate object is composed.

Chapter 5 covers the object-communication diagram, which shows the messages (and actual arguments) passed between objects at run-time, and the object-interaction/timing diagram, which shows objects' methods scaled roughly to their execution times. This diagram is particularly useful for designing systems with concurrent execution and asynchronous messaging.

Chapter 6 addresses the state-transition diagram, which shows how objects may make transitions from state to state within the state-space defined for their class. Many of the issues in Chapter 6 relate to the adaptation of traditional state-transition diagrams for object-oriented software.

Chapter 7 wraps up Part II with a miscellany of more specialized diagrams that don't warrant a chapter apiece. Although you probably won't use all of the notation of Chapter 7 on your next project, you will find some of its notation to be useful in particular circumstances. Chapter 7's diagrams are: the database-access diagram, which shows various ways of interacting with a persistent-storage mechanism; the technology-interconnect diagram, which shows units of technology and their physical communication links; the processor-interconnect diagram, which shows how a software system is partitioned across components of technology; the window-layout diagram, which shows the content of an individual window; and the window-navigation diagram, which shows the application-meaningful paths between windows.

In Part II, I occasionally point out alternative styles of OODN that you may choose to depict a given construct. Which style you choose will depend on your taste and your drawing technique. Since the alternative symbols are usually semantically identical, a good CASE tool should allow you to switch among them at will.

Note, as you go through Part II, that OODN is intended strictly as a design notation, rather than a requirements-analysis notation.

The Basic Notation for Classes and Methods

This chapter describes the Object-Oriented Design Notation (OODN) for classes and methods. I first introduce the symbol for the class itself and then explore notation for the various kinds of methods that you may allocate to a class. The chapter continues with notation for packages (a rudimentary construct in which classes and objects aren't differentiated) and concludes with notation for the internal design of classes.

But, before I launch into the notation itself, let me present the nine goals of OODN.

3.1 The Goals of OODN

Although it has a more sophisticated repertoire of notation than UON, OODN's goals are the same as those that I set with Larry Constantine and Steve Weiss for UON. They are:

1. Simplicity and straightforwardness

There are many baroque notations for object-oriented design. But, because many of these have turned out to be unteachable and unlearnable, we've learned that a successful system-design notation must be sparse and clear in its set of symbols. On the other hand, since object orientation yields complex software constructs, we can't get by with a notation quite as simple as those invented in the 1970s.

2. Balance between the sparseness of the symbol alphabet and richness of expression

Although OODN seeks to avoid a mob of marauding symbols, it shouldn't restrict a designer's ability to express designs. Thus, I had to choose a symbol set that covers all necessary design constructs, whichever object-oriented environment a designer uses. However, because of this generality, you probably won't use the whole panoply of OODN symbols on any one project or even within any one shop.

3. Capability to express bad designs (within reason) as well as good ones

This isn't a primary goal for the notation, but I feel that OODN shouldn't editorialize. If someone wants to depict a miserable design (perhaps that of an existing system), he should be able to use OODN to do it. Obviously, the depiction of a bad design wouldn't be a pretty sight; it would be the very reflection of the underlying mess.

4. Alignment of symbols and structure with intuition

Over a beer in the days of UON, Larry Constantine said: "If we show the public-method symbol to a paleolithic inhabitant of a remote island, he should be able to understand that the method symbol protrudes a few millimeters outside the underlying class symbol because the method has external visibility beyond the class." Well, having failed to find a Stone Age islander, we tried the experiment on some object-oriented programmers, who (by and large) bestowed reality upon Larry's wish.

5. Correspondence to code close enough to permit reengineering

OODN depicts the structure of object-oriented code at the level just above that of the code itself. Therefore, it should be possible to take existing code and, by automated or manual means, represent its structure in OODN.

6. Wide applicability

I don't want to tie OODN to the idiosyncrasies of any single object-oriented language, however popular that language might be. As I was working on OODN, I kept at the front of my mind the constructs of about half-a-dozen mainstream object-oriented languages.

Sometimes it was tough to decide which language features to include. For example, I decided not to introduce special notation to handle the dynamic object-delegation that's found in the language Self, because the language doesn't seem popular enough to warrant the inclusion.

It also wasn't easy to come up with a notation that could depict most of the constructs of the major object-oriented languages and still be natural enough for users of any single language. The result was inevitably a superset of what any one person might need. So, again, don't feel obliged to use the entire set of OODN just because it's there. It's okay to choose only those symbols that are relevant to your language, your environment, and your project.

7. Consistency with Structured Design Notation

Structured Design Notation (SDN) has been a popular choice for depicting traditional procedural systems.[1] I want OODN to be compatible with SDN for two reasons. First, I'd like people to be able to reuse their knowledge and experience in their move to object-oriented systems. Second, many so-called object-oriented systems are actually hybrids of object-oriented code and standard procedural code. (For example, a project team may want to use some library routines or salvage some code from previous systems.) Therefore, I aimed for a notation that can depict a hybrid system as well as a "pure" object-oriented system.

8. As far as possible, consistency with other object-oriented notations

Over the years, I have dissected many object-oriented design notations and looked for their good and bad points. Wherever possible, I tried to adopt from them what made sense, rather than to strain myself to be gratuitously different. Of course, because there's not much discernible consistency among the competing notations, it was impossible to be consistent with *all* of the existing object-oriented notations.

9. Computer-aided, as well as manual, usage

Since Computer-Aided Software-Engineering (CASE) tools are widespread, I tried to create a notation suitable for the province of the screen, mouse, and printer. But, despite the availability of CASE, plenty of system modeling still takes place on whiteboards and on the backs of envelopes. So, I made most of OODN's symbols sketchable with humble pencil and paper too, prior to their subsequent glory in an electronic medium. For this reason, I offer alternatives to some symbols, which are easier to draw by hand than are the original forms.

---

[1] See, for example, [Page-Jones, 1980] and [Yourdon and Constantine, 1975].

3.2 The Class Symbol

The class (or object-module) symbol on the left of Fig. 3.1 is the basis of OODN.[2] Its shape—part curved, part rectilinear—is a metaphor taken from Structured Design Notation, where a circle symbolizes data and a rectangle symbolizes procedure. Therefore, the class symbol evokes the part-data, part-procedure nature of the class.[3]

Fig. 3.1: Symbol for a class and an abbreviated alternative.

People refer to the class symbol informally as the "bread slice," the "stained-glass window," the "stone tablet," or, more grimly, "the tombstone." (Perhaps your project can come up with a better nickname than any of those.)

An alternative symbol for a class appears on the right side of Fig. 3.1. This abbreviated symbol is handy when you want to show only a class and its name.

A generic class is shown with a [ ] suffix to its name. For example, a balanced tree class that holds CUSTOMER objects in its nodes might be named BALANCED-TREE [CUSTOMER].

3.3 Modifier and Accessor Methods

To define the external properties of a class, you begin with a diagram of the class and the methods defined on it. Figure 3.2 shows a class with two methods.

Notice in Fig. 3.2 that the method symbols at the left have different shapes. Method **a** (with a rectangular shape) is a method that may change the state of an object of class CLASS1. For example, the method **turn-left** of HOMINOID (Chapter 1), which updates the direction of a hominoid, is such a method. Such methods

[2] I use the blanket term *object module* to cover both *classes* and *objects* in those languages that make little distinction between them.

[3] Or, more precisely: part state, part behavior.

are termed *modifier methods*. Informative and imperative messages (see Section 1.5.4) typically invoke modifier methods.

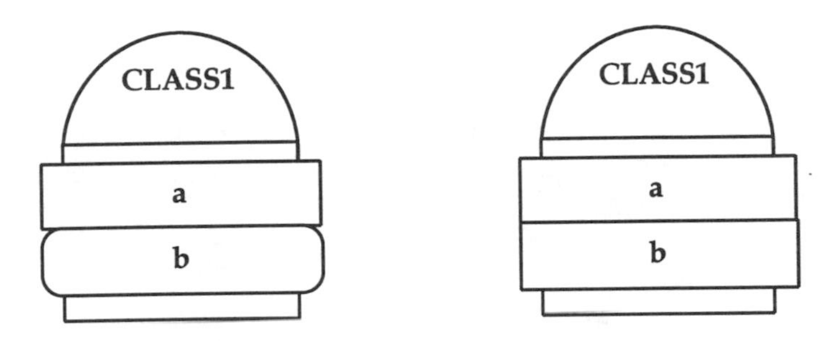

Fig. 3.2: Modifier and accessor methods.

Method **b** (with a rounded corner shape known in the trade as a roundangle) is a method that doesn't change the state of an object. It's an example of a read-only method whose job is to convey information about the state of the object. For example, the method **location** of HOMINOID, which returns the square on which a hominoid finds itself, is such a method. Such methods are termed *accessor methods*. Interrogative messages (see Section 1.5.4) typically invoke accessor methods.

Some shops choose not to distinguish between modifier and accessor methods. These shops show both kinds of methods as a rectangle, as shown at the right side of Fig. 3.2. This is a reasonable approach, since most object-oriented languages don't distinguish between modifier and accessor methods either.[4]

3.4 The Class-External-Interface Diagram

The OODN diagram on the left side of Fig. 3.3 shows the formal interfaces to the methods of a class. Each formal interface consists of the method's name, together with the list of formal arguments comprising the method's interface.[5] (The list of formal arguments is also known as the method's *formal signature*.)

---

[4] Eiffel is an example of a language that *does* distinguish between them, with its procedure and function routines, respectively. See [Meyer, 1992].

[5] *Formal argument* is a traditional term in computer science. It means an argument that appears in the definition of a function (usually in the function header, which defines the function's interface). By contrast, an *actual argument* is one that's supplied by a caller of the function. In object orientation, the same distinction between *formal* and *actual* applies to the arguments of methods.

Each formal argument of methods **a** and **b** is shown as a little object with a label. The label has two parts: the argument's formal name and the class to which the argument belongs. The single argument of method **c** is a data-type (such as INT) and is shown with a data symbol (as denoted by the circular tail on the argument arrow).

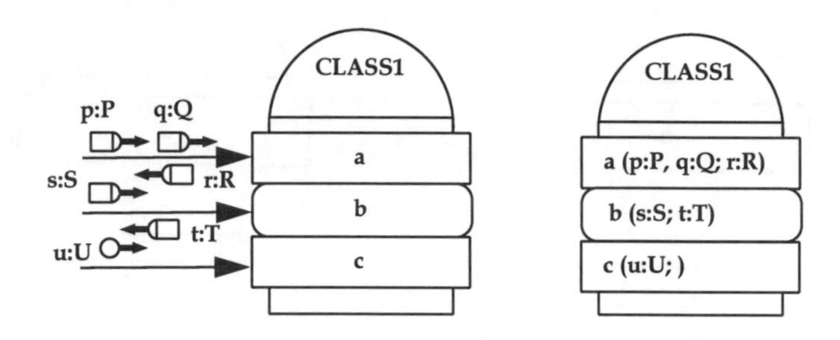

Fig. 3.3: Three methods with their formal interfaces—a pin-out diagram.

On the right side of Fig. 3.3, I show an alternative, more textual, style of depicting a class-external-interface diagram. In this style, you write the input-argument list and output-argument list for a method inside the method symbol, separated by a semicolon. (Note that since method **c** has no output-argument list, there's nothing after the semicolon in its signature.) Since the world seems divided as to which style is more convenient, I show examples of both styles throughout this section.

Taken as a set, the formal interfaces to the methods represent the formal interface to the whole class. Many people refer to this class-external-interface diagram as the pin-out diagram, because it so much resembles the diagram of IC pins in an integrated-circuit catalog.[6]

[6] Some authors refer to this diagram as an *ADT-definition* or *object-type-definition diagram*, where "ADT" stands for "abstract data-type."

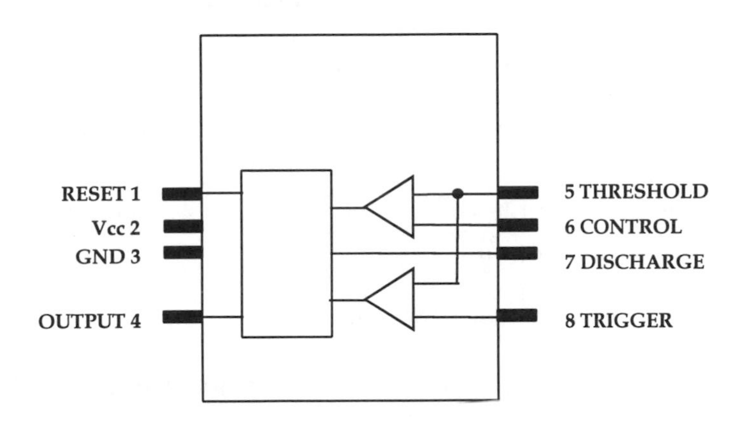

Fig. 3.4: A pin-out diagram for a fictitious IC, a timer.

To reinforce the analogy between a class and an integrated circuit, I show (in Fig. 3.4) an example of a pin-out diagram for an electronic IC, a fictitious timer. The diagram shows what each of the eight pins requires as input or provides as output. The behavior of some of the pins is also implied by their names. The pins of the IC correspond to methods of a class.

3.5 Function-Style Methods

A *function-style method* (or, in some languages, simply a *function*) transmits a value via the name of the method itself. (The term arose in the early days of FORTRAN, where such a component was termed a *function*.) Usually, a function-style method is used as an accessor method. However, it may be used either as a modifier method or as an accessor method or both. (Eiffel follows this practice by using functions only as accessors.[7] C++ uses them as both accessors and modifiers.)

[7] Eiffel uses the simple terms *function* and *procedure*, respectively, for *function-style method* and *procedure-style method*.

The following is an example of a function-style method used as an accessor method (which is, as I mentioned, the most common use):

```
cust-ship-addr := cust1.shipping-address;
```

Here, the function-style method **shipping-address** passes information out from the object known as **cust1**.

The following is an example of a function used as a modifier method (which isn't possible in some languages):

```
cust1.shipping-address := new-ship-addr;
```

In this example, the function-style method **shipping-address** is being used to receive a new shipping address, with which it updates the state of the object known as **cust1**.

Figure 3.5 shows two function-style methods of the class CUBOID (a "stretched" cube). OODN shows a function-style method used as a *modifier* with a right-pointing arrow (>) after the method name. A function-style method used as an *accessor* has a left-pointing arrow (<) before its method name. (Mnemonic: The symbol points in the direction of the allowed assignment.)

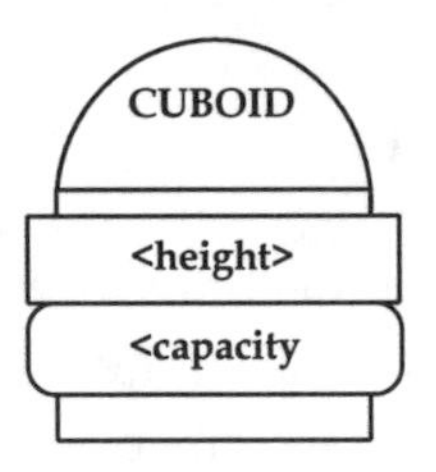

Fig. 3.5: Two function-style methods.

The method **<height>** is therefore a function-style method that can be used both as a modifier and an accessor method. In other words, this function-style method may appear on either the left or right side of an assignment. For example,

```
cuboid1.height := new-cuboid-height;        // height as a modifier method
cuboid-height := cuboid1.height;            // height as an accessor method
```

The method **<capacity** depicts a function-style method that can be only on the right side of an assignment. For example,

```
cuboid-capacity := cuboid1.capacity;
```

We know that **<capacity** is solely an accessor method because it has a single < symbol. (Presumably, the reason that **capacity** can't be updated is that it isn't stored, but is computed by multiplying the cuboid's **length**, **breadth**, and **height**.)

Figure 3.6 shows the formal interface to these two methods in part of CUBOID's class-external-interface diagram. The use of an asterisk symbol (*) in the graphic style indicates that the argument is being returned by the method name itself. (You could repeat the name of the method on the returned argument if you didn't mind the redundancy.)

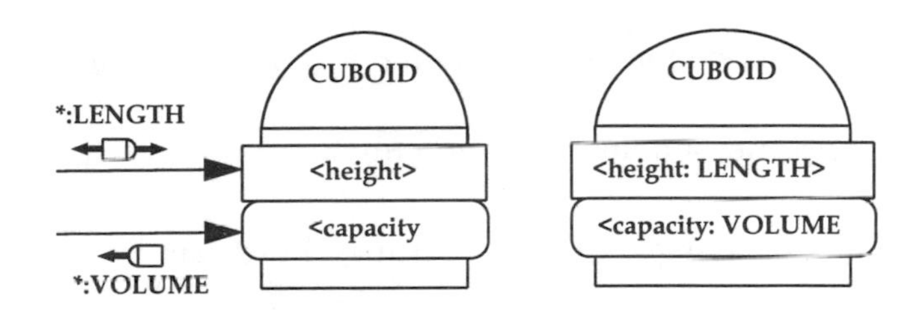

Fig. 3.6: Function-style methods with their formal interface.

Note that you have some flexibility in designing a function-style method's internals. If you're not concerned about exposing the representation of a variable, the easiest implementation is to make a variable public. Then, it would be straightforward to access or modify its value. Alternatively, you may use a pair of simple methods to hide a private variable from the outside world: One method would be **set-variable** and the other **get-variable**.

You will probably implement simple accessors to an object's attributes as function-style methods. However, OODN is much more precise in its design representation for so-called attributes than are many other notations.[8] Not only does OODN differentiate between updatable and non-updatable attributes, but the notation also permits attributes to be accessed with additional (input or output) arguments.

For example, Fig. 3.7 shows a function that returns the area of a segment (the part of a circle cut off by a chord). To determine this attribute of the circle (namely, the area of the portion that's cut off), we must supply an argument, such as the length of the cutting chord.

---

8 An attribute may be designed in one of several ways, each way depicted by different OODN. I mention three such ways in this section.

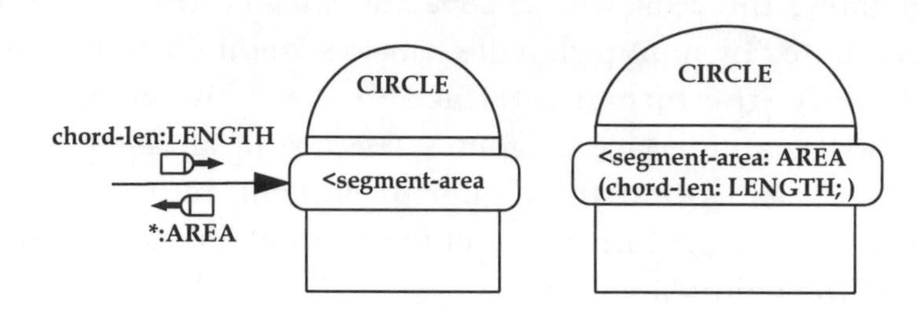

Fig. 3.7: A function-style method with one (input) argument.

The function-style access method **segment-area** might be used as follows:

cut-off-seg-area := circle1.segment-area (cutting-chord-len;);

The alternative to a function-style method is termed a *procedure-style method.* This kind of method cannot transmit a value via its name; all values must be transmitted via input and output arguments. By convention, procedure-style methods are used to implement modifiers, although this convention is by no means universal. Some programming languages encourage the convention, while others remain neutral on it. For example, Eiffel uses procedures to implement all modifiers. On the other hand, C++, which has procedure-style methods in the form of void functions, uses them chiefly (but not exclusively) as modifiers.

3.6 Overloaded Methods

Methods that are overloaded will appear many times on the pin-out diagram, each time with a different signature (that is, with a different number of arguments or with different classes of arguments).[9] For example, the method **mark-down**, which reduces the price of an item, may have two versions. The first **mark-down** takes an argument, which is a percentage discount. The second **mark-down** takes no argument; it always reduces the price by the same (default) amount. (Notice that this version of **mark-down** has no input arguments and so has nothing before the semicolon in the textual version of its signature.) See Fig. 3.8.

[9] You may recall from Chapter 1 that an overloaded method is one that is defined more than once on the same class.

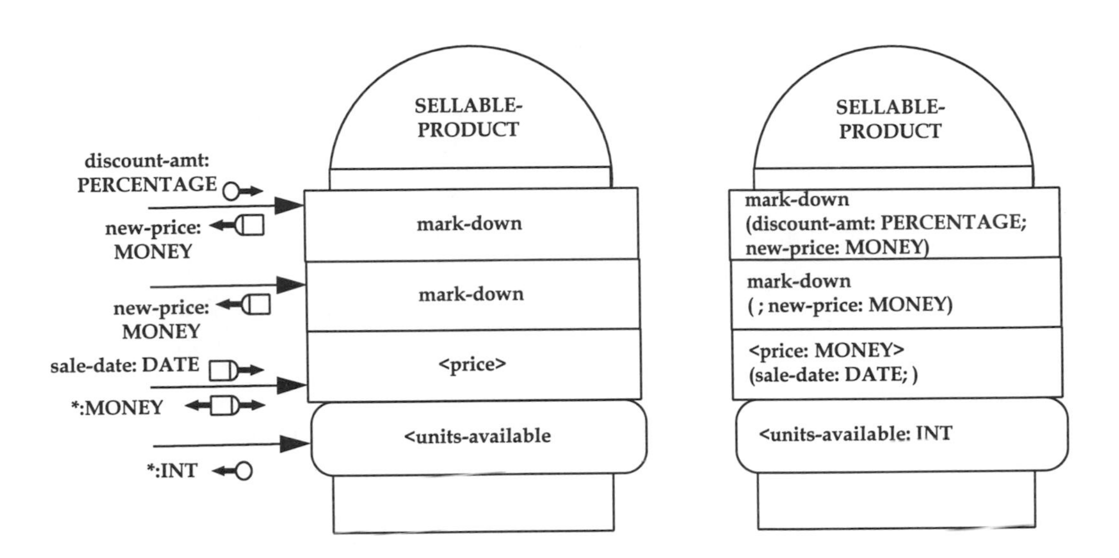

Fig. 3.8: Two overloaded methods.

The two other methods of SELLABLE-PRODUCT that appear in Fig. 3.8 also have some points of interest. The function-style method **<price>** serves both as a modifier and an accessor. In this design, it appears just once on the pin-out diagram. However, you may choose to program **<price>** in one of three ways: as a single method as currently designed, if your language permits this; as two overloaded methods (one accessor, one modifier), again if your language permits; or as two methods with different names (such as **price** and **set-price**).

The final method of Fig. 3.8 is the accessor method **<units-available.** Its point of interest isn't related to overloading but is the fact that it returns data rather than an object. (Notice the little circle on the arrow next to *:INT, which as we saw in Fig. 3.2 is OODN's way of showing a data argument.) This is an example of a hybrid design, where some arguments (typically those of INT, CHAR, BOOL, and so on) are treated as pure data, while others are treated as objects. As I mentioned in Section 1.5.3, how much hybridity you introduce into your application depends greatly on your language. Smalltalk allows no hybridity, Eiffel allows a little, and C++ allows as much (or as little) as you wish.

3.7 Further Notation for Methods

This section covers notation to depict special properties of, or restrictions on, some methods.

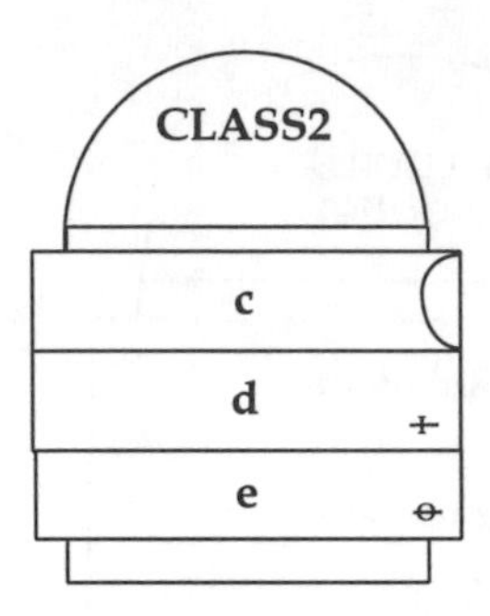

Fig. 3.9: A class method, a non-inheritable method, and a non-overridable method.

In Fig. 3.9, the stylized "C" symbol on the right side of method **c** tells us that **c** is a class method. As you may remember from Chapter 1, a class method is part of the machinery for a class as a whole. It doesn't "belong" to any individual object and so isn't instantiated for any object.

Several languages allow a designer to restrict inheritance in certain ways, so that some methods and/or variables of a superclass are protected from inheritance by any subclass. This can be useful in limiting the effect of any change to the superclass.[10] In addition to this, some languages place restrictions on the overriding of method implementations in subclasses.

Inheritance of a method may be mandatory, optional, or forbidden. Overriding may also be mandatory, optional, or forbidden. The possible combinations of inheritability and overridability define nine kinds of method, of which only four kinds are useful in practice. I show these four kinds of method, together with the typical term for each kind, in the lists below:

Inheritance	Overriding	Typical term for this kind of method
Mandatory	Mandatory	Deferred (or virtual) method
Optional	Optional	Standard method
Optional	Forbidden	Frozen method
Forbidden	Forbidden	Non-inheritable method

[10] Note that this concept is analogous to, but different from, the notion of privacy. A method that is private cannot be invoked by a message from another object; it may or may not be inheritable. OODN treats privacy and inheritability as distinct concepts.

A frozen method—the term *frozen* comes from the Eiffel language—is one whose definition must be the same wherever it is used. Frozen methods are useful to restrict overriding of basic-language operations, such as **is-equal**. Non-inheritable methods are well implemented in C++ through the use of the *private member* term in a base class (that is, a superclass in an inheritance hierarchy).

OODN shows mandatory overriding as O̲, forbidden overriding as Θ, and forbidden inheritance as Ɨ. (Again, see Fig. 3.9.) Optional overriding and inheritance are so common that they're not indicated on the method. In other words, an unadorned method is a standard method, which may be inherited by a subclass and may also be overridden.

Inheritance and overriding lead to the subject of deferred methods and deferred classes. A deferred method (equivalent to a base-class, pure-virtual function in C++) is a method without an implementation. In other words, it has an interface and defined functionality, but no working code! A deferred class (called an abstract class in C++) is a class that cannot instantiate objects, usually because it has at least one deferred method defined on it. (It can't create an object, because a message invoking that object's deferred method would cause a run-time error).

In other words, the following message is illegal on a deferred class:

```
DEFERRED-CLASS.new;   // illegal code![11]
```

On the face of it, a deferred method and the class on which it's defined both seem useless. So why have them in an object-oriented language?

The answer lies in inheritance. A deferred method in a class C is like a common placeholder that indicates to the reader that classes below C in the inheritance hierarchy will provide a real, working implementation of the deferred method. Of course, each of the ultimate subclasses will probably provide a *different* implementation of the method, each one optimized in some way for the special needs of that subclass.

For example, in the POLYGON class of Chapter 1, we could have made **area** a deferred (alias, pure-virtual) method of POLYGON and thus have rendered POLYGON a deferred (alias, abstract) class. This would have had two implications:

[11] In Exercise 4 of Chapter 1, we also saw that instantiation from literal classes (as in **INT.new**) is illegal. A deferred class is similar in this respect to a class of literals. Otherwise, however, it's a distinct concept. A deferred class never has objects, but a literal class can be considered to have many predefined objects.

1. We'd have been *obliged* to provide a method **area** for TRIANGLE, RECTANGLE, *and* HEXAGON.

2. We should never instantiate an object of class POLYGON. That is, we should never write **POLYGON.new**, because a message to its method **area** would cause an error. We should instantiate an object only of one of the classes TRIANGLE, RECTANGLE, or HEXAGON. (Indeed, Eiffel and C++ both enforce this guideline as a rule.) However, we could still have written **var p:POLYGON**. This would allow **p** (polymorphically) to hold the handle of an object of any of the classes TRIANGLE, RECTANGLE, or HEXAGON.

Figure 3.10 shows an example of POLYGON as a deferred class. Notice that the deferred functional method **area** has mandatory overriding, because it's a deferred method. POLYGON appears with a dotted outline in its pin-out diagram to indicate that it's deferred. Although OODN could have shown the deferred method as dotted too, having the I and O together already indicates the method's deferred nature. For that reason, you may decide not to bother with the dotted notation for methods at all.

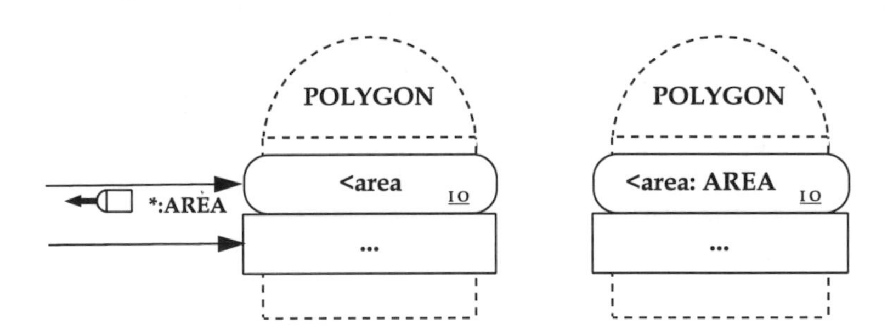

Fig. 3.10: A deferred class, with a deferred method **area**.

3.8 The Package

The package, as exemplified by Ada-83's package construct, is an assembly of procedural modules encapsulated with private data into a single unit. It differs from the class in that it cannot instantiate individual objects.[12] So you could regard

[12] You cannot instantiate objects from deferred classes either. However, you *can* instantiate objects from deferred classes' descendants (so long as they're not deferred, of course).

the package as a class with no objects: Its only methods and variables are class methods and variables.[13]

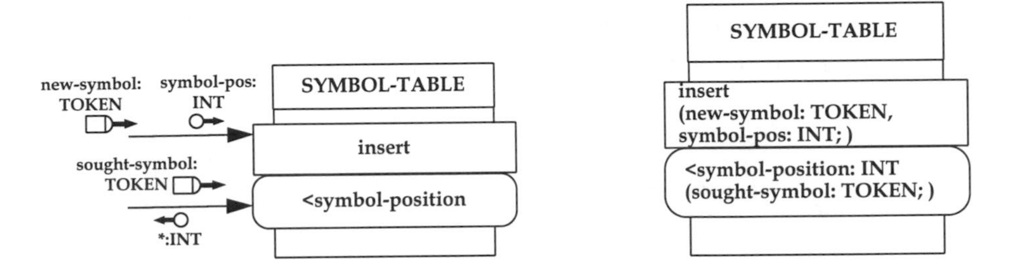

Fig. 3.11: A package to handle a symbol table, with a procedure-style modifier and a function-style accessor.

Figure 3.11 shows the OODN for a package. Although the symbol is almost identical to the class in shape, its rectangular top reveals that it depicts a package. (I chose this departure from the metaphorical "rounded top" of the class in order to retain compatibility with other authors' notation for the package.)

The package is valuable for implementing a software component with only one instance, such as a daemon.[14] The package is also useful because it can give some measure of object orientation to traditional languages such as C or COBOL.[15]

3.9 The Class-Internal-Design Diagram

The class internal-design diagram depicts the interactions among the methods and variables within a class. It therefore includes the constructs within a class

---

[13] In Ada, you can create new packages from a generic package through the keyword **new**. However, this falls short of full object instantiation. In structured design, the term for a package is *information cluster* or *information-strength module.*

[14] A daemon is a piece of software that acts as a monitor for changing conditions. For example, it may watch system inputs for the occurrence of events in the environment or it may watch a database for some condition to become true.

[15] The usual COBOL implementation for a package is a subprogram with multiple, discrete entry points. A system designed around packages rather than classes is usually termed *object-based.*

that are *not* visible from outside and were therefore not shown on the class-external-interface diagram. For example, Fig. 3.12 shows three methods (**method-a**, **method-b**, and **method-c**) and their interactions with four variables (**p**, **q**, **r1**, and **r2**).[16] In Fig. 3.12, the CLASS3 symbol serves as a header for the diagram to indicate which class's methods are being shown.

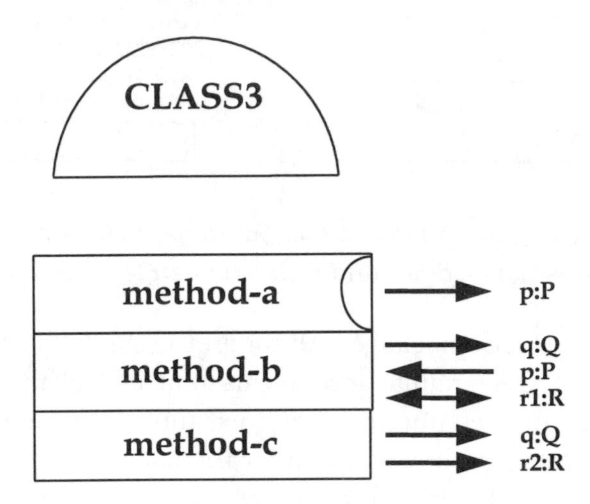

Fig. 3.12: A class-internal-design diagram, summarizing interaction between methods and variables.

There are three kinds of little arrows between methods and variables. Each kind denotes a different way in which a method uses a variable, as I describe below.

(i) An arrow from the variable to the method. The method sends an accessor message to the object pointed to by the variable in order to get some information. This symbol is also used to show the access to the entire object, for example, to assign the object's handle to another variable or to pass the object handle out as an argument in a message.

(ii) An arrow from the method to the variable. The method sends a modifier message to the object pointed to by the variable. This symbol is also used to show the handle of an object being assigned to a variable.

(iii) An arrow pointing both ways. This indicates that both kinds of interaction listed above occur between a method and a variable.

---

[16] Exercise 4 at the end of this chapter shows another, more concrete example of this diagram, based on the HOMINOID class.

The class-internal-design diagram assists a designer to sketch out ideas for implementing a class, but it isn't meant to be a profound diagram. It's also useful as a summary diagram to give a reader an overview before he plunges into the pseudocode-level details of a method's algorithm or the specifics of the method's outgoing messages, which would be shown on an object-communication diagram (as described in Chapter 5).

Figure 3.13 has two points of interest. First, the instance methods, **method-b** and **method-c**, of CLASS3 both use **shared-component**. We see this because of the fan-in from **method-b** and **method-c** to **shared-component**. (Incidentally, Fig. 3.13 is very similar to a diagram with fan-in that we might see in structured design.)

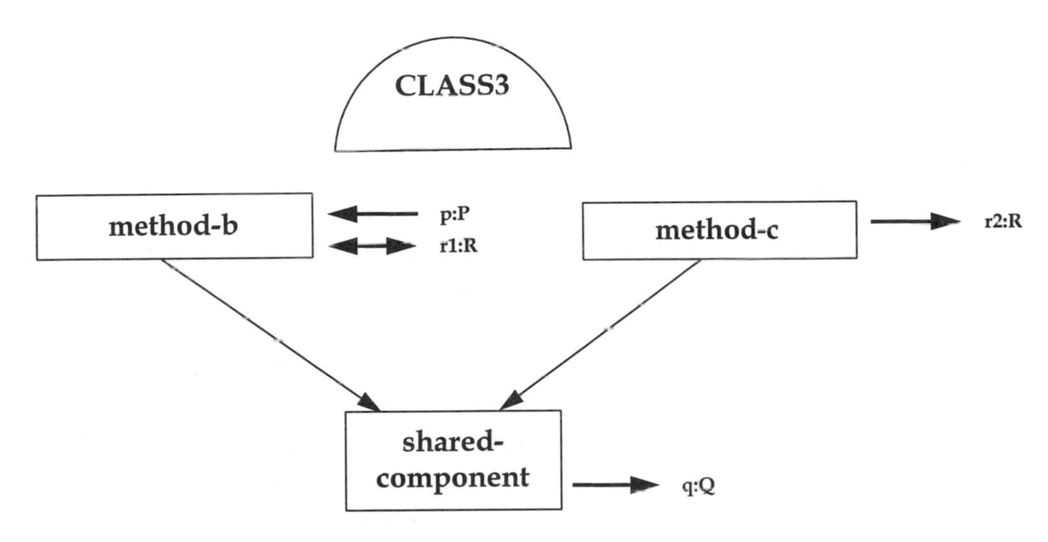

Fig. 3.13: A class-internal-design diagram with calls from methods to a shared procedure.

The second point of interest in this class-internal-design diagram is that **shared-component** is a private method. (We know it's a private method, because it didn't appear on CLASS3's pin-out diagram.) There are two approaches to designing and implementing accesses to a private method. One, which is shown in Fig. 3.13, is as a simple call to a local, stand-alone function or procedure. (The code would be **call shared-component**.)

The other approach, which I'll cover in Chapter 5, is as a message to **self**. (The code would be **self.shared-component**.) The approach that you choose in order to invoke a private method depends somewhat on your programming language. For example, Smalltalk favors the second approach (via **self**), whereas Eiffel and C++ mildly favor the first.

3.10 Summary

The basic symbol of Object-Oriented Design Notation (OODN) is the class symbol. Its shape (partly curved, partly rectangular) symbolizes the part-data, part-procedure nature of a class. (OODN depicts a package, which is similar to a class in structure but which cannot spawn instances, with the package's traditional flat-topped symbol.) Methods appear superimposed on the class (or package) symbol as rectangles. Accessor methods (which do not change an object's state) have rounded corners; modifier methods (which may change an object's state) have normal corners.

The class-external-interface diagram (the pin-out diagram) shows a class and its methods, together with the methods' formal input and output arguments. These arguments may appear either as symbols on an arrow to each method or textually within each method symbol. Overloaded methods appear several times on a pin-out diagram, each time with a different signature (number and classes of arguments).

Many languages have function-style methods, from (and, in some languages, to) which an argument may be passed in the name of the method itself. (Methods without this facility are termed procedure-style methods.) Some languages employ function-style methods solely as accessor methods and procedure-style methods solely as modifier methods. OODN prefixes a function-style method whose name serves as an output argument (the more common situation) with **<**; in the case that the name serves as an input argument (a rarer situation), OODN suffixes the method name with **>**. When the method name serves both as an input and an output argument, OODN sandwiches it between **<** and **>**.

Further annotations for methods include: a stylized C, denoting a class method; I̲, denoting mandatory inheritance of the method by a subclass; Ɨ, denoting forbidden inheritance by any subclass; O̲, denoting mandatory overriding of the method by a method of an inheriting class; and Ɵ, denoting forbidden overriding.

The class-internal-design diagram documents the internal structure of a class, comprising the interactions between methods and variables. An arrow from a variable to a method indicates the method's accessing information held by the object to which the variable refers. An arrow from a method to a variable indicates the method's updating information in the object to which the variable refers. This diagram is used chiefly for sketching out design ideas for the internals of a class. The object-communication diagram (which we'll cover in Chapter 5) further formalizes a class's internal design.

3.11 Exercises

1. In Section 3.3, I explained that, in shops that make this distinction, a method with a rectangular symbol is one that "changes the state of an object." Could a method deserve a rectangular shape although it does not change the state of the object to which it's directly applied?

2. Summarize the properties of classes (such as deferred versus nondeferred) that we covered in this chapter and Chapter 1.

3. Summarize the properties of methods (such as modifier versus accessor) that we covered in this chapter and Chapter 1.

4. Draw a class-external-interface (pin-out) diagram for a class of your choice, such as the HOMINOID class of Chapter 1.

3.12 Answers

1. In OODN, a method certainly gets a rectangular symbol if it may modify the state of the object to which the method is bound at run-time. However, a method may be a modifier method without always changing the state of *that particular object.* For example, a method may generate a message to another object, which causes that second object to change state. Also, an **if** statement in a modifier method may mean that the method doesn't change an object's state on all occasions that it's executed.

   Use the roundangle accessor-method symbol only where you know that a method's execution will *always* leave *every* object's state unchanged.

2. Here are some differentiating properties of classes that we've considered in this chapter and in Chapter 1:

   (i) Class or package. The former gives rise to distinct objects. The latter doesn't (or should be considered to be the sole object of its "class").

   (ii) Non-literal or literal. The former is a normal class, with run-time instantiation of objects. The latter has all its objects instantiated implicitly by the compiler and the objects' handles are their literal values.

   (iii) Mutable or immutable. The former is a normal class, whose objects are mutable, that is, they may change state after instantiation. The latter has objects that are immutable, that is, they do not change state. Most immutable classes are literal classes and most literal classes are immutable classes.

   (iv) Nondeferred or deferred. (Concrete or abstract.) The former is a normal class, with objects. The latter has no objects, although its subclasses usually do.

   (v) Nongeneric or generic. The former is the simple, more common class. The latter is a class that takes class name(s) as argument(s) upon instantiation of objects.

To complete the list, I'll add a property that we'll see in Chapter 5.

(vi) Concurrency (of instantiated objects of the class), which may occur at one of three levels: none, object-level, or method-level.

3. Here are some differentiating properties of methods that we've considered in this chapter and in Chapter 1:

(i) Instance or class. The former method is defined on an individual instance (object). The latter is defined on a class and does not directly access variables of individual objects.

(ii) Modifier or accessor. The execution of the former changes the overall state of the system. Execution of the latter does not.

(iii) Function-style or procedure-style. The former passes a value via the name of the method. The latter does not pass a value via the name of the method.

(iv) Public or private. The former is visible outside the class or object on which it's defined. The latter is not.

(v) Inheritability. Optional, forbidden, or mandatory.

(vi) Overridability. Optional, forbidden, or mandatory.

(vii) Nondeferred or deferred. (Real or pure-virtual.) The former is the normal kind of method. The latter method lacks an actual implementation and should be inherited and overridden by a real implementation.

Again, to complete this list, I'll add a property that we'll see in Chapter 5.

(viii) Concurrency, which may occur at one of two levels: None or method-level.

4. Figure 3.14 shows the methods that may be defined on HOMINOID.

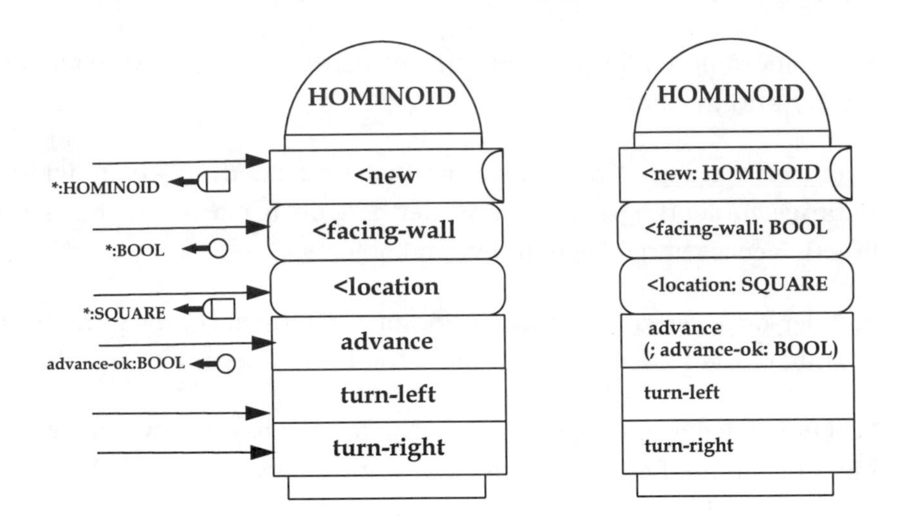

Fig. 3.14: One possible class-external-interface diagram for HOMINOID, showing both graphical and textual styles of OODN.

There are a few points to note in this example:

1. The methods **new**, **facing-wall**, and **location** are all function-style methods; hence, the **<** notation.

2. Since **facing-wall** and **location** return values without changing any states, they have the roundangle symbol.

3. Although most methods have input or output arguments, the methods **turn-left** and **turn-right** have none. This is legal, but it's often a hint to a designer that a method could be generalized. We could replace the two methods with a single, more general method, for example, **turn (angle;)**.

4. The method **advance** may fail (perhaps because a hominoid is at a wall). If so, it sets its return argument, **advance-ok**, to **false**. I show **advance-ok** as data of type BOOL, as indicated by the data symbol on the argument. If your language has BOOL as a class, then you can change **advance-ok** (and the return argument of **facing-wall**) to an object of class BOOL.

Inheritance and Aggregation Diagrams

This chapter introduces OODN for two important object-oriented structures. Section 4.1 covers the superclass/subclass inheritance structure, depicted by the class-inheritance diagram. As we saw in Chapter 1, inheritance is a vital structure for building classes upon other classes. It's also the major framework upon which you build a class library. OODN copes with both single and multiple inheritance.

Section 4.2 covers the aggregate/component structure, depicted by the object-aggregation diagram. This is the whole/part (or composition) structure, by which, for instance, a chair comprises a back, a seat, and four legs. This structure is as common and as useful in object orientation as it is in everyday life.

4.1 The Class-Inheritance Diagram

Figure 4.1 shows the notation for class inheritance. Notice that the direction of the arrow is from the subclass (inheriting class) to the superclass (inherited-from class). This may seem odd: In everyday life, doesn't inheritance "travel" *downward*? That is, doesn't one inherit Trans-Siberian Railway Shares and a large Etruscan pot *from* one's great-uncle?

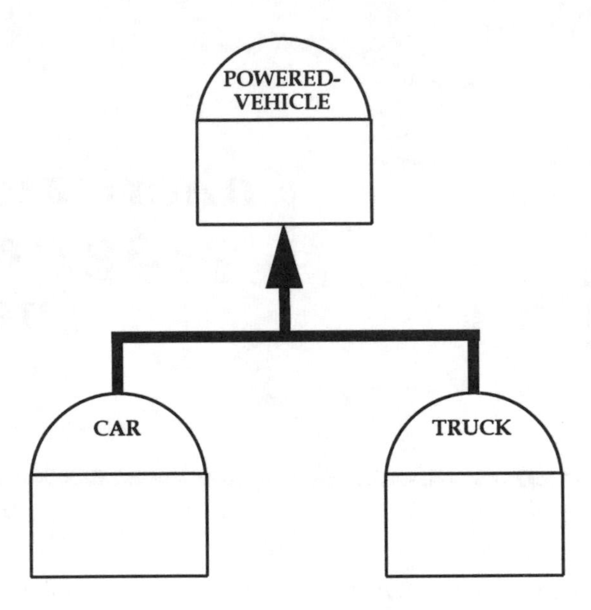

Fig. 4.1: A (single) inheritance hierarchy.

The inheritance arrow points upward in the hierarchy, however, because the direction of class reference is upward. In other words, a subclass HEXAGON may refer to its superclass, POLYGON, but POLYGON normally has no reference to HEXAGON. The arrow turns out to have another valuable intuitive connotation: It also depicts the path along which an object of a given class will search for a required method. (First, it searches within its own class, then its parent class, then its grandparent class, and so on.)

Notice, too, how broad the arrow shaft is. Its breadth reflects the broad coupling between classes that inheritance induces. Coupling via inheritance is very similar to that induced by lexical inclusion in block-structured programming languages—for example, an inner **begin** . . . **end** in Pascal. In such languages, the features of the outer block are visible in the inner block (although they may be overridden by local redeclaration in the inner block). On the other hand, the features of the inner block are invisible to the outer block.

The graphic notation of OODN handles single inheritance or multiple inheritance. But, for single inheritance, a diagram isn't necessary. So, if you work entirely in a single-inheritance environment, you may choose to document your single-inheritance class hierarchies with simple indented text. This is exactly how many vendor-supplied library-browsers depict inheritance.[1]

For example, if CAR and TRUCK are subclasses of POWERED-VEHICLE, you could write:

POWERED-VEHICLE
        CAR
        TRUCK

However, the indented-list portrayal of inheritance cannot simultaneously show methods (as in a pin-out diagram) very easily, whereas OODN can show methods superimposed on the class symbols of a class-inheritance diagram.

Sometimes, a class inherits from a superclass not only its public methods but also the private variables that the superclass uses in its internal implementation. (However, as I discuss in Section 8.2.5, this kind of inheritance may violate good object-oriented encapsulation.) If you wish to emphasize this inheritance of internal implementation, you can use the "little hat" notation, as shown in Fig. 4.2.

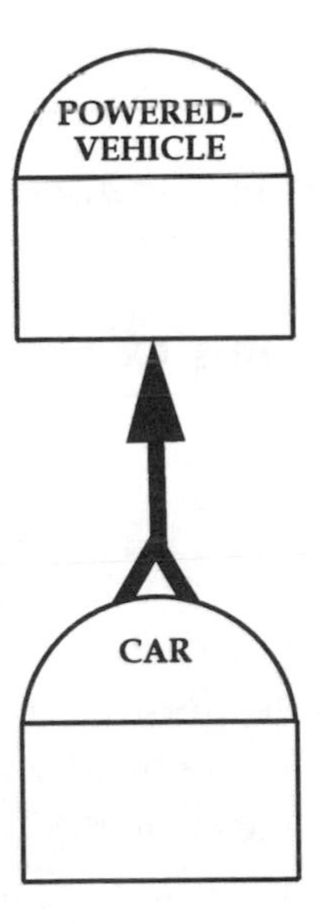

Fig. 4.2: Inheritance for the purpose of inheriting internal implementation.

[1] Multiple inheritance can also be expressed textually in the form of a direct-inheritance matrix, a Boolean matrix that shows which class is a direct superclass of which. The total-inheritance matrix is derived from this first matrix by computing its so-called transitive closure. This is a job for a CASE tool.

Figure 4.3 shows OODN for multiple inheritance, whereby a class inherits directly from more than one superclass. There's nothing significant in the left-to-right ordering of a class's direct superclasses.

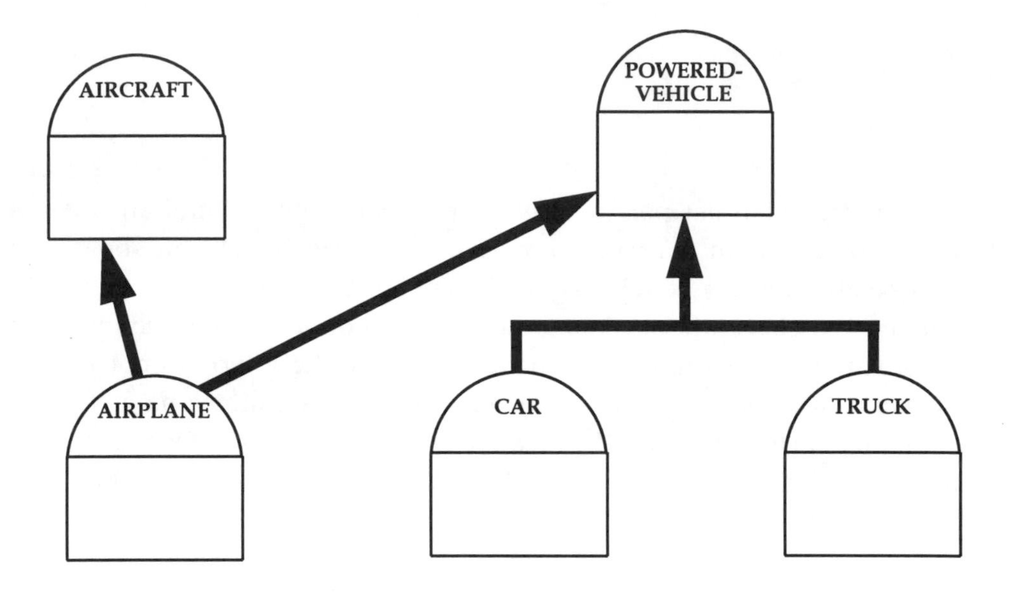

Fig. 4.3: A multiple-inheritance hierarchy.

4.2 Aggregate Objects and Their Components

A common structure in all software systems, including object-oriented ones, is *aggregation* (also known as *composition*). Many aggregate objects derive from structures that occur in real life, such as a dog's being an aggregation of a head, a body, and a tail, together with a leg at each corner. Other aggregations are more software-specific, such as an e-mail missive's being an aggregation of a header and a few text paragraphs. In turn, the header is an aggregation of the sender's name, the receiver's name, and the message title.

Object orientation provides a natural way of implementing aggregation. In this section, we'll examine what this way is and how it's depicted in OODN.

4.2.1 The object-aggregation diagram

A class contains declarations of variables. In the run-time objects created from the class, these variables will point to other run-time objects. For example, since a glider object is the aggregate of its components, the class GLIDER may have the following variables declared within it:

fuselage: FUSELAGE;
tail: TAIL;
left-wing: WING;
right-wing: WING;

When an object—let's refer to it as **glider1**—of class GLIDER is instantiated (and initialized), the variable **tail** will point to an object representing the tail of **glider1**. Similarly, **fuselage**, **left-wing**, and **right-wing** are variables that hold the handles of the other components of a GLIDER object.

OODN shows this aggregate relationship graphically in the object-aggregation diagram of Fig. 4.4.[2]

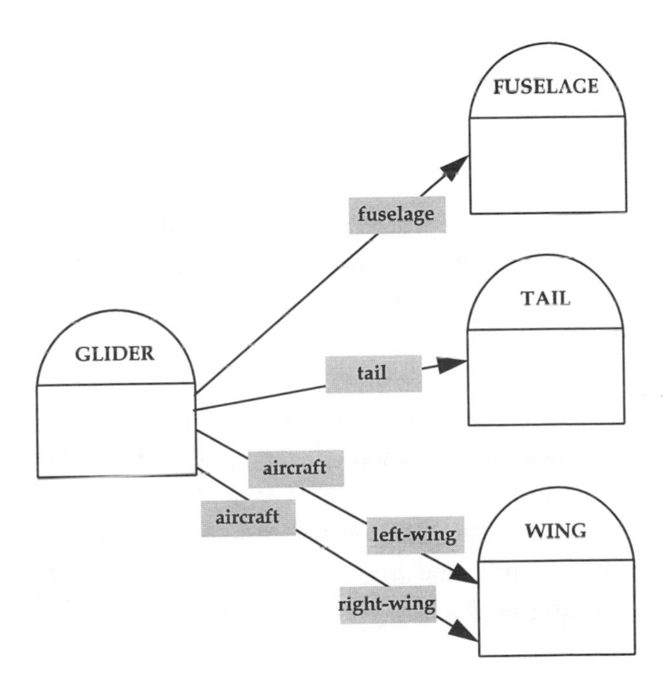

Fig. 4.4: An aggregate object and its components.

Again, the arrow denotes the direction of reference: from the aggregate object to its components. Notice that each of the four components (respectively, **fuselage**, **tail**,

[2] I use gray boxes (for example, around the variable **tail**) for graphical clarity only. The gray box has no semantic significance.

left-wing, and **right-wing**), although it's an object, appears on the diagram under the name of the class to which it belongs (respectively, FUSELAGE, TAIL, WING, WING). The reason for this is that, as we saw in Section 1.4, objects have no names. They have only handles—bit-patterns stored in pointer variables, which no human ever sets eyes on.

The prototype version of OODN, UON, stayed true to the above ideal of object orientation, leaving the component objects anonymous and indicating *only* their classes in the diagram. However, among the first users of UON, there was a great wailing and gnashing of teeth, and they rose up and came unto us and beseeched us thus: "Hey, could you somehow stick the *names* of the aggregate object's variables on the diagram?"

We sympathized with their problems. In UON, there was no way to indicate what role a component was playing in the aggregate—no way to distinguish between, say, a left wing and a right wing. Yet we didn't want our notation to lie by showing a name on the component object itself, for—as I keep saying—an object has no name of its own. The solution in OODN is to place the name of the relevant variable on the message arrow, rather than on the referred-to component. (The relevant variable is the one in the aggregate that holds the handle of the component.) An example in Fig. 4.4 is **left-wing**.

People who are purer in mind than myself have pointed out that the object-aggregation diagram breaks the notion of encapsulation by revealing an object's internal components. They're right! You may therefore choose to use the aggregation diagram to depict only the publicly visible components of an object, those components that may be accessed via a method.

You may also choose to use this diagram only for "significant" aggregations, for example, one based on the physical composition of real things, such as a glider or a chair. Another example of "significant" aggregation is aggregation with several layers, where component objects themselves aggregate yet other components. The e-mail missive at the start of this section was a small example of this.

Conversely, you wouldn't use an object-aggregation diagram—although you *could*—to show that a dog is "composed of" height, weight, color, and date of birth.

These are properties, rather than components, of a dog. If you used object-aggregation diagrams merely to depict properties, you'd create huge diagrams without much lasting value.

Very often, aggregation goes hand-in-hand with message propagation. For example, in order to find the weight of a chair, you need to send the same message to each component of the chair—a message that will return a weight. As another example, if you want to move a rectangle symbol on a screen, you could tell the rectangle object to move itself. In turn, the rectangle would send a message to each of its component lines in turn, to tell them to move. (In Chapter 5, where I introduce OODN for messages, I offer an example of messages sent to components of an aggregate object.)

4.2.2 Aggregate objects with generic classes in their components

What should we do with multiple component objects, possibly organized by so-called container classes such as LIST, SET, or TREE? (As we saw in Chapter 1, a container class is one whose objects can hold structures of other objects.) For example, the aggregate class CHAIR might have in it:

back: CHAIR-BACK;
seat: CHAIR-SEAT;
legs: SET[CHAIR-LEG];

OODN addresses the issue of multiple instances of a component by marking cardinality on the reference arrow. The cardinality notation shows the minimum and maximum number of participating component objects. For example, **1..N** means "at least one." (You could show this exactly as **1..1**, except that "exactly one" is so common that **1..1** is conventionally left off the diagram.)

Where the instances are organized into some structure—as with the legs of the chair—you typically name the structuring class (for example, SET) and don't bother to note any further cardinality at that end of the line.[3] See Fig. 4.5.

[3] Some people have told me that the word "SET" should be enclosed in a class symbol, since SET is a (generic, container) class. However, I find that that's an unnecessary refinement that adds little to the meaning of the diagram.

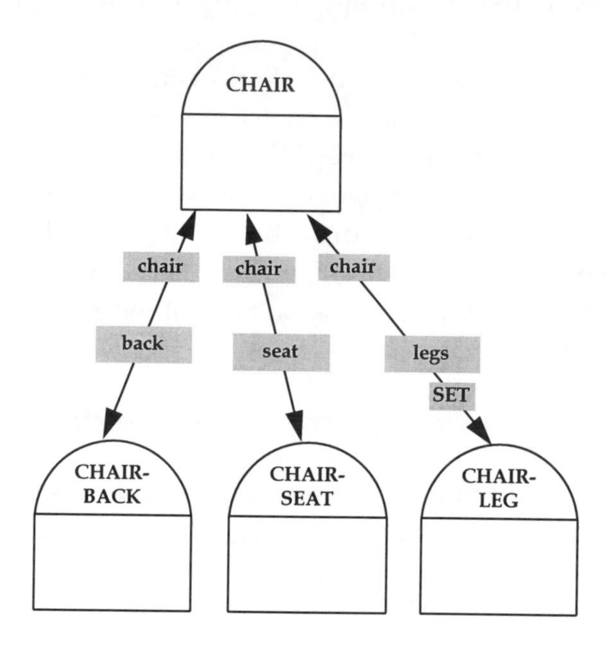

Fig. 4.5: An aggregate object with an iterated component.

Note that the arrows to **back**, **seat**, and **legs** are bidirectional. This means that not only does a chair object point to its component parts but also that each part points to the chair to which it belongs. (There's no intrinsic design reason for bidirectionality in this chair example; I just wanted to show a variation in the notation.) Notice the name **chair** near the arrowheads at the aggregate object. This indicates that the component objects **back**, **seat**, and **legs** each refer to the aggregate object through a variable named **chair**.

(Incidentally, you can show an object-aggregation diagram horizontally across the page or vertically down the page. Thus, there's nothing special about Fig. 4.5's vertical orientation or Fig. 4.4's horizontal orientation. Indeed, in practice, you'll often wind up using both vertical and horizontal orientations to exploit the real estate on your page.)

Sometimes, component objects may be part of several aggregate objects. One example is an object of, say, class PHOTOGRAPH, which might appear in many reports or dossiers. Another example is an object of class TEXT-PARA, which may be simultaneously embedded in several different objects of class MGMT-REPORT. In these examples, we'd expect to see **1..N** or **0..N** at the aggregate-object end of the arrow. See Fig. 4.6.

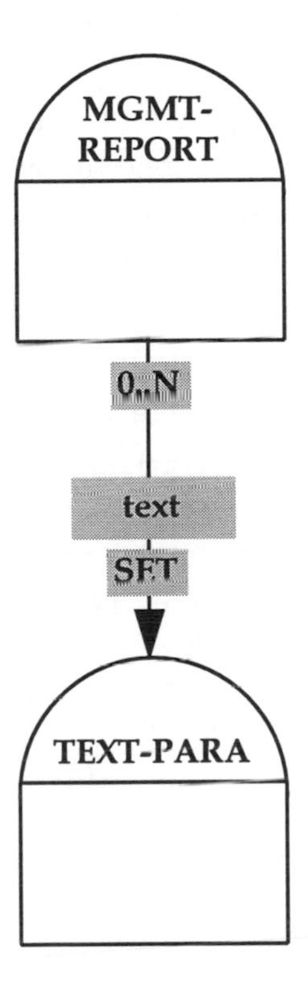

Fig. 4.6: An object (a text paragraph) that may be a component of several aggregate components.

4.3 Summary

The OODN for inheritance shows a broad arrow from the inheriting subclass to the "inherited from" superclass. If the inheritance includes the private methods or variables of the superclass, then the origin of the arrow bears a "little hat." This notation handles both single inheritance and multiple inheritance (in which a class may inherit from several superclasses). However, you may choose to represent single inheritance as an indented list of classes. For large hierarchies, the textual representation may be more concise, though less graphically immediate, than OODN.

OODN shows object aggregation by means of reference arrows from the aggregate object to the component objects. These arrows are of normal width, that is, they aren't as broad as the inheritance arrows. At the component-object end of each arrow is the name of the component object (as referred to by a variable in the aggregate object). If the component object is aware of the aggregate to which it belongs, then the arrow also has a head at the aggregate end. The name alongside this end of the arrow is the name of the aggregate object (as referred to by a variable in the component object).

The cardinality between the aggregate object and the component object is shown by means of a range, if known, or by the name of a structure. Range is expressed as **min..max** and structure is usually expressed by the name of a generic container class, such as SET.

4.4 Exercises

1. Draw a class-inheritance diagram that captures the situation in which a company has customers that fall into two categories: external customers and internal customers. External customers are other companies. Internal customers are divisions within the company. (All divisions are internal customers.)

2. Draw an object-aggregation diagram for a book chapter with the following structure: A chapter comprises several sections, each of which comprises several paragraphs and figures. A paragraph comprises several sentences, each of which comprises several words. (You may ignore punctuation and you needn't pursue the structure of a figure any further.)

4.5 Answers

1. Figure 4.7 shows one class-inheritance diagram for the internal/external customer situation. The interesting portion of the structure centers on the class INTERNAL-CUSTOMER, which inherits multiply from CUSTOMER and CORPORATE-DIVISION.

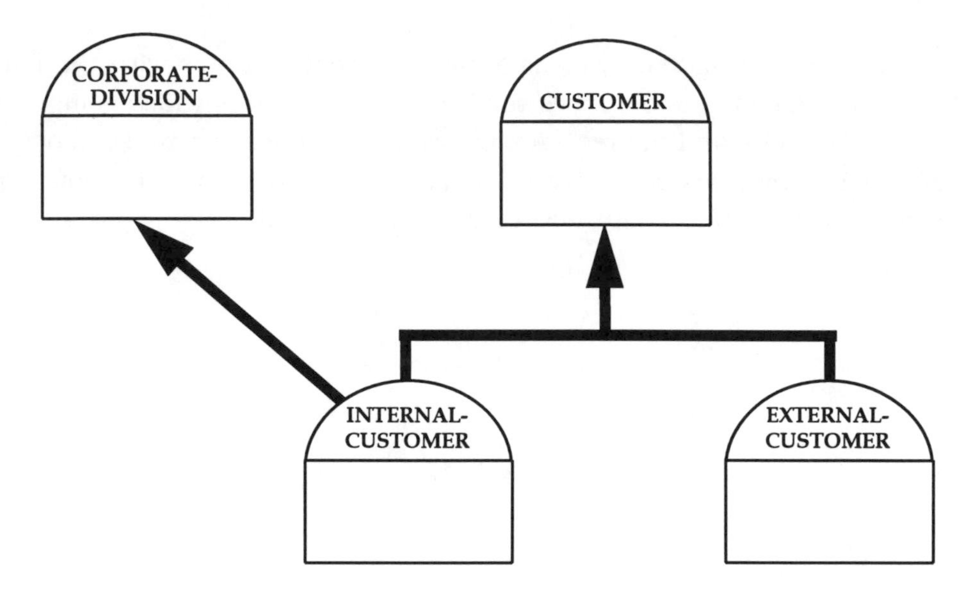

Fig. 4.7: The CUSTOMER inheritance hierarchy.

You could refine this class-inheritance diagram by introducing another class, EXTERNAL-COMPANY, and then having EXTERNAL-CUSTOMER inherit multiply from CUSTOMER and EXTERNAL-COMPANY. This approach would separate customer properties completely from corporate-entity properties and would also improve the symmetry of the class structure.

2. Figure 4.8 shows one possible aggregate structure for the book chapter.

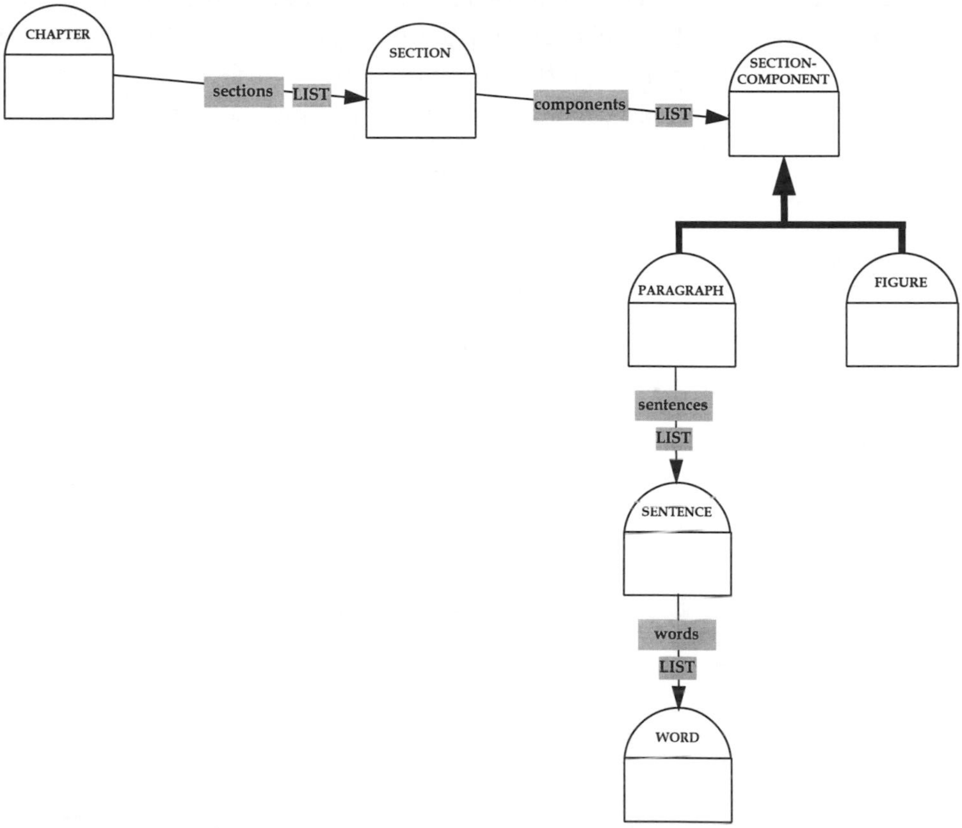

Fig. 4.8: An object-aggregation diagram for a book chapter.

The object-aggregation diagram shows that a chapter is a list of sections. I use LIST to structure the sections in sequence because LIST is normally defined as an ordered sequence of components. To be less implementation-specific, I could use ORDERED-COLLECTION instead. (If order were irrelevant, I could use SET or simply **1..N**.) The structures for a paragraph and a sentence are similar to the structure of a chapter.

The structure of a section is a little tricky, because a section comprises paragraphs and diagrams intermixed. A good way to design this is to create a class, SECTION-COMPONENT, from which both PARAGRAPH and FIGURE inherit. This allows each component of a section to be either a paragraph or a figure.

Finally, Fig. 4.8 contains two implicit assumptions. The first is that a chapter refers to its sections, but a section doesn't refer to its parent chapter.

If a section did refer to its parent chapter, then the reference arrow would have a head at each end. The second assumption is that a section appears in exactly one chapter. If a section could appear in multiple chapters, then there should be a **1..N** at the "chapter end" of the referencing arrow. (Of course, other parts of Fig. 4.8 contain similar implicit assumptions.)

The Object-Communication Diagram

So far in this discussion of OODN, we've looked mainly at the static structure of the object-oriented source code that sits calmly on your listing. Now we turn to the execution, run-time, or dynamic structure of an object-oriented system. (Obviously, static and dynamic structures are highly related, for it is the compiled lexical code that actually runs!)

Central to the execution of an object-oriented program is the sending of messages. As we saw in Chapter 1, a message is a request by a sender object to execute a method of a target object. In OODN, the object-communication diagram depicts the messages and message arguments that objects send to one another. The two kinds of messages that an object-communication diagram shows are the synchronous message (in which a sender object must wait for the target to finish) and the asynchronous message (in which a sender object does not need to wait).

In Section 5.1, I explore synchronous messages, the usual form of messages in most object-oriented systems. In Section 5.2, I explore asynchronous messages, which are important in some real-time object-oriented systems.

5.1 Synchronous Messaging

In this section, I first show the OODN for a straightforward synchronous message and then add further notation for special kinds of synchronous message.

A *synchronous message* requires the sender of the message to wait for the target object to process the message before the sender continues executing.

5.1.1 Depicting a synchronous message

OODN shows a synchronous message by means of a solid arrow that points from the "calling" method of the sender to the "called" method of the target.[1] The OODN arrow represents the code for a message within a method of the sender object. This message code, as we saw in Chapter 1, comprises the name of a target-object method, followed by that method's signature (the actual input and output arguments).

The example in the top diagram of Fig. 5.1 shows the method **land** (in a sender object of class AIRCRAFT) sending a message to a target object **left-flap** (of class FLAP). The message requests **left-flap** to set itself to an appropriate landing angle. The return argument **landing-angle-ok** is set to **true** whenever the value of **landing-angle** is valid. (The message that you'd read in the code of the sender's method **land** would be **left-flap.set (landing-angle; landing-angle-ok)**.)

Notice the difference between Fig. 4.3 (the aggregate relationship) and Fig. 5.1 (the sender-message-target relationship). In the aggregate relationship, there's a static reference to an entire object; the arrow points to a whole object. (Used in this way, "static" means that the reference is to a name or a handle, but doesn't imply any run-time execution.)

In the sending of a message, there's a dynamic reference to a single method; the arrow points to the method. (Here, "dynamic" implies an invocation of the method at run-time.) Following the SDN tradition, we made no graphic distinction between static and dynamic references because using the same style of arrow doesn't cause any ambiguity in practice.

But, again, there surfaces the same problem that arose with component objects: What's the name of the target object? The solution is the same as before: the name of the sender's variable that holds the handle of the target. This variable name appears at the start of the message arrow. The example here is **left-flap**. (Again, see the first diagram of Fig. 5.1.)

---

[1] The sender and target objects are usually, but not necessarily, different objects. Usually, but not necessarily, they also belong to different classes.

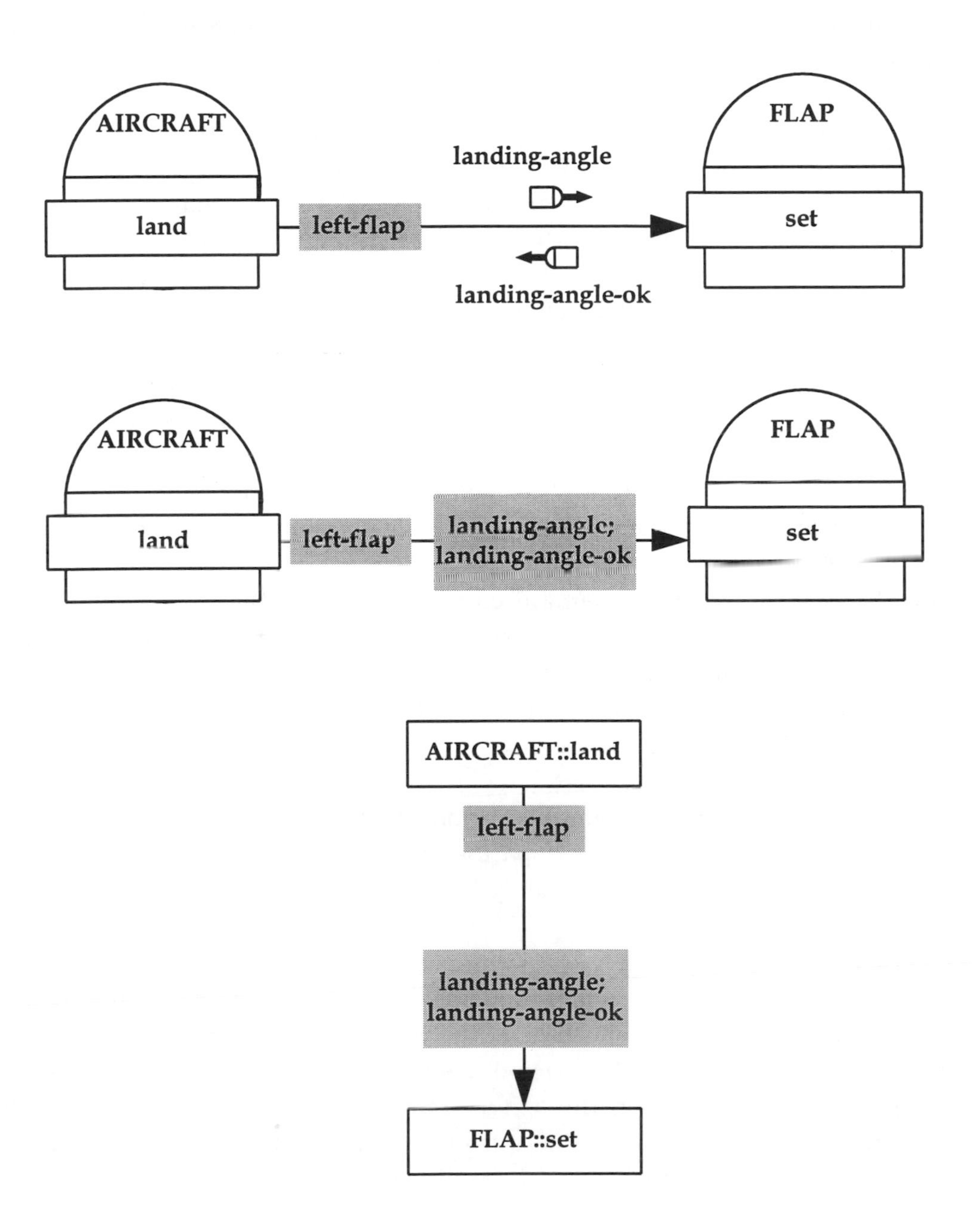

Fig. 5.1: Three styles of object-communication diagram for the message **left-flap.set (landing-angle; landing-angle-ok)**.

A message, of course, is not solely a request for the execution of a method; arguments pass back and forth with the message just as they do in an old-fashioned subroutine call. Therefore, OODN uses a notation similar to SDN to show message arguments. However, where the arguments are pointers to objects rather than pointers to data, OODN depicts them with the same little object symbols that we saw in Fig. 3.6.[2]

The label of an actual argument in a message is similar to that of a formal argument in the pin-out diagram: the argument's name and the class to which it belongs. However, this time the name is the *actual* argument name, that is, the name of the argument as used by the *sender* in its argument list, as opposed to the formal name used by the target in the header of its method. An example of an actual argument name is **landing-angle** of Fig. 5.1. (The formal argument name inside the method **set** is perhaps **required-flap-angle**.)

The second diagram of Fig. 5.1 is semantically identical to the first one. It shows the message in a more textual format: The actual signature of a message (the input and output arguments) appear as text, rather than as small symbols. The advantage of this style is that it's easier to draw quickly by hand. However, it doesn't graphically depict whether the arguments are pointers to objects or simply data.

The third diagram, again semantically identical to the first, shows each method name qualified with a prefix stating its class (for example, **FLAP::set**, which means the **set** method, as defined on the class FLAP). The double colon is called the *qualifier* (or *scope-resolution*) *symbol*; its purpose is to show which method we're talking about when the same method is defined on more than one class.

Although this style departs somewhat from the OODN symbology, the diagram is both easy to draw manually and sparing of real estate on screens and whiteboards. Owing to its minimalist quality, this third style of Fig. 5.1 has gained great popularity.

A couple of graphical tips: First, it's quite acceptable to repeat symbols (objects and/or methods) on an object-communication diagram. Such repetition may help out if message lines begin to cross or curve very tightly (when, for instance, an object sends a message to itself). Second, it's usually a good idea to place the target name (the name by which the sender refers to the target object) near the sender object. This keeps the name out of the way of the arguments traveling back and forth near the arrowhead and so reduces clutter.

---

[2] But, if you used OODN to model a hybrid system (with both data and objects), you'd show data arguments using the standard structured-design symbol (the little arrow with the circle on its tail), as in Fig. 3.8.

5.1.2 Polymorphism in the object-communication diagram

Polymorphism brings great power to object orientation. And now the bad news. Polymorphism and dynamic binding, which is polymorphism's run-time implementation mechanism, also bring headaches to notation developers. In the SDN world, we always knew where we were: **call** A always meant **call** A. But, in object orientation, the question becomes: What *is* the class of an object to which a message is sent? This section covers OODN's answer to that question.

If the class of the target object is known absolutely at design time (that is, if no polymorphism applies), then the class name in the target-object symbol is the name of the target object's class. But, if polymorphism applies, the sender object may not be aware of the exact class of the target object. So, in this case, what name should we give to the class of the target?

The answer is this: the lowest class in the inheritance hierarchy that is a superclass of all the classes to which the target object could possibly belong. For example, if the message is **shape.area** and the target object (pointed to by **shape**) may be of class TRIANGLE, RECTANGLE, or HEXAGON, then the class name on the OODN target object would be POLYGON (assuming that POLYGON is the direct superclass of those three classes).

Another example: If we had **x.print**, where **x** could point to a target object of class SPREADSHEET, TEXTDOC, CUSTOMER, or several others, then we'd probably be obliged to choose as the target class name the highest class of all, which may be the class OBJECT, because there's unlikely to be another class that's a superclass of all those classes.

Some shops emphasize the polymorphism of a target object by means of parentheses. When the exact class of the target object can be determined absolutely at design time (which is equivalent to static binding), these shops show the target class name without parentheses. Where the exact class will be determined only at run-time (dynamic binding), they show the target class name in parentheses. (They derive the class name in the parentheses as I described above.) See Fig. 5.2.

I go much further into the ramifications of polymorphism in Section 11.2.

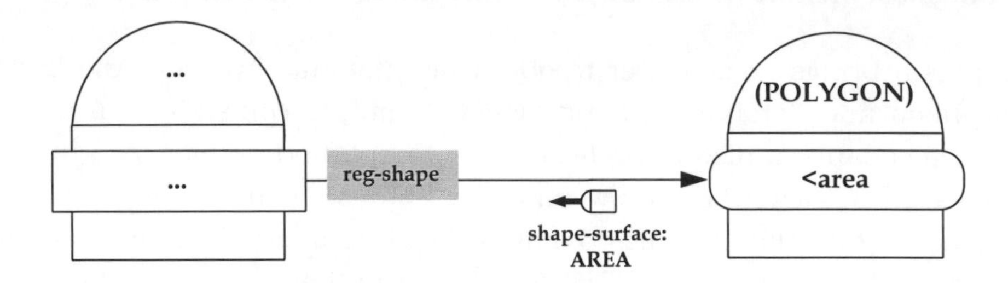

Fig. 5.2: The method that will be dynamically bound to the target will be from POLYGON or one of its subclasses.

5.1.3 Iterated messages

An iterated message is one that's sent repeatedly, typically to each component of an aggregate object. For an example of an iterated message, let's first assume that a shipment unit (in a product-shipping company) is a wooden box that contains a few dozen packages. In an object-oriented application, the following variables (among others) might be declared within the class SHIPMENT-UNIT:

containing-box: SHIPMENT-BOX;
content-packages: SINGLY-LINKED-LIST [SHIPMENT-PACKAGE];

I show this graphically in Fig. 5.3:

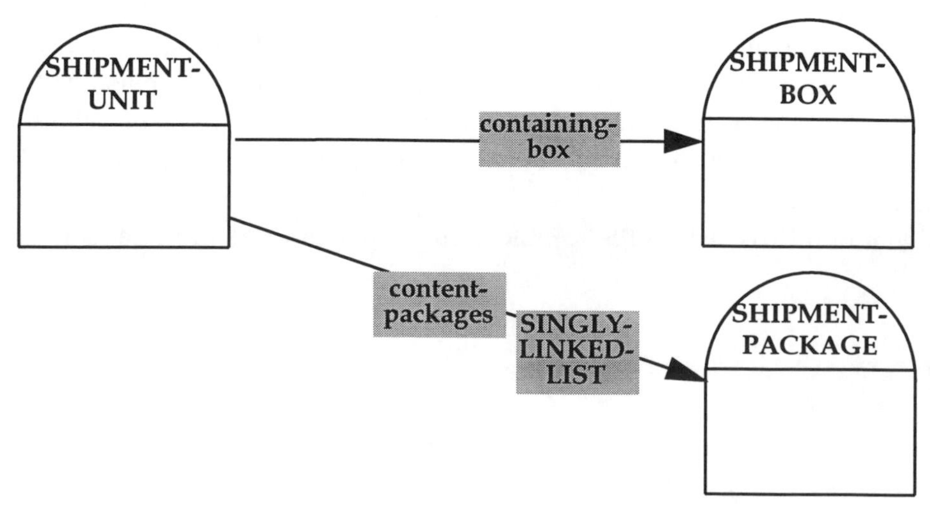

Fig. 5.3: The structure of an aggregate object of class SHIPMENT-UNIT.

Given this structure, to find the total weight of the entire shipment unit, we need to sum the weights of the individual packages. In other words, we need to send the same message iteratively, that is, to each object in the aggregation.

In a case such as this, in which a message is to be sent to each object in a SET, LIST, TREE, and so on, OODN uses the iterator symbol. See Fig. 5.4.

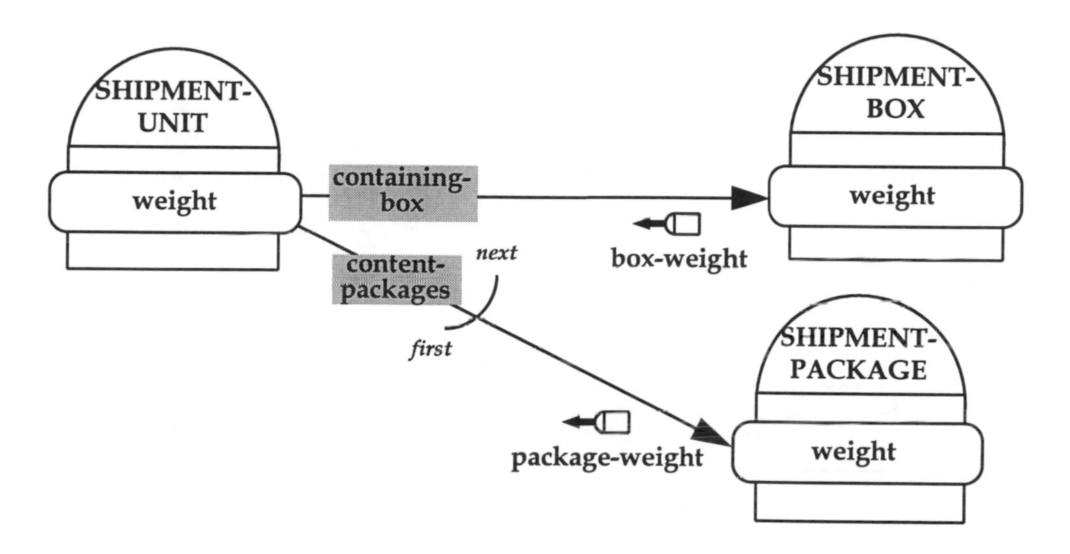

Fig. 5.4: A message sent iteratively to a SINGLY-LINKED-LIST of component objects.

If you wish, you may annotate the iterator symbol with the sequence in which the target objects will be sent their messages. Thc style of the annotation depends on what the generic class is. For linear sequences, annotation will comprise two parts: how the first target object of the collection is chosen and how the next target object is chosen. (If you can, you should use method names taken from the generic class itself.)

For example, for SINGLY-LINKED-LIST (as in the example in Fig. 5.4), we might have the terms *first* and *next* annotating the iterator. For a TREE, the annotation might be an informal comment such as *left-right, depth-first.* (On a SET, sequence is normally undefined.)

However, these annotations are simply meant to be a convenience for a reader of the diagram; they're not meant to replace a method's full specification. So, for example, you would write a specification of **weight**'s algorithm either as pre- and postconditions, or as PDL, pseudocode, or a more formal language.

5.1.4 *Use of* **self** *in messages*

The term **self** often appears in messages on OODN diagrams.[3] **self** is an instance constant (that is, not a variable) that holds an object's own handle. This allows an object sending a message to either

1. Pass **self** as an argument, thereby telling the target object which object sent the message, or

2. Send a message to itself.

In OODN, you would show the first usage (passing **self** as an argument) simply by labeling one of the message arguments **self**. See Fig. 5.5.

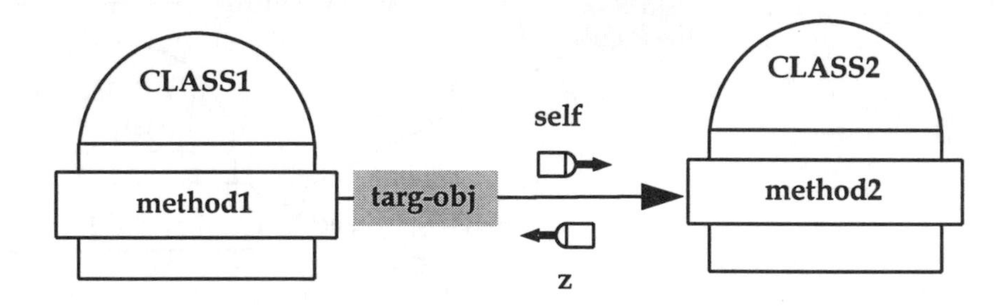

Fig. 5.5: **self** *passed as an argument.*

Passing **self** as an argument occurs most often when the target needs to look up the sender's handle in a table that, perhaps, relates the sender to some other object(s). Some beginners to object orientation splatter their diagrams with **self** arguments, thinking that a target object needs the handle of the sender to "somehow get the output arguments back to the right object." Not so! The message arrow implies automatic return of execution control from the target object to the sender object. All major object-oriented programming languages, in fact, take care of return of control to the sender object in this way.[4]

So, use **self** judiciously as an argument. Beware, too, of "yo-yo messaging," wherein sender and target objects continually swap roles and engage each other in

---

[3] **self** is a term from Smalltalk. You may prefer the C++ term **this**, or the Eiffel term **Current**.

[4] However, in some asynchronous callback mechanisms, the target *does* need the handle of the sender. I cover this in Section 5.2.1.

a seemingly endless dialogue of messages! The clue on the object-communication diagram will be **self** arguments flying back and forth like shuttlecocks.

In OODN, you would show the second usage of **self** (for an object's sending a message to itself) by placing **self** at the start of the message arrow. The class of the target object is the same as the sender object. Figure 5.6 shows two ways to depict this. The first way (shown in the upper diagram) is easier to draw, but the second way is more evocative.

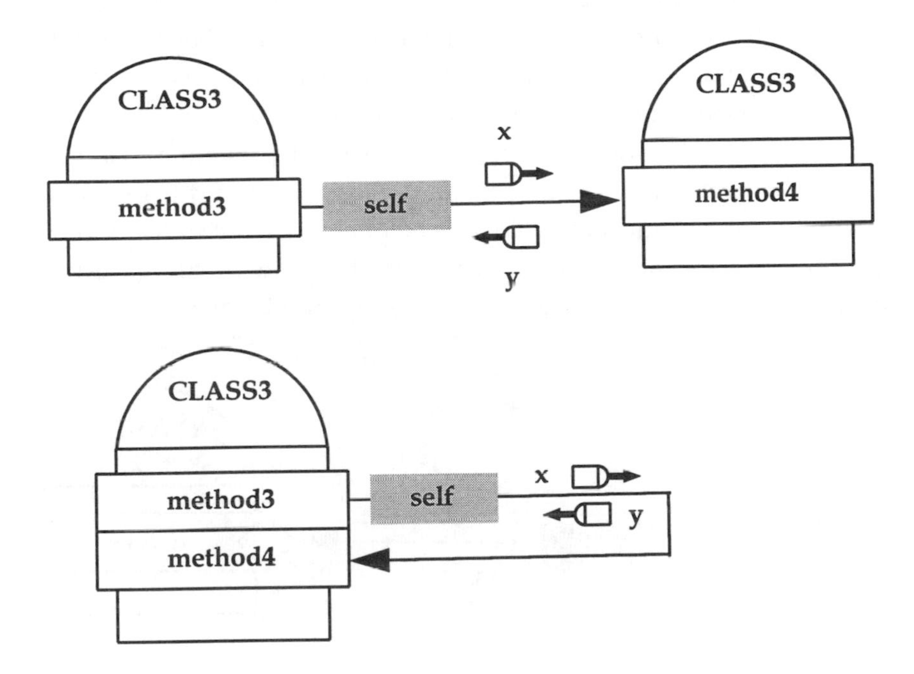

*Fig. 5.6: Two depictions of a sender sending a message to itself (**self** is the target object).*

In the example depicted in two ways in Fig. 5.6, **method3** sends a messagc to invoke **method4** on itself, the same object. Strictly speaking, this message is unnecessary. Because **method3** has access to all the object's variables, it *could* directly manipulate the same variables as **method4**. However, that approach has two drawbacks: First, it may duplicate some code in the two methods. Second, it spreads knowledge of the representation of the variables to too many methods.

Having an object send a message to itself is therefore useful when a designer wants to use the key idea of implementation hiding to hide the implementation of one method from another method in the same class. The design of some classes therefore contains "rings of methods," a topic that we'll return to in Chapter 12.

5.1.5 Messages that result in exceptions

No matter how well software designers and programmers accomplish their crafts, something may go wrong during software execution. For example, a peripheral may unexpectedly time-out (fail to respond within a reasonable time), a hardware error may cause an arithmetic overflow, or an object's instantiation may exhaust available memory. No matter how defensively you write your code, such problems can cause an unexpected run-time crash.

As I mentioned in Chapter 2, an excellent way to improve the robustness of software is through *exception detectors* and *exception handlers*, the latter being known in Eiffel as *rescue clauses.* (The modern jargon for detecting and handling an exception is "throwing and catching an exception.")

When an exceptional condition arises that would prevent normal execution from continuing, an exception detector traps the exception and transfers control to the appropriate exception handler.[5] This piece of software tries to fix the problem, or, at least, prevents the application from crashing and burning. An exception handler should also clean up any inconsistencies in an object's state.

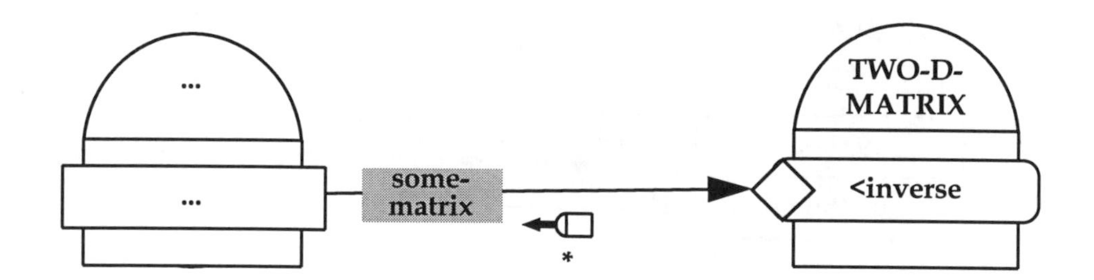

Fig. 5.7: A method with exception-detection capability.

OODN shows the exception-detection ability of a method by a small diamond on the left of the method's symbol. The example in Fig. 5.7 is a function-style method **<inverse** that computes the inverse of a two-dimensional matrix. This method has an exception detector that traps exceptions (such as arithmetic overflow or available-memory exhaustion).

Some languages allow methods that detect exceptions also to return an *exception indicator.* Many exception indicators simply return one of two values: **true**, if

[5] Since languages such as Ada, Eiffel, and C++ have different ways of transferring control to an exception handler, OODN doesn't attempt to depict this transfer.

the method executed successfully, or **false**, if otherwise. More sophisticated exception indicators may bear several values that discriminate among several possible reasons for failure.

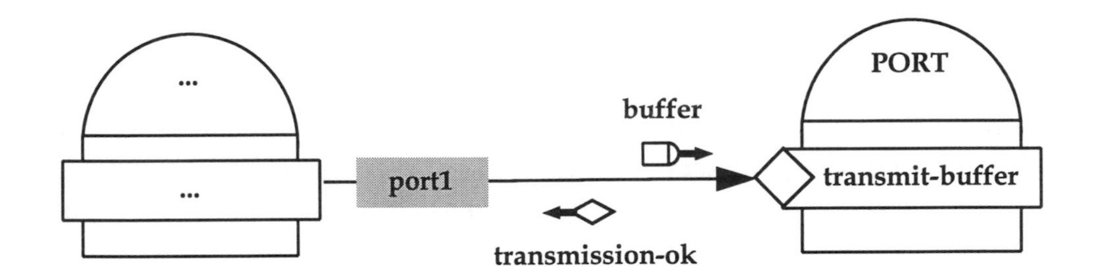

Fig. 5.8: The return of an exception indicator (signifying perhaps a time-out or other problem).

The OODN symbol for the exception indicator is a diamond-headed arrow. Figure 5.8 shows **transmission-ok** as an example. **transmission-ok** will be set to **true** if **transmit-buffer** did its job successfully, and to **false** otherwise (if there was, say, a communications time-out).

Note that an exception indicator bears more serious news than a typical application flag (such as **cust-num-ok**). An exception represents a severe failure on the part of a method to carry out its job, possibly due to trouble in the computer or operating system. An application flag usually signals a more innocuous situation (such as an input error by a user).

5.2 Asynchronous Messaging and Concurrent Execution

In Section 5.1, I tacitly assumed that all messages are synchronous, that is, that a sender object waits while the target of the message processes the message. I also assumed that all execution in an object-oriented system is single-threaded, meaning that only one object is active at a time.

To put it more explicitly, I assumed the following: that only one object in a system can send a message at a given time; that the sender object must wait for the target object to process the message; and that the target object will process only one message at a time. Although this is indeed the way that many mainstream object-oriented environments currently work, it is but a special case of object execution in general.

In this section, I explore the more general *asynchronous* message.

> An *asynchronous message* allows the sender of the message to continue executing while the target object is processing the message.

Asynchronous messages demand multiple threads of control in the system, in order for several objects to execute at the same time. Without multiple threads of control, known more often as *concurrency*, all messages would have to be synchronous messages.

To give OODN the ability to model systems with concurrent execution, we must have a way for an object-communication diagram to depict the following:

1. A sender object's ability to continue execution after it sends a message (possibly until such point that the sender needs the results of the message). This, of itself, implies some concurrency in the system.[6]

2. The capability of a target object to receive multiple messages in an orderly way (from concurrently executing senders).

3. The capability of a target object to process multiple messages concurrently.

4. The capability of a target object to broadcast messages that can be picked up by any object. Such messages are termed *broadcast*, or *nontargeted, messages.*

In Section 5.2.6, I also introduce the object-interaction/timing diagram, which emphasizes time and sequence in the execution and interaction of objects. However, I don't dwell on the specific mechanisms by which concurrency is achieved, which may include remote procedure calls, non-blocking message-sends, and so on.[7]

---

[6] A processor may simulate concurrency by means of, say, time-slicing. This technique, known as *pseudo-concurrency*, is invisible to the executing software.

[7] To read more about various forms of concurrency, you may wish to see [Booch, 1994] or [Atkinson, 1991].

5.2.1 Depicting an asynchronous message

OODN borrows notation for an asynchronous message from SDN (which uses the term *asynchronous transfer*). The notation is an arrow with a dashed shaft, as shown in Fig. 5.9.

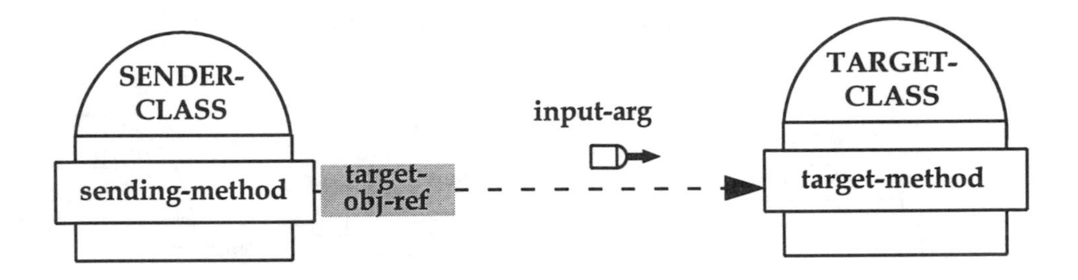

Fig. 5.9: An object-communication diagram showing a basic asynchronous message.

Once a sender sends an asynchronous message, there are (at least) two loci of execution in the system, because the target begins to execute while the sender remains executing. If the sender needs nothing more from the target, then we have total asynchrony: Each object continues exactly as it wishes. However, there are subtle variations on asynchrony.

The most common variation is that the sender's method must stop executing at some point and wait for the target to complete execution of *its* method (and probably deliver some answer). OODN shows this with the notation of Fig. 5.10, which is loosely based on the *incremental module* notation of SDN. Note that the arrow is set apart from the sender, indicating the method's need to wait.

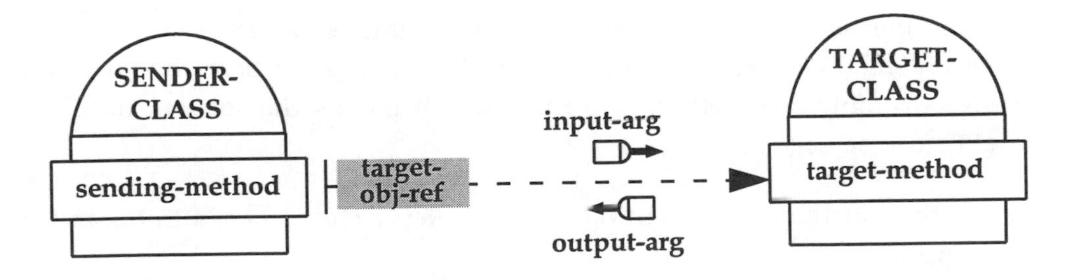

Fig. 5.10: An asynchronous message where the sender waits for the result.

Of course, a sender may reach some point and choose whether to wait or not, or to wait only for some period of time, or to wait for the first of several (concurrently executing) target objects' methods to finish. OODN doesn't differentiate among these possibilities; such complexity belongs properly within the method definition of the sender (written in pseudocode, for example). OODN shows only that the sender takes note of the target's completion of the message.[8]

Another mechanism in a concurrent, asynchronous system that allows a sender to wait for the target's completion is the *callback*. Figure 5.11, which I explain below, shows one way that the callback mechanism may work.

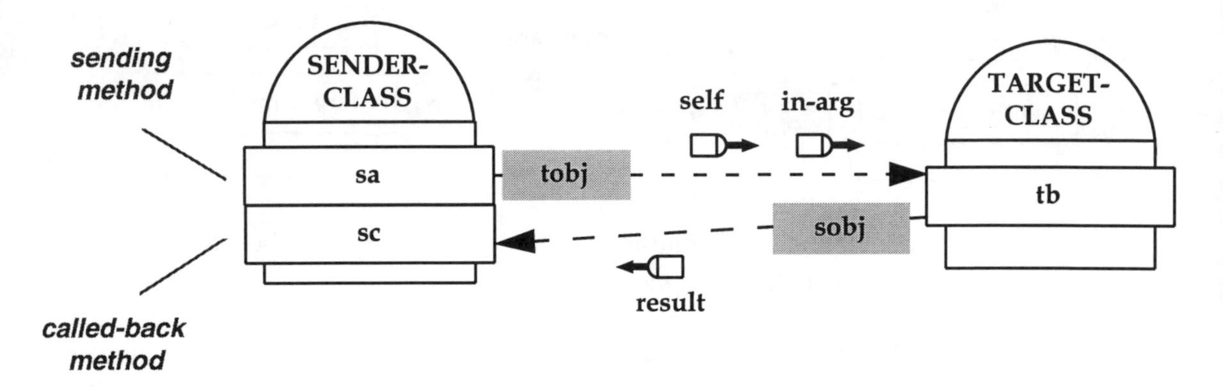

Fig. 5.11: The callback mechanism via asynchronous messages in a concurrent environment.

1. Method **sa** in the sender object **sobj** sends an asynchronous message **tobj.tb** to a target object **tobj** with an input argument **in-arg**. The sender also supplies its handle (via **self**), which will provide the return address for later callback.

2. Method **sa**, which is still executing, terminates.

3. When method **tb** has consumed the message and computed the result, it sends back another asynchronous message to the original sender object—probably to a different method—such as **sobj.sc (;result)**. (I assume here that the sender can execute only one method at a time, which means that **sa** will have terminated before **sc** begins.)

4. Method **tb**, which is still executing, does whatever else it needs to do and then terminates.

---

[8] It's possible that the sender that sets the target executing receives the **process-id** of the executing target method. With this **process-id** the sender may later kill, pause, or inquire about the state of the target method. (The **process-id**, which is normally assigned by the computer's operating system, is different from the target object's handle.)

The object-communication diagram of Fig. 5.12 clarifies this game of O.O. telephone tag with a more concrete example of the use of the callback mechanism.

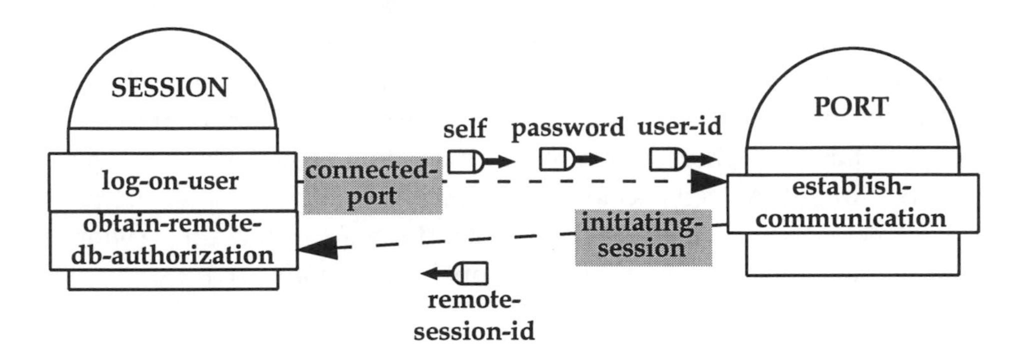

Fig. 5.12: The callback mechanism used to initiate a session with a remote machine.

The job of the system fragment shown in Fig. 5.12 is to get a user logged on to a remote computer system. First, the object on the left (of class SESSION) sends an asynchronous message to a target object **connected-port** (of class PORT) asking to establish communication with the remote computer. Establishing this communication may take a while. When the method **establish-communication** has eventually completed its job, it sends another asynchronous message—the callback message—to the SESSION object, whose **obtain-remote-db-authorization** method is activated. The SESSION object then continues the logging-on procedure.

5.2.2 Depicting a target object's capability to receive multiple messages

Once we allow concurrency, we also allow the possibility for a target object to be bombarded by messages from lots of concurrently executing sender objects. Since these messages may arrive faster than the target can process them, they'll have to go somewhere to wait their turn. They go into a "waiting room," more often known as a *message queue*.

The target object ushers arriving messages into the message queue. The object then repeatedly removes a message from the front of the queue, sends the message to the method that will process it, and takes the next message from the queue. Messages that overflow the queue will be rejected. An object with no queuing facility will reject all messages that cannot be immediately processed. (Rejected messages may be returned to sender with an exception indicator.)

Messages in a queue may be ordered by priority. You can picture this as a set of parallel queues at the target, each queue with its own priority level.[9] (See Fig. 5.13.) Sender objects may also have priority levels. If so, a rule such as "a message may not have a higher priority than its sending object" will allow parts of a system to obtain guaranteed execution priority. (For example, if a nuclear reactor is about to melt down, it may be a good idea to ensure that the reactor-cooling software executes before the monthly-personnel-report software.)

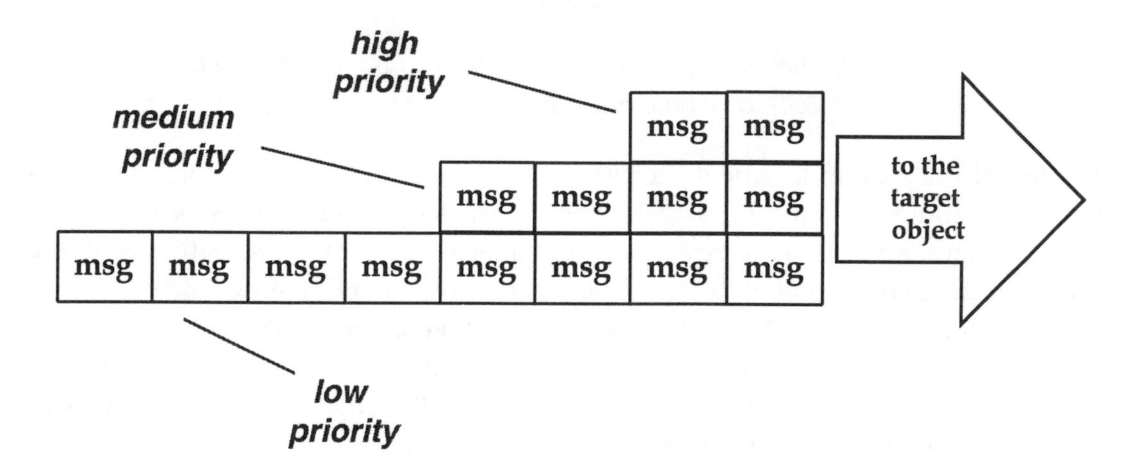

Fig. 5.13: Three parallel queues, each with its own priority.

Later in this section (in Fig. 5.16), I show an example of OODN for the priority level of an asynchronous message.

5.2.3 Depicting a target object's capability to process multiple messages concurrently

In the previous section, I assumed that, although the system as a whole has concurrency, a target object takes one message at a time from its queue. This is *sys-*

[9] Presumably, these messages are processed in priority sequence: first, all the highest-priority ones; next, the lower-priority ones; and finally, all the lowest-priority ones. But, of course, a real implementation could use a much more sophisticated sequencing scheme.

tem-level concurrency. However, a target object may handle multiple messages at a time (*object-level concurrency*). Even a single method may be able to handle multiple messages at a time (*method-level concurrency*).[10]

Obviously, method-level concurrency implies object-level concurrency, which in turn implies system-level concurrency. OODN can indicate both object-level and method-level concurrency. The degree of concurrency that you can use is constrained by your programming language and operating environment.

OODN shows a class whose objects are capable of object-level concurrency with a small reversed-L in the lower-right corner of the class symbol, as Fig. 5.14 shows.

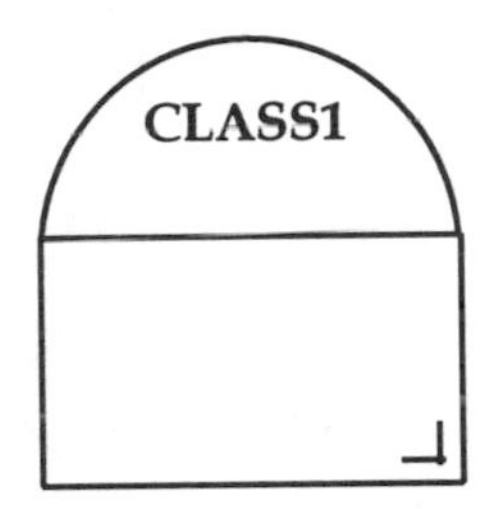

Fig. 5.14: A class whose objects have object-level concurrency.

Figure 5.15 shows a class whose objects have methods with method-level concurrency. As the figure shows, only two of the three methods have concurrency.

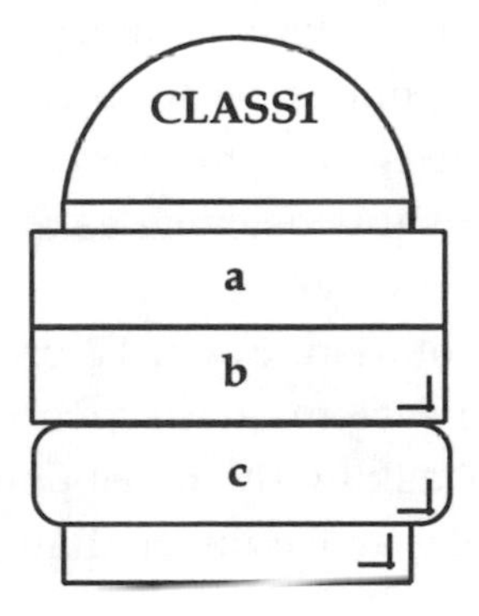

Fig. 5.15: A class whose objects have two methods with method-level concurrency.

[10] Technically speaking, a method could simultaneously process several messages by having several execution threads through re-entrant code. Alternatively, the system could simply run several copies of the method.

Incidentally, people often ask me whether object-level concurrency requires multiple copies of an object. Conceptually, no: There is still but a single object, with a single handle, and (at a given moment) a single state. Nevertheless, since that single object is being processed (accessed, even updated) in many ways all at the same time, the environment may make several temporary object copies for its own, private convenience. The environment will keep the copies synchronized with one another and will eventually remerge them all.[11]

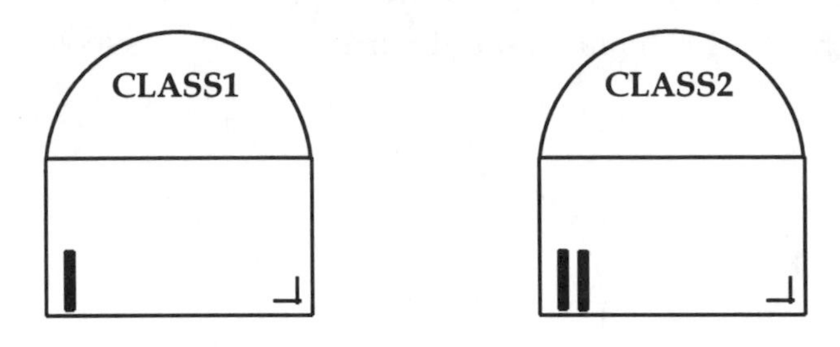

Fig. 5.16: A class whose objects support a single-priority message queue and one whose objects support a multiple-priority message queue.

Figure 5.16 shows OODN for classes whose objects will support message queues at run-time. The single bar in the class on the left denotes a single-priority queue; the double bar in the class on the right denotes a multiple-priority queue. (This is the same kind of multiple-priority queue that appeared in Fig. 5.13.)

Although queue support and object-level concurrency are separate concepts, in practice you can assume that an object with object-level concurrency will also support a queue of waiting messages. Furthermore, since many concurrent operating environments support queues intrinsically, as a designer, you probably won't need to use OODN's queue notation very often.

However, if you do need this notation, Fig. 5.17 provides an example of its use. Here, in part of an electronic-mail system, an asynchronous message is being sent to an object of class EMAIL-PORT asking the **email-port** to transmit some outgoing e-mail. Since e-mail messages may arrive faster than they can enter the informa-

[11] The replicated objects share the same handle, although the operating environment may append suffixes to the normal handle in order to keep track of the copies. Distributed object-oriented DBMSs may employ replicated objects for the sake of efficiency. The DBMS is then responsible for maintaining the replicated objects' consistency with one another, relieving the designer of this burden.

tion superhighway, they have to go into a queue (a multiple-priority queue at the method level) at **transmit-email-message**.

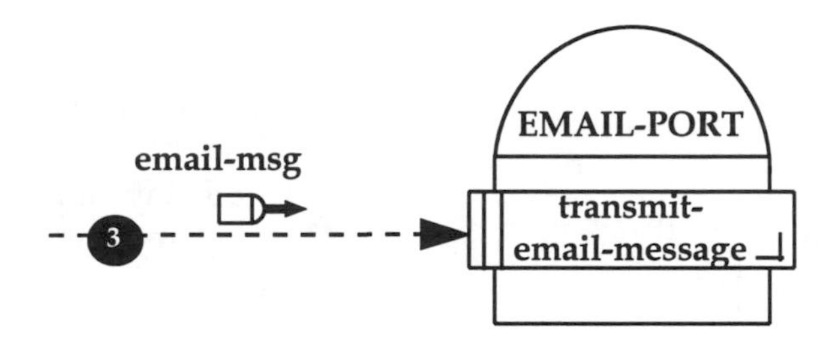

Fig. 5.17: An asynchronous message (with priority 3) invoking a method with a multiple-priority message queue.

The figure shows a sender object using a priority-3 asynchronous message, as depicted by the numeral **3** on the message arrow. The double-bar symbol within the method **transmit-email-message** reveals that this method supports a multiple-priority queue.

5.2.4 Depicting a broadcast (nontargeted) message

An object sending a message normally holds the handle of the object that's the target of the message. However, in systems with concurrency and asynchronous messaging, this isn't always true. In the extreme case, a sender may *broadcast* a message—that is, treat every object in the system as a potential target. A copy of the message goes into the queue of every object in the system.

An object may broadcast a "to whom it may concern" message in response to some external event that it detects. For example, an object might detect a security compromise and broadcast to all objects the need for a priority system shutdown. An object may ignore a broadcast message because it has no method with which to process it. Another object may choose to ignore the message temporarily until it reaches a suitable state.[12] But a handful of objects will take some action immediately upon receiving the message.

A broadcast message is similar to an iterated message in that it goes to many objects. Unlike the sender of an iterated message, however, the sender of a broadcast message doesn't need to know which objects are interested in the event that

[12] I cover object states in Chapters 6 and 10.

has taken place and so doesn't need to have the handles of the target objects. Figure 5.18 shows the OODN for a broadcast message.

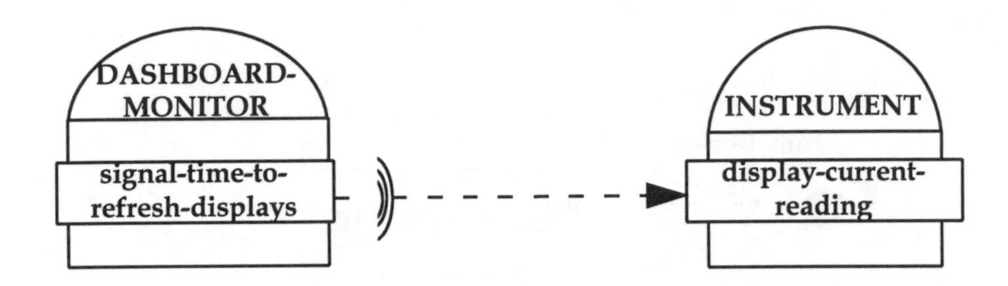

Fig. 5.18: A broadcast message.

In the real-time application shown in Fig. 5.18, the method on the left (**signal-time-to-refresh-displays**) "watches a clock" to determine when it's time to refresh the instrument displays on a vehicle dashboard. The class name of the target indicates the class of the objects receiving the broadcast. The class name INSTRUMENT, therefore, tells us that every object of class INSTRUMENT is getting the message. (The class name OBJECT or ANY would indicate that the message goes to every object in the whole system.) Incidentally, here we see again the beauty of polymorphism: Each object of a subclass—such as SPEEDOMETER or TACHOMETER—is presumably carrying out its own version of the method **display-current-reading**.

5.2.5 Depicting other mechanisms to support concurrency

Concurrency comes with a well-known problem: What happens when a bunch of object methods, executing at the same time, all start updating the same object's private variables? Couldn't all manner of chaos and inconsistency ensue? Since the answer is, "Yes," we need some way to control conflicting usage of a target object.

There are two major approaches: *pessimistic concurrency control* and *optimistic concurrency control*. The best-known example of pessimistic concurrency control is *locking*, which temporarily reduces concurrent access to an object.

You may implement a locking request as a **lock** message to the target object to be locked, shown in OODN like any other message. The **lock** message goes into the target object's queue. When the target object retrieves the message from the queue, it carries out steps such as the following: First, it ceases to take any more messages out of its queue; second, it waits for all methods currently executing to complete; third, it thenceforth takes from its queue only messages from the sender of the locking message.

The sender object has thus acquired a lock on—and so exclusive use of—the target object.[13] The lock will normally remain in place until the sender sends an **unlock** message.

Another way to effect locking is to send a message to a special system object called the *lock manager*. The lock manager also has the ability to lock "in one swoop" a group of target objects across which a sender object wishes to maintain consistency.

Pessimistic concurrency control isn't ideal for a system in which an object may become locked for hours. (What if a user goes to lunch or sets off on a trek to Nepal, just after starting a transaction?) Although there are work-arounds to the problem, a more generally useful approach is optimistic concurrency control.

With optimistic concurrency control, a sender (say, sender A) merrily updates target objects hither and thither. However, these updates are not committed (that is, they can be undone at any time). When sender A has finished updating, it must explicitly commit the updates. If another sender (sender B) has also been updating a target object, then the commit will fail and sender A will have to try all over again. Updates to multiple objects require a *two-phase commit*: All updated objects are asked whether they're okay to commit. If they *are* all okay, then all commit together; otherwise, none of them commits.[14]

5.2.6 Object-interaction/timing diagrams

Being able to depict what's executing when is especially valuable in systems with concurrency. To do this in OODN, you can use the object-interaction/timing diagram as an adjunct to an object-communication diagram, particularly where timing issues are complex or tricky.

The object-interaction/timing diagram shows time increasing down its vertical axis. Horizontally, along the top, the diagram lists objects that will receive messages (or just their class names, if that's precise enough). The body of the diagram

---

[13] I don't pursue any further the myriad varieties of possible locks. There are, for example, arrogatory locks (which force all messages currently executing to cease and roll back) and locks that allow read-only messages to proceed normally. There are also arrogatory unlocks (which force a sender object to relinquish its lock and the target object to roll back).

[14] To read further on concurrency mechanisms (such as transaction begin/end, pause, kill, and forced rollback), see [Atkinson, 1991], for example.

shows the activated methods, drawn to rough chronological scale: The vertical length of an activated-method symbol corresponds to the length of time during which the method is active. The arrows between methods depict messages, just as they do in the object-communication diagram.

Figure 5.19, for example, shows a piece of a real-time system that authorizes personnel to pass through electronically controlled doors. (The employee inserts an ID card, which is read, and the system then sounds a buzzer, lights up a sign, and holds the door open.)

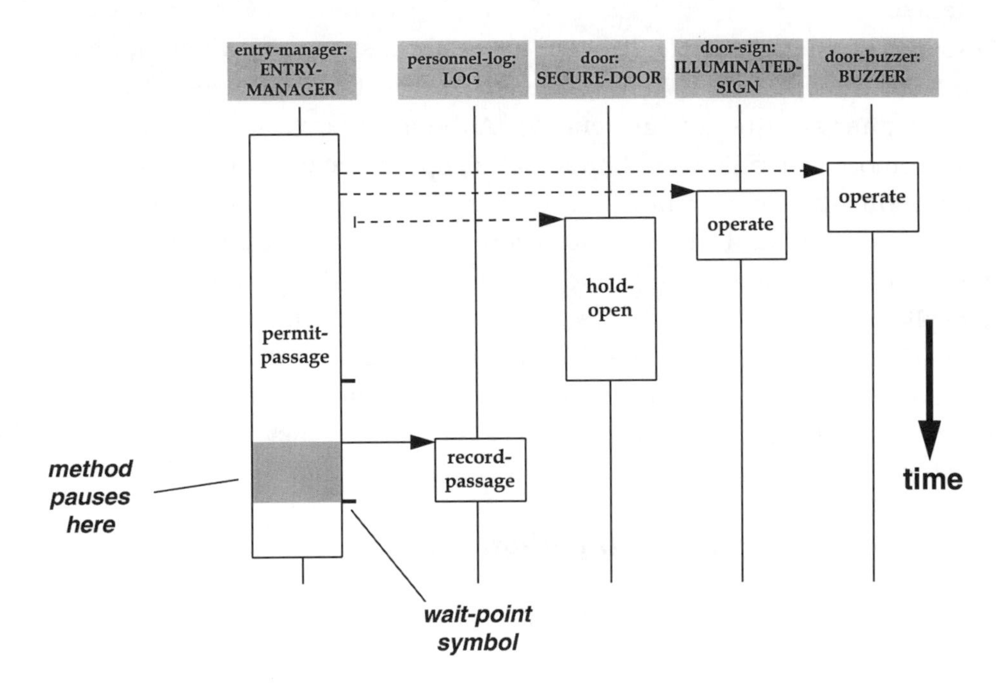

Fig. 5.19: Object-interaction/timing diagram for concurrently executing objects.

The method that manages this piece of the application is **permit-passage** (defined on the class ENTRY-MANAGER), which appears on the left of Fig. 5.19. When this method begins executing, it sends two asynchronous messages—one to invoke **door-buzzer.operate** and one to invoke **door-sign.operate**. **permit-passage** lets those two methods execute concurrently and pays no further heed to them. **permit-passage** then asynchronously invokes **door.hold-open**, which also runs concurrently. However, at a certain point (marked with a tiny tab-line extending from the method), **permit-passage** waits to hear that **hold-open** has finished executing.[15] Finally, **permit-passage** invokes **personnel-log.record-passage** synchronously, which means that **permit-passage** cannot execute until **record-passage** returns. (Although I emphasize **permit-passage**'s period of enforced idleness by a shaded area in Fig. 5.19, this shading isn't normally shown in an object-interaction/timing diagram.)

In this example, the names along the top of the diagram refer to objects. Alternatively, you could use this diagram to model the execution behavior of a system's architectural components by showing tasks or entire CPUs along the top of the diagram.

Figure 5.20 shows another pair of concurrently executing objects—the pair we saw in Fig. 5.12 as an example of the callback mechanism.

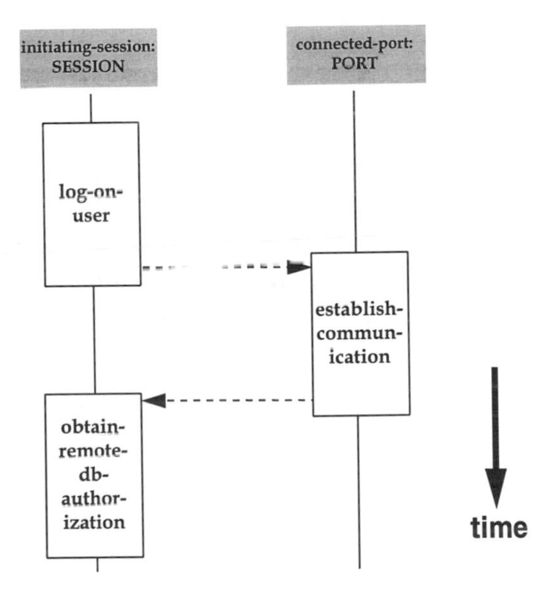

Fig. 5.20: Object-interaction/timing diagram for a callback mechanism.

Figure 5.21 is a variation on Fig. 5.20, wherein the object **initiating-session** of class SESSION has object-level concurrency. The two methods, **log-on-user** and **obtain-remote-db-authorization**, may thus execute concurrently with each other.

[15] The small horizontal tab-lines on the right side of a method show *synchronization-* or *wait-points*, at which a method must pause until another method has completed its job.

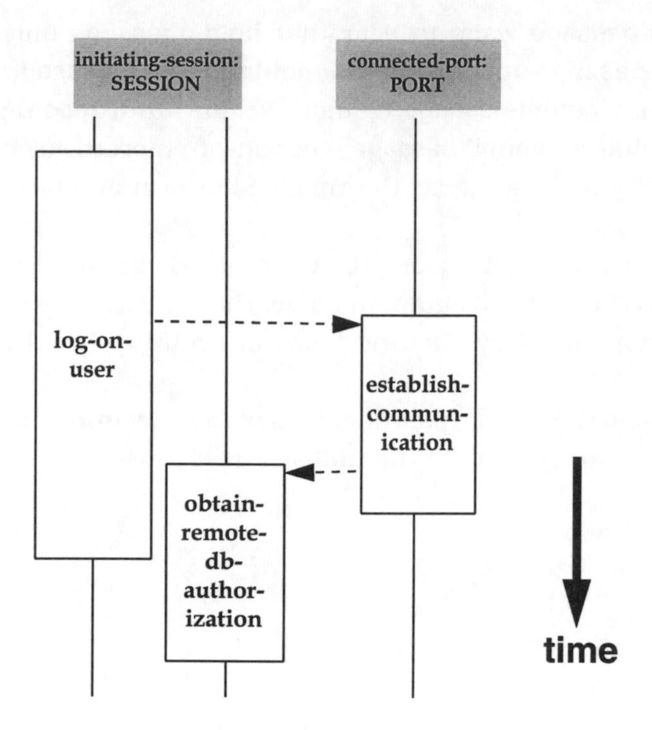

Fig. 5.21: Object-interaction/timing diagram for a callback mechanism with object-level concurrency.

5.3 Summary

In this chapter, we look at OODN diagrams for depicting the execution of an object-oriented system. The object-communication diagram depicts the messages that objects send at run-time. The diagram may show synchronous messages (in which the sender object waits for the target object to complete execution) and asynchronous messages (in which the sender object continues execution after sending the message).

OODN shows a message by means of a reference arrow from the sender object to the target object. This arrow is identical in form to the reference arrow in an object-aggregation diagram. However, the message arrow is distinctive because it points to a specific method—the method to be invoked—rather than to a whole object. The name of the target object, from the point of view of the sender, appears near the start of the message arrow. The message arrow may also be accompanied by argument symbols, depicting the arguments, if any, of the message.

The name of the target object's class appears at the top of the target-object symbol. Polymorphism complicates the naming of this class, because the sender may not precisely know the target's class. The rule is this: Use the name of the lowest class in the inheritance hierarchy that is a superclass of all the classes to which the target object could belong. If you wish, you may emphasize the polymorphism by enclosing this name in parentheses.

OODN shows iteration of a message with the iterator symbol, alongside which you may note the sequence of iteration, if that's important. OODN depicts exception detectors with a small diamond, which is attached to the side of a method, and shows exception indicators with a small diamond-tailed arrow, which is returned as a message argument. However, OODN does not depict any unconstrained transfer of control as a result of an exception.

OODN depicts asynchronous messages with a dotted arrow shaft. In OODN, to indicate that a message sender must wait at some point for the result of a message, you show the origin of the arrow slightly detached from the sending method.

Asynchronous messaging requires some concurrency of execution in the system. This, in turn, implies that many messages may need to be queued up at an object or a method within that object. The notation shows both multiple-message queues and priority levels on the messages themselves. (Higher-priority messages are executed before lower-priority ones.) OODN uses the broadcast symbol to show an object broadcasting the same message to many objects at once.

Finally, OODN provides the object-interaction/timing diagram to emphasize sequence of execution of objects. This diagram, in which time flows down the vertical axis, is useful for clarifying the sequence of interactions among several communicating, concurrent objects.

5.4 Exercises

1. The annotations that forbid the inheritance (Ɨ) or overriding (Ɵ) of a method appear on the class-interface (pin-out) diagram. They do not annotate a method when it's shown on an object-communication diagram. Why not?

2. Draw the different kinds of argument symbols that might appear alongside a message in an object-communication diagram.

3. Draw a class-internal-design diagram for a class of your choice, such as the HOMINOID class of Chapter 1. (Although we covered class-internal-design diagrams in Chapter 3, I present this exercise in this chapter because your answer may employ messages, such as a message to **self**.)

4. For the class you chose in Exercise 3, is any object-level concurrency possible? What methods could execute simultaneously on the same object? Are there any pairs of methods that you *wouldn't* want to execute simultaneously on the same object?

5. In OODN, how might you depict the friend function of C++? (This is a function to which a class grants access to the components of the class's objects that would normally be private.)

5.5 Answers

1. The anti-inheritance and anti-overriding annotations denote restrictions on a class's ability to inherit and override a method. The object-communication diagram depicts objects communicating at run-time and does not explicitly model inheritance. In other words, the object-communication diagram concerns itself with what information passes from one object's method to another, rather than whether a method can be inherited.

2. Figure 5.22 shows four kinds of argument symbol, three of which we saw in this chapter. The fourth is a pointer to a function or procedure, which you might also find in a non-object-oriented system.

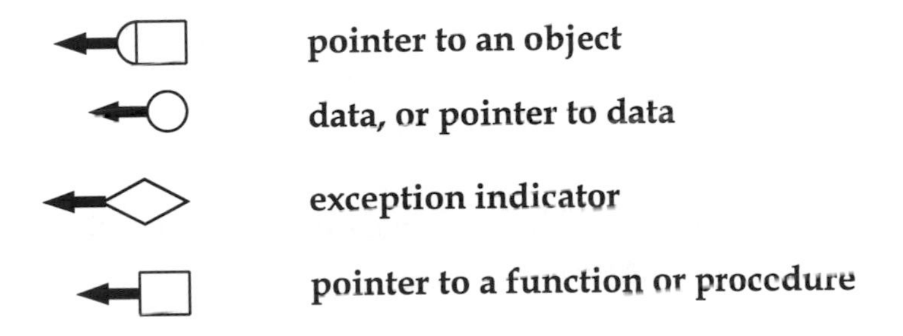

Fig. 5.22: Four kinds of argument symbol.

3. Figure 5.23 shows one approach. In this example, both **turn-left** and **turn-right** use the private method **turn** in order to do their jobs. The OODN reveals that **turn** is messaged (rather than simply called) because the arrows are annotated with **self**, which is the target object of the message.[16]

---

[16] But, as I mentioned in Section 3.9, many languages implement **self.method** simply as **call method**. In the latter case, you would not annotate the arrow with **self**.

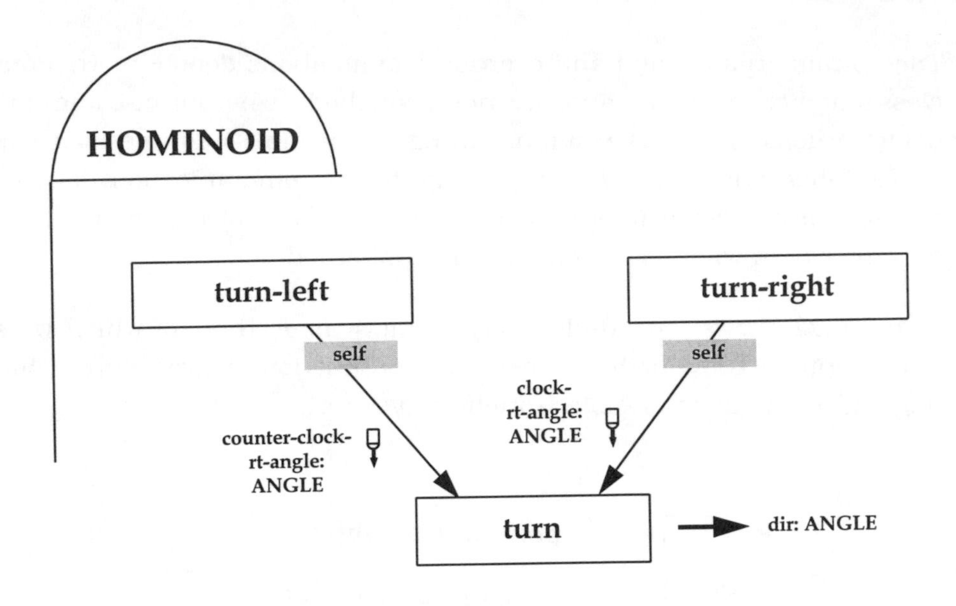

Fig. 5.23: A possible class-internal-design diagram for part of HOMINOID.

The method **turn** does the job of updating the hominoid's direction. The code of the message from the method **turn** to the object referred to as **dir** might be something like

```
dir.increment (turn-angle; )
```

4. In HOMINOID, the methods **facing-wall** and **location** (for example) could execute together. (Indeed, it would be okay for each method to have method-level concurrency.) However, there would have to be some restrictions on object-level concurrency. I doubt, for example, that the method pairs **turn-left/turn-right** or **advance/turn-left** could execute simultaneously. (Imagine what that would do to the hardware!)

5. Figure 5.24 illustrates C++'s friend function in OODN. The upper diagram shows the static declaration of friendship. The arrow points to the friend function since the reference direction is from class to function. The "little hat" at the end of the arrow differentiates the notation from the inheritance arrow and also symbolizes the granting of access to the private implementa-

tion of the class. (We first saw the "little hat" used to emphasize inheritance of implementation in Fig. 4.2.)

The lower diagram is an object-communication diagram that shows the use of friendship at run-time. In this diagram, the friend function refers to a private instance variable (namely, **some-inst-var**) of the object being befriended.

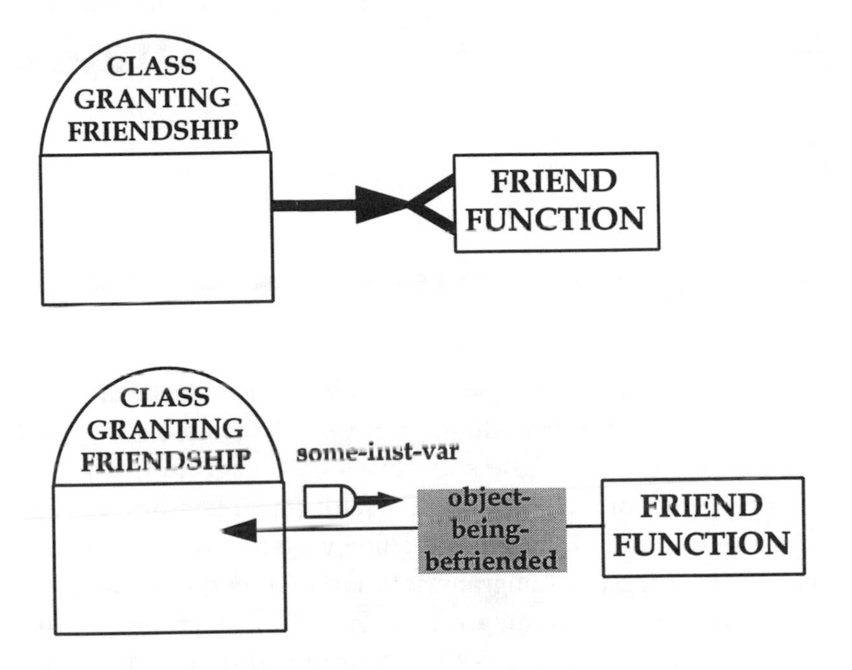

Fig. 5.24: OODN's depiction of C++'s friend function.

State-Transition Diagrams

A state-transition diagram shows the states that objects of a given class may assume and the transitions from state to state that are legal for those objects. Although the state-transition diagram has proven useful in traditional design, in order for it to be useful for object-oriented design we must augment the traditional diagram in some ways.[1] To this end, OODN has extended basic state-transition-diagram notation by incorporating nested states and object messages into the standard notation. In this chapter, I first briefly describe the traditional state-transition diagram and then outline OODN's extensions to it.

6.1 Basic State-Transition Diagrams

A state-transition diagram is ideal for modeling a variable with few values and restrictions on its permitted value transitions. For example, consider the class SELLABLE-PRODUCT, containing the variables **base-price:MONEY** and **curr-stock-status:STOCK-STATUS**. There are two qualitative differences between these two variables, as follows:

[1] See [Ward and Mellor, 1985], for example. Note that state-transition *tables*—described in several of the references—are also valuable, although I don't cover them as part of OODN.

1. **base-price**, being an instance of MONEY, has a large number of possible values, such as $1.98, $4.95, $5.95, and so on. **curr-stock-status**, on the other hand, has only a small set of possible values, such as **in-stock**, **out-of-stock**, **on-order**.

2. There's probably little business restriction on permitted changes to **base-price**. In other words, an object's **base-price** may change from $4.95 to $5.25, or from $6.50 to $5.99, or whatever. However, an object's **curr-stock-status** may perhaps not be able to change directly from **out-of-stock** to **in-stock** without first passing through the value **on-order**.

base-price is not a suitable candidate to be modeled by means of a state-transition diagram, because it has lots of possible values and has almost no restrictions on its transitions among those values. The variable **curr-stock-status**, on the other hand, has the two properties that make it ideal for a state-transition diagram. As we saw above, this variable has only a few possible values and there are significant restrictions on its transitions from one value to another.

Figure 6.1 shows a state-transition diagram for **SELLABLE-PRODUCT::curr-stock-status**. In Fig. 6.1, each of the boxes containing a value of **curr-stock-status** represents a state of a SELLABLE-PRODUCT object.[2] The arrows represent transitions between states. Each transition is annotated with a two-part label. Above the line are the inbound message(s) to the object that can trigger that transition from one state to the other. The presence of multiple messages above the line indicates that *any one* of the listed messages may cause the transition.[3]

Below the line are the outbound message(s) from the object that are triggered by a transition between states. The presence of multiple messages below the line indicates that *all* of the listed messages are emitted during the transition. For some transitions, the list of outbound messages may be empty.

The initial transition of a state-transition diagram, such as the one at the top of Fig. 6.1, takes an object to the state that it first acquires on its instantiation or initialization. The final transition of a state-transition diagram shows an object's transition from its final state to deletion. (There's an example of a final transition at the upper left of Fig. 6.7.)

---

[2] As we'll see in Chapter 10, a box on a state-transition diagram denotes a region in the state-space of the class. The region may comprise a single point or a large group of points.

[3] Usually, you may omit messages' arguments in a state-transition diagram (as I did in Fig. 6.1). However, in some state-transition diagrams you'll need to show the arguments, as we'll see in later examples.

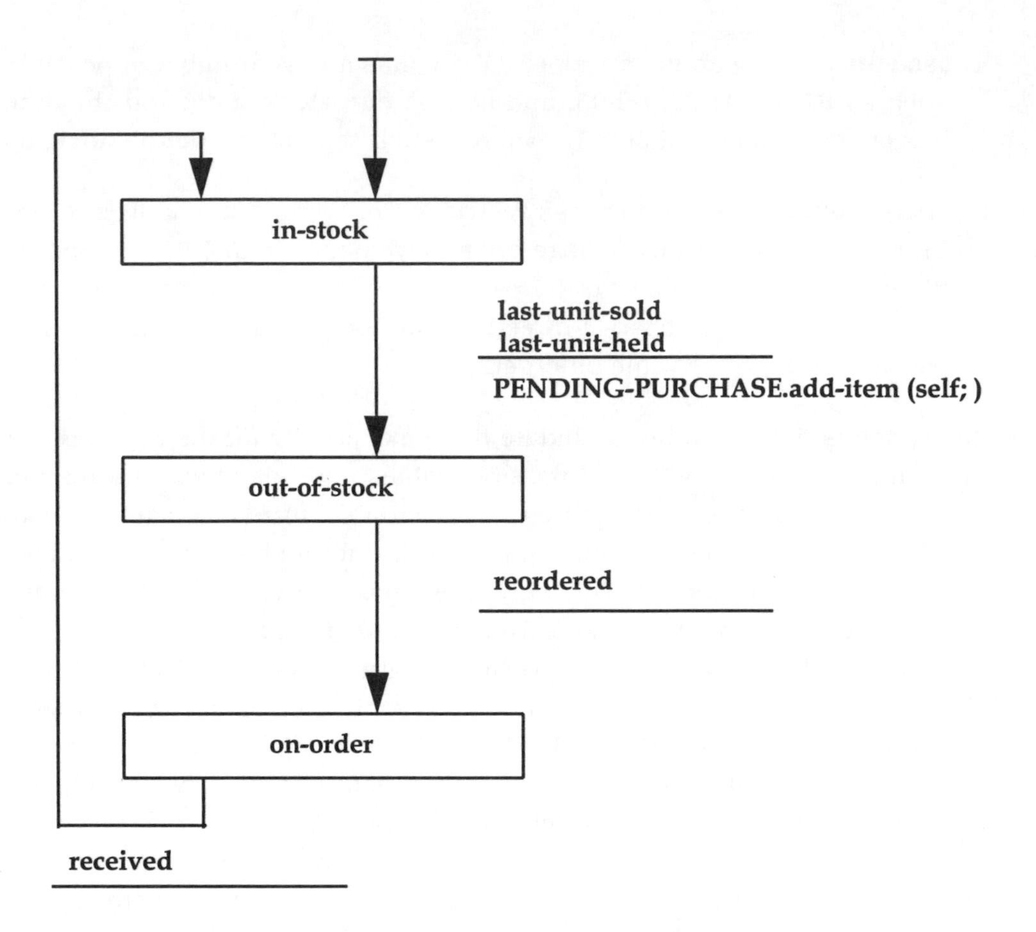

Fig. 6.1: State-transition diagram for **SELLABLE-PRODUCT::curr-stock-status**.

Note that OODN tends to use Mealy state-transition diagrams, which place outbound messages on transitions. However, Moore state-transition diagrams, which place outbound messages on states, are equally valid (and I show one later in this chapter). In OODN, you may choose to use the Mealy convention, the Moore convention, or even a convention that combines both Mealy and Moore.[4]

6.2 Nested States

Not all state-transition diagrams are as simple as the one in Fig. 6.1. Some state-transition diagrams require inner states nested within outer ones. To furnish an example of such a state-transition diagram, let's consider the state-transition diagrams for a machine in a factory.

[4] See [Mealy, 1955] and [Moore, 1956].

The machine's operating status (**MACHINE::op-stat**) has four states: **standing-by**, **accelerating**, **running**, and **decelerating**. The machine also has a maintenance status (**MACHINE::maint-stat**) with three states: **operating**, **waiting-for-repair**, and **in-repair**. Each of the variables **maint-stat** and **op-stat** has its own state-transition diagram, as shown in Fig. 6.2.

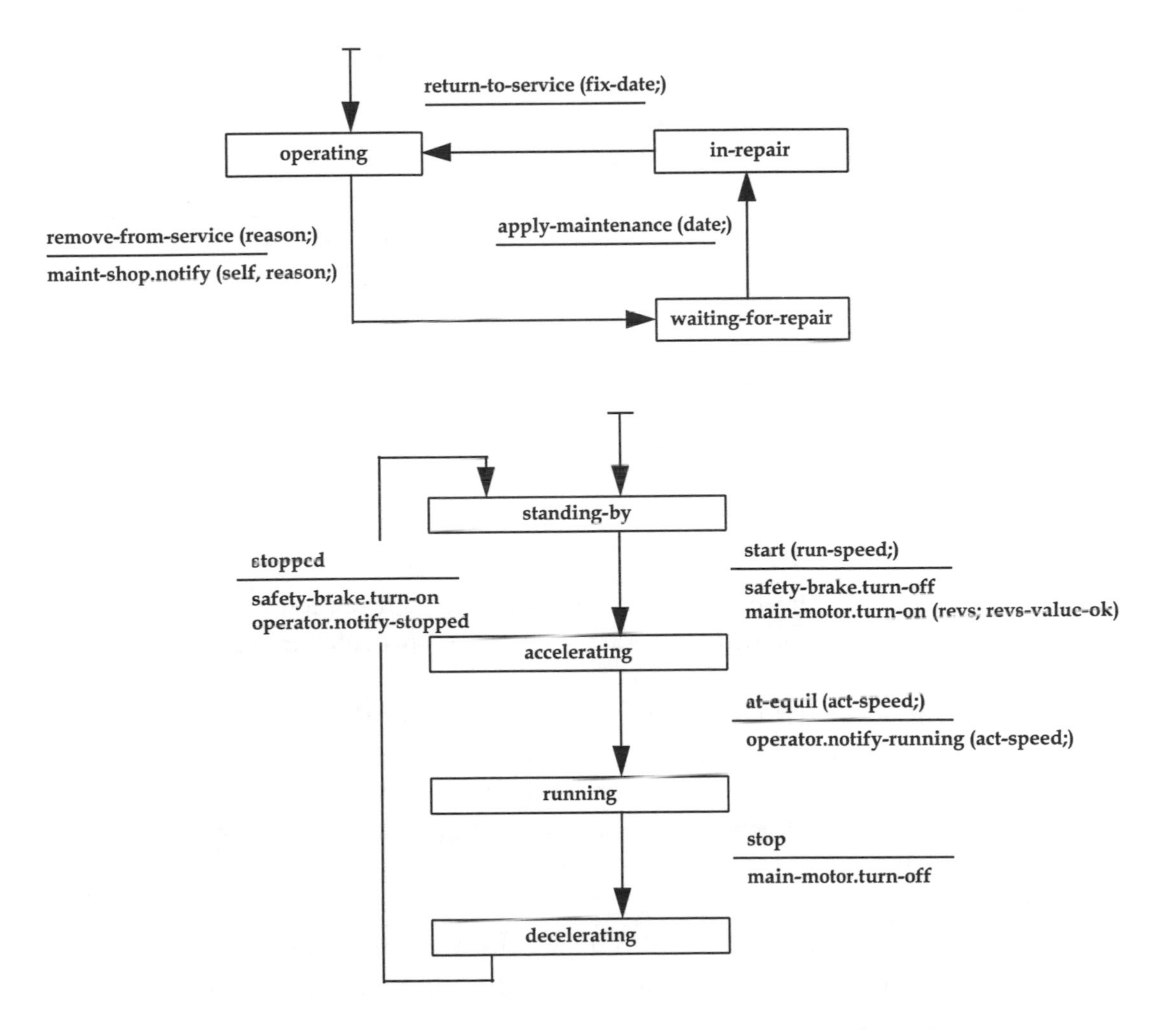

Fig. 6.2: The state-transition diagrams for **MACHINE::maint-stat** *and* **MACHINE::op-stat**.

At first glance, MACHINE appears to have twelve possible states (three for **maint-stat** times four for **op-stat**). But that's not true if we reasonably assume that only an *operating* machine can accelerate, decelerate, and so on. Thus, there are really only *six* legitimate states, because the two variables, **maint-stat** and **op-stat**, aren't mutually independent. **op-stat** has meaning only when **maint-stat = operating**.

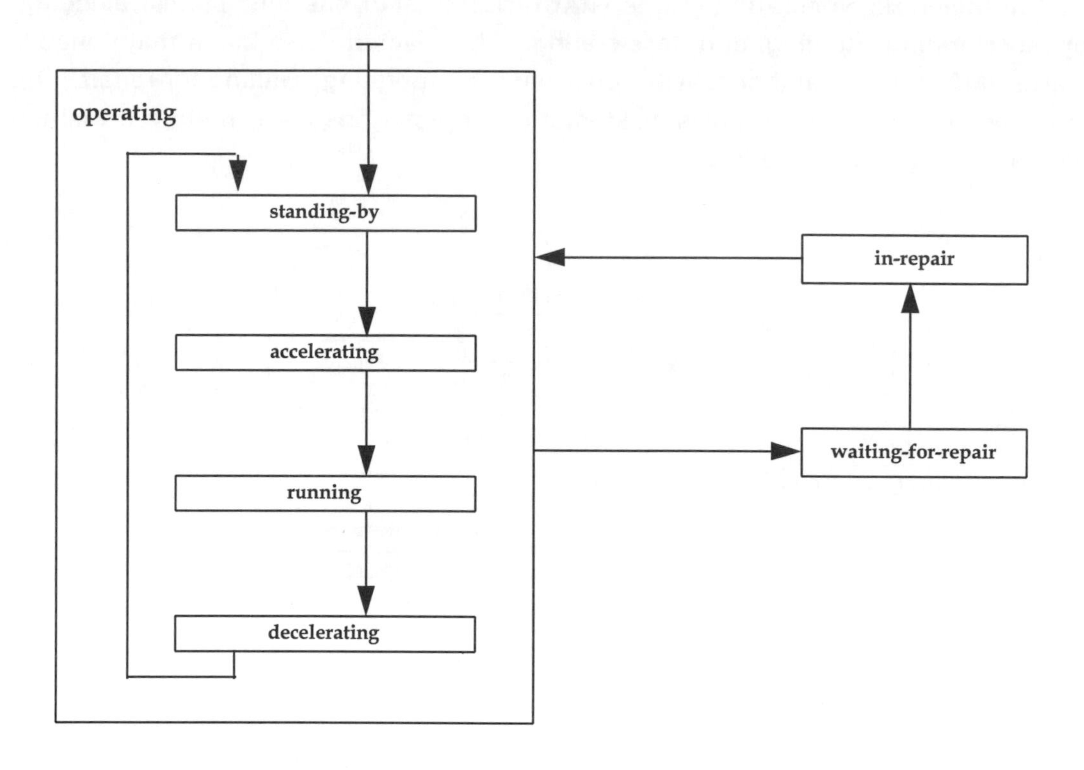

Fig. 6.3: The combined, or nested, state-transition diagram for **MACHINE::maint-stat** *and* **MACHINE::op-stat**.

Figure 6.3 shows the two state-transition diagrams of Fig. 6.2 combined into one by nesting the second diagram into the **operating** state of the first.[5] This nesting of the four **op-stat** states within the **operating** state is a graphic depiction of the constraint that **op-stat** has meaning only when **maint-stat = operating**. Indeed, this nesting is useful only when there are constraints such as these across state-transition diagrams for a class.

The idea of using nested boxes to depict the combination of inner states within outer ones comes from David Harel.[6] The meaning of, say, the **running** state is

[5] Note that I omitted the annotations on the transitions only for purposes of clarity in this example.

[6] In this book, I concentrate on the enhancements to Harel's notation for state-transition diagrams that OODN has found useful for object orientation. For a discussion of the original notation, see [Harel, 1987] or [Henderson-Sellers and Edwards, 1994]. [Cook and Daniels, 1994] also has an excellent discussion of the application of state-transition diagrams to object-oriented design.

that the machine has both the operating status of **running** and the maintenance status of **operating**. The **in-repair** state has no nested state(s). This means that, when the machine has the maintenance status of **in-repair**, the operating status is undefined.

6.3 Message Arguments

So far, so good. But object orientation introduces an extra nuance into state-transition diagrams in the form of message arguments, which traditional state-transition diagrams ignore. In OODN, arguments may appear either on inbound *trigger messages* or on outbound *action messages*.

Once we have message arguments on state-transition diagrams, we may also have *conditional transitions*. A conditional transition is one whose target state depends on the value(s) of inbound arguments, the value(s) of results of outbound message(s), the value(s) of an object's variable(s), or sometimes all three.

As an example, consider an application at a small seminar company. For simplicity, I'll assume that the company offers only one seminar and has only one (worn-out and frazzled) instructor. Each week of the teaching calendar is an instance of the class SEMINAR-WEEK. The reservation status of a given week is held in **SEMINAR-WEEK::reservation-stat**, which has the possible values **available**, **tentatively-reserved**, and **firmly-reserved**. These three values of **reservation-stat** are shown as the three states of the state-transition diagram of Fig. 6.4.

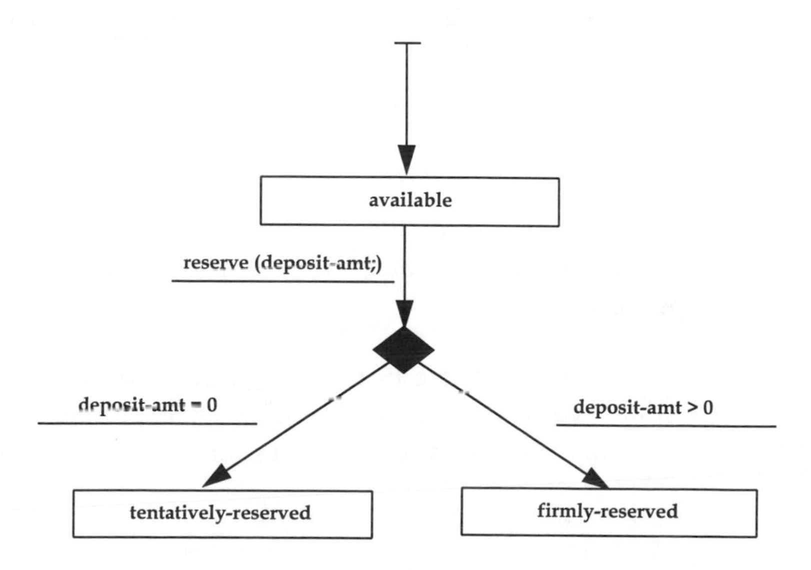

Fig. 6.4: Part of the state-transition diagram for **SEMINAR-WEEK::reservation-stat**.

A customer makes a reservation for a given week with an optional deposit. The deposit entitles the customer to a "firm reservation"; without the deposit, the customer gets only a "tentative reservation." The state-transition diagram shows each conditional transition as a filled diamond, with the specific conditions stated on the arrows to the target states.

One day, the seminar company realizes that some weeks are more in demand than others. So, the company establishes the concept of peak (highly popular) weeks, as opposed to normal weeks. The variable **popularity-stat** captures the popularity of a week. Only firm reservations are allowed in peak weeks; to secure a firm reservation, a customer must plunk down a large deposit. ("Large" is defined as "greater than the sum of money represented by **peak-deposit**.") Figure 6.5 shows this new twist to reservations.

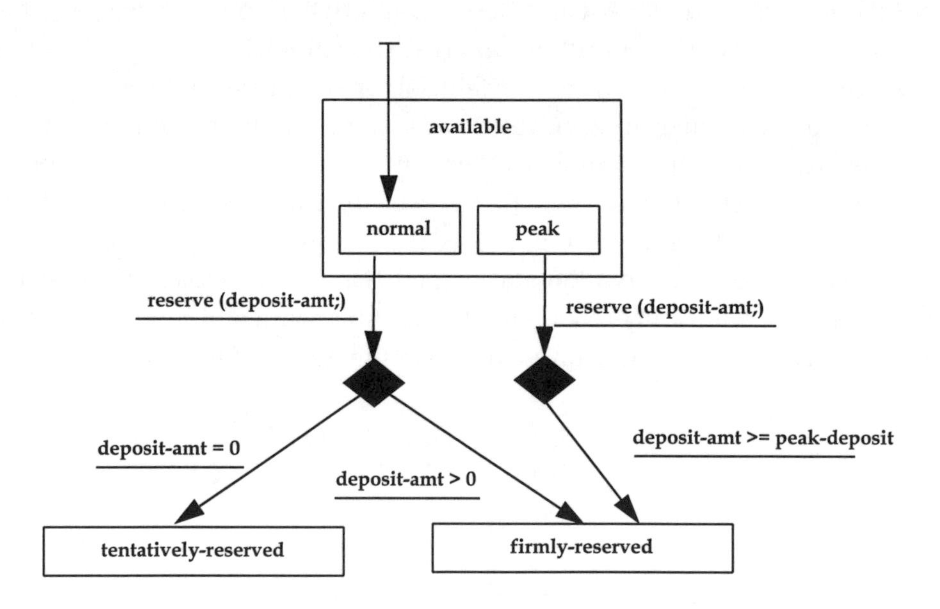

Fig. 6.5: Part of the state-transition diagram for **SEMINAR-WEEK::reservation-stat** *and* **SEMINAR-WEEK::popularity-stat**.

In Fig. 6.5, the transition arrows emanate from the two inner states (**normal** and **peak**) within the outer state (**available**).[7] The different sets of conditions on the two black diamonds reflect the different **reservation** policies for the two kinds of weeks.

[7] The names of the states are abbreviations for **popularity-stat = peak**, **reservation-stat = available**, and so on.

There is only one arrow from the **peak** state because a transition is allowed only when **deposit-amt >= peak-deposit**.

Finally, note that the initial state of this state-transition diagram is the nested state **available** and **normal** (which you can alternatively read as "**normal** within **available**"). When each instance of SEMINAR-WEEK is created, this is the state to which that object will be initialized.

As another example of conditional transitions, consider the MACHINE application of Section 6.2 again. Figure 6.6 shows a conditional transition from the state **standing-by**, a transition governed by the value of **revs-val-ok**.

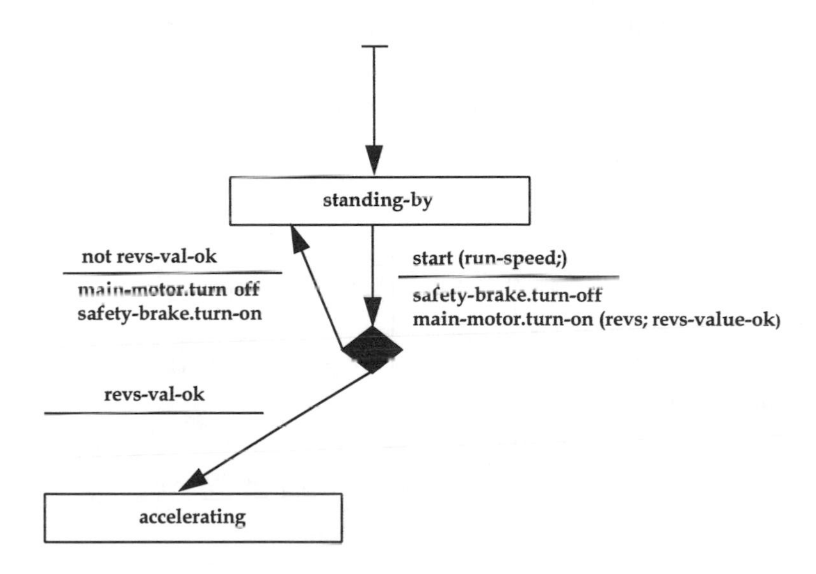

Fig. 6.6: Part of the state-transition diagram for **MACHINE::op-stat**.

revs-val-ok is the output argument of the message **main-motor.turn-on** from the machine to the motor. **revs-val-ok** is set to **true** when the motor can handle the requested revolutions per second (revs) and to **false** when the motor's speed limit is exceeded (in which case, the motor refuses to obey the message and does nothing).

Obviously, we can't say that the machine has an **op-stat = accelerating** if the motor has refused to carry out the machine's message to turn on. Therefore, the state-transition diagram has a condition diamond directing the transition to the **accelerating** state only when all's well. The interesting transition, however, is the one back to the **standing-by** state. Notice how this transition causes further outbound messages to be issued (to ensure that the motor really is turned off and the brake applied).

6.4 Continuous Variables

Some quantities in the real world vary continuously in time (conceptually, at least). Nothing noteworthy happens to cause them to change: They just go up and down, down and up, all day. Such quantities are represented in a computer system by *continuous variables*.

For example, a reaction in a chemical factory's tank has a current temperature, which is continuously varying. The variable **REACTION::curr-temp** represents the reaction's temperature in the system (where REACTION is the class of chemical reactions in a vessel). Although **curr-temp** is a continuous rather than a discrete variable, it warrants a state-transition diagram, as Fig. 6.7 shows.

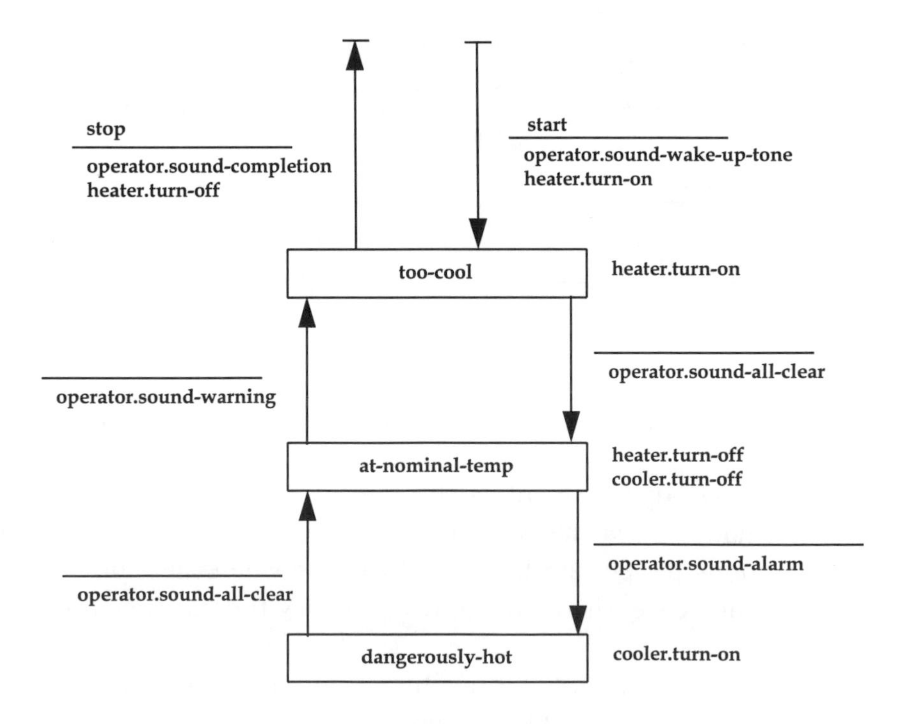

Fig. 6.7: State-transition diagram for **REACTION::curr-temp**.

Notice that each of the three states on the state-transition diagram is a range of values of **curr-temp**, as shown below. (Each range serves as the definition of the state.)

> crit-temp // dangerously-hot
≤ crit-temp **and** ≥ min-temp // at-nominal-temp
< min-temp // too-cool

Notice, too, that the transitions, apart from the initial and final ones, have no inbound messages on them. This is a modeling idiom: Because we're interested only in the actual value of **curr-temp** and there are no explicit events that change its value, we can leave every inbound message blank.

If you don't like this idiom, then you can simply label each inbound message as **set-curr-temp (measured-temp;)**. But remember that transitions triggered by this message would be conditional and that the conditions on the diamonds would be the same as the assertions for the states themselves. Somewhat tedious!

This state-transition diagram also illustrates the Moore convention of placing outbound messages on states, rather than on transitions (which is the Mealy convention). For example, whenever the state **too-cool** is reached, the message **heater.turn-on** is sent. (Actually, in Fig. 6.7, I've combined the Mealy and Moore conventions, which is perfectly acceptable in OODN.)

6.5 State Definitions

For each state on a state-transition diagram, you should ask yourself whether that state needs a definition. The state definition is an assertion that's correct for all objects (and only those objects) that are in the state.[8] For example, the assertions for REACTION's states **at-nominal-temp** and **dangerously-hot**, which are based on ranges of **curr-temp**, are (respectively)

curr-temp ≤ crit-temp **and** curr-temp ≥ min-temp // at-nominal-temp
curr-temp > crit-temp // dangerously-hot

If a class has dedicated state variables (which you can usually recognize by their "-stat" or "-status" suffixes), many of its state definitions become trivial. For instance, the state definition for the state **peak** (in the SEMINAR-WEEK example) is simply **popularity-stat = peak**. In other words, the state definition is no more

[8] As we'll see in Chapter 10, any such assertion is actually equivalent to the definition of a region of the class's state-space.

than the full name of the state. Nevertheless, although such a definition may seem trivial, it's still worth writing it down for clarity and verification.

States that are nested within other states on a state-transition diagram almost invariably have compound assertions in their definitions. (A compound assertion combines two separate assertions, with different variables, by means of an **and**.) For example, the full definition of the state **peak** in Fig. 6.5 would be

reservation-stat = available **and** popularity-stat = peak

6.6 Summary

A state-transition diagram shows the permitted states that objects of a given class may assume and the permitted transitions between pairs of states. The diagram is useful for modeling classes whose objects have a variable with these two properties: The variable can take on a small number of allowed values, and the permitted transitions among those values are restricted.

Each possible value of the variable appears as a state on the state-transition diagram. Each transition between a pair of states appears as an arrow on the state-transition diagram. Inbound messages that cause a transition and outbound messages (if any) resulting from a transition both appear alongside the transition arrow. If you use the Moore convention, rather than the Mealy one, then outbound messages will be attached to states. In OODN, you may mix the Mealy and Moore conventions within a state-transition diagram if you wish.

A class may have two (or sometimes more) variables that can be profitably modeled with state-transition diagrams. This leads to more than one state-transition diagram for the class, or—if the variables are not completely independent of each other—nested state-transition diagrams. A nested state-transition diagram shows inner states within outer states.

Object orientation complicates the traditional state-transition diagram, because both inbound and outbound messages often have arguments that affect transitions among states. If an argument modulates a transition, the transition may result in one of two (or more) states. The value of the argument will determine the specific resultant state at run-time. Such a transition is termed a conditional transition.

Some classes—especially those in real-time systems—have variables that are continuous, rather than discrete, in the values that they may assume. Some continuous variables may yield a worthwhile state-transition diagram. The states of a state-transition diagram based on a continuous variable are typically ranges of the variable's values. Often, there are no interesting inbound messages on such a state-transition diagram. On the other hand, there may be many outbound messages attached to transitions (if you use the Mealy convention) or to states (if you use the Moore convention).

6.7 Exercises

1. Suppose a designer has created a state-transition diagram with 57 states and 93 transitions, many of them conditional. The consensus of reviewers is that the diagram is hopelessly tangled and incomprehensible. What would you advise this designer? ("Emigrate to Baffin Island" is not an acceptable answer.)

2. What if another designer had spent a day staring at a class and was about to leap from the 38th floor because he couldn't come up with a worthwhile state-transition diagram for the class? What would be your advice to *this* designer?

3. The example in Section 6.4 implied that continuous variables are to be found only in the real-time (for example, process-control) world. Is that true? In what sense might **SHARE::price** be a continuous variable? Could it have a meaningful state-transition diagram?

6.8 Answers

1. Make sure that your state-transition diagrams are *abstractions* of class behavior. A state-transition diagram doesn't—and shouldn't—capture *every* possible facet and algorithm of the class. If you find that your state-transition diagram is becoming a hodgepodge of states and conditions, then you probably want to rethink your notion of the class—or at least further abstract your diagram.

   If your state model of a class becomes horribly complicated, then you should consider factoring out subclasses, each subclass taking on the behavior of one major state of the original class. For example, you could introduce two or three subclasses of MACHINE in this way: perhaps OPERATING-MACHINE, WAITING-FOR-REPAIR-MACHINE, and IN-REPAIR-MACHINE. (This idea of subclassing based on states is very strongly emphasized in [Shlaer and Mellor, 1992].)

2. Don't worry if the class on which you're working reveals nothing profound via a state-transition diagram. Many classes have no worthwhile state-transition diagram, because their variables can take on hundreds of values or because their transitions are unrestricted. Capture such classes' behavior through class invariants and the definitions of the classes' methods and variables, and don't bother with state-transition diagrams for these classes. (I cover these definitions in Chapter 10.)

3. Although continuous variables crop up most obviously in process-control systems, you may also encounter them in some business systems. The variable **REACTION::curr-temp** of Section 6.4 is continuous in two senses: First, it is a real number with (in principle, if we measured it with great precision) an infinite list of values. Therefore, it varies continuously, rather than jumping discretely as an integer would. Second, if we measure its value often (in principle, infinitely often), its value changes continuously over time.

   The variable **SHARE::price** shares these two continuities. Although we may not measure **SHARE::price** quite so often as **REACTION::curr-temp**, and, although we might not store it more precisely than to the nearest cent, we may (in principle, again) treat it as a continuous variable, both in value and over time.

   SHARE::price could have a state-transition diagram very similar to that of **REACTION::curr-temp** (with the state names changed to preserve the application). The states would be, perhaps, **fairly-priced**, **over-priced**, and **under-**

priced. A transition to **over-priced**, for example, could cause an outbound message to sell the position in that share. The message may be one such as

```
equity-account.sell-position (self; )
```

Additional OODN Diagrams

Chapters 3 to 6 covered the heart and soul of OODN, the notation that you'll use daily in object-oriented design. Chapter 7 introduces OODN for three major modeling areas: database access, system architecture, and the human interface. Because OODN in Chapter 7 addresses these special aspects of design, you won't use this chapter's notation as often as the notation we explored in previous chapters.

Indeed, you may argue that some of the notation in this chapter depicts constructs that aren't intrinsically object oriented. Nevertheless, we need such notation for completeness. To put it another way, although some of Chapter 7's notation isn't object oriented *per se*, you may still need to use it in order to build an object-oriented system.

The first section of the chapter deals with notation for access to databases, both object-oriented databases and more traditional ones (such as relational databases). The second section covers notation for showing the technology deployed in a system and for partitioning the software application across multiple processors. The third section shows notation both for modeling windows in the human interface and for the navigation paths among the windows.

7.1 Depicting Database Access

How should OODN show the creation, deletion, and messaging of objects in an object-oriented database? The answer is, It shouldn't! The very principles of object orientation mean that the site and medium of an object—semiconductor memory, ferrous disk, optical disc, or whatever—is, like any other aspect of its implementation, hidden from the users of that object.

7.1.1 Persistence

But the above argument isn't really valid. There's more to persistence than the medium in which an object is held.

In Section 1.4, I said that an object persists only while some other object holds its handle. However, in a database, an object must stay around even when all other objects—including the one that instantiated it—have disappeared. We certainly don't want the garbage collector to run rampant through our database, deleting our persistent objects under the same rules by which it removes volatile objects.[1]

> A *logically persistent object* is an object able to exist after all pointers to its handle have been deleted.
>
> A *physically persistent object* is one that is stored on a medium with physical permanence, such as a hard disk.

OODN shows a class whose objects are capable of both logical and physical persistence with a small black circle. See Fig. 7.1. (I don't differentiate between logical and physical persistence in OODN, because you normally need the two forms of persistence together for an object to "survive.")

Although OODN depicts an object's *ability* to persist, it doesn't have a way to depict an object's actually being *made* persistent. For example, Figs. 7.1 and 7.2 show two ways of making an object persistent: the first, by sending a message "make yourself persistent" to the object itself; the second, by sending the object's handle to a facility within an ODBMS.[2] You would depict the persistence mechanism that's actually supported by your environment.

---

[1] A volatile object is one that hasn't been made persistent.

[2] Some ODBMSs make persistence a default property. Others have diverse ways of accomplishing object persistence that are beyond the scope of this book. See, for example, [Bertino and Martino, 1993].

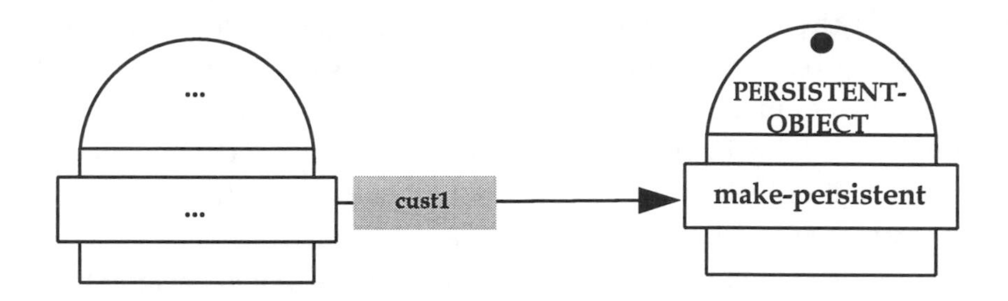

Fig. 7.1: Establishing persistence by a message to the object itself.

Notice that, in this example, although the object pointed to by **cust1** is probably of the class CUSTOMER, the method **make-persistent** is defined on PERSISTENT-OBJECT. This implies that CUSTOMER (and any other classes whose objects are to be made persistent) inherits from PERSISTENT-OBJECT.[3]

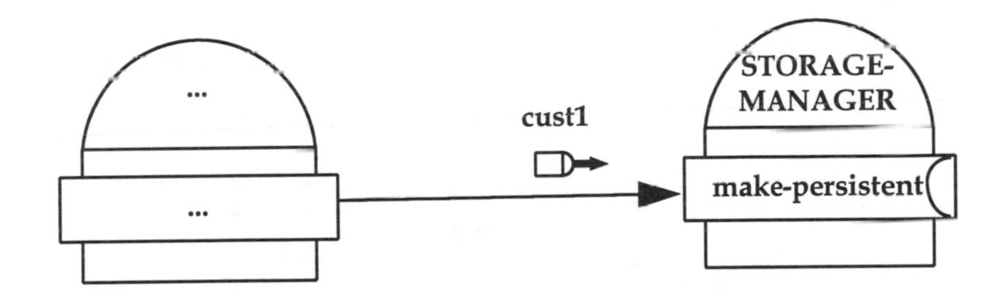

Fig. 7.2: Establishing persistence by means of a class message to a DBMS facility.

In the second example, **make-persistent** is a class method of a system class named STORAGE-MANAGER. Persistence is achieved by "registering" an object with that method. I prefer this approach because it doesn't burden the class-inheritance hierarchy with a layer of complexity due solely to the system implementation, as the PERSISTENT-OBJECT approach would.

7.1.2 Navigational and scanning queries

Now that we've made an object persistent, we have another problem: How do we ever find it again if we don't have its handle? This is where an object-oriented

[3] PERSISTENT-OBJECT is an example of a mix-in class. See Chapter 12.

DBMS is like any other DBMS. We need to be able to construct a query that will return pointers to the objects that we want. The query should be based on some publicly available properties of the stored objects. (Although queries are also relevant to volatile objects in memory, they're vital for retrieving persistent objects.)

Fair enough. But this brings up a difficult problem for OODN (which, incidentally, was not solved in SDN either). The problem is to find a happy middle ground between two extremes of representation. Let's say that we want to find the name of the project leader of the project to which a given employee is assigned.

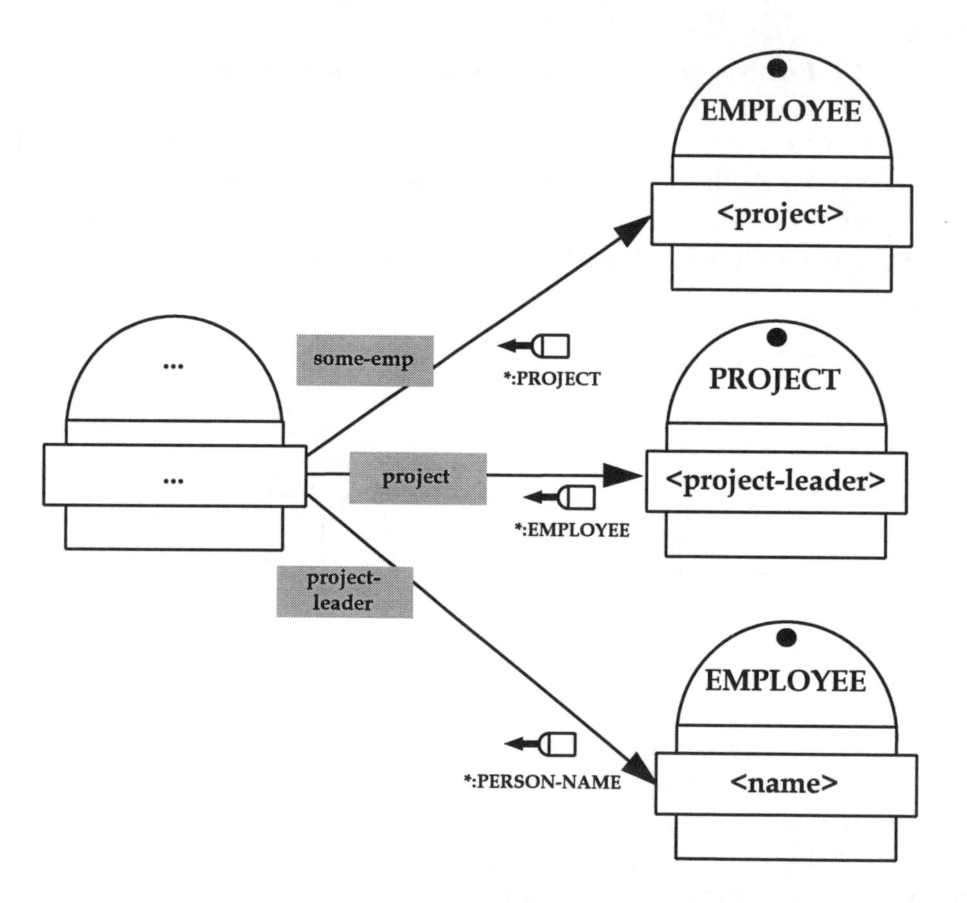

Fig. 7.3: "Blow by blow" navigation through related objects.

The elaborate extreme is to show three separate accesses, as in Fig. 7.3. The first access uses the **some-emp** handle to retrieve the **project** object; the second uses the **project** handle to retrieve the **project-leader** object; the third uses the **project-leader** handle to retrieve the **name** of the project-leader. This is rather tedious and wasteful of real estate on the diagram. It also seems to be overkill, since it's possible that the actual object-oriented code may simply be

some-emp.project.project-leader.name

The terse extreme is to create an "answer-query" method that would be invoked for any query. This would be a simple, but bland and uninformative component, as shown in Fig. 7.4.

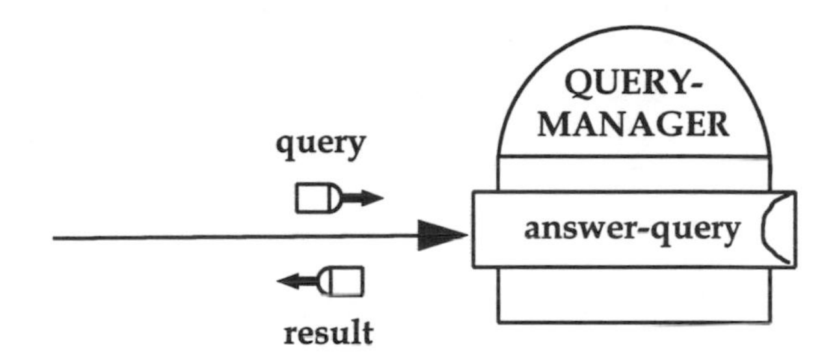

Fig. 7.4: The one-size-fits-all "answer-query" method.

Although OODN will happily show either the elaborate or terse extreme, I typically adopt a compromise between the two extremes. In this compromise, I use standard SDN to show a black-box procedural component labeled "find something or other." I show as input arguments to this component the information that I have available and, as output arguments, the information, that is, the object(s), that I want. Figure 7.5 shows an example.

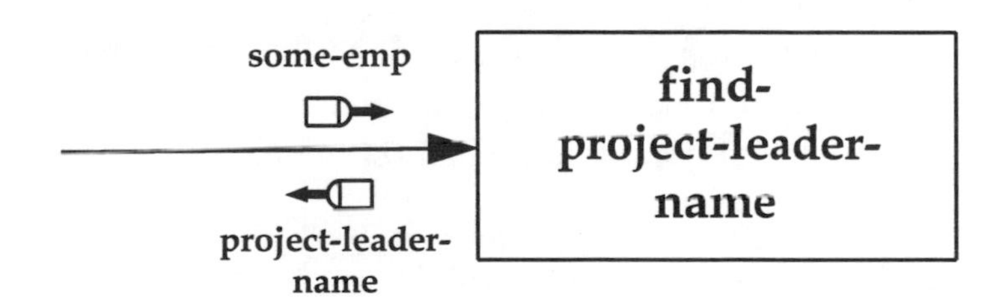

Fig. 7.5: A navigational query, showing the "information I have" and the "information I want."

I would place the actual definition of the navigation paths of the query in the module specification for **find-project-leader-name**.

Figure 7.6 shows another example, in which we're looking for the set of customers with credit balances of less than a deadbeat level of, say, $1,000. This time, we approach the query with no object handles at all (except the handle of the MONEY object held in **deadbeat-level**) and the DBMS scans for us, returning the required set of objects.

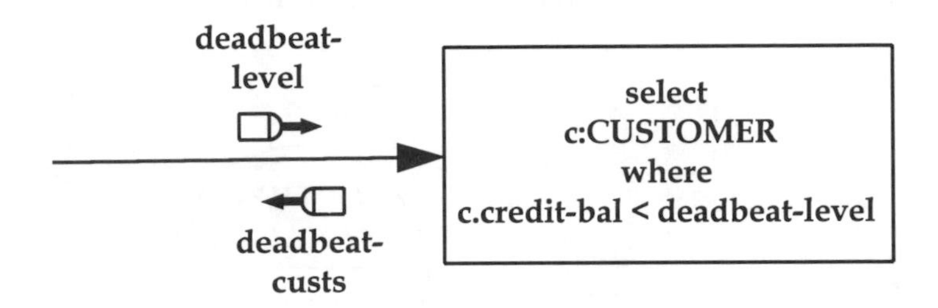

Fig. 7.6: A scanning, rather than navigational, query.

7.1.3 Access to data files

Many object-oriented systems use a relational DBMS to store information in data rather than object form. This calls for the unpacking of objects down to their most elementary, data components. OODN shows the access to a data file (such as a relational table), as in Fig. 7.7. Note that I show **customer-record** as an SDN data argument, rather than an OODN object argument. The reason, of course, is that **customer-record** contains just the data (numbers and strings) that can be stored as a row in a standard RDBMS table, in this case **customer-table**.

Note, too, that I don't show the persistence symbol (of Fig. 7.1) here, because the object *per se* is not being made persistent. Rather, the information within it is being transferred to a database. Later, that information will be reassembled into an object, albeit a different object with a different handle.

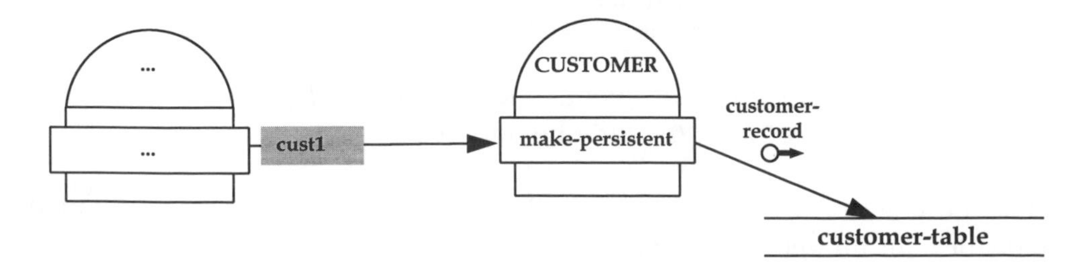

Fig. 7.7: The addition of a customer instance to a relational table.

7.1.4 Class migration

An object-oriented DBMS or language may allow an object to acquire and lose classes during its lifetime. For example, an object pointed to by **fred** may at first be of class UNMARRIED-PERSON. Then, **fred** may acquire the class EMPLOYEE. Later, **fred** may migrate from the class UNMARRIED-PERSON to the class MARRIED-PERSON.

> *Class migration* (from class A to class B by object **o**) is **o**'s simultaneous loss of membership of class A and its acquisition of membership of class B. (Most object-oriented languages do not support class migration directly.)

Although there's no special OODN for modeling class migration, Figs. 7.8, 7.9, and 7.10 show how you may accomplish it by means of a message invoking a class method of, say, OBJECT. The arguments **old-class** and **new-class** are strings bearing the respective class names.

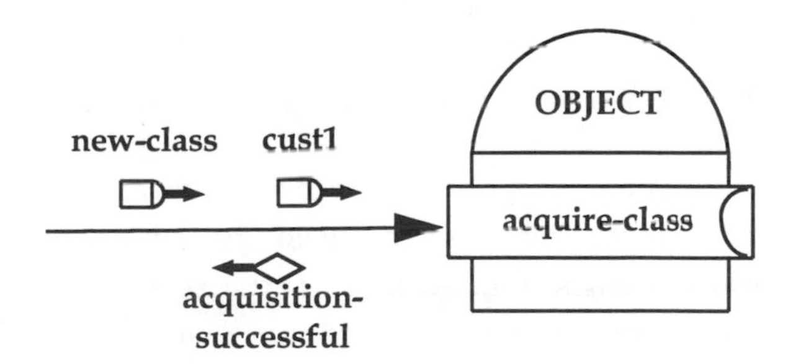

Fig. 7.8: The addition of a further class to an object.

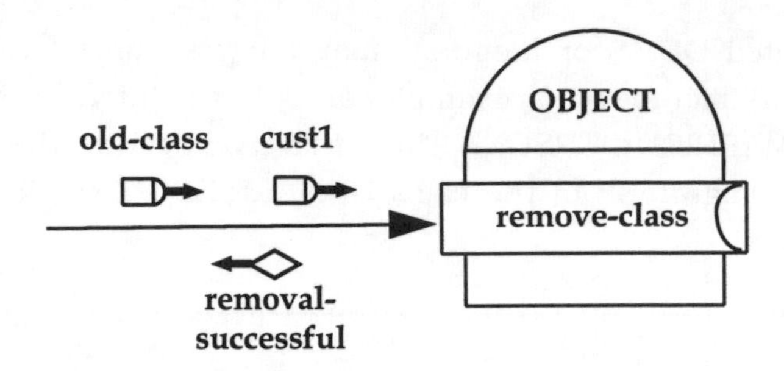

Fig. 7.9: The removal of a class from an object.

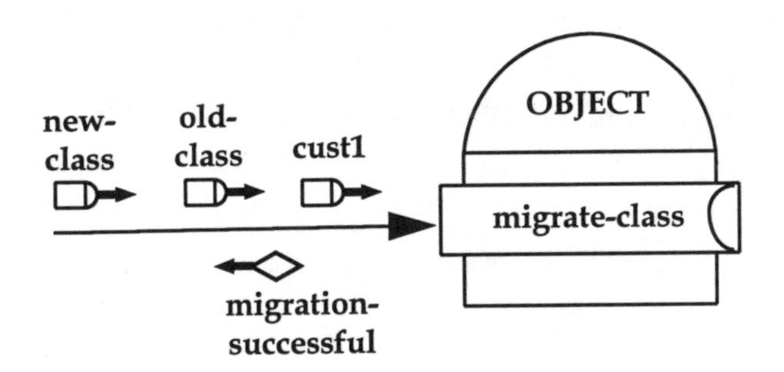

Fig. 7.10: The migration of an object from one class to another.

Notice the use of returned exception indicators (such as **migration-successful**) that indicate whether the messages were successfully carried out. Note, too, that an object's migration from class to class is often the result of a state transition modeled on a state-transition diagram. (For example, states of PERSON, based on the variable **marital-status**, may include **married** and **unmarried**.)

7.2 Depicting System Architecture

Architecture modeling is the mapping of an essential model of system requirements onto chosen technology. You can use OODN both to show the interconnections between technology components and to show how you intend to distribute your software system across these technology components.

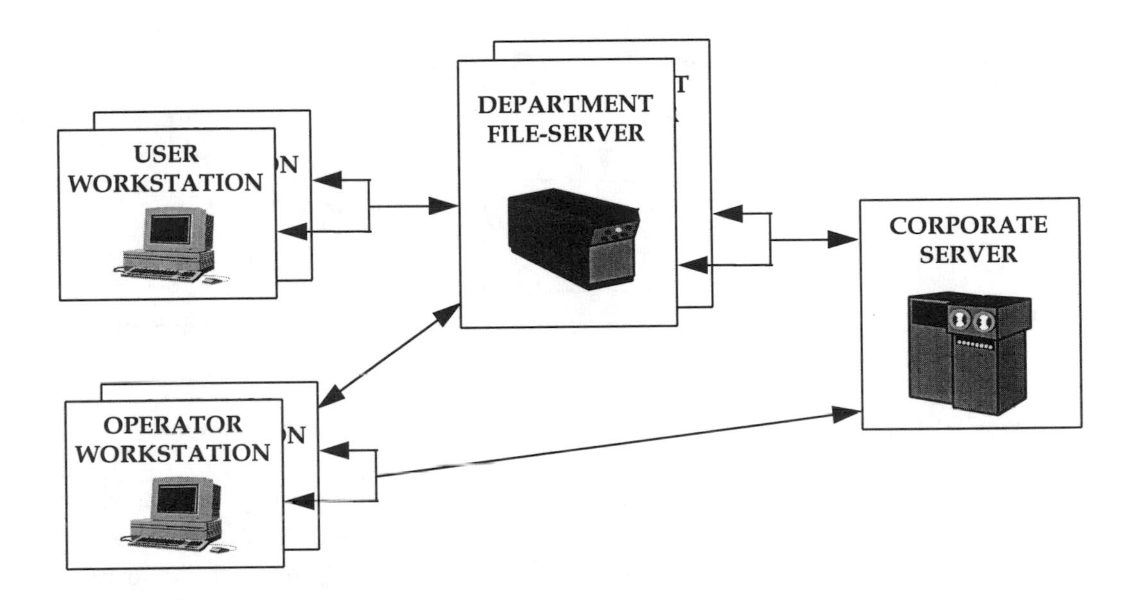

Fig. 7.11: A picture of the technology in a three-tier client-server system.

Figure 7.11 shows the hardware technology of a three-tier client-server system in pictorial form. On the users' desks are workstations, which are connected via a local-area network (LAN) to a departmental file-server. The departmental file-server may hold executable code for object classes and/or some objects themselves. The departmental file-servers are, in turn, connected via a wide-area network (WAN) to the corporate server. The corporate server may contain information that is central to the corporation or that needs to be kept securely.

There's one operator workstation per department. This is directly connected (via LAN) to the file-server and (via WAN) to the corporate server.

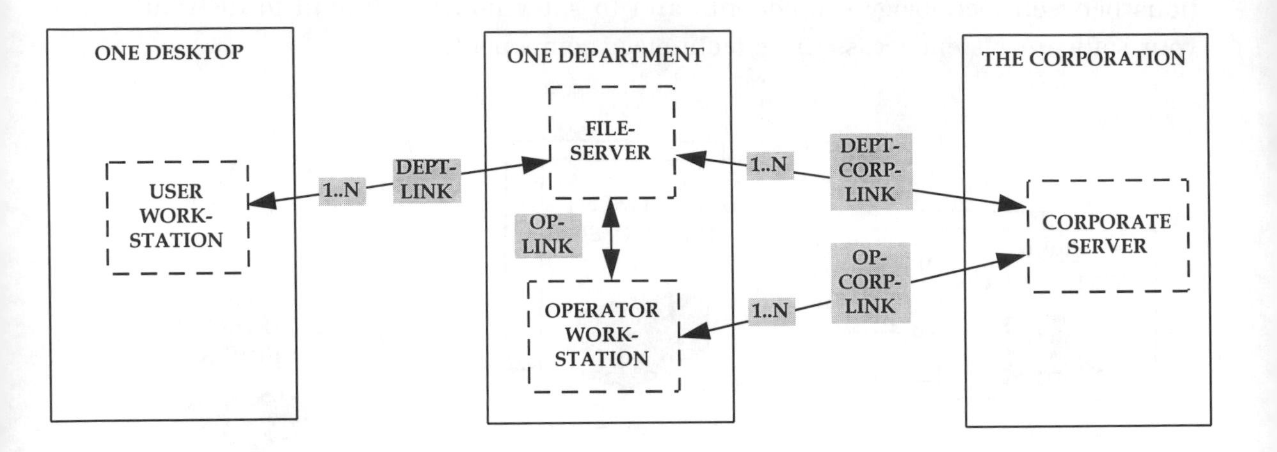

Fig. 7.12: A technology-interconnect diagram for the business system.

Figure 7.12 is OODN's *technology-interconnect diagram* for the system described above. This diagram is an abstraction of Fig. 7.11, which emphasizes the location of technology units and the communication links between them.[4] The example in Fig. 7.12 shows that several user workstations are connected to a single departmental file-server via a local communication link (called DEPT-LINK). Each departmental file-server is attached to an operator workstation via a link (called OP-LINK). Both the departmental file-servers and the operator workstations are connected to the corporate server via links (called DEPT-CORP-LINK and OP-CORP-LINK, respectively, which are presumably wide-area communication links).

A technology-interconnect diagram, such as the one in Fig. 7.12, is a framework to which you can attach all kinds of numbers to specify the technology units and their links. For example, you might specify a certain workstation to be a BLATZ/888-100 with so many megabytes of RAM and so many gigabytes of fixed-disk. Or, you might define DEPT-LINK to run on a LAN from a certain vendor, with a certain protocol and bandwidth.

[4] This is equivalent to the architecture-interconnect diagram of [Hatley and Pirbhai, 1988].

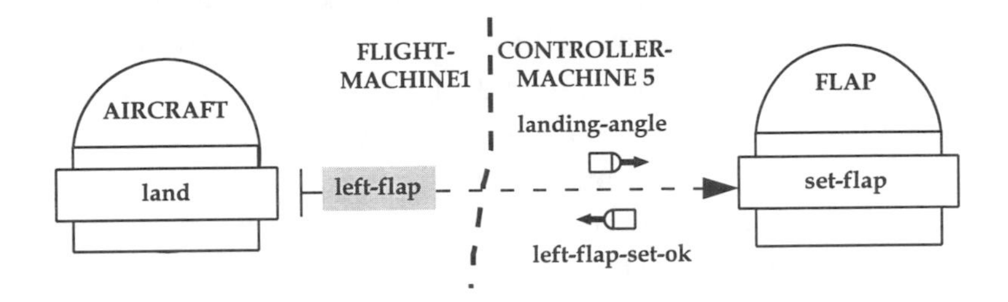

Fig. 7.13: An asynchronous message crossing technology (machine) boundaries.

Figure 7.13 shows how you can informally annotate an object-communication diagram to indicate that a message crosses physical boundaries. In this example, the object on the left (running on FLIGHT-MACHINE1) sends an asynchronous message to an object on a different computer (CONTROLLER-MACHINE5), and then waits for the reply. The dashed line symbolizes the machine-machine boundary. (You can also use a dotted line to show task-task boundaries.)

If you gather together all the components that execute on one processor into a single symbol (represented by a dashed rectangle) and show the communication between pairs of processors, then you have a *processor-interconnect diagram*, an example of which is shown in Fig. 7.14.[5]

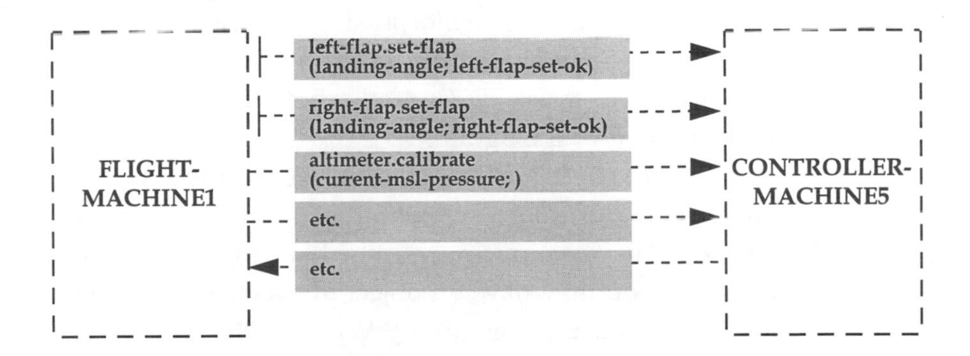

Fig. 7.14: A processor-interconnect diagram for two processors: FLIGHT-MACHINE1 and CONTROLLER-MACHINE5.

[5] This is equivalent to the architecture-flow diagram of [Hatley and Pirbhai, 1988] or the processor model of [Ward and Mellor, 1985].

This diagram differs from the technology-interconnect diagram in two ways. First, it shows the information crossing from one processor to another, rather than the form of communication link between processors. Second, the information that it shows is specific to the application being designed. I prefer to use the textual style of message naming on this diagram (as I introduced in Fig. 5.1 of Chapter 5) because it renders the diagram graphically clearer.

To show the structure of concurrent tasks executing within a single processor, you can use a *task-interconnect diagram*. This is very similar to the processor-interconnect diagram, but shows information passing among tasks. If you wish to distinguish tasks from processors graphically, you can use dotted, rather than dashed, rectangles.

7.3 Depicting the Human Interface

This section covers the OODN that you need to model a system's human interface, especially a typical modern interface comprising windows. A system that presents itself to its users as a cooperating set of windows follows the so-called *object-action paradigm*. This means that a user first selects an object (perhaps an icon) in a window and then applies an action to the object (perhaps via a menu selection or a simple double-click).

The object-action paradigm brings object orientation out to the human interface. I say this because the idea of first identifying an object and then requesting it to do something corresponds exactly to sending a message, where we first identify an object by its handle and then invoke one of its methods.

Another object-oriented concept, polymorphism, may also be important in the human interface. You may highlight an object on a window and then "tell it to print itself." *How* it prints itself will depend on whether the selected object is a spreadsheet, a text document, or a diagram.

From the above paragraphs, it appears that object-oriented design might be a very appropriate approach to building the human interface to a system. You design the interface as if it were an application like any other object-oriented application. For example, you may have an object of class UPDATABLE-WINDOW, which, when it closes, sends a message to a SAVE-IGNORE-OR-CANCEL window to warn the user that changes may be lost. The class UPDATABLE-WINDOW may inherit from the class WINDOW.

However, a windows interface has a couple of special characteristics beyond those that we've considered so far, which you need to capture by means of two additional OODN diagrams. These characteristics are

1. the properties of each individual window

2. the transitions among the windows that form the users' navigation paths

The two OODN diagrams that capture these characteristics are, respectively, the window-layout diagram and the window-navigation diagram. I describe each of these diagrams below, beginning with Fig. 7.15's example of a window-layout diagram for a window in a sales system.

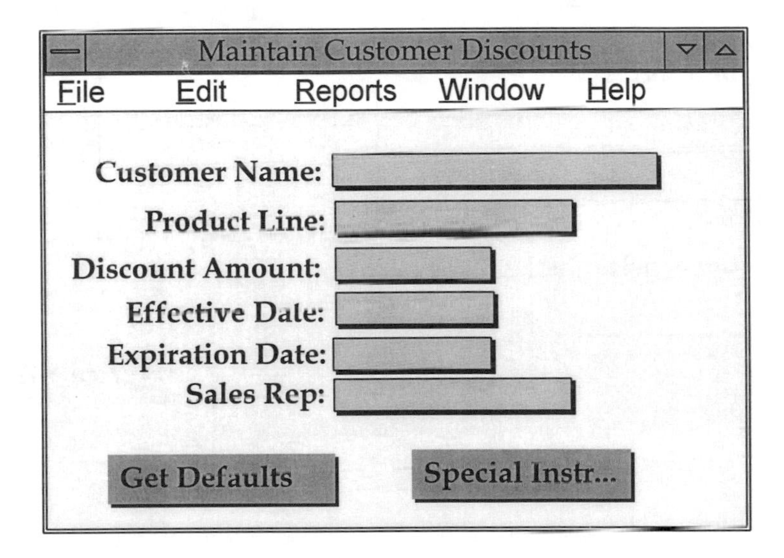

Fig. 7.15: Example of a window-layout diagram.

As Fig. 7.15 shows, a window-layout diagram corresponds almost exactly to the actual window that will be delivered for this part of the application. It shows the fields, buttons, and menus of the windows, but it may not be cosmetically correct. (For example, it may not have the fields properly aligned and the colors and fonts may be wrong.) This simple diagram forms the framework for further design specification, which includes the required field cross-validations, field synchronizations, database lookups, and so on.

The purpose of a window-navigation diagram is to show how the users may traverse from one window to another along major, application-meaningful paths.[6] Figure 7.16 shows an example of a window-navigation diagram for the product-pricing part of a sales system. (Note that "w_" is a standard abbreviation for "window.")

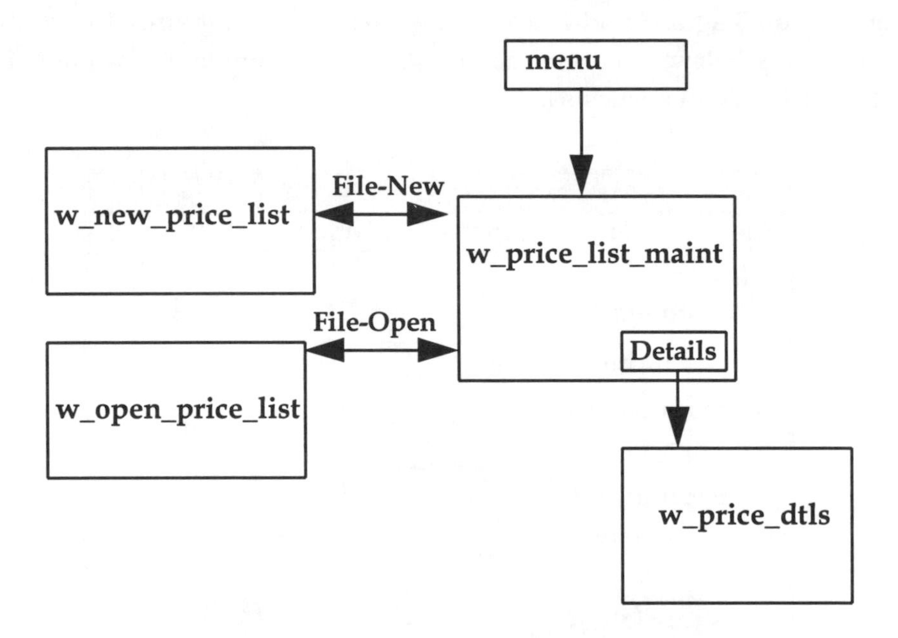

Fig. 7.16: Example of a window-navigation diagram

From a menu, the user arrives at the main window for (product) price-list maintenance. Thence, he may select **New** from the pull-down menu under **File**, which will take him to the window for starting a new price list. Alternatively, he may select **Open** from the pull-down menu under **File**, which will take him to the window that retrieves an existing price list. In any case, he must return to the main

---

6 My colleague David Ruble created the window-navigation diagram in its current form, by adapting the screen-transition diagram. ([Yourdon, 1989, p. 392], for example, describes the screen-transition diagram, which is itself an adaptation of the state-transition diagram of Chapter 6.)

window, where he may then inspect the details of the price list by clicking the **Details** button. He need not return from the price-details window (because, presumably, he may exit from the entire price-list maintenance while he still has that window open).

A window-navigation diagram shows only an abstraction of each window. (The window-layout diagram has the job of showing a window's details.) It shows just the buttons, double-clicks, and so on, which cause transitions from one window to another. Similarly, it shows only menu items and sub-items that cause transitions. Figure 7.17 gives the key to the straightforward symbols of the window-navigation diagram.

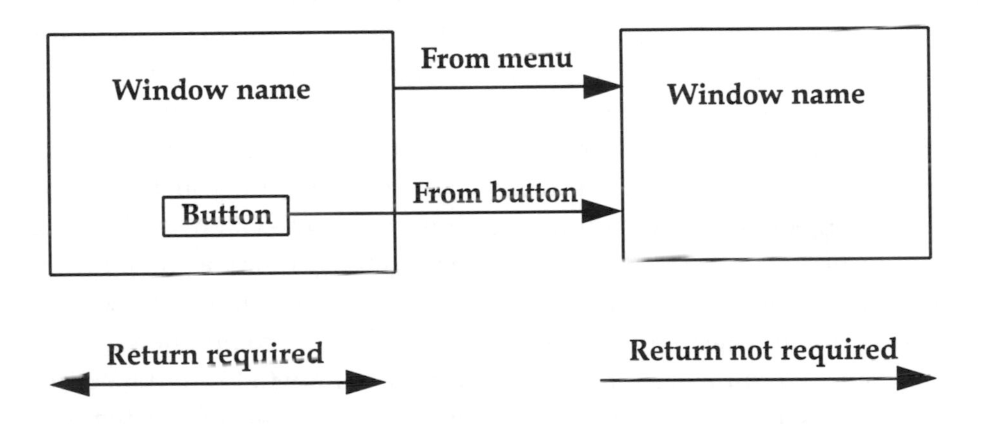

Fig. 7.17: Key to symbols on a window-navigation diagram.

7.4 Summary

This chapter presents the OODN for database access, system architecture, and human interfaces. The first issue in diagramming database access is, How should we show an object's being made persistent? The notional answer of "not at all" is unsatisfying. The best way is explicitly to show a **make-persistent** message to the database manager (or to the object itself, depending on how your environment handles it). Like SDN, OODN shows a query to a database as a call to a module and shows an object being stored in a relational database as the addition of a row (or record) to a table. Finally, OODN offers no special notation for class migration. Instead, for those few DBMSs that allow an object to change classes, OODN shows class migration as a message that invokes, say, **OBJECT::acquire-class**.

Modeling system architecture involves mapping the model of the software to be implemented onto the chosen implementation technology. OODN represents this technology by means of the technology-interconnect diagram, which shows units of technology and the physical communication links among them. To model the distribution of software across the technology components, you may informally annotate the object-communication diagrams for your system with processor-processor boundaries. Or you may, more formally, gather together the components that execute on each processor to form a processor-interconnect diagram, which depicts the messages that cross from one processor to another.

The window-layout diagram defines the content of a window to be delivered as part of a system's human interface. It approximates the layout of the windows, but doesn't contain every eventual cosmetic refinement. The window-layout diagram serves both as a prototype of the ultimate window and also as a framework on which to specify field validations, database lookups, and so on.

The window-navigation diagram depicts application-meaningful paths between windows. It abstracts each window as a skeletal rectangle that bears the window's navigational buttons. The paths between windows appear as arrows, annotated where necessary with menu-selection choices. The window-navigation diagram allows interface designers and users to explore interface navigation before the system is built.

7.5 Exercises

1. Persistent objects may persist for several months or years. What problem could this cause for an object with respect to the class from which it was instantiated? (Hint: Think about an old spreadsheet that you have. What happened when the vendor issued a new release of the spreadsheet package?)

2. The partitioning of software across units of technology can occur at several "levels of granularity." For example, an entire subsystem could live on one processor and another subsystem on another processor. Can you think of other levels of partitioning, especially ones that are finer than the subsystem level, which would be possible with an object-oriented system? (Hint: In what ways could you partition objects and the classes to which they belong?)

3. The fragment of a window-navigation diagram that appears in Fig. 7.18 shows three windows forming part of the interface to a customer-information system. Start with the window **w_cust_select** and, judging from the navigation paths and the names of the windows and buttons, guess what happens at each window shown. To which diagrams would you turn to confirm (or refute) your speculation?

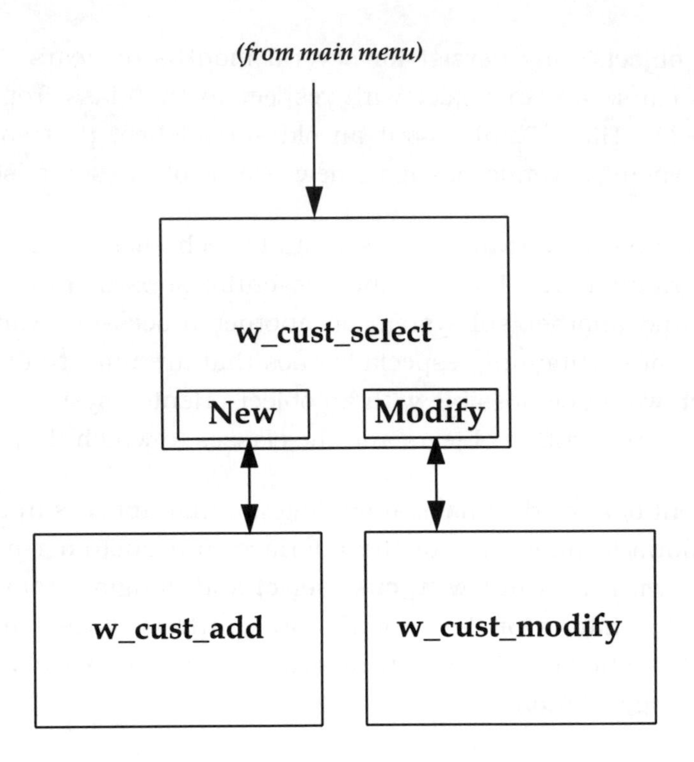

Fig. 7.18: Three windows in part of a window-navigation diagram.

7.6 Answers

1. The problem with storing an object indefinitely is that during its lifetime the definition of its instantiating class may change. There are three ways to handle this situation (the same three options that you have with your spreadsheet): First, keep the old and new versions of the class and use the appropriate version for each object. Second, convert the old object on the fly to suit the new class whenever the object becomes active (that is, receives a message). Third, when you introduce a new version of a class, run a conversion program that permanently converts each object instantiated under version *N-1* of its class to the form required by version *N*.

   The first option has the advantage of simplicity. However, it can become a configuration-management nightmare, especially when you need to retain more than two versions of the class. The second option has the advantage that the objects on the database can be left as is. However, you must include code in version *N* of each class that can handle objects instantiated under version *N-1*, *N-2*, and so on. The third option is usually the best, for you remove the problem by bringing all the objects in the database up to date in a single *coup de grace*.

   All three options that I outline assume that version *N* of a class is upwardly compatible with previous versions. If that's not so—for example, if you change the name of a method—then you will have to modify software in addition to the class and its persistent objects. For example, any software containing messages to the previous version of the objects will need to be recompiled with the new method name in the affected messages. The three approaches are easier to implement if every object remembers its version number with a simple version tag.

   Finally, notice how in this discussion it was absolutely vital to maintain the distinction between the term "class" and the term "object." This distinction, which I hammered upon in Chapter 1, is not mere pedantry!

2. One possibility is that the objects of a particular class are distributed across processors. For example, we may have a machine in Paris, a machine in Tokyo, a machine in Rio de Janeiro, and a machine in Terre Haute. The objects of class CUSTOMER could then be distributed across these machines, for the obvious reason of efficiency: We want to access our Japanese customers quickly on the Tokyo machine, for example. The code for the class CUSTOMER would presumably be fully replicated on the four machines, because the code must execute on all four machines. Partitioning a population of objects like this is termed *horizontal partitioning.*

The objects could also be fully replicated, perhaps to allow the Paris office to quickly access information about *les Hoosiers*. However, such redundancy would complicate maintaining mutual consistency across copies of the same object.

You could even split an individual object into parts that abide on different machines. This is a very fine partitioning, but one which could be useful in some circumstances. For example, say you've designed a class CUSTOMER for an application handling both shipping and finances. CUSTOMER's objects will thus contain financial information, shipping information, and so on. If the Rio office is purely a shipping office, then perhaps the objects at that location will never be asked to provide customers' financial information. Therefore, financial variables and methods could be stripped out of the objects on the Rio machine in order to save space (and possibly to enhance security).

Splitting objects apart in this manner is termed *vertical partitioning*. It introduces problems of consistency again (for example, ensuring that the physically separated pieces are kept consistent), and is usually implemented so that at least one machine holds whole objects.

A third possibility is that a class lives on one machine and its objects live on another. In this case, the second machine may specialize in holding and manipulating large volumes of information (as a so-called database engine). The first machine may specialize in processing (as a so-called number cruncher). To execute a message, the appropriate object is transferred from the second machine to the first. For this approach to be worthwhile in efficiency, the two machines should normally be close to each other.

Although there are several other ways to partition object-oriented software, the above three are the most typical. Incidentally, notice again how important it was in the above paragraphs to maintain the distinction between the term "class" and the term "object."

3. From the main menu in Fig. 7.18, the user arrives at a window for selecting customers. Presumably, this window lists a group of customers (objects of class CUSTOMER), from which the user can select a customer by means of a mouse. The window is, no doubt, tabular, with columns that present enough information (such as name and address) for the user to recognize a specific customer. Once he's selected a customer, the **Modify** button becomes enabled. Clicking this button takes the user to the window for modifying customer information.

   On the modify window, the user sees all (externally visible) information for a CUSTOMER object, and he can modify any of the updatable fields on the window. He must return from this window to the selection window (as indicated by the two-way arrow). In other words, he can only close the **w_cust_modify** window and return focus to the **w_cust_select** window; he cannot, for example, open some other window.

The window for adding a new customer operates similarly to the window for modifying an existing one. However, the **New** button on the **w_cust_select** window is presumably always enabled, whether the user has a customer selected or not. (There's no need to select an existing customer in order to add a new one.)

Some of the above explanation is speculative. To confirm my speculations in practice, we should also look at the window-layout diagrams for the three windows, which list the fields that each window contains. More importantly, the definitions behind the diagrams tell us what each window does when it opens and closes, when each of its buttons becomes enabled and disabled, what happens when a button is clicked, what the validation rules are for fields, and so on. Together with the window-navigation diagram, window-layout diagrams would complete our understanding of this piece of the graphical user interface.

Part III: The Principles of Object-Oriented Design

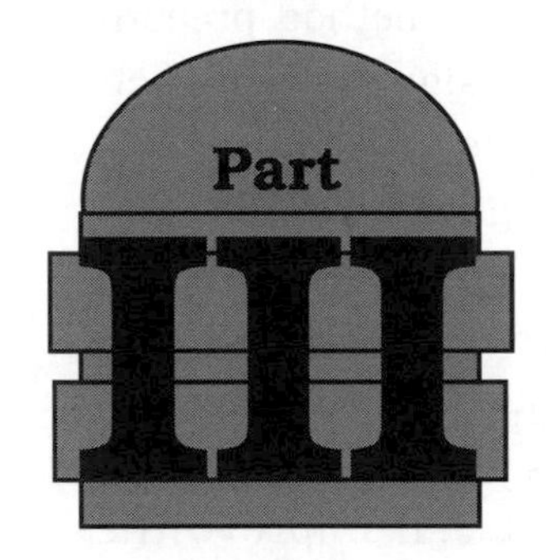

"The logic of our understanding contains the laws of correct thinking upon a particular class of objects."

—Immanuel Kant, *Critique of Pure Reason*

The chapters of Part III cover the principles behind good object-oriented design and the criteria by which you can evaluate the quality of your designs. In other words, Part III addresses the question, What makes a good object-oriented design and what makes a bad one? The question is certainly meaningful, for I've seen object-oriented code in one application that was extensible and modifiable, and object-oriented code in another application that was hideous, gnarled, and infuriating to maintain. Since the programming of the two applications was similar and the requirements that the applications were trying to implement were similar, the variation must have been due to their design structure.

Chapter 8 begins by contrasting the encapsulation structure of object-oriented software with that of traditional software. I then build the idea of connascence upon the principle of encapsulation. Connascence, which is a generalization of structured design's coupling and cohesion to more complex encapsulation structures, is a yardstick of how well a designer has exploited the potential encapsulation that object orientation offers.

Classes at distinct levels of design abstraction have distinct design characteristics and properties. They also have different degrees of reusability. Chapter 9 outlines the domains of classes that you're likely to find in an application, and what the classes are in each domain. The chapter introduces a quantitative metric, the encumbrance of a class, and shows how it relates to class domains. The chapter uses the idea of domains and encumbrance to evaluate three kinds of class cohesion. (Class cohesion indicates how closely knit the methods of a given class are and whether they "belong together" in that class.)

Chapter 10, which is the heart of Part III, explores the design fundamentals of object orientation. It addresses the ideas of class invariants and method preconditions and postconditions, which are the foundations of design by contract. Chapter 10 also looks at the properties of subclasses in terms of state-spaces, together with the design principle of type conformance, which guides the development of robust class hierarchies.

In Chapter 11, I use class cohesion and other concepts from earlier chapters to identify and remedy dangers that lurk in the valuable object-oriented mechanisms of inheritance and polymorphism. Chapter 12 dissects a particular object-oriented design to illustrate some design techniques that can improve the resilience of class design. This chapter, and the book, closes with an answer to the original question, What makes a good object-oriented design? by showing the conditions under which a class implements a true abstract data-type.

Encapsulation and Connascence

This chapter covers the two fundamental aspects of object-oriented system structure: encapsulation and connascence. Although both these aspects of software structure were present in traditional systems, object orientation, with its new complexities, elevates their significance considerably. The understandability and maintainability of object-oriented software—even the value of object orientation itself—rest fundamentally on encapsulation and connascence.

In the first section of this chapter, I discuss encapsulation; in the second, I discuss connascence and then explore how good object-oriented software depends on a combination of good encapsulation and connascence.

8.1 Encapsulation Structure

In the 1940s, software emerged from the primeval swamp as a collection of unicellular creatures known as machine instructions. Later, these evolved into other unicellular creatures known as lines of assembler code. But grander structures soon appeared, in which many lines of code were gathered into a procedural unit with a single name. As I mentioned in Chapter 1, this was the subroutine (or procedure), with examples such as **compute-loan-repayment** and the all-time star of The Subroutine Hall of Fame, **compute-square-root**.

The subroutine introduced encapsulation to software. It was the encapsulation of lines of code into a structure one level higher than that of the code itself.

8.1.1 Levels of encapsulation

I term the subroutine's level of encapsulation *level-1* encapsulation. (Raw code, with no encapsulation, has *level-0* encapsulation.) Object orientation introduces a further level of encapsulation. The class (or object) is a gathering together of subroutines (known as methods) into a yet higher-level structure. Since methods, being procedural units, are already at level-1 encapsulation, the class is at *level-2* encapsulation. See Fig. 8.1.

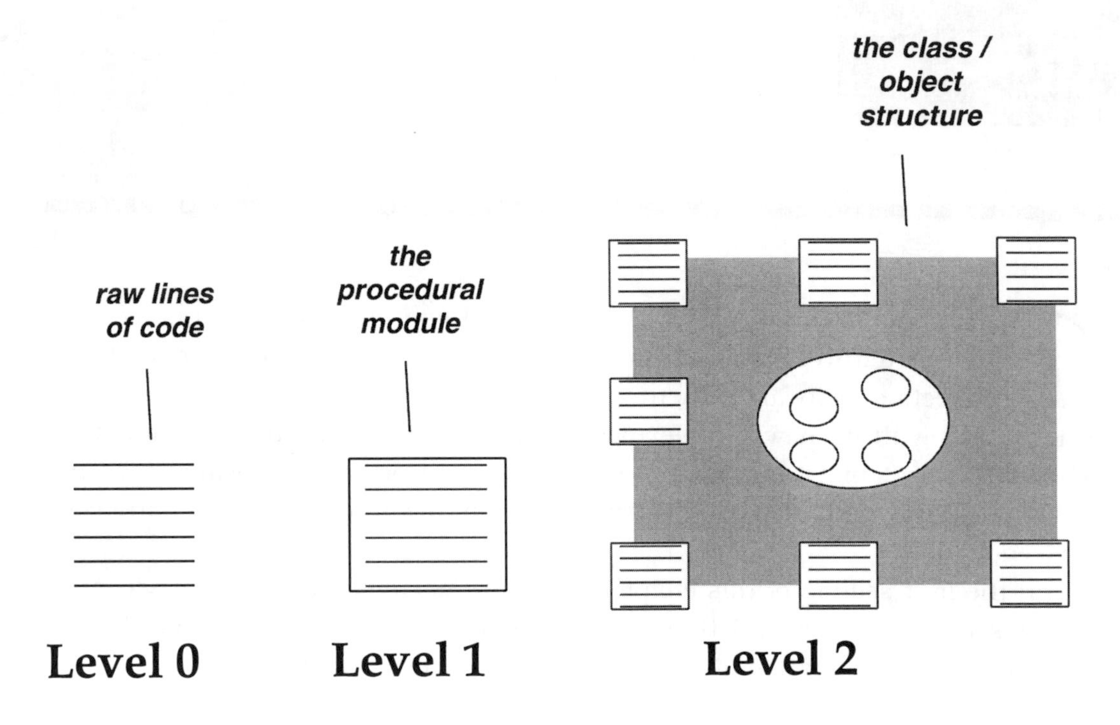

Fig. 8.1: Three levels of encapsulation exhibited by software constructs.

My analogy between organisms and software structures, though far from profound, isn't entirely gratuitous. Procedural modules, such as those found in structured design, didn't realize the reusability for which people had hoped. (The Module of the Month Club offered an illustration of this. After joining this club, one could order the latest in tremendously reusable procedural modules. Unfortunately, the club soon went out of business.) Classes stand alone far better than procedures do. Classes come closer to biological organs in their ability to be transplanted from application to application.

"But why stop at level-2 encapsulation?" you ask. A good question! In the future, we may see level-3 encapsulation, in which classes are grouped into even higher-level structures. Outside these structures only *some* classes (or parts of their interfaces) would be visible.

Already, we're seeing some level-3 encapsulation in large object-oriented systems, in which groups of classes are gathered into their respective subject areas. For example, in an airline application there may be a subject area related to the passenger, another for the airport, another for personnel, and another for the aircraft. Since a class related to a passenger's frequent-flyer program wouldn't have much to do with a class for aircraft inventory, the two classes could be encapsulated into different subject areas.

8.1.2 Design criteria governing interacting levels of encapsulation

Table 8.1 summarizes some traditional structured-design criteria in terms of the encapsulation levels of Section 8.1.1. It shows which criterion applies to each pair of encapsulation levels. For example, cohesion is a classic measurement of the quality of the relationship between a procedure (a level-1 construct) and the lines of code (level-0 constructs) within the procedure. I briefly describe each criterion in the paragraph following the table.

Table 8.1.

The Structured-Design (or Level-1) Criteria Governing Interrelationships Among Components at Each Pair of Encapsulation Levels.

To: / From:	level-0 construct (line of code)	level-1 construct (procedure)
level-0 construct (line of code)	Structured programming	Fan-out
level-1 construct (procedure)	Cohesion	Coupling

The principles of structured programming govern the relationship between a line of code and other lines of code within the same procedure. Fan-out, cohesion, and coupling are terms from structured design. Fan-out is a measure of the number of references to other procedures by lines of code within a given procedure. Cohesion is a measure of the "single-mindedness" of the lines of code within a given procedure in meeting the purpose of that procedure. Coupling is a measure of the number and strength of connections between procedures.[1]

Table 8.2.

An Extension of Table 8.1 to Include Level-2 Encapsulation (Classes).

To: From:	level-0 construct (line of code)	level-1 construct (procedure)	level-2 construct (class)
level-0 construct (line of code)	Structured programming	Message fan-out	—
level-1 construct (procedure)	Cohesion	Coupling	—
level-2 construct (class)	—	Class cohesion	Class coupling

Table 8.2 is an extension of Table 8.1 to include level-2 encapsulation. Notice that although the original (level-0 and level-1) section remains basically the same, level-2 encapsulation gives us five more boxes to name.

Class cohesion is an obvious analogue to the cohesion of a procedure, but is at one higher level of encapsulation. It means the single-mindedness of a set of methods in meeting the purpose of the class. Class coupling is a measure of the number and strength of connections between classes.

Although the other three boxes don't have names, we could give them names—or we could dig out names from the darker crevices of the object-oriented literature. Then we'd have nine names. And, if we included level-3 encapsulation, we'd have sixteen names.

But enough names already! When the number of fundamental particles of physics exploded, physicists began to wonder whether their particles were quite so fundamental after all. When the number of fundamental design criteria explodes like this, perhaps we should look for a deeper criterion behind them all. If we can

[1] See, for example, [Page-Jones, 1980] and [Yourdon and Constantine, 1975] for detailed discussions of fan-out, cohesion, and coupling.

find such a criterion, then it should apply to software components at all levels of encapsulation—even level-4, if we're ever blessed with such a level.

In the next section, I propose such a criterion: *connascence*.

8.2 Connascence

Connascence, which derives from Latin, means "having been born together." An undertone to this meaning is "sharing the same destiny in life." Two software components that are *connascent* (or *connate*) are born from some related need and share the same fate for at least one reason.[2] Below, I give the definition of *connascence*, as it applies to software.

> *Connascence* between two software components A and B means either
>
> 1. that you can postulate some change to A that would require B to be changed (or at least carefully checked) in order to preserve overall correctness, or
> 2. that you can postulate some change that would require both A and B to be changed together in order to preserve overall correctness.

In this section, I explore the varieties of connascence. My chief purpose is to present the concept as a general way to evaluate design decisions in an object-oriented design as well as in any subsequent design methodology that you may use.

8.2.1 Varieties of connascence

I begin with a simple example of connascence. Let's take software component A to be the single line of traditional code declaring

```
int i;                    // line A
```

2 No, I didn't make up the word "connascence." It's in, for example, *Chambers' Twentieth Century Dictionary* and (as "connate") in *Webster's Third International Dictionary*.

and component B to be the assignment:

```
i := 7;                // line B
```

There are at least two examples of connascence between A and B. For instance, in the (unlikely) situation that A were changed to **char i;** then B would certainly have to be changed, too. This is *connascence of type*. Also, if A were changed to **int j;** then B should be changed to **j := 7;**. This is *connascence of name*.

Now some variations on the theme of connascence: The above example of **i** on lines A and B showed *explicit connascence*, which is in effect connascence that's detectable by a good text editor. In other words, it's connascence that leaps off the page and says, "This component is connascent with that one."

Some connascence, however, is *implicit*. For example, in an assembler routine I once saw:

```
X: JUMP Y+38
...
Y: CLEAR R1
...                    // 38 bytes here
CLEAR R2               // This is the instruction being jumped to from X—call it Z
...
```

There are 38 bytes between CLEAR R1 and CLEAR R2. Exactly 38 bytes! This *connascence of position* between these two innocent instructions at Y and Z is forced upon them by the nasty jump at line X. Although the need for this offset of precisely 38 bytes isn't apparent in the code after line Y, woe betide anyone who inserts another instruction somewhere in those 38 bytes.[3]

Clearly, explicitness and implicitness are neither binary nor absolute. Instead, connascence has a spectrum of explicitness. The more implicit connascence is, the more time-consuming and costly it is to detect—unless it's well documented in an obvious place. Connascence that spans huge textual distances in a class-library specification or other documentation is also likely to be time-consuming and difficult to discover.

Note that:

1. Two software components needn't communicate with each other in order to be connascent. (We saw an example of this in the connascence of position between lines Y and Z in the above assembler routine.)

---

[3] That, by the way, is exactly what a maintenance programmer did. The next time the system ran, it crashed shortly after line X was executed.

2. Some forms of connascence are *directional.* If component A refers to a component B explicitly, although B contains no reference to A, then A and B would be directionally connascent (the direction being *from* A *to* B). Many examples of connascence of name are directional, for example, the connascence of name introduced when one class inherits from another.

3. Some forms of connascence are *nondirectional.* Components A and B would be nondirectionally connascent if neither one referred explicitly to the other. For example, A and B are connascent if they use the same algorithm, although neither one refers to the other at all.

8.2.1.1 Varieties of static connascence

Most of the connascence I've described above is *static connascence.* That's connascence that applies to the code of the classes that you write, compile, and link. It's connascence that you can assess from the lexical structure of the code listing. The following list (which isn't exhaustive) gives some further varieties of static connascence.

1. Connascence of name

We saw this in the first example (lines A and B) above, in which two variables needed to have the same name in order to refer to the same thing. Another example: A subclass that uses a variable of its superclass must obviously use the same name for the variable that the superclass uses. If the variable name is changed in the superclass, then it must also be changed in the subclass if correctness is to be preserved.

2. Connascence of type or class

We also saw connascence of type in the example with the data-type **int**. If **i** is assigned the value **7** on line B, then **i** should be declared to be of type **int** on line A.

3. Connascence of meaning

Let's say that the class ACCOUNT-NUMBER has instances in which positive account numbers, such as 12345, belong to people; negative ones, like

–23456, belong to corporations; and 00000 belongs to all internal departments. The code will be sprinkled with statements like

if order.acct-num > 0
then ...

There's connascence of meaning among all the software components touching an account number. Unless this convention of account-number meaning is encapsulated away, these components may be widespread across the system.[4]

4. Connascence of algorithm

Connascence of algorithm is similar to connascence of meaning. Example: A software component inserts symbols into a hash-table. Another component searches for symbols in the table. Clearly, for this to work, they must both use the same hashing algorithm. Another example: the encoding and checking algorithms for check-digits in a customer's account number.

A bizarre example of connascence of algorithm that I saw recently was caused by a bug in one of a class's methods. This method was supposed to return an array of values, sorted into ascending order. But, because of the bug, the last two array values were always switched. Owing to the absence of the source code, no one was able to correct the bug.

So the "fix" was this: Every class that invoked this method had code added to it that switched back the two offending array values. This yielded horrid connascence of algorithm, which hurt everyone badly when the offending class was finally rewritten. Then, all the added code (in more than forty places) had to be found and removed.

5. Connascence of position

Most code in a procedural unit has connascence of position: For two lines of code to be carried out in the right execution sequence, they must appear in the right lexical sequence in the listing. There are several kinds of connascence of position, including *sequential* ("must appear in the correct order") and *adjacent* ("must appear next to each other"). Another example of connascence of position is the connascence in a message between the formal arguments in the

[4] This is actually a connascence of "value/meaning convention." It's similar to hybrid coupling in structured design and has caused many a maintenance problem in systems.

sender and the actual arguments in the target. In most languages, you must set out actual arguments in the same sequence as the formal ones.

8.2.1.2 Varieties of dynamic connascence

Dynamic connascence is connascence that's based on the execution pattern of the running code—the objects, rather than the classes, if you like. It, too, has several varieties:

1. Connascence of execution

Connascence of execution is the dynamic equivalent of connascence of position. It comes in several kinds, including *sequential* ("must be carried out in a given order") and *adjacent* ("must be carried out with no intervening execution"). There are many examples of connascence of execution, including initializing a variable before using it, changing and reading values in global variables in the correct sequence, and the setting/testing of semaphores.

2. Connascence of timing

Temporal connascence crops up most often in real-time systems. For example, an instruction to turn off an X-ray machine must be executed within *n* milliseconds of the instruction to turn it on.

3. Connascence of value

Connascence of value usually involves some arithmetic constraint. For example, during the execution of a system, the **low-pointer** to a circular buffer can never be higher than the **high-pointer** (under the rules of modulo arithmetic). Also, the four corners of a rectangle must retain a certain geometric relationship in their values: You can't move just one corner and retain a correct rectangle.

Connascence of value arises famously when two databases hold the same information redundantly, often in different formats. In that situation, procedural software has to maintain a bridge of consistency between the databases to ensure that any duplicated data has identical values in each database. This software, perhaps needing to perform awkward format translations, may be cumbersome.

4. Connascence of identity

An example of connascence of identity is provided by a typical constraint in an object-oriented system: Two objects, **o1** and **o2**, each of which has a variable pointing to another object, must always point to the same object. That is, if **o1** points to **o3**, then **o2** must point to **o3**. (For example, if the sales report points to the March spreadsheet, then the operations report must also point to the March spreadsheet.) In this situation, **o1** and **o2** have connascence of identity; they must both point to the same (that is, identical) object.

8.2.2 Contranascence

So far, I've tacitly equated connascence with "sameness" or "relatedness." For example, two lines of code have connascence of name when the variable in each of them must bear the same name. However, connascence also exists in cases where *difference* is important.

First, I'll offer a trivial example. Let's say that we have two declarations:

```
int i;
int j;
```

For correctness—merely for the code to compile!—the variable names, **i** and **j**, must differ from each other. There's a connascence at work here: If, for some reason, we wanted to change the first variable name to **j**, then we'd also have to change the second name *from* **j** to something else. Thus, the two declarations are not independent.

I've heard this kind of connascence called "connascence of difference" or "negative connascence." I use the shorter term *contranascence*. Although it sounds like the opposite of connascence, contranascence is actually a form of connascence in which difference rather than equality must be preserved.[5]

A famous example of contranascence crops up in object-oriented environments with multiple inheritance (the ability of a subclass to inherit from multiple superclasses). If class C inherits from both classes A and B, then the methods of A and B should not have the same names: There's a contranascence of name between A's methods and B's methods.

As a more concrete example of contranascence, consider an application in a video-rental store. The class PROGRAM-RENTAL-ITEM may inherit from both

---

[5] The true opposite of connascence is *disnascence*: Two software components are disnascent if one has absolutely nothing to do with the other.

PHYSICAL-INVENTORY-ITEM and RECORDING-MEDIUM. These two classes (or their superclasses) may each have a method named **length**.

But PHYSICAL-INVENTORY-ITEM's **length** may mean the physical length of an item in inches and RECORDING-MEDIUM's **length** may mean the playing time of the program (the movie or whatever is on the video tape). Although you could argue that **duration** would be a more appropriate name for the second method, you may have to take what you get from your class library.

If the class PROGRAM-RENTAL-ITEM needs to inherit both of the methods named **length**, then there's a serious problem because of this clash in names. Across an entire library of classes, any pair of which may share a subclass, there's a similar contranascence of name across *all* classes because of this risk of name clashes under multiple inheritance. No wonder multiple inheritance has a bad reputation, and no wonder good object-oriented languages contain mechanisms that remove this rampant contranascence.[6]

8.2.3 Connascence and encapsulation boundaries

I'll go so far as to say that connascence and contranascence are at the heart of modern software-engineering constructs. To explain this, I'd like to return to Section 8.1's topic of encapsulation. Although I defined encapsulation and the levels to which it may aspire, I didn't say much about why encapsulation is important.

Encapsulation is a check on contranascence. Imagine a system comprising 100,000 lines of code. Imagine further that the entire system resides in a single module, say a main procedure. Imagine next that you have to develop and maintain this system. The contranascence among the hundreds of variable names would of itself be a nightmare: Just to pick a name for a new variable you'd first have to check dozens of other names to be sure of avoiding a clash.

Another problem would be the deceptive nature of the code. Consider two lines of code that are adjacent on a source listing. You might wonder *why* the two lines are adjacent: Is it because they *must be* adjacent (owing to connascence of position) and that inserting a line would wreck the system? Or did they just *happen to* wind up adjacent when the code was all shoveled into the same module?

So, a system that's not broken into encapsulated units has two problems: rampant connascence (chiefly through contranascence), and the confusion over what is true connascence and what is fortuitous similarity or adjacency. (An example of fortuitous similarity would be two variables named **i**, in two entirely separate and

---

[6] One of the best language mechanisms is Eiffel's **rename** keyword. See [Meyer, 1992], for example. See also Exercise 4 in Chapter 11 for another look at this example.

unconnected classes. There would be no connascence of name here; either variable could be renamed **j** with no sad consequences.)

Connascence is also why object orientation "works." Object orientation eliminates—or at least tames—some of the connascence that runs wild in traditional modular systems with only level-1 encapsulation. Again, I'll explain with an example: the hash-table example of Section 8.2.1.

I'll assume a system that maintains a single hash-table and is designed with only level-1 encapsulation (which is the level of encapsulation of, say, structured design). The system must access the hash-table from several (at least two) places in the code: location(s) that update the table, and location(s) that look up symbols in the table. The code in these locations will have connascence of algorithm; if you think up a better hashing algorithm, then you'll have to find all the code locations that use the current algorithm and make the necessary changes.

Level-1 encapsulation will neither guide you to where these places are nor tell you how many places there are. Even if there are only two places with the hashing algorithm, they may be close together or far apart in the system listing. You'll be on your own (unless you can find some friendly and accurate documentation).

An object-oriented system, which has level-2 encapsulation, has a natural home for the hashing algorithm in the single class SYMBOL-TABLE. Although there will still be a connascence of algorithm between the method **insert-symbol** and the method **lookup-symbol**, the connascence will be under control. It will be encapsulated within the boundary of a single component (the class SYMBOL-TABLE). If good object-oriented design has been used, then there will be no connascence due to the hashing algorithm anywhere else in the system (that is, anywhere outside SYMBOL-TABLE).

8.2.4 Connascence and maintainability

Connascence offers three guidelines for improving system maintainability:

1. Minimize overall connascence—this includes contranascence, of course—by breaking the system into encapsulated components.

2. Minimize any remaining connascence that crosses encapsulation boundaries. (Guideline 3, below, will help here.)

3. Maximize the connascence within encapsulation boundaries.

The above guidelines transcend object orientation. They apply to any software-construction approach with level-2 encapsulation or level-3 encapsulation, or higher levels. Also, as you may have noticed, the guidelines express a very old principle in design: Keep like things together and unlike things apart. However, this old principle never told us what "like things" were; in fact, they're software components with mutual connascence.

Figure 8.2 shows two classes with connascence between them. (The connascence is directional, with the direction indicated by arrowheads.) Some of this connascence (shown by the broad lines) violates the rules of object orientation by connecting the internal design of one class to the internal design of another: "Like things" have been placed in different software components.

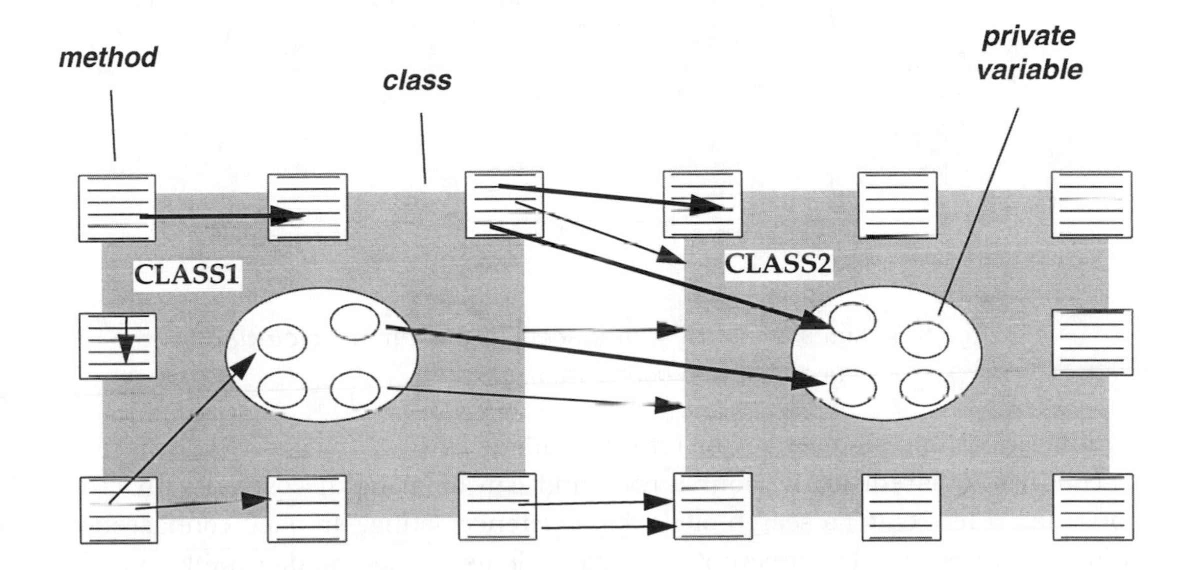

Fig. 8.2: Lines showing connascence (for example, connascence of name), with broad lines violating encapsulation boundaries.

For example, a line from the method of CLASS1 that refers to a variable within CLASS2 violates object-oriented encapsulation. (Note that directional connascence violates encapsulation only when it crosses *into* an encapsulated unit.)

Figure 8.3 shows two other classes that have no offending encapsulation-busting connascence.

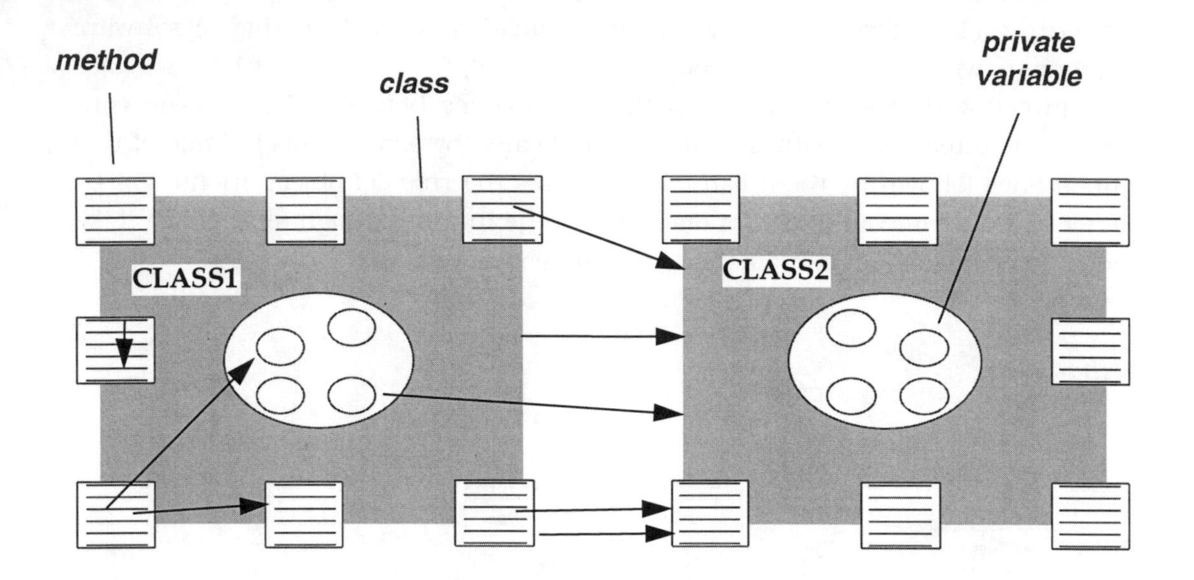

Fig. 8.3: Lines showing connascence, with none violating encapsulation boundaries.

Connascence represents a set of interdependencies in software. Explicit connascence is apparent in the source code and can often be discovered with little more than a text editor's search or a cross-reference listing. Implicit connascence (connascence not readily apparent from the code itself) may be detectable only by human ingenuity, aided by whatever documentation exists for the system under examination.

The human mind is a very expensive (and fallible) tool for keeping track of widespread connascence. Implicit connascence, especially when it straddles encapsulation boundaries, presents an extra challenge to system maintainers. Implicit connascence becomes particularly difficult to track several months after the code has been designed and written. Perhaps future CASE tools will assist people in monitoring connascence and in revealing implicit connascence. This would be especially helpful in large systems that exhibit level-2 (or higher) encapsulation.

8.2.5 Connascence abuses in object-oriented systems

As we saw in Section 8.2.3, the level-2 encapsulation capabilities of object orientation are a tremendous boon for a designer trying to tame connascence. However, in this final section on connascence, I give three examples of how object-oriented designers sometimes violate the principle of "keeping connascence at home"—that is, within class boundaries. The first concerns the friend function of C++, the second concerns a misuse of inheritance, and the third concerns a gratuitous introduction of connascence in breach of object-oriented principles.

1. The friend function of C++

The friend function of C++ was created expressly to violate encapsulation boundaries. It's a component outside the boundaries of a class that has access to the private elements of objects of that class. So, if a friend function FF gets the handle of an object of class C1, it can mess about in the internals of that object willy-nilly. The connascence between FF and C1 is therefore high; it includes connascence of name, type, meaning, and so on. Every change that a designer makes to the internal design of C1 will require FF to be thoroughly checked and possibly changed.

If FF is the friend of only one class, then you could argue that FF is really part of that class and to all intents lies within its boundary. Fair enough. However, if FF is also the friend of C2, C3, and C4, then that argument fails. Unfortunately, many C++ designs have exactly that structure . . . and with friends like those, who needs enemies!

One legitimate use of the friend construct, however, is as a scaffold to inspect the internal states of objects under test. Since object-oriented encapsulation limits white-box scrutiny of objects, it ironically hinders the testing of object-oriented systems. The friend function lifts the veil of secrecy from the implementation of the class under test.

2. Unconstrained inheritance

The construct of inheritance—although wildly popular in most object-oriented shops—may sometimes introduce raging connascence. If you allow a class to make use of both externally visible and internally visible components of a superclass, then you will introduce a great deal of connascence across major (class) encapsulation boundaries. This will include connascence of name, connascence of class, and other varieties of connascence.

In a shop where I consulted last year, an analysis/design team had begun to build their class library with some very well-thought-out hierarchies of classes. For example, DOMESTIC-SHIPMENT and EXPORT-SHIPMENT were both (reasonably enough) subclasses of SHIPMENT. However, their design strategy allowed subclasses unbridled access to private variables of superclasses. This meant that the maintainers of subclasses C1, C2, and so forth, had to stay aware—almost on a minute-to-minute basis—of any changes to the internal design of the superclass C, because C's maintainer could create disastrous results in descendant classes just by an innocuous change to an (ostensibly private) variable name.

The team worked around this problem by having Jim be responsible for, say, the classes DOMESTIC-SHIPMENT, EXPORT-SHIPMENT, SHIPMENT, and other related classes. Jim would make sure that any changes he made to SHIPMENT were propagated to classes connascent with SHIPMENT—and there were actually quite a lot of them. Unfortunately, however, the rampant connascence couldn't be parceled out to individual team members quite so neatly. The result was that every class maintainer had the tedious chore of keeping abreast of internal design changes to all that class's superclasses. Even more unfortunate, however, was that each change to the class library caused high anxiety all round, since time pressures denied the team any chance to keep the library documentation up to date.

If Jim and his colleagues had taken into account the guideline that connascence should not cross encapsulation boundaries, it would have told them that inheritance by a subclass should be restricted to only those features of the superclass that are already externally visible. (Another way to say this is: The notion of inheriting abstract behavior should be divorced from the notion of inheriting the internal implementation of such behavior.[7]) Had their library been designed according to this principle, their lives would have been less fraught with trouble, and maybe they wouldn't have called their shop The Land of the Midnight Fix.

3. Relying on accidents of implementation

In another shop of yore, a programmer named The Weasel—don't ask me why!—had created a class SET that furnished the behavior of a mathematical set. (Its methods included: **add**, **remove**, **size**, and so on.) It appeared to be well designed and written and it always performed fine.

The Weasel used SET in several places in his own applications. For example, he used the **retrieve** method, which retrieved elements of the set one by one in random order until every element had been provided. However, The Weasel knew that **retrieve** happened to retrieve elements in exactly the *same* order in which they'd been added to the set—although that wasn't documented

[7] See [Porter, 1992] for further discussion of this point.

or supposed to be a property of the method. He made use of this accidental, undocumented fact several times in his application. He had thus created a connascence of algorithm across the encapsulation boundary between his application and the internals of the **retrieve** method.

When SET was later replaced by a different implementation—one that happened not to preserve order in the same way—many of The Weasel's applications blew up. Many of the users also blew up, but The Weasel was nowhere to be found. It was rumored that he had taken up another identity and had gone underground in the Middle East. So, let's all hope that the Day of The Weasel has passed forever.

8.3 Summary

Encapsulation is a venerable concept in software. The subroutine, invented in the 1940s, introduced encapsulation of code into procedural modules; this is level-1 encapsulation. However, object-oriented structures are more sophisticated than traditional procedural structures like the subroutine. Object orientation involves at least level-2 encapsulation. In level-2 encapsulation, subroutines (known as methods) are themselves encapsulated, together with variables, into classes.

The complexities of level-2 encapsulation introduce many novel interrelationships among design components. Rather than give each kind of interrelationship its own term, I introduce a general term, "connascence." Connascence exists when two software components (say, A and B) must be changed together in some circumstance in order to preserve software correctness. Contranascence is a form of connascence in which difference, rather than similarity, must be preserved. Disnascence is the absence of connascence.

Connascence comes in several forms. Static connascence derives from the lexical structure of a code listing. Examples are: connascence of class and meaning. Dynamic connascence depends on the execution pattern of code at run-time. Examples are: connascence of time and value. Explicit connascence is immediately apparent from reading a code listing. An example is connascence of name. Implicit connascence is apparent only from a study of the code or its attendant documentation. Connascence of execution or algorithm is usually implicit. Copious implicit connascence raises software-maintenance costs.

The level-2 encapsulation of object orientation addresses the problem of potentially rampant connascence in large, modern systems. This encapsulation provides solid class structures within whose boundaries unbridled connascence can be corralled.

However, there are several ways that connascence may escape encapsulation boundaries—even in an object-oriented design. In this chapter, we saw three examples of poor design: The first was the use of C++'s friend function deliberately to nullify the benefits of object-oriented encapsulation. The second was the misguided use of inheritance to allow a subclass to inherit the implementation of a superclass. The third was allowing the internal (and probably volatile) details of a class's algorithm to be relied on by code in other classes.

The three examples above violate the central principle of object-oriented design: Minimize overall connascence—this includes contranascence, of course—by breaking the system into encapsulated components. Minimize any remaining connascence that crosses encapsulation boundaries by maximizing the connascence within encapsulation boundaries.

8.4 Exercises

1. A man I met in a pub told me that every idea in modern music can be found somewhere in Haydn's works. One could say something similar about Yourdon and Constantine's book on structured design [Yourdon and Constantine, 1975]: Its pages form a magnum opus of oft-overlooked design ideas, which are "rediscovered" time after time. Check this book to see whether Yourdon and Constantine have anything to say on the subject of connascence.

2. Use of the **go to** statement has become notorious over the past few decades as a cause of incomprehensible software. From the standpoint of connascence, can you justify the **go to**'s bad reputation?

3. Assume that you've become tired of object orientation and you're creating a new software paradigm, which employs levels of encapsulation and has various forms of connascence. Explain (in a general way) how you would set forth the design criteria and guidelines for connascence and encapsulation in your paradigm.

4. This chapter discussed connascence mainly in terms of programming code. Are there any other examples of connascence that crop up in the wider context of the overall software-development project?

5. In Section 8.2.4, I suggested that implicit connascence that crosses encapsulation boundaries usually proves particularly troublesome to maintainers of an object-oriented system. Can you give examples of such connascence and suggest how to make it more explicit, and thus easier to track?

6. Further research is needed into the forms of connascence that apply to modern software-design paradigms, especially as object-oriented design becomes popular. Set up an experiment to elicit the degrees of ill caused by the different varieties of connascence (for example, connascence of name and position). The experiment could measure the effects of connascence (both within and across encapsulation boundaries) on presumed dependent variables, such as human comprehension time/cost, debugging time/cost, and modification time/cost. Perhaps you can recruit volunteers to review source code and measure their time to detect bugs deliberately seeded into the code.

8.5 Answers

1. Yes; Yourdon and Constantine begin an exploration of what is essentially connascence in Chapter 3 of their book. However, after introducing connascence (under the vague term *structure*) and touching on it briefly, the chapter goes off at an angle from the general concept. Later, the book again flirts tantalizingly with the topic, and their Chapter 6, on coupling, and Chapter 7, on cohesion, cover many issues related to connascence.

2. It has long been known that the undisciplined use of the **go to** statement causes the static and dynamic structures of code to diverge. In terms of connascence, it implies that static connascence of position (in the code listing) gives little clue to dynamic connascence of execution (at run-time). Since maintainers make modifications to the static code, **go to**s increase the risk that a static change will violate some connascence of execution. Furthermore, any **go to** induces an additional connascence of name between the **go to** itself and the label that's the target of the **go to**, together with contranascence among the label names themselves.

3. Here's one possible framework on which to base a definition of a future software paradigm:

    a. State the intended purpose and scope of applicability of your paradigm.

    b. State the paradigm's encapsulation structure. State what the paradigm's components are and which components are contained within which.

    c. In terms of the above encapsulation structure, state the default visibility rules of the paradigm. This will prescribe the allowed connections among components and will state the "boundaries of privacy" established by the encapsulation structure.

    d. List the possible forms of connascence inherent in the paradigm. There will be explicit connascence, which appears in the source code, and implicit connascence, which will be more difficult to perceive because it is "invisible." As we saw, implicit connascence becomes especially subtle when it transcends the official encapsulation structure of the paradigm.

    e. Classify as much as possible the pernicious effects of each form of connascence in various contexts.

f. Suggest heuristics for deriving or modifying software designed under this paradigm in order to minimize the above pernicious effects.

4. Yes, there are many examples of connascence that spans project deliverables. For instance, connascence is to be found between the model of user requirements and the design model of a software implementation of those requirements. Recently, I encountered a distressingly vast connascence of name when a business decided to change the word CUSTOMER to CLIENT. The havoc caused was immense! A good CASE tool should keep track of these hundreds of lines of connascence across deliverables and thereby reduce the onus on the human mind to keep track of them.

5. I recently saw the following examples of implicit connascence in two object-oriented systems: A pair of classes in a business system each contained the number **5** (representing the number of office buildings the company owned). This created implicit connascence of value between the two classes, because to change one **5** (but not the other) to **6** would cause an error. If the literal constant **5** were instead denoted by **num-of-offices**, then the connascence would become explicit and less of a problem: Change the value once, and it would be changed everywhere. To do this, you would presumably store the value of **num-of-offices** in a database.

   A real-time communications application contained two objects that would issue voluminous communications across a network at exactly the same time. This caused the network to clog unnecessarily, because there was no reason that the objects *had to* start communicating simultaneously. The problem was solved when the two objects were made to stagger their transmissions. In other words, this system had an implicit contranascence of timing, which was made explicit by setting up a scheduling table for the objects' communication.

Domains, Encumbrance, and Cohesion

Classes in an application are not all alike. For example, in a brokerage system you might find the classes EQUITY, ACCOUNT-POSITION, DATE, TIME, LIST, and SET. In an avionics system, you might find the classes FLAP, FUEL-TANK, DATE, TIME, SET, and TREE.

Notice that there's something about the classes EQUITY and FUEL-TANK that intuitively makes them seem different from the classes DATE and SET. For example, EQUITY seems more complex and intricate than the simple DATE class. There's a reason for this: EQUITY and FUEL-TANK are from the business domain, whereas DATE and SET are from the foundation domain.

I begin this chapter by defining class domains and subdomains. In the chapter's second section, I introduce encumbrance as a quantitative measure of a class's "sophistication" and show how classes from higher domains normally have higher values of encumbrance. In the chapter's third section, I define a qualitative measure of a class, class cohesion, one of whose recommendations for "class goodness" is that a class should be based in one and only one domain.

9.1 Domains of Object Classes

A given object-oriented system will contain classes from four major domains. They are the application domain, the business domain, the architectural domain, and the foundation domain. Each of these domains is further refined into subdomains. Below I list the four domains, together with their respective subdomains:

- The *application domain*—comprising classes valuable for one application

  Event-activity management subdomain
  Event-stimulus recognition subdomain

- The *business domain*—comprising classes valuable for one industry or company

  Relationship subdomain
  Role subdomain
  Attribute subdomain

- The *architectural domain*—comprising classes valuable for one implementation architecture

  Human-interface subdomain
  Database-manipulation subdomain
  Machine-communication subdomain

- The *foundation domain*—comprising classes valuable across all businesses and architectures

  Semantic subdomain
  Structural subdomain
  Fundamental subdomain

In the next sections, I explain the significance of each domain and subdomain by means of examples. I begin with the most straightforward classes, which are at the bottom of this list,

9.1.1 The foundation domain

The classes in the foundation domain are usable in many applications from many different industries running on a broad range of computer architectures. In other words, the foundation domain comprises classes with the widest possible reusability. The foundation domain contains three subdomains: the *fundamental*, *structural*, and *semantic* subdomains. Below I give examples of classes in each of these subdomains.

- *Fundamental classes* are those such as INT, BOOL, CHAR, and so on. These classes are so basic that many object-oriented languages include them as built-in, simple, traditional data-types.

- *Structural classes* implement structures. They read like a Data Structures 101 curriculum, with representative examples being STACK, QUEUE, LIST, BINARY-TREE, SET, and so on. They're also known as *container classes*, and they're very often designed with genericity.

- *Semantic classes* include DATE, TIME, ANGLE, MONEY, and MASS. (Some people also include in this subdomain basic geometric shapes, such as POINT, LINE, POLYGON, and CIRCLE.) Semantic classes have a richer meaning than plain INT or CHAR. Additionally, their values are often expressed in units, such as hours, dollars, or meters.

Classes in the foundation domain, by definition, may prove useful in any application in any business anywhere. A LIST or a DATE class is as likely to show up in a medical system as in a video-library system.

A foundation class may be built upon other foundation classes. For example, ANGLE may use REAL in its implementation, and POLYGON may use SET. The way I've ordered the class domains is no accident; the classes lower down in the list tend to be used by the classes higher up, as we shall see when we look at class cohesion later, in Section 9.3.

9.1.2 The architectural domain

The classes in the architectural domain are usable in many applications from many different industries. However, the reusability of architectural classes is limited to a single computer architecture. The architectural domain contains three subdomains: the *machine-communication*, the *database-manipulation*, and the *human-interface* subdomains. Below I give examples of classes in each of these subdomains.

- *Machine-communication classes* include PORT and REMOTE-MACHINE.

- *Database-manipulation classes* include TRANSACTION and BACKUP.

- *Human-interface classes* include WINDOW and COMMAND-BUTTON.

Architectural classes are useful in any application in any business, so long as the application is implemented on a physical architecture supported by those classes.

In other words, there can't be a single architectural-domain class library for the whole world, because classes such as PORT or BACKUP will have to exist in several versions for the various computer architectures that exist. So, the particular architectural-domain library that you choose for your shop will depend on the hardware and software architecture(s) in your shop.

9.1.3 The business domain

The classes in the business domain are useful in many applications—but only those *within a single industry*, such as banking, medicine, or avionics. The business domain contains three subdomains: the *attribute*, *role*, and *relationship* subdomains. Below I give examples of classes in each of these subdomains.

- *Attribute classes* capture the properties of things in the business world. Examples are BALANCE (of a bank account) or BODY-TEMPERATURE (of a patient). Although these classes are obviously similar to MONEY and TEMPERATURE (which are semantic foundation classes), they are not identical. A bank account's balance and a patient's body temperature will be subject to certain business rules that don't apply to general foundation classes. For example, the value of an account balance may be constrained to lie within certain limits. Transgression of those limits may signal an error or trigger off some other business activity.

- *Role classes* are classes derived from "roles that things play" in the business.[1] Examples are CUSTOMER and PATIENT.

- *Relationship classes* derive from associations among things in the business world. They include ACCOUNT-OWNERSHIP (by a bank customer) and PATIENT-SUPERVISION (by a nurse).

Some business classes' applicability may be even more narrow than a whole industry: They may be useful only to a single corporation. Indeed, since some large corporations are in several businesses, the usability of a given business class may not span more than one division. For example, I know a corporation that is developing seven different classes named PURCHASE-ORDER—and the company has only nine divisions! I suspect that they could reengineer the corporation to reduce the number of incompatible PURCHASE-ORDERs. But I doubt that they

[1] A role in object-oriented analysis is analogous to the entity-type in information modeling.

could ever reduce the number to one, because no two divisions carry out purchasing in exactly the same way.

Again, we see the pattern of classes in higher domains being built on classes in lower ones. For example, ACCOUNT-OWNERSHIP will refer to the classes CUSTOMER and ACCOUNT, and at least one variable within ACCOUNT will be of class BALANCE.

9.1.4 The application domain

A class in the application domain is used only within a single application (or a small group of related applications). The application domain contains two subdomains: the *event-stimulus-recognition* and *event-activity-management* subdomains. Below I give examples of classes in each of these subdomains.

- *Event-stimulus-recognition classes* (also termed *event-recognizer classes*) are event daemons, software components that monitor input to check for the occurrence of specific events in the environment. An example might be the class MONITOR-PATIENT-TEMPERATURE, which would be chartered to look for the events **patient develops fever** and **patient becomes hypothermic**, among others.[2]

- *Event-activity-manager classes* (also termed *event-manager classes*) carry out the appropriate business policy when an event of a given type occurs. An example of event-activity management would be WARM-HYPOTHERMIC-PATIENT, which might immediately increase the warmth to the patient and then sound an alarm at a nurse's station to summon medical attention for the patient. (Of course, this piece of software would become active only when a patient became hypothermic.) Another example, from a different hospital application, would be SCHEDULE-PATIENT-FOR-SURGERY. An avionics example might be SET-FLAP-LANDING-CONFIGURATION.

A class in the application domain has very narrow reusability. Indeed, most classes in this domain are relevant to only one application and so have no reusability at all. For example, SCHEDULE-PATIENT-FOR-SURGERY would probably be useful only in the Surgery-Management System.

---

[2] Shops with a noun convention for class names would label this class PATIENT-TEMPERATURE-MONITOR.

9.1.5 The source of classes in each domain

For most people, the ability to stock libraries with reusable classes is the *sine qua non* of object orientation, and many shops rightly devote much of their design effort toward the exquisite reusability of the classes that they build. But, as we saw in the preceding sections, classes in different domains have different degrees of reusability. Classes in the lowest domain have the greatest reusability; classes in the highest domain have the least, as Fig. 9.1 illustrates.

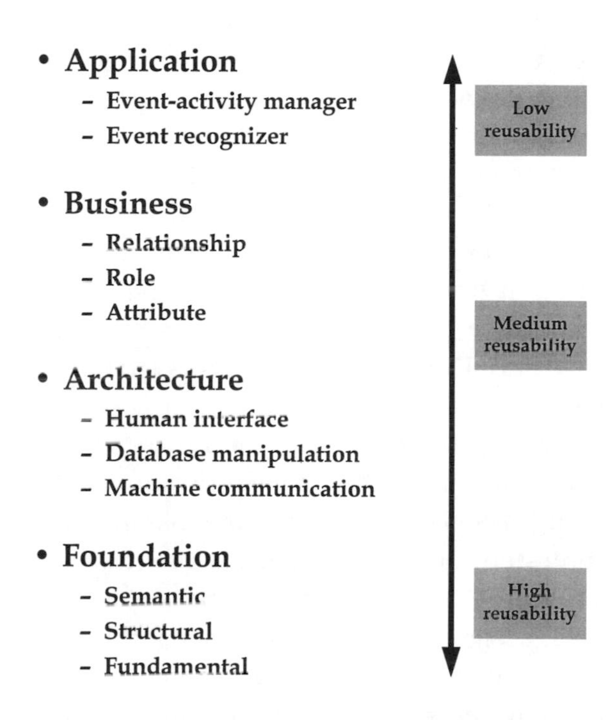

Fig. 9.1: Domains of classes and their reusability.

I realize that this is a circular argument. After all, I defined the foundation domain to be the domain of classes with universal reusability and the application domain to be that of components useful only with one application. Nevertheless, the issue of reusability is important when it comes to the famous old question, Where do classes come from? The answer depends greatly on the domain of class concerned.

For the foundation classes, the answer is simple: You buy them from a class vendor. Developing a foundation library is a difficult and expensive undertaking. Don't try it at home. If you make that mistake—and I've seen this happen—you may spend a thousandfold more than you would if you purchased the library.

You'll certainly have to augment your purchased foundation library with some classes of your own. That's okay. But buy, borrow, and beg any foundation classes you need before you fall back on the option of building them.

The source of classes in the architectural domain is similar to that of the foundation domain, but has four differences. First, you may have to buy architectural classes from the vendor(s) of your hardware and software infrastructure (although third-party vendors will supply libraries for popular architectures). Second, you may have to suffer incompatibilities across portions of the architectural library that come from different vendors.

Third, your architectural-library vendor(s) may have built on a different foundation library from yours. Fourth, because of the two previous points, your purchased architectural library may cause you more tailoring, custom-building, and modification than your purchased foundation library.

The classes in the business domain are especially interesting—and challenging. These are classes that—for at least two reasons—you can't go out and buy. First, general vendors don't have the industry expertise to develop classes for hospitals or banks or aviation or telecommunication. Second, the marketplace for such a class library would be a nightmare. Every purchaser would want special tailoring—"The class CUSTOMER that you sold to us isn't quite right for our company's business needs."

So, you'll have to develop the classes in the business domain yourself. And you'll have to take great care in analyzing their requirements—using techniques such as role-relationship modeling or entity-relationship modeling—because they will become a treasure store of your company's business acumen. Also, you'll have to take great care in their design, because these classes will have significant reusability if they're well designed (but virtually none if they're not).

The competitiveness of your company may depend on the time-to-deployment of new software systems, which will depend on the quality of the business classes in your shop library. So, although you'll get a lot of mileage from your foundation and architectural libraries, the strategic success of object orientation in your corporation will rest on how well you build your home-grown business-domain library.

The topmost domain is the application domain. Don't worry too much about design for reusability here; however well you design, you won't get much reusability. The main source for the classes in this domain is the business events that you discover during analysis.

Although I used the term "classes" in the previous paragraph, many software components in the application domain may be traditional procedures or single-instance packages, rather than full-blooded classes. For example, the event-activity manager WARM-HYPOTHERMIC-PATIENT could become a stand-alone function. (Alternatively, it could become the single method of a new class, or it could become a method of the existing class PATIENT.) Thus, your "object-oriented" design may in reality comprise a mixture of procedural and object-oriented constructs.

9.2 Encumbrance

Section 9.1 treated class domains in a qualitative way. In this section, I offer a quantitative way to tell how far a class sits above the fundamental domain. The measure is called *encumbrance*.

9.2.1 Definition of encumbrance

Encumbrance measures the total ancillary machinery of a class. "Total ancillary machinery" comprises all the other classes that the given class must rely on in order to work. In other words, if you count all the classes referred to by a class C, and then count the classes that *they* refer to, and so on, the total number will be the encumbrance of C.

In order to define "encumbrance" formally, I first define the terms "direct class reference set" and "indirect class-reference set." (Note: The next few paragraphs look more difficult than they really are. Please stay tuned, because I need to define "encumbrance" formally just once—and then it will be over. If you wish to avail yourself of anesthetic, go ahead!)

> The *direct class reference set* of a class C is the set of classes to which C refers directly.

In practice, a class C can refer directly to another class D in the following ways:

C inherits from D.
C has a variable of class D.
C has a method with an input argument of class D.
C has a method that sends a message with a returned argument of class D.
C has a method containing a local variable of class D.
C supplies D as an actual generic parameter to a generic class.
C has a friend class D.

> Let the direct class-reference set of C comprise the classes D_1, D_2, ..., D_n.
>
> Then, the *indirect class-reference set* of C is the union of the direct class-reference set of C and the indirect class-reference sets of D_1, D_2, ..., D_n.[3]

This definition is obviously recursive. I can stop the recursion by saying that the class-reference set—both direct and indirect—of every class in the fundamental domain (INT, REAL, BOOL, for example) is empty. (What you choose as your fundamental domain is arbitrary; it doesn't matter what classes you pick so long as you stick to them and you define their class-reference sets to be empty.)

And now—at last—here's the definition of encumbrance:

> The *encumbrance* of a class is the size of its indirect class-reference set.[4]

At this point, you're probably tearing your hair out. Fortunately, however, there's a much clearer and more intuitive way to look at encumbrance. Let's use an arrow to show a direct class reference. Thus, in the example of Fig. 9.2, the direct class-reference set of C is C_1, C_2, C_3.

[3] If you prefer an even more mathematical definition: The indirect class-reference set of C is equivalent to the transitive closure on the direct class-reference set of C.

[4] Some authors use the term *class coupling* for the size of a class's direct-reference set.

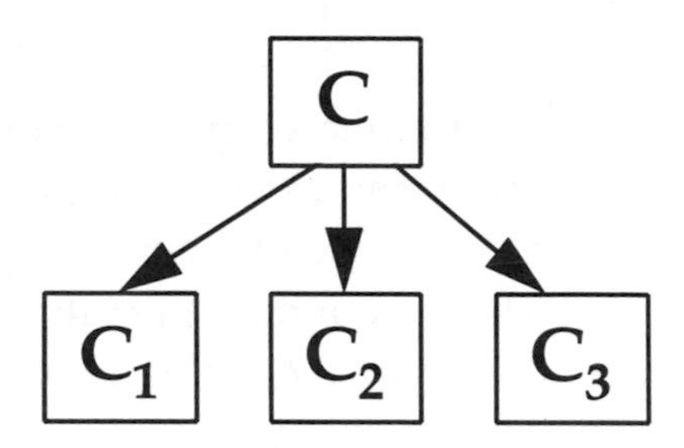

Fig. 9.2: C and its direct class-reference set.

Figure 9.3 shows C's indirect reference set. You find the encumbrance of C by counting all the classes in this diagram, that is, all the classes in the tree whose root is C and whose leaves are the fundamental classes at the bottom (denoted by F_1 and so forth). The encumbrance of C is therefore 12.

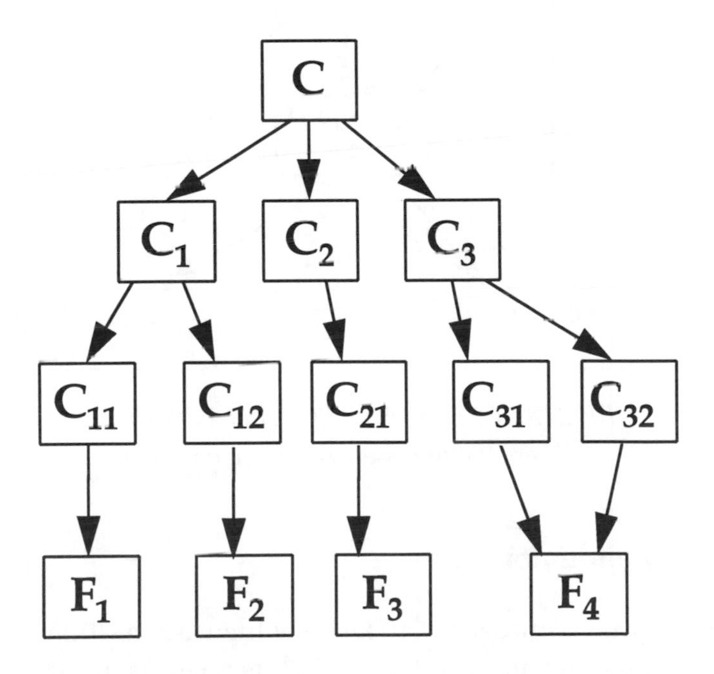

Fig. 9.3: C and its indirect class-reference set.

Notice that I've set the encumbrance of the fundamental-subdomain classes (F_1 through F_4) to zero, although some of the foundation classes refer to one or two other classes. This is the convention of setting the fundamental classes' encumbrances to zero, which I mentioned above. (You *could* assign a nonzero encumbrance to a fundamental class. If you did, your measure of each class's encumbrance would be slightly higher.)

Figure 9.4 shows a concrete example of encumbrance, in which the encumbrance of RECTANGLE is 4, since it has the four classes POINT, LENGTH, REAL, and BOOL in its indirect reference set.[5] Although REAL may refer to BOOL (in a comparison operation) and INT (in a rounding operation), I've adopted the usual "zero" convention to set the encumbrance of REAL (and its fundamental companions) to zero.

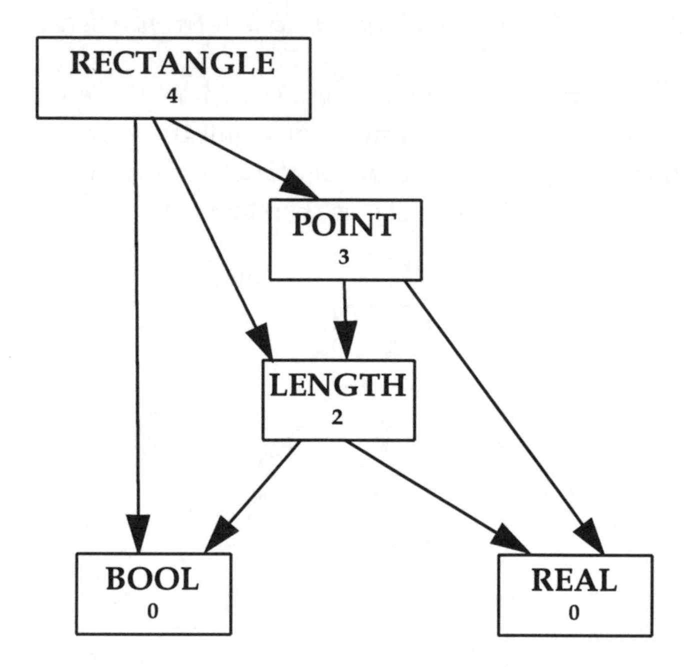

Fig. 9.4: RECTANGLE and its indirect class-reference set, with each class's encumbrance marked.

9.2.2 The use of encumbrance

Encumbrance gives us a measure of class sophistication—that is, how high the class is above the fundamental subdomain. Thus, classes in higher domains have high encumbrance and those in lower domains have low encumbrance.

---

[5] A different design for RECTANGLE would give it a slightly different encumbrance.

An unexpected encumbrance may indicate a fault in class design. For example, if you find a class with high encumbrance to be in a low domain, then there may be a problem with the class's cohesion. (I cover class cohesion in Section 9.3.) Alternatively, if a class in a high domain has low encumbrance, then it has probably been designed from scratch; that is, the designer has built it directly from INT, CHAR, and other fundamental classes, rather than by reusing intermediate classes from the library.

9.2.3 The Law of Demeter

Lieberherr and Holland offer the Law of Demeter as a guiding principle for limiting the encumbrance of a class by limiting the size of its direct reference set.[6] (However, the authors didn't actually employ the terms "encumbrance" and "direct class-reference set.")

A general phrasing of the *Law of Demeter* is

> For a class C, and for any method **m** defined on C, all target objects of messages within **m** must be instances of one of the following classes:
>
> 1. C itself.
> 2. The argument classes of **m**.
> 3. The classes of C's variables.
> 4. Classes of objects created by **m** (or by functions or methods that **m** calls).
> 5. Classes of objects in global variables.

The law also permits messages to **self** and **super** (Smalltalk), to **this** (C++), or to **Current** (Eiffel).

There are two versions of the law, differing only in their interpretation of Point 3: The Strong Law of Demeter defines C's variables as being just the variables defined

[6] In Greek mythology, Demeter was the goddess of the harvest. However, this Law of Demeter derives its name from an object-oriented project named Demeter. See [Lieberherr and Holland, 1989] for further details.

in C itself. The Weak Law of Demeter defines C's variables as being the variables of C, together with those that C inherits from other classes.

The Law of Demeter is eminently reasonable, for it restricts arbitrary references to other classes within a given class. I prefer the Strong Law of Demeter to the Weak Law, because it limits connascence across encapsulation boundaries—the boundaries in this case being the class boundaries of C's superclasses.

As we saw in Section 8.2.4, limiting connascence across encapsulation (that is, class) boundaries eases system maintenance and evolvability (because it frees the designer of C's superclasses to redesign their internal implementation) and enhances the understandability of C (because someone trying to understand the design of C isn't continually dragged into the implementation details of C's superclasses).

9.3 Class Cohesion: A Class and Its Methods

Class cohesion is the measure of interrelatedness of the methods in the external interface of a class. In Table 8.2, I placed the term "class cohesion" in the quadrant formed by level 2 and level 1 to indicate that class cohesion is one encapsulation level higher than module cohesion.[7] A less formal way to think of class cohesion is as how well a class "hangs together as an implementation of some abstract data-type."

A class with low (bad) cohesion has a set of methods that don't belong together. A class with high (good) cohesion has a set of methods that all contribute to the type abstraction implemented by the class.

People have tried to define class cohesion by considering how a class's methods use the class's private variables. The idea: The more overlap in the methods' use of the variables, the higher the cohesion of the class. Although I've tried this approach, I don't find it very attractive—for the following two reasons.

The first reason is that cohesion is a property that should be apparent from the "outside" of an encapsulated software unit. Therefore, it seems wrong to have to look at a class's internals in order to assess its cohesion. (Perhaps we should even think of class cohesion as *type cohesion*.) The second reason is that such a measurement is unstable and too dependent on the particular internal design of the class, which can change over a class's lifetime. Therefore, an immature class (one that you're just beginning to design) may appear to have lower cohesion than a mature one (one that has grown its final, adult set of methods). That isn't good.

---

[7] Module cohesion, a term from structured design, is a measure of how well lines of code belong together within a single procedural module.

During my recent meanderings through object-oriented shops, I've observed three telltale cohesion problems in the allocation of methods to classes: three problems that are observable from a class's external design. I call these three problems: *mixed-instance*, *mixed-domain*, and *mixed-role cohesion*. Of the three, mixed-instance cohesion is typically the greatest sin, and mixed-role cohesion the least.

A class can have all, some, or none of these cohesion problems. A class with none of these three mixed cohesions is entirely cohesive and is said to have *ideal cohesion*. In the following sections, I define each of the three mixed cohesions and assess their design symptoms.

9.3.1 Mixed-instance cohesion

> A class with *mixed-instance cohesion* has some components (typically methods) that are undefined for some objects of the class.

For example, let's say that a sales department has both commissioned and non-commissioned salespeople. Fred is commissioned and Mary is noncommissioned. In the object-oriented application that supports the department, there is a class SALESPERSON, of which the objects pointed to by the variables **fred** and **mary** are instances.

Given the above, the first of the following two messages makes sense, but the second does not:

```
fred.issue-commission-pmt;
mary.issue-commission-pmt;
```

We *could* set the commission of the object **mary** to zero. However, that would be a lie. Mary doesn't have zero commission; she has an undefined commission. We would also need a variable **whether-commissioned:BOOL** in SALESPERSON. And we should include in the method **SALESPERSON::issue-commission-pmt** an **if** statement that prevents the printing of commission checks of $0.00 for "noncommissioned objects." That would all work, but it would be an ugly design.

The real problem is that the class SALESPERSON has mixed-instance cohesion, because it is too coarse for the application: It lumps both commissioned and noncommissioned salespeople together as one class. We need to add the finer-grained subclasses COMM-SALESPERSON and NONCOMM-SALESPERSON to our design. These two new subclasses will inherit from their superclass, SALESPERSON. A commissioned salesperson would be represented by an instance of COMM-SALESPERSON, while a noncommissioned salesperson would be represented by an instance of NONCOMM-SALESPERSON.

The method **commission** would then be allocated to COMM-SALESPERSON, as shown in Fig. 9.5.

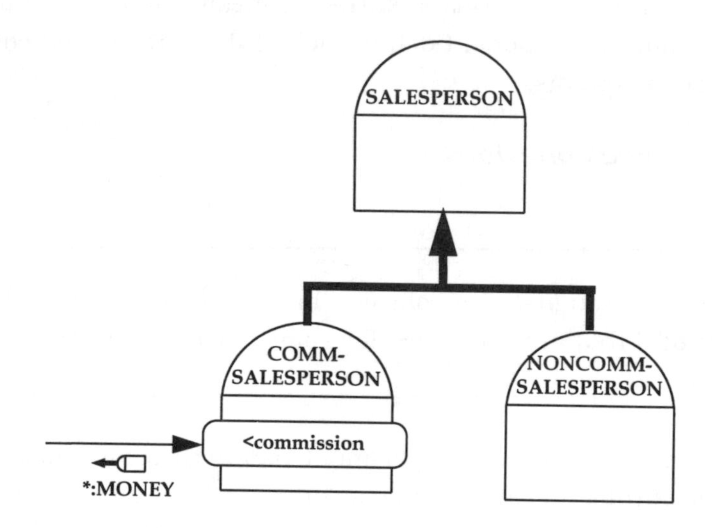

Fig. 9.5: Removing the cohesion problem of SALESPERSON by adding subclasses.

Mixed-instance cohesion usually indicates a class hierarchy that isn't thoroughly thought through or simply isn't correct. As we saw, it also implies some gnarled code (extra **if** statements) within the offending class itself.

9.3.2 Mixed-domain cohesion

> A class with *mixed-domain cohesion* has a component that encumbers the class with an extrinsic class of a different domain.

In the above definition, I use "domain" in the same sense that I did in Section 9.1. But now I need to define "extrinsic."

> The class B is *extrinsic* to A if A can be fully defined with no notion of B.
>
> B is *intrinsic* to A if B captures some characteristic inherent to A.

For example, ELEPHANT is extrinsic to PERSON, because in no sense does "elephant" capture some characteristic of a person. However, DATE (as in, date of birth) may well be intrinsic to PERSON. Intrinsicality is therefore not absolute: It depends on the application in which PERSON is being used.

There are many examples of mixed-domain cohesion, some of which are obvious, some subtle. The first example that I ever saw was subtle: It was the REAL (real number) class in a vendor's class library, which had a method **arctan**.[8] I stared for a long time at this method, for I perceived something gravely wrong with its being allocated to the class REAL. However, although I realized the gravity of the problem, I couldn't figure out exactly *why* I thought that **arctan** didn't belong in REAL.

One day, as I was sitting beneath an apple tree in my garden, an insight suddenly hit me. (Lacking a sense of historical precedent, I shouted "Eureka!") REAL has no business messing around with objects of class ANGLE. Where would the designer stop with this encumbrance?

How about adding a method **convert-temp** to REAL so we could convert Fahrenheit to Celsius and Kelvin to Réaumur? That would encumber REAL with TEMPERATURE. Or, if we wanted to get marks for our dollars, we could encumber REAL with MONEY. Or REAL could even return the set of customers whose bank balances were (to the nearest cent) equal to some real number. The list of absurd possibilities is endless, as Fig. 9.6 shows.

[8] In case your school trigonometry is a little rusty, I should explain that **arctan** is the inverse-tangent function. It takes a real number **r** and tells you the angle whose tangent is **r**. (**arccos** is the inverse cosine.)

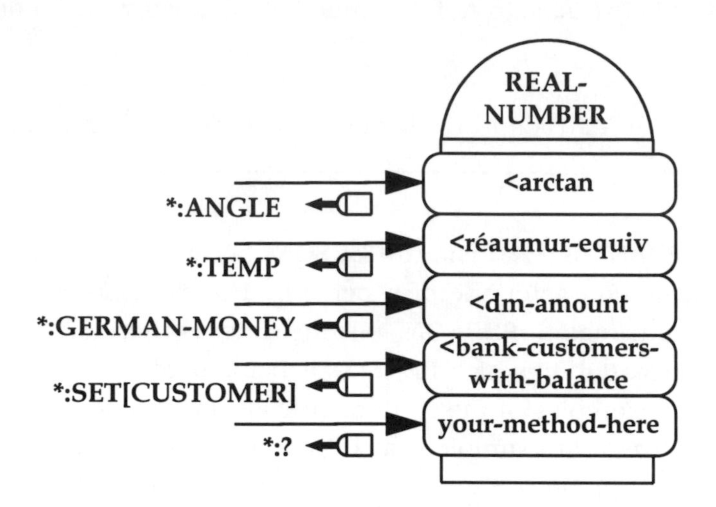

Fig. 9.6: REAL-NUMBER with rampant, mixed-domain cohesion.

When you design a class of a given domain, you'll have to include classes from lower domains in your design—that's what reusability's about. But make sure that you need those classes because of intrinsic properties of your class. For example, it would be fine for the class ACCOUNT to have a method that returned an object of class MONEY or even a variable of class DATE. However, I'd be very suspicious if the class returned an object of the architectural-domain class WIRE-XFER-LINK.

The architectural domain is one that often (and wrongly) gets mixed into a business-domain class. The old object-oriented motto of "a something should know how to something itself," as in "a document should know how to print itself," can be a little *too* appealing. A DOCUMENT class with specific knowledge of a printer has mixed-domain cohesion.

When you design a class of a given domain, you should be particularly wary of introducing classes of higher domains into the class you're designing. That's why the class REAL (above) was a problem. REAL is a fundamental class, and it shouldn't be encumbered with classes of higher (sub)domains. Yet, its method **arctan** forced it to deal with ANGLE, a class from a higher subdomain (namely, the semantic subdomain).

Another way to get a sense of the relative domains or subdomains of two classes is to ask the question, Can I imagine this class being built without this other class? I can imagine REAL being built without the class ANGLE ever existing.

However, I cannot picture my building the class ANGLE without having the class REAL available to me. This implies that ANGLE is in a higher (sub)domain than REAL.

(Incidentally, the class REAL that I encountered had another method, **arccos**, which isn't even defined for most real numbers. This saddled the poor class with mixed-instance cohesion as well.)

9.3.3 Mixed-role cohesion

> A class C with *mixed-role cohesion* has a component that encumbers the class with an extrinsic class that lies in the same domain as C.

Unlike a class with mixed-domain cohesion, a class with mixed-role cohesion doesn't straddle domains. However, it does include more than one role from a single domain, where "role" means the abstraction of the real world that a class represents.

A famous example concerns persons and dogs. Let's say that we have a class PERSON with a method **num-of-dogs-owned** (which, not surprisingly, returns the number of dogs that a given person owns). We would use the method in this way:

```
freds-num-of-dogs-owned := fred.num-of-dogs-owned;
```

This class doesn't have mixed-instance cohesion, because non-dog-owning objects could simply return a value of zero. It doesn't have mixed-domain cohesion, because PERSON and DOG are both in the business domain. But it does have mixed-role cohesion, because PERSON and DOG are distinct concepts, extrinsic to each other.

In pure design terms, mixed-role cohesion is the least serious transgression of class cohesion. However, if you're designing your classes for reusability, then you should pay careful attention to mixed-role cohesion. What if you wanted to reuse PERSON in an application that had no dogs? You could do so, but you'd have extra, useless baggage in the class, and you might get some pesky warnings about missing dogs from your compiler or linker.

And where should we stop with this design philosophy? Why not include these methods in PERSON: **num-of-cars-owned**, **num-of-boats-owned**, **num-of-cats-owned**, **num-of-frogs-owned**, . . .? Not only would these methods severely encumber PERSON with other classes, but each of these methods also implies yet another method to update the number of things owned.[9]

Mixed-role cohesion, as exemplified by "person owns dog," is all-too appealing because

- It's very easy to write the message code to find out how many dogs someone owns: It's simply **fred.num-of-dogs-owned**.

- In many information-modeling approaches, **num-of-dogs-owned** is an attribute of PERSON.

- In real life, if you want to find out how many dogs a person owns, you would probably ask that person.[10]

However, you shouldn't be distracted by any of the above arguments into automatically creating a class PERSON with mixed-role cohesion. There are many other design options that don't compromise the cohesion of PERSON; I explore four of these in detail in the final exercise of Chapter 12.

As an object-oriented designer, you should aim to create classes with ideal cohesion, that is, classes with no mixed-instance, mixed-domain, or mixed-role cohesion. Classes with ideal cohesion have the utmost reusability, which is (especially for classes in the business domain) a primary objective of object orientation.

---

[9] Yes, you could generalize all these methods to **num-of-things-owned**, with **type-of-thing** passed as an argument. But the basic cohesion problem would remain.

[10] I find this anthropomorphic view of object orientation to be specious and irrelevant. I include it because I've often heard it used as an object-oriented "design principle."

9.4 Summary

A class may belong to one of four domains. These domains are: the foundation domain, which comprises classes valuable across all businesses and architectures; the architectural domain, which comprises classes valuable for one implementation architecture; the business domain, which comprises classes valuable for one industry or company; and the application domain, which comprises classes (as well as some simpler procedural components) that are valuable within one application.

Classes of the foundation domain have the greatest reusability, while those from the application domain have the least. (This follows directly from the definitions of the domains, of course.) Each of the four domains has several subdomains within it.

Encumbrance is the size of a class's indirect class-reference set, which is the set formed by the transitive closure of the class's direct class-reference set. Informally speaking, the encumbrance of a class is the number of other classes that it needs in order to "work." Classes from higher domains normally have higher encumbrance than classes from lower domains. The Law of Demeter (named after the Demeter Project in which it was first postulated) offers guidelines for bounding a class's encumbrance by limiting its references to other classes.

The cohesion of a class is the measure of how well the components of the class (its methods and variables) belong together in a single class. A class departs from ideal cohesion if it has mixed-instance, mixed-domain, or mixed-role cohesion. (It may have more than one. See Exercise 4 below.)

A class with mixed-instance cohesion has components that are undefined for some objects instantiated from the class. A class with mixed-domain cohesion has a component that refers to an extrinsic class belonging to a different domain. A class with mixed-role cohesion has a component that refers to an extrinsic class belonging to the same domain.

Of the three types of cohesion above, mixed-instance cohesion results in the greatest design and maintenance problems, whereas mixed-role cohesion tends to result in the least.

9.5 Exercises

1. A class library that you purchase from a general class vendor will probably contain only foundation classes. Why do you think this is?

2. How should we handle inheritance when we compute encumbrance? For example, some class hierarchies emanate from a single root class (named, for example, OBJECT or ANY). Since every class in such a hierarchy inherits ultimately from OBJECT, doesn't this imply that the encumbrance of every class will be approximately equal?

3. Did the HOMINOID class of Chapter 1, as it was designed, have any cohesion problems? If so, suggest alternative designs for HOMINOID.

4. If a class may have mixed-instance, mixed-domain, or mixed-role cohesion, how many combinations of cohesion are possible for a class?

5. I once saw a class BANK-CUSTOMER with a method **gender**, which returned the gender of a customer. The method returned one of four possible values: **0** (customer's gender was unknown), **1** (male), **2** (female), and—this one took me by surprise—**3** (other!). It turned out that this last value was used for corporate bank customers, whose gender is undefined.

   What is the cohesion of BANK-CUSTOMER? What design change would you introduce to improve its cohesion?

6. If you have a collection of trigonometric methods, such as **tan**, **cos**, **sin**, and so on, you could make them instance methods of the class ANGLE. Methods such as **arctan**, **arccos**, **arcsin**, and so on, would be class methods of the class ANGLE, because they don't apply to individual instances of ANGLE. In what other way (other than as class and instance methods) could you gather all these methods into a single construct? (Hint: The construct appeared in Section 3.8.)

9.6 Answers

1. There are several reasons: First, most vendors aim for the maximum marketplace. By definition, foundation classes are useful to the widest possible group of industries and applications. Second, most foundation classes demand a knowledge of general computer science, rather than of any specific business. Thus, a typical class vendor can claim (with credibility) an understanding of foundation classes that's as good as anyone else's.

   Third—and this is the reason that most vendors' libraries *don't* contain business classes—business classes are difficult to analyze and often embody business policy and information that companies consider proprietary. Most companies aren't currently in the business of selling their business expertise as software classes to be reused. Nevertheless, I believe that this will change and that we'll see banking class libraries, telecommunication class libraries, medical class libraries, and so on, available in the commercial marketplace.

2. No. A class is unlikely to derive much of its encumbrance from a class high in the class-inheritance hierarchy for two reasons: First, inheritance is only one way in which a class refers to other classes; a class's encumbrance is due to many other kinds of reference, too. Second, the highest classes in a class-inheritance hierarchy tend to have low-to-medium encumbrance, because they refer to few other classes. Thus, the contribution of a class high in the hierarchy to the encumbrance of its subclasses isn't likely to be dramatic.

   Nevertheless, an alternative definition of encumbrance (which I saw a shop investigating recently) excludes from an indirect class-reference set of a class C any classes whose features aren't actually used by methods of C. This variety of encumbrance will yield a finer measure of C's encumbrance, but it's also more complicated to compute than the variety I describe in this chapter.

3. The HOMINOID class had mixed-domain cohesion, because it had a method **display** that presented a hominoid on a screen. Since HOMINOID is therefore mixed up with devices and their formats, we might even need a different version of HOMINOID for every architecture—printer, screen, plotter—around the shop.

   If that doesn't bother you (perhaps because portability and reusability are not issues), then okay. But if it does, then you should have HOMINOID return an object of class BIT-PATTERN or LINE-PATTERN. Then, you can send that object in a message to an output-device object, which would then display it.

   However, you may dislike the above design approach, because you may consider that exporting the bit-pattern representation of a hominoid shouldn't be part of the abstraction of HOMINOID. If so, you could write another class, DISPLAYABLE-HOMINOID, which inherits from HOMINOID as in Fig. 9.7.

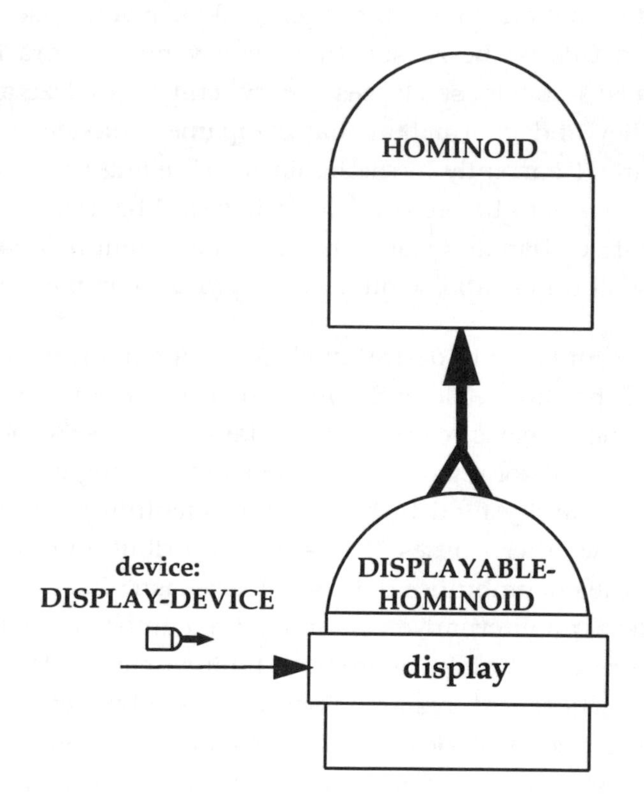

Fig. 9.7: The design of DISPLAYABLE-HOMINOID.

Notice that, in this design, I've used inheritance for the purpose of implementation (as indicated by the "little hat" symbol). Although I said in Section 8.2.5 that inheriting implementation isn't normally a good idea, it's useful here for this reason: We don't want to export any information on the appearance of a hominoid from HOMINOID and yet the method **display** needs access to that information, which is encapsulated within HOMINOID.

The disadvantage of this design is that I've tied the class DISPLAYABLE-HOMINOID tightly to the class HOMINOID. I will, therefore, have to ensure that any change made to the internal design of HOMINOID is reflected in DISPLAYABLE-HOMINOID.

Yet another design approach would be to separate the appearance of a hominoid from its other information and keep "hominoid appearance" in another class. I cover such a design approach in Section 11.1.4, when I discuss the design of the class ROOM.

4. Table 9.1 shows the six possible combinations of mixed-instance, mixed-domain, and mixed-role cohesion that a class may possess. The reason that there are six (rather than eight) combinations is that a class with mixed-domain cohesion must also have mixed-role cohesion, as combinations 3 and 6 of Table 9.1 indicate. The first combination represents ideal class cohesion. (In the table, the abbreviations MI, MD, and MR stand for mixed-instance, mixed-domain, and mixed-role cohesion.)

Table 9.1.
The Six Possible Combinations of Mixed-Instance, Mixed-Domain, and Mixed-Role Cohesion.

	MI	MD	MR
1.	N	N	N
2.	N	N	Y
3.	N	Y	Y
4.	Y	N	N
5.	Y	N	Y
6.	Y	Y	Y

5. BANK-CUSTOMER has mixed-instance cohesion, because one of its methods (**gender**) applies to only some of its instances (that is, only to objects representing *human* customers). The designer of this class should factor it into two subclasses, HUMAN-BANK-CUSTOMER and CORPORATE-BANK-CUSTOMER. The first subclass would have methods such as **gender** and **mothers-maiden-name**. The second subclass would have methods such as **corporation-type** and **num-of-shareholders**. The superclass, BANK-CUSTOMER, would have methods such as **customer-num** and **customer-name** (although corporate customers may have a different name format from human customers).

   Once these two subclasses have been factored out from BANK-CUSTOMER, all three classes will have ideal cohesion (so long as they don't have other cohesion problems, such as mixed-domain cohesion, of course).

6. You could group these methods together as a trigonometry package of functions, with signatures such as

   tan (angle: ANGLE): REAL;

   arctan (real: REAL): ANGLE;

   This design approach would also avoid the problem of mixed-domain cohesion that I pointed out in Section 9.3.2.

Properties of Classes and Subclasses

Chapter 10 investigates two fundamental properties of classes in order to determine what it takes to achieve sound design in class hierarchies. In the first section of the chapter, I introduce these two properties of classes: state-space and behavior. In the second section, I explore the state-spaces of subclasses; and then, in the third section, I analyze the behavior of subclasses.

The fourth section introduces class invariants as restrictions on state-spaces, and the fifth section explores method preconditions and postconditions, which together form the contract between a method and a client of that method. In the sixth section, I bring together the ideas of the previous sections to introduce the principle of type conformance.

The seventh section of this chapter applies the principle of type conformance to answer the question of what makes a subclass a subtype, a vital issue in the correct design and use of class hierarchies. Understanding subtypes in object-oriented systems is tricky because of the interaction among object orientation's three major sophistications: level-2 encapsulation, inheritance, and objects passed as message arguments. Fortunately, however, the ideas of preconditions, postconditions, and class invariants greatly clarify the important, but tricky, subject of subtypes.

The chapter's final section returns to the topic of subclass behavior, this time from the point of view of subtypes and type conformance, and presents the important principle of closed behavior in classes and subclasses.

10.1 State-Space and Behavior of a Class

A class should represent a uniform abstraction of the properties of the individual objects that belong to that class. Although that's a grand-sounding sentence, what do the words in it really mean?

By "abstraction" I mean that we don't necessarily have to consider *every* possible facet of the real-world things that are represented by software objects. For example, although we may have a class HUMAN-BANK-CUSTOMER, we don't have to include in that class information about a customer's head size (although of course we could if we wished to).

By "uniform" I mean that the abstraction we choose for a class applies in the same way to each of the objects belonging to the class. For example, if we're interested in date of birth for HUMAN-BANK-CUSTOMER, then we're interested in date of birth of *all* human bank customers.

By "properties" I mean simply this:

> The two *properties* of a class are its *state-space* and its allowed *behavior.*

Most of Chapter 10 is an exploration of the concepts of state-space and behavior and their practical implications for object-oriented design. But, before I formally define "state-space" and "behavior," let me illustrate these terms with a concrete example: a knight on a chessboard—that is, an object of class CHESS-KNIGHT—as in Fig. 10.1.

Fig. 10.1: A chessboard with a queen and a knight.

The total *state-space* of CHESS-KNIGHT amounts to every square on the board. Next consider the queen. The total state-space of CHESS-QUEEN is also every square on the board. Nevertheless, we know that the class CHESS-QUEEN is different from CHESS-KNIGHT. So, what's different? The answer is, her behavior.

The queen is permitted to move along any row, column, or diagonal to get to another square. Therefore, she can reach any other square on an empty board—that is, any other state in her state-space—in only two moves. The knight, on the other hand, with his peculiar behavior, may need up to six moves to reach a particular square.

Therefore, the classes CHESS-KNIGHT and CHESS-QUEEN have identical state-spaces but unlike behaviors. Let's imagine another kind of knight, one that moves like the traditional knight but is not allowed on the central four squares of the chessboard. (See Fig. 10.2.) So, why is this knight different? The answer is that, although he shares identical behavior with the traditional knight, his state-space differs.

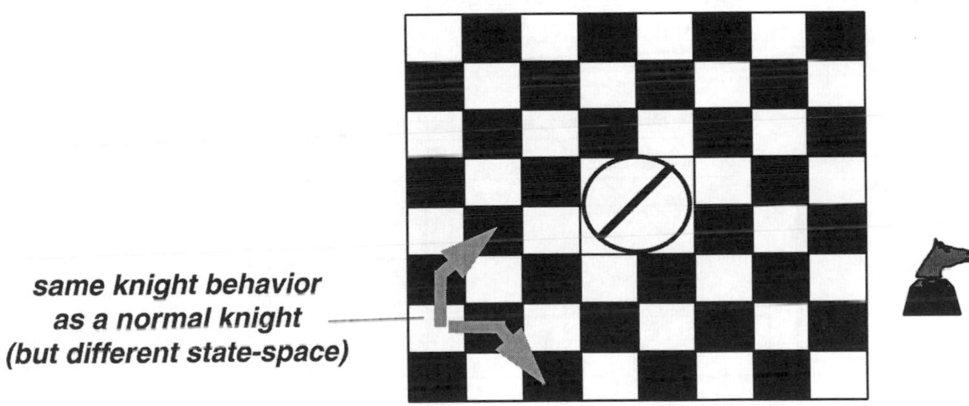

Fig. 10.2: A knight that's not permitted in the center of the board.

From the above, we see that two classes may differ either in their state-space or in their behavior (or both). Now, I'll define "state-space" more exactly. (In Section 10.3, I define "behavior.")

> The *state-space* of a class C is the ensemble of all the permitted states of any object of class C.
>
> The *dimensions* of a state-space are the coordinates needed to specify the state of a given object.

Informally, the state of an object is the "value" that it has at a given time. More properly, an object's state is the ordered set of objects to which the object refers at a given time. For example, the state of a SWIMMING-POOL object right now might be 30, 2, 25 (being meters long, meters deep, and temperature in Celsius, respectively). In other words, this SWIMMING-POOL object currently points to an object of class LENGTH (30 meters), another one of class LENGTH (2 meters) and one of class TEMPERATURE (25 degrees Celsius).

I picture a class's state-space as a grid of points, each point being a state. Each object that's an instance of the class is like a little dot, which spends its lifetime hopping around from place to place (from state to state) within the state-space of its class. A "hop from place to place" is known technically as a transition.

Figure 10.3 shows such a grid in three dimensions, the state-space for the class PRODUCT-LINE. (Although the state-space of the actual class may have many more dimensions, three is the most I can manage to draw!) The three dimensions that I've shown are **weight**, **price**, and **qty-available**. Since these three dimensions are mutually independent, an object (a given product line) may be found almost anywhere within the grid. Figure 10.3 shows several objects sitting as little dots within the PRODUCT-LINE grid.

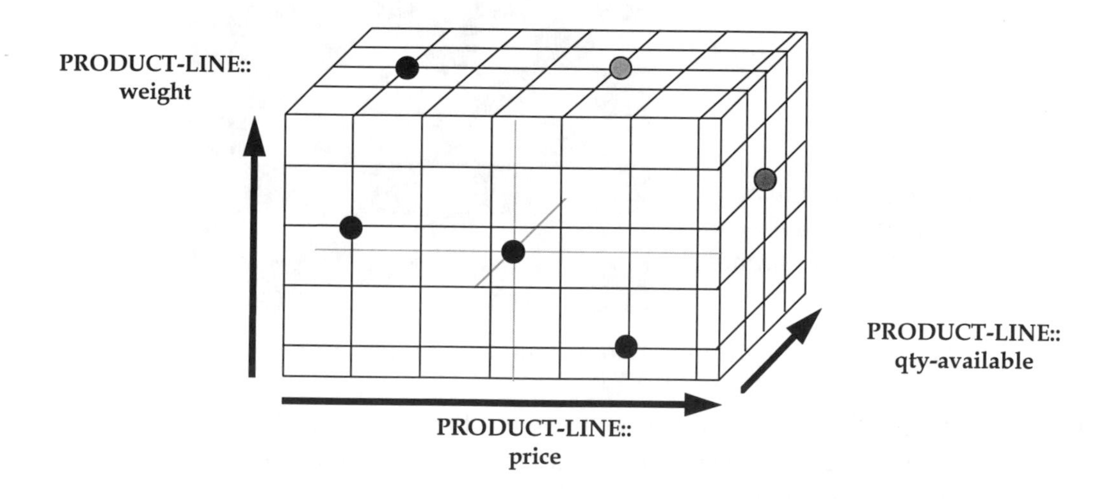

Fig. 10.3: The state-space of the class PRODUCT-LINE as a grid, with each product line as a "little dot."

As another example, the PATIENT class may have such dimensions as **age**, **height**, **weight**, **current-temperature**, and so on. A given PATIENT object may be at (almost!) any point in this multidimensional grid.

The dimensions of a state-space are, in effect, the attributes defined on a class. The values marking off the dimensions are the values that the attributes may take on. Since each dimension is itself of some class, the values along that dimension are objects of the dimension's class. For example, the **price** dimension of PRODUCT-LINE would be marked off with objects of class MONEY, and the **height** of a patient would be marked in inches or centimeters, objects of class LENGTH.

But the classes that mark dimensions aren't always from such a lowly domain as MONEY and LENGTH. For example, HAMMER's state-space has two dimensions—HANDLE and HEAD—because you make a hammer by selecting one handle and one head. Each of these classes is itself from the business domain and itself has several dimensions (such as **length**, **weight**, and so on).

10.2 The State-Space of a Subclass

This section begins our exploration into subclasses with a look at the state-spaces of two famous classes, A and B.

> If B is a subclass of A, then the state-space of B must be entirely contained within the state-space of A.[1] We say that B's state-space is a *confinement of* A's.

The best way to clarify this is with a more concrete example. Let's say that the class A is ROAD-VEHICLE. For simplicity, we'll assume that its state-space has only one dimension: **curr-weight**. We'll set lower and upper limits of, respectively, 0.5 tons and 10.0 tons on **ROAD-VEHICLE::curr-weight**.

Let's take the subclass B to be AUTOMOBILE. If we set lower and upper limits of, respectively, 1.0 tons and 3.0 tons on **AUTOMOBILE::curr-weight**, then we're in good shape. The state-space of AUTOMOBILE is confined within that of ROAD-VEHICLE and so AUTOMOBILE is legal as a subclass of ROAD-VEHICLE. Figure 10.4 shows the ranges of **ROAD-VEHICLE::curr-weight** and **AUTOMOBILE::curr-weight** graphically.

[1] Technically, it's the *projection* of B's state-space onto A's that must lie within A's state-space.

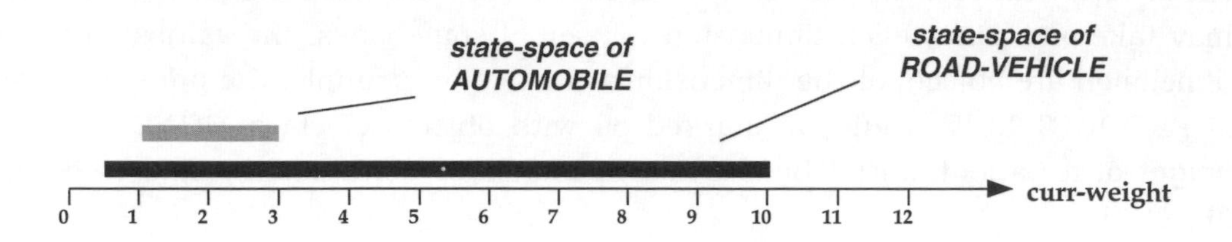

Fig. 10.4: The 1-D state-spaces of AUTOMOBILE and ROAD-VEHICLE.

However, had we set lower and upper limits of, respectively, 0.2 tons and 13.0 tons on **AUTOMOBILE::curr-weight**, then we'd be in trouble. The state-space of AUTOMOBILE wouldn't be confined within that of ROAD-VEHICLE, and so AUTOMOBILE couldn't be a subclass of ROAD-VEHICLE.

For instance, a 13-ton automobile couldn't be a legal road vehicle by the above definition of ROAD-VEHICLE. This state-space violation would allow an object to be a legal instance of its own class but to be illegal as an instance of the superclass. In other words, my car could be an automobile but not a road vehicle—an absurdity.

Ironically—and this surprises many people—the state-space of a subclass may have *more* dimensions than that of the superclass.

> If B is a subclass of A, then B's state-space must comprise at least the dimensions of A's—but may be made up of more. If it comprises more dimensions, we say that B's state-space *extends from* A's.

The state-space of AUTOMOBILE, for example, might have the dimension **AUTOMOBILE::curr-passenger-count**, which would not be a dimension of a general non-passenger road vehicle. If so, AUTOMOBILE's state-space would be an extension from ROAD-VEHICLE's.

Perhaps this has left you a little bewildered. How can a subclass' state-space both be *confined by* and *extend from* the state-space of its superclass? The answer is this: Within the dimensions defined on the superclass, the state-space of a subclass may be smaller than that of the superclass. But the subclass' state-space may at the same time extend into other dimensions that are undefined for the superclass.

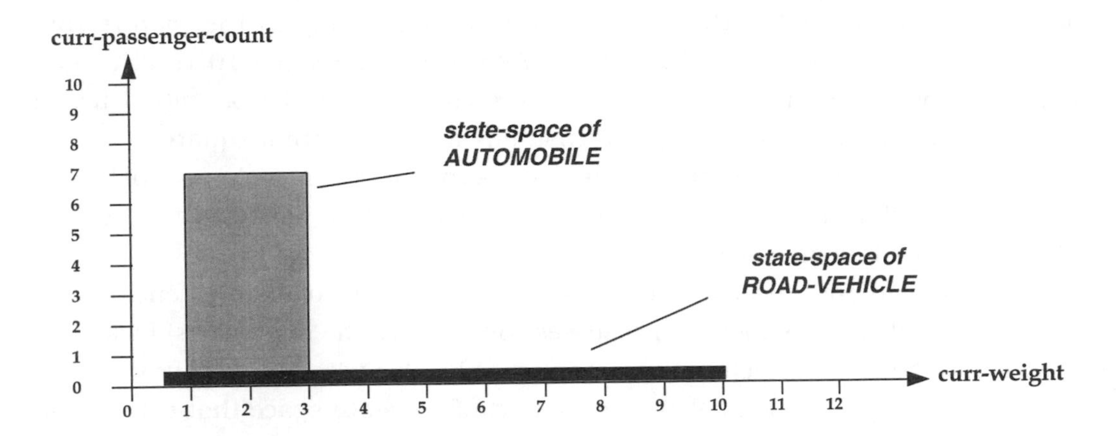

Fig. 10.5: The 2-D state-space of AUTOMOBILE and the 1-D state-space of ROAD-VEHICLE.

Figure 10.5 shows AUTOMOBILE's state-space simultaneously being confined by and extending from ROAD-VEHICLE's state-space. In the **curr-weight** dimension, AUTOMOBILE's state-space is still confined within ROAD-VEHICLE's, because **AUTOMOBILE::curr-weight**'s range still falls within **ROAD-VEHICLE::curr-weight**'s range.

Now, however, AUTOMOBILE has an extra dimension (**curr-passenger-count**) in its state-space. Thus, its state-space (shown as a gray area in Fig. 10.5) extends into that second dimension; specifically, as we see, an automobile may have zero to seven passengers aboard. For ROAD-VEHICLE, **curr-passenger-count** remains undefined.

10.3 The Behavior of a Subclass

Most objects (unless they're immutable) make transitions within their class's state-space as one or more of their attributes change value. These transitions constitute a class's allowed behavior, whose definition follows:

> The *behavior* of a class is the set of transitions that an object of the class is permitted to make between states in the state-space of the class.

This definition implies that not all possible transitions are legal for an object. An object hops around within the state-space of its class only in the manner prescribed for it by the behavior of the class. As we saw in Section 10.1, although a knight may be found on any of the 64 chessboard squares, its permitted transitions are quite limited (at most, eight transitions from its current square).

What about behavior in subclasses? Do superclass and subclass behaviors have a relationship like state-spaces do? Specifically, does behavior get extended and/or confined in a subclass?

The answer to both these questions is, Yes. First, let's consider extension, that is, behavior that B (the subclass) possesses, but that A (the superclass) lacks. It's obvious that such extra behavior in B must exist, for without it, how would an instance of B manage to leap about in the part of B's state-space that extends out from A's?

Let's return to ROAD-VEHICLE and its subclass AUTOMOBILE as our example. AUTOMOBILE will have behavior such as **pick-up-passenger** and **drop-off-passenger**, to allow it to increase and decrease its number of passengers. This behavior is clearly beyond any behavior that ROAD-VEHICLE may have; after all, ROAD-VEHICLE doesn't even have a notion of passengers!

(To put it more technically: ROAD-VEHICLE lacks the dimension of **curr-passenger-count** in its state-space. Therefore, any behavior that lets an object mosey around in the **curr-passenger-count** dimension couldn't possibly be defined on ROAD-VEHICLE.)

This example shows that AUTOMOBILE may *extend* the behavior of its superclass, ROAD-VEHICLE, just as AUTOMOBILE extended the state-space of ROAD-VEHICLE.

AUTOMOBILE's behavior may also be *confined by* the behavior of ROAD-VEHICLE, just as AUTOMOBILE's state-space was confined by the state-space of ROAD-VEHICLE. A simple example would be the fact that we can usually add five tons to the weight of many road vehicles (which have a limit of ten tons), whereas we can never add five tons to an automobile's weight (which has a limit of three tons).

In Section 10.8, I return to behavior confinement, whose implications lead to an important principle in the design of bulletproof subclasses: closed behavior.

10.4 The Class Invariant As a Restriction on a State-Space

Most of the state-spaces that we've looked at in this chapter have been complete in the sense that an object may occupy any of the places in the state-space grid. However, many classes don't allow their objects such free rein. We saw one such restriction in Fig. 10.2's example of the knight that had to keep out of the middle. In Section 10.4, we look at how to define legal state-spaces more precisely.

The legal state-space of a class is defined by its class invariant.

> A *class invariant* is a condition that every object of that class must satisfy at all times (when the object is in equilibrium).

The expression "when the object is in equilibrium" means that an object must obey its class invariant at all times when it's not in the middle of changing states. In particular, an object must toe the invariant line when the object is initialized at instantiation, and before and after any (public) method is executed.

Let's take as an example the class TRIANGLE.[2] If the sides of a triangle are **TRIANGLE::a**, **TRIANGLE::b**, **TRIANGLE::c**, then part of TRIANGLE's class invariant would be

$$a + b \geq c \textbf{ and } b + c \geq a \textbf{ and } c + a \geq b$$

This says that, no matter what object of class TRIANGLE we have, the sum of the lengths of any two of its sides must be greater than or equal to the length of its third side. (No doubt you can come up with several other, similar constraints on TRIANGLE.)

The three-dimensional grid of Fig. 10.6 (with axes labeled **a**, **b**, and **c**) represents the state-space of TRIANGLE. But that's not strictly true; it's an overstatement. Only some of the points in the grid—the ones that satisfy the above invariant for TRIANGLE—belong to TRIANGLE's true state-space. For example, we couldn't have a triangle with sides of 1, 2, and 5.

---

[2] To keep this example simple, I'll ignore the position and orientation of triangles and concentrate on their size.

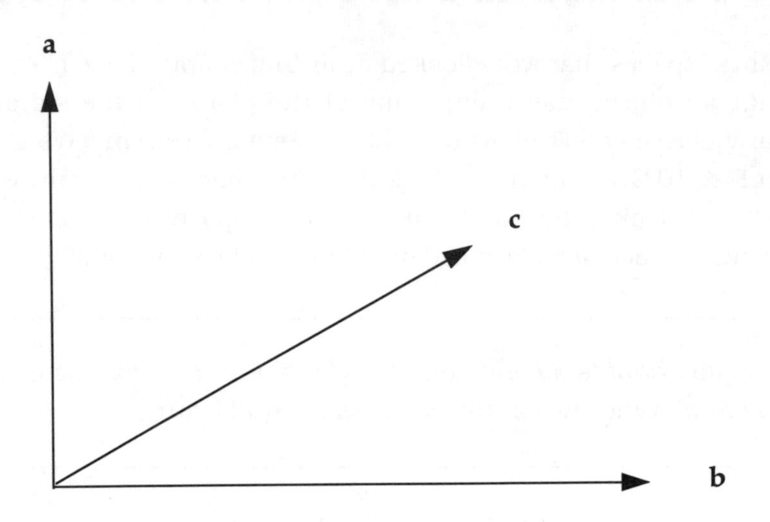

Fig. 10.6: The 3-D state-space of TRIANGLE—but not all positions represent valid triangles!

Figure 10.7 shows a hierarchy of triangle varieties. The class ISOSCELES-TRIANGLE has the invariant

a = b **or** b = c **or** c = a

and the class RIGHT-TRIANGLE has the invariant (due to the late Mr. Pythagoras)

a * a + b * b = c * c // I assume for simplicity that **c** is the hypotenuse[3]

[3] See Exercise 5 for more details.

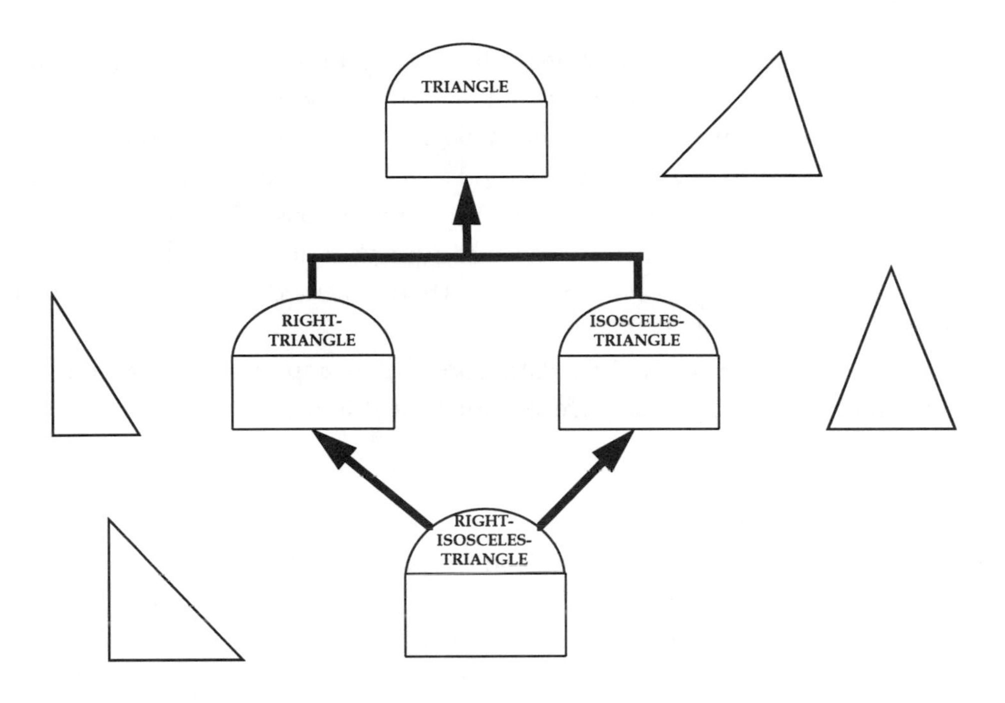

Fig. 10.7: Four varieties of triangle.

Because invariants are inherited, a given class must obey the invariant(s) of its superclass(es). So, since both ISOSCELES-TRIANGLE and RIGHT-TRIANGLE are subclasses of TRIANGLE, they also inherit the invariant

$a + b \geq c$ **and** $b + c \geq a$ **and** $c + a \geq b$

Therefore, ISOSCELES-TRIANGLE objects will always obey this entire invariant:

($a + b \geq c$ **and** $b + c \geq a$ **and** $c + a \geq b$)
and ($a = b$ **or** $b = c$ **or** $c = a$)

To pursue this further, the class RIGHT-ISOSCELES-TRIANGLE (which inherits both from RIGHT-TRIANGLE and ISOSCELES-TRIANGLE) has a state-space made up of points that are legal for *both* RIGHT-TRIANGLE and ISOSCELES-TRIANGLE. Its class invariant is therefore the logical **and** of the invariants of RIGHT-TRIANGLE and ISOSCELES-TRIANGLE, namely:

($a + b \geq c$ **and** $b + c \geq a$ **and** $c + a \geq b$)
and $a * a + b * b = c * c$
and ($a = b$ **or** $b = c$ **or** $c = a$)

10.5 Preconditions and Postconditions

So far, we've looked chiefly at the rules—the invariants—governing classes as a whole. Now, let's turn to the conditions that govern *individual methods*.

Every method has a *precondition* and a *postcondition*. The precondition is a condition that must be true when the method begins to execute. If it is not true, then the method may legitimately refuse to execute and possibly raise some exception condition. The postcondition is a condition that must be true when the method ends its execution. If it is not true, then the method has a defect and must be redesigned or recoded.

Take, for example, the method **STACK::pop**, which pops the top element off a normal last-in, first-out stack. The precondition for this method is

not empty

If the precondition of a method is met, then the method must ensure that, at the point at which the method ends its execution, the method's postcondition will be met. For example, the postcondition for **pop** might be

num-elements = **old** num-elements - 1 **and not** full

wherein the keyword **old** means "whatever value this had before the method began executing."

Bertrand Meyer and others describe the pre- and postconditions of a method as a contract between a method and a client who sends a message to that method.[4] The metaphor of the contract implies that

1. If the sender of the message can guarantee that the precondition is true, then the target method will guarantee that the postcondition will be true after execution.

2. If, on the other hand, the sender of the message cannot guarantee that the precondition is true, then the whole deal is off: The method is neither obliged to execute nor to guarantee the postcondition.

---

[4] See, for example, [Meyer, 1988], [Meyer, 1992], or [Wiener, 1995].

Remember that the class invariant is true both when a method begins and when it ends. So the full story of pre- and postconditions is that a method is sandwiched between two compound conditions, like this:

Class invariant **and** method precondition

Method executes

Class invariant **and** method postcondition

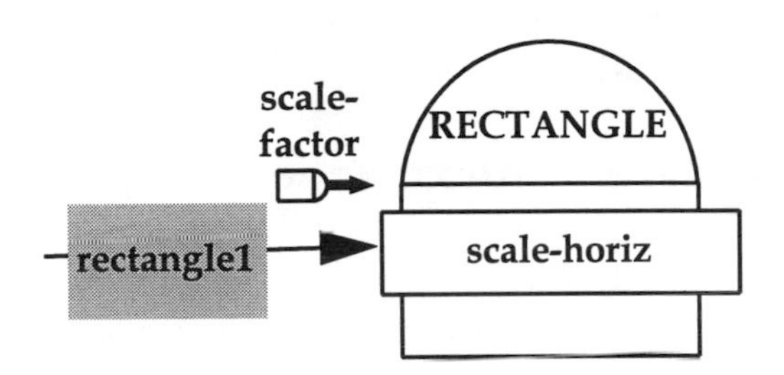

Fig. 10.8: **RECTANGLE::scale-horiz.**

As an example, let's take the method **scale-horiz**, defined on the class RECTANGLE. (The method, which appears in Fig. 10.8, stretches or shrinks a rectangle's horizontal width by a multiplicative factor and takes one argument, **scale-factor**.) Let's assume that the rectangle has sides **w1**, **h1**, **w2**, and **h2**. Its class invariant will be **w1=w2 and h1=h2**.[5]

A precondition on **scale-horiz** will be

max-allowed-width ≥ w1 * scale-factor

The obvious postcondition will be

w1 = **old** w1 * scale-factor

[5] You may wonder why my RECTANGLE class has all *four* sides of a rectangle, when just **width** and **height** would do. I do so to provide a simple example of a class invariant. In Sections 12.1 and 12.2, I look in detail at several designs for RECTANGLE.

Taking everything together gives

```
w1=w2 and h1=h2 and max-allowed-width ≥ w1 * scale-factor
                                                  // complete precondition
    scale-horiz (scale-factor;)                   // the method
w1=w2 and h1=h2 and w1 = old w1 * scale-factor    // complete postcondition
```

Needless to say, no one ever actually writes out the class invariant as part of every method pre- and postcondition: That would be tedious and redundant. Nevertheless, the class invariant is there implicitly and you should take it into account when you design a method to work correctly.

10.6 The Principle of Type Conformance

A robust class hierarchy is heavy-duty and a joy forever. A miserably designed one may be an albatross that brings a premature end to your project and even to object orientation in your shop. The design principle of type conformance is extremely important in creating the hierarchies of reliable and robust classes that form your class library.[6]

The principle of type conformance comes from the theory of abstract datatypes, upon which object orientation is founded.

> The *principle of type conformance* states that, if S is a true subtype of T, then S must *conform* to T.
>
> Type S *conforms* to type T if an object of type S can be provided in any context where an object of type T is expected and correctness is still preserved when any accessor method is executed.

[6] For more on the principle of type conformance in an object-oriented environment, see [Meyer, 1992] and [LaLonde and Pugh, 1991]. The principle of type conformance is very similar to what authors such as Barbara Liskov term the principle of substitutability [Liskov et al., 1981].

For example, CIRCLE is a subtype of ELLIPSE. Any object that's a circle is also an ellipse—a very round ellipse. So, any method that's expecting to receive an ellipse as an argument in a message should be very happy to get a circle.[7]

But how does this apply to classes and subclasses? The best way to think of a class is as the implementation of a type, which is the abstract or external view of a class. In other words, type includes the purpose of the class, together with its state-space and behavior. (Specifically, the type of a class is defined by the following components: the purpose of the class; the class invariant; the methods of the class; and the methods' preconditions, postconditions, definitions, and signatures.)

A class *in toto*, however, entails an internal design, as well as a type. The internal design, as we saw in Chapter 1, includes the private variables of the class and the code of its algorithms. Indeed, a single type may be implemented as several classes, each class having its own particular internal design.

You might create several classes of the same type in order to give each class its own efficiency advantage in some special circumstance. For example, one design of ORDERED-COLLECTION might have very efficient traversals, while another might have very efficient insertions and deletions. Yet, both versions of ORDERED-COLLECTION would implement the same type.

Although type represents the outside guise of a class, a subtype isn't necessarily the same as a subclass. The proof of this is straightforward, because I can come up with two counterexamples to indicate the difference.

First, I'll show that a subclass isn't necessarily a subtype. Syntactically, any class can be made a subclass of any other. For instance, you could make ELEPHANT inherit from RECTANGLE and SALES-REP inherit from BRICK. Although these *are* legal class/subclass structures, they are, of course, semantic nonsense because the subclasses aren't subtypes of their respective superclasses.

For example, it would make no sense to apply Pythagoras to an elephant in order to find its diagonal! And a **post-commission** method wouldn't be very happy to get a piece of building material as an argument when it was expecting a sales representative. (Most customers wouldn't be happy either, although I concede that some sales representatives are indistinguishable from large pieces of building material.)

Next I'll show the converse, that a subtype needn't be a subclass. In a language without a superclass/subclass inheritance construct, you can still design

[7] Of course, this doesn't work if the method tries to stretch the circle! This explains the caveat "when any *accessor* method is executed" (which implies that no object changes state) in my definition of conformance. I address this restriction in detail in Section 10.8.

and implement subtypes by hand (by tediously duplicating code) so long as you take care to obey the principle of type conformance.

10.7 Subclasses As Subtypes

I spent the last few paragraphs explaining that a subclass and a subtype are distinct concepts. Now, however, I'm going to turn around and say:

> In a sound object-oriented design, the class/subclass inheritance hierarchy should follow the type/subtype hierarchy. Therefore, you should design each subclass to be a subtype of its superclass; it should follow the principle of type conformance.

But how do we ensure that a subclass is a true, honest, and upright subtype? I'd like to examine in some detail just what you have to do to make the type of a subclass conform to the type of its superclass. To do that, I'll make use of the notions of class invariants, method preconditions and postconditions, state-space, and behavior, all of which we've covered in this chapter.

> MENTAL HEALTH WARNING: The concepts of Section 10.7 are important, but counterintuitive on first reading. Be prepared to read this section twice. When I first encountered these concepts, I had to think about them *three* times before they made sense.

To ensure type conformance in a subclass, you first need to ensure that the invariant of the subclass is at least as strong as that of the superclass. For example, RECTANGLE has the invariant **w1=w2 and h1=h2**. SQUARE has the invariant **w1=w2 and h1=h2 and w1=h1**. That's okay, because SQUARE's invariant is stronger than RECTANGLE's. (In other words, an object that meets SQUARE's invariant is bound to meet RECTANGLE's; an object that meets RECTANGLE's invariant may not meet SQUARE's.)

Second, you need to ensure the following three constraints on methods:

1. Every method of the superclass has a corresponding method in the subclass with the same name and signature.

2. Every method's precondition is no stronger than the corresponding method in the superclass. This is called the *principle of contravariance*, so named because the strength of method preconditions in the subclass goes in the *opposite* direction to the strength of the class invariant. That is, the methods' preconditions get, if anything, weaker.

3. Every method's postcondition is at least as strong as the corresponding method in the superclass. This is called the *principle of covariance*, so named because the strength of method postconditions in the subclass goes in the *same* direction as the strength of the class invariant. That is, the methods' postconditions get, if anything, stronger.

Incidentally, the terms "stronger" and "weaker" in the above constraints don't describe quality or robustness in any way. "Stronger" isn't "better" and "weaker" doesn't mean "worse."

These constraints are trivially satisfied if a subclass inherits a method *as is* from its superclass: Then, the name and signature and pre- and postconditions are identical in both the superclass and the subclass. More interesting issues arise when the subclass overrides a superclass' method with a method of its own, as in the following example.

The class EMPLOYEE has a subclass MANAGER. (Yes, managers comprise a subclass of employees!) What must we do to ensure that MANAGER is a valid subtype of EMPLOYEE?

First, let's say that an invariant of EMPLOYEE is **grade-level > 0** and an invariant of MANAGER is **grade-level > 20**. That makes MANAGER's class invariant stronger than EMPLOYEE's, so we're in good shape there.

Second, let's consider **calc-bonus**, a method of EMPLOYEE. The method takes a performance evaluation and calculates a bonus, which is a percentage of the employee's regular salary. The OODN of Fig. 10.9 shows the method's signature.

We'll say for simplicity that the passed argument, **perf-eval**, is an integer between 0 and +5. The return argument, **bonus-pct**, is between 0 and 10 percent.

The algorithms to compute bonuses may be different for managers and non-managers. Therefore, the class MANAGER may override **calc-bonus** with a method of its own (with the same name and signature).

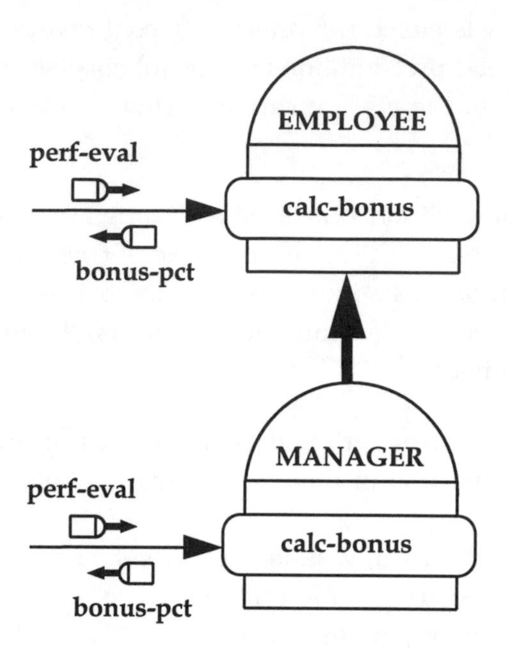

Fig. 10.9: OODN for **calc-bonus (perf-eval; bonus-pct)**, *defined on EMPLOYEE and MANAGER.*

Now let's turn to **MANAGER::calc-bonus**. Remember that, for MANAGER to conform to EMPLOYEE, **MANAGER::calc-bonus** must have a precondition equal to or weaker than **EMPLOYEE::calc-bonus**. This means, in particular, that the range of **MANAGER::calc-bonus'** input argument **perf-eval** must be equal to or larger than the range of **EMPLOYEE::calc-bonus'** input argument **perf-eval**. (To help me remember that "larger range = weaker condition," I think of "larger" as "looser" or "weaker," and "smaller" as "tighter" or "stronger.")

Therefore, each of the following ranges for **MANAGER::calc-bonus'** input argument **perf-eval** would be legal:

```
 0 to 5   // equal in both classes MANAGER and EMPLOYEE
 0 to 8   // larger (weaker) in MANAGER
-1 to 9   // larger (weaker) in MANAGER (assuming a
          // negative evaluation makes sense!)
```

Conversely, the following ranges for **MANAGER::calc-bonus'** input argument **perf-eval** would be illegal:

1 to 5   *// smaller (stronger) in MANAGER*
2 to 4   *// even smaller (stronger) in MANAGER*

Figure 10.10 shows the legal and illegal ranges for **perf-eval** in graphic form.

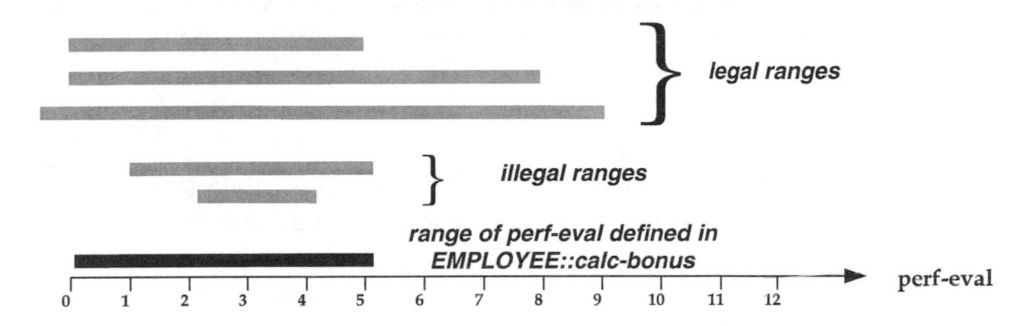

Fig. 10.10: Contravariance: possible ranges for **perf-eval** *in* **MANAGER::calc-bonus (perf-eval; bonus-pct).**

For MANAGER to conform to EMPLOYEE, **MANAGER::calc-bonus** must have a postcondition equal to or stronger than **EMPLOYEE::calc-bonus**. This means, in particular, that the range of **MANAGER::calc-bonus'** output argument **bonus-pct** must be equal to or less than the range of **EMPLOYEE::calc-bonus'** output argument **bonus-pct**.

Therefore, each of the following ranges for **MANAGER::calc-bonus'** output argument **bonus-pct** would be legal:

0% to 10%   *// equal in both classes MANAGER and EMPLOYEE*
0% to 6%   *// smaller (stronger) in MANAGER*
2% to 4%   *// even smaller (stronger) in MANAGER*

Conversely, each of the following ranges for **MANAGER::calc-bonus'** output argument **bonus-pct** would be illegal:

0% to 12%   *// larger (weaker) in MANAGER*
-1% to 13%   *// larger (weaker) in MANAGER (assuming a*
// negative evaluation makes sense!)

Figure 10.11 shows the legal and illegal ranges for **bonus-pct** in graphic form.

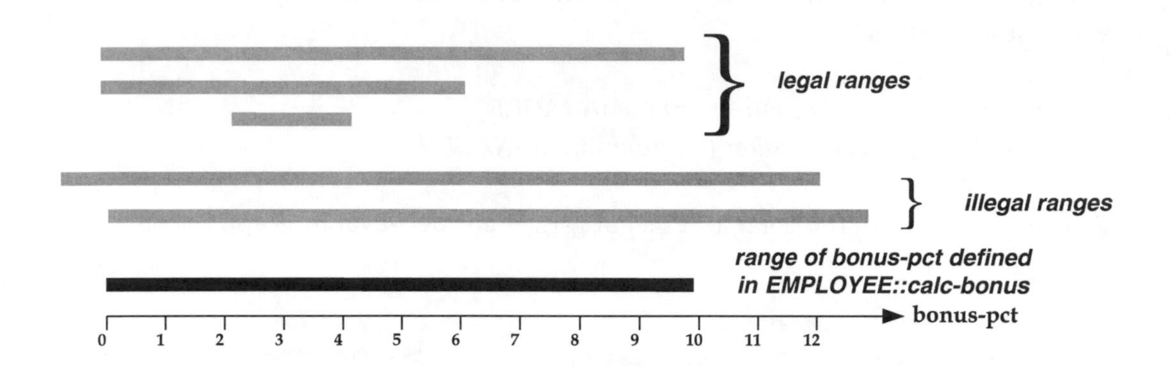

Fig. 10.11: Covariance: possible ranges for **bonus-pct** *in* **MANAGER::calc-bonus (perf-eval; bonus-pct).**

The principles of weaker preconditions and stronger postconditions in subclasses' methods aren't intuitive (to say the least!). Indeed, when I present them in seminars, I leave my car engine running in case I need to make a quick getaway from infuriated students. So, I think I should explain further *why* these principles are important to you when you design your class hierarchy correctly to follow a true type hierarchy.

The importance of type conformance stems from the nature of second-order design, which means that a message argument in an object-oriented system, being an object, carries "the entire genetic code of its class" along with it.[8] For example, let's assume that we pass, one at a time, each object representing an employee to a method (**conduct-year-end-review**) that conducts a year-end review of the employee. **Conduct-year-end-review** figures out a value for **perf-eval** (the evaluation of the employee's performance), and then sends a message to the object pointed to by **emp** to carry out the object's method **calc-bonus**.

[8] Second-order design arises when message arguments have level-2 encapsulation—in other words, when message arguments are (references to) objects. In first-order design, software components communicate by passing arguments with level-1 encapsulation (functions or procedures). In zeroth-order design, arguments are simply data. (Structured design is mainly zeroth-order design, with some first-order design occurring where procedures are passed as arguments.)

Textually, this message would be **emp.calc-bonus (perf-eval; bonus-pct)**. I show it in OODN in Fig. 10.12.[9]

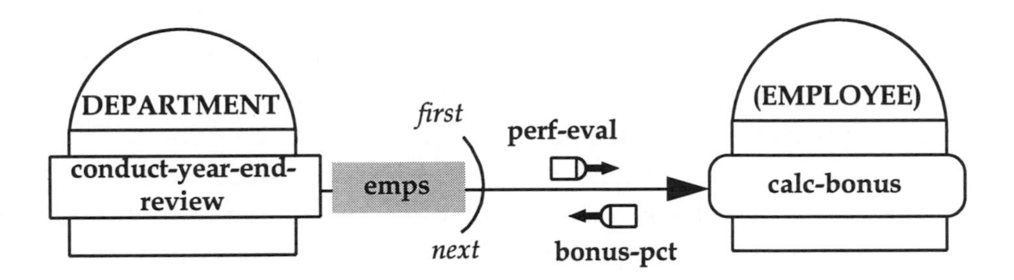

Fig. 10.12: **Conduct-year-end-review** *invoking* **calc-bonus** *on each* **emp** *object (a given* **emp** *may be either of class EMPLOYEE or of its subclass, MANAGER).*

When the method **conduct-year-end-review** gets the next object (which I'll term **emp**) from a list of employees (termed **emps**), all this method knows is that it has hold of some kind of employee, either an ordinary employee or a manager. But **conduct-year-end-review** doesn't worry about what kind of employee it has; the method knows that, through the miracle of polymorphism, when the **emp** object gets the message **emp.calc-bonus (perf-eval; bonus-pct)**, the object will respond correctly.

The method **conduct-year-end-review** also knows **calc-bonus'** precondition, the rule for using **calc-bonus** correctly: So long as **perf-eval** is between 0 and 5, **calc-**

[9] A note on the notation: The message is sent iteratively to each employee in a list of employees for a department. The parentheses around EMPLOYEE (as shown in Fig. 10.12) signify that polymorphism is at work and that the sender of the message doesn't know which version of **calc-bonus** will be used to satisfy the message.

bonus will work fine. But let's assume that we violated type conformance by *strengthening* the acceptable range for **MANAGER::calc-bonus**' input argument, **perf-eval**, to range from 2 to 4. Then, if **conduct-year-end-review** innocently sends **perf-eval=1** to an object that happens to be a manager, then **calc-bonus** would blow up, complaining that the passed **perf-eval** was out of range.

If, on the other hand, we followed the type-conformance principle and *weakened* the acceptable range for **MANAGER::calc-bonus'** input argument, **perf-eval**, to 0 to 8, we'd have no problem. Then, whatever **MANAGER::calc-bonus** received for **perf-eval** in the range 0 to 5, it could handle without skipping a beat.

The inverse applies to the postcondition. Here, if we violated the conformance principle of stronger postconditions, it would be **conduct-year-end-review** that would suffer. Let's say we *weaken* the acceptable range for the output argument, **bonus-pct**, to the range –1 to 12 percent. Since the range for employees is supposed to be 0 to 10 percent, **conduct-year-end-review** would be taken completely by surprise to get a negative number returned to it. It might even be so surprised that it would blow up.

To summarize this principle: The principle of type conformance demands that for a subclass S to be a true subtype of the class T, the following six constraints are necessary. (The first two apply to whole classes; the last four apply to individual methods.)

1. The state-space of S must have the same dimensions as T. (But S may have additional dimensions that extend from T's state-space.)

2. In the dimensions that S and T share, the state-space of S must either be equal to or lie within the state-space of T. (Another way to say this is, The class invariant of S must be equal to or stronger than that of T.)

For each method of T (say, **T::m**) that S overrides with **S::m**:

3. **S::m** must have the same name as **T::m**.

4. **S::m**'s formal signature must list its arguments in the same order as **T::m**'s formal signature.

5. The precondition of **S::m** must be equal to or weaker than that of **T::m**. In particular, each formal input argument to **S::m** must be a supertype of (or the same type as) the corresponding formal input argument to **T::m**. (This is the principle of contravariance.)

6. The postcondition of **S::m** must be equal to or stronger than that of **T::m**. In particular, each formal output argument from **S::m** must be a subtype of (or the

same type as) the corresponding formal output argument from **T::m**. (This is the principle of covariance.)

10.8 The Principle of Closed Behavior

In the preceding sections, we looked at the principle of type conformance. Although respecting type conformance is necessary for us to be able to design sound class hierarchies, type conformance isn't enough. Informally speaking, type conformance alone leads to sound designs only in read-only situations, that is, only when accessor methods are executed. (Perhaps you recall the fine print "when any accessor method is executed" in Section 10.6's definition of type conformance.)

To handle situations in which modifier methods are executed, we also need the *principle of closed behavior*. This principle requires that the behavior inherited by a subclass from a superclass should respect the invariant of the subclass. Without this principle, we may design subclasses with modifier methods that have error-prone behavior.

> In an inheritance hierarchy based on a type/subtype hierarchy, the behavior of each class—including the inherited behavior of its superclass(es)—should obey the invariant of the class when any method (modifier or accessor) is executed. This is the *principle of closed behavior.*

As an example of the principle of closed behavior, let's look at how behavior defined on a superclass POLYGON might affect objects of a subclass TRIANGLE. It's important to remember, as we go through this example, that the behavior in each of the two cases below is behavior defined in a method of POLYGON.

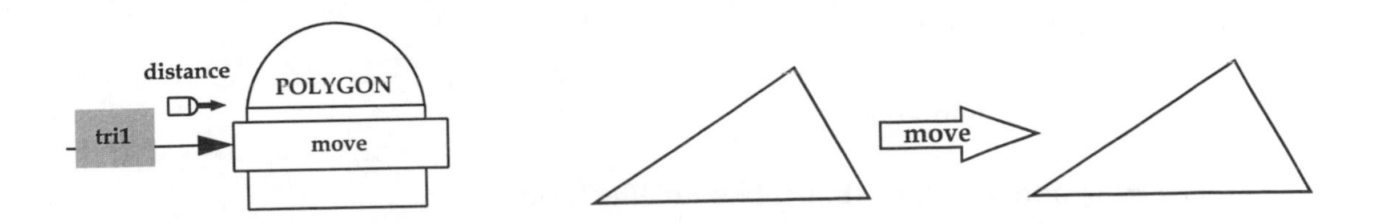

Fig. 10.13: **POLYGON::move**, *as applied to the triangle* **tri1**, *preserves its "triangle-ness."*

Case 1: For this, we'll take the object **tri1** to be the triangle of Fig. 10.13, and the method to be POLYGON's method **move**, which causes an object to move to the right by, say, a centimeter.

After the move, **tri1** is still a triangle. This piece of POLYGON's behavior leaves an object that's in the state-space of TRIANGLE in that same state-space. We say that the subclass TRIANGLE is *closed* under the behavior defined by the superclass' method **move**.

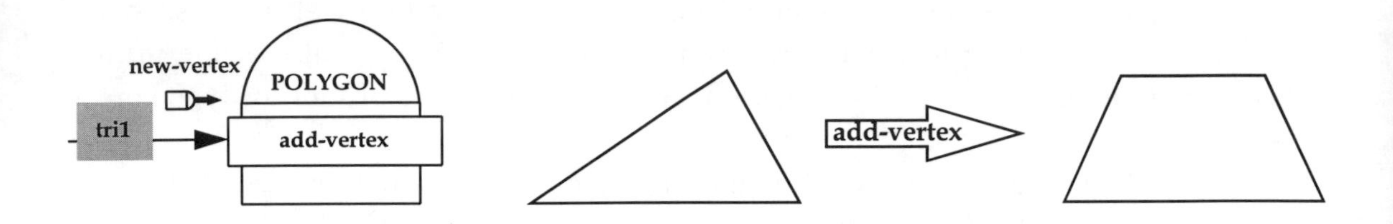

Fig. 10.14: **POLYGON::add-vertex**, *(wrongly!) applied to the triangle* **tri1**, *destroys its triangular property.*

Case 2: Again we'll take **tri1** to be a triangle. However, this time we'll consider a method **add-vertex** that adds a vertex to a polygon. (See Fig. 10.14.) After this transition, **tri1** won't be a triangle; it will be a quadrilateral. TRIANGLE is not closed under the behavior defined by POLYGON's method **add-vertex**.

Closure of a subclass under its superclasses' behavior doesn't happen automatically, as we saw in the example of Case 2. You have to "design it in." Therefore, as the designer of a subclass, you must often deliberately and explicitly override methods of the superclass that would otherwise violate the invariant of the subclass.

In this example, as the designer of TRIANGLE, you must take one of the following three corrective actions:

- Do not inherit **add-vertex**, or
- Override **add-vertex** so that it has no effect, or
- Be prepared to reclassify the TRIANGLE object as RECTANGLE, if that

behavior, which *doesn't* preserve TRIANGLE's closure, is acceptable to the application.[10]

In general, the designer of a class has the duty to ensure the class's closure of behavior. Designers of other classes shouldn't have to worry about maintaining the invariant of the class.

However, it never hurts to check. If you're designing a class that sends a message to an object to invoke a modifier method, you should check for closure of behavior on the target's class. If you send the message assuming the general (superclass) case, you must be prepared for the object to refuse the message or simply to return without any action. If this is a problem, then before you send the message you need to do one of the following:

- Check the run-time class of the target, or
- Restrict polymorphism on the variable that points to the target, or
- Design the message on the assumption that the target is of the most specific, lowest class in the relevant hierarchy, that is, the class with the greatest constraint on its behavior.

In the next chapter, we'll use the concepts and principles of this chapter to examine specific problems that arise from inheritance, polymorphism, and genericity.

[10] See also Exercises 6 and 7, which follow up this last point.

10.9 Summary

The properties of a class A are its state-space and its allowed behavior. The state-space is the ensemble of the states permitted to an object of class A. The dimensions of a state-space are the coordinates needed to specify an object's state. The allowed behavior of A is the set of transitions in A's state-space that an object is legally able to make.

If B is a subclass of A, then B's state-space must be entirely confined within A's. However, B's state-space may extend from A's, which means that it has dimensions that A's state-space lacks. Similarly, B's behavior may be both a confinement and an extension of A's behavior.

Every object of a given class must satisfy the class's invariant. This invariant acts as a constraint, limiting the size of the class's state-space. A subclass both inherits the class invariant(s) of its superclass(es) and adds a further restriction of its own.

Each method of a class has a precondition and a postcondition, which together form a contract between the method and a client of that method. The precondition states what must be true for the method to execute. The postcondition states what will be true when the method has completed execution. Formally speaking, the class invariant is part of every method's pre- and postconditions. (Practically speaking, however, no one actually writes the class invariant as part of pre- and postconditions.)

If class B is a true subtype of class A, then B must conform to A. That is, in any context in which an object of class A is expected and no modifier method will be executed, an object of class B will be acceptable. A sound superclass/subclass hierarchy will follow a supertype/subtype hierarchy.

To achieve this, you must ensure that: The invariant of each subclass is at least as strong as that of its superclass; each superclass method has a corresponding method in the subclass with the same name and signature; each subclass method's precondition is no stronger than the corresponding method in the superclass; and each subclass method's postcondition is at least as strong as the corresponding method in the superclass. These last two principles are termed, respectively, the principle of contravariance and the principle of covariance; they are very important in determining the correct classes for arguments of subclass methods.

Finally, each class in a sound class hierarchy will obey the principle of closed behavior. This requires that the behavior that a subclass inherits from superclass(es) must respect the subclass' invariant. A subclass designer may achieve this by: not allowing inheritance of conflicting behavior; overriding inherited methods that have conflicting behavior; or migrating to another class an object that has violated its class invariant.

You may have found some of the topics in this chapter to be difficult or abstruse. But if you refer to them continually as you build class hierarchies and design object-oriented code, you'll find that they soon become second nature to you. Fortunately, you'll also find that ninety percent of the object-oriented design situations you face are straightforward and don't call for deep design knowledge. But when you do run into that awkward ten percent, knowing the principles of this chapter will set you apart from the object-oriented herd.

10.10 Exercises

1. Assume a class VISA-ACCOUNT with two dimensions (among others) named **current-balance** and **credit-limit**. Why don't we simply name these dimensions, or "attributes," after their class, MONEY?

2. What is the dimensionality of the class RECTANGLE's state-space? In other words, how many dimensions does RECTANGLE have? Before you answer, "Two—height and width. That's easy!" let me point out that the question is undefined until you have a good idea of what abstraction RECTANGLE actually represents. So, let me define RECTANGLE to be a class whose objects are rectangles that may rotate, stretch in height and width, and wander around the plane.

   So, how many dimensions does the class RECTANGLE, with the above definition, have? In other words, how many degrees of freedom does each RECTANGLE object have? If you were to design the internal implementation of RECTANGLE, how many degrees of freedom would your internal design permit? Could this number be different from your first answer? If so, why?

3. What if, in Section 10.7's example of the EMPLOYEE class with the subclass MANAGER, you couldn't make **calc-bonus**' precondition at least as weak and its postcondition at least as strong in the subclass? (For example, the users' business demands may drown out the cries of your design conscience.) Since that would mean that MANAGER isn't a true subtype of EMPLOYEE, should you then revamp your class structure accordingly?

4. How can the behavior of a subclass be considered more constrained (with respect to its superclass) if a subclass may have extra dimensions in its state-space that its superclasses do not?

5. The class invariants for the classes RIGHT-TRIANGLE, ISOSCELES-TRIANGLE, and RIGHT-ISOSCELES-TRIANGLE were complex and also similar to one another. Could you factor out the similarities in some way and thereby also simplify the expression of the invariants?

6. Take the class RECTANGLE and consider one of its methods, **rotate**, which rotates a rectangle in its plane by some angle:

   rotate (rotation-angle;)

   After the rotation, a rectangle is still a rectangle; the same class invariant still applies. Consider also SQUARE, a subclass of RECTANGLE. It inherits the method **rotate**. After a square is rotated, it also remains a square and obeys its class invariant. No problem!

But now take another method of RECTANGLE, **scale-horiz**, which stretches a rectangle in one dimension:

scale-horiz (scale-factor;)

A stretched rectangle is still a rectangle. But a stretched square is no longer a square! The class invariant **w1=h1** is broken. The behavior prescribed by **scale-horiz** keeps a rectangle within the state-space of its class, but it doesn't keep a square within its state-space. RECTANGLE is therefore closed under **scale-horiz**, but SQUARE is not. What are your options in the design of SQUARE that will preserve its closure under **scale-horiz**?

7. As we saw in Section 10.8, adding a vertex to a triangle, rectangle, or hexagon violates the principle of closed behavior. Does this fact suggest another class that should go between POLYGON and TRIANGLE, RECTANGLE, and HEXAGON?

10.11 Answers

1. There are two reasons that we shouldn't name the dimension with something as banal as MONEY. The first reason is that the name would be ambiguous. Since at least two dimensions of VISA-ACCOUNT's state-space are monetary, how would we know which dimension was the **current-balance** and which was the **credit-limit**? Therefore, we label the dimension **current-balance**. **current-balance**, of course, is likely to be one of VISA-ACCOUNT's private variables, of class MONEY.

   The second reason is that a typical dimension doesn't correspond precisely to a class like, say, LENGTH. For example, in PATIENT, a height dimension named LENGTH would imply that *any* height of patient were possible—including a patient eight miles high! **PATIENT::height** should have some restrictions on permitted heights. One way to do this is by placing ad hoc restrictions on the variable **height:LENGTH** within PATIENT. A more elegant (and more extravagant) solution would be to create a subclass of LENGTH named PATIENT-HEIGHT. It's more extravagant because it gives us another class in our library to maintain. This would be worth doing only if PATIENT-HEIGHT had important or complicated business properties.

2. I'll answer the questions in this exercise in reverse order. First, let's explore three possible approaches to the internal design of RECTANGLE and assess the dimensionality (or degrees of freedom) of each. Each design approach—I'll call them A, B, and C—will apparently yield a different dimensionality! After examining each approach, I'll resolve this apparent conflict through the class-invariant concept in order to come up with the true dimensionality of RECTANGLE.

   Approach A: Consider each RECTANGLE object to be represented by four points in a plane. Because each point has two dimensions (**x** and **y**), RECTANGLE's state-space will have eight (that is, 4 times 2) dimensions.

   Approach B: Consider a RECTANGLE object to be just two points: a **top-left** point and a **bottom-right** point. Although this would appear to give the state-space just four dimensions, it's not quite enough. Two points will work for horizontal rectangles, but they're ambiguous for rectangles that can turn. (Try it with pencil and paper.) We therefore need to know the rectangle's angle of orientation, too. This makes five (that is, 2 plus 2 plus 1) dimensions.

Approach C: We can also specify a RECTANGLE object by stating its **center**, its **height**, its **width**, and its **orientation**. This also yields a five-dimensional state-space (that is, 2 plus 1 plus 1 plus 1).

So which answer should it be? Does RECTANGLE have an eight-dimensional state-space or a five-dimensional one? The answer is: the minimum of all those values—in other words, five dimensions.

But why the *minimum*? To answer that question, let's take another look at each of the three design approaches to see how the class invariant reduces the degrees of freedom in an internal design of RECTANGLE that appears to have more than five dimensions.

Approach A: Although four points on a plane can certainly specify a rectangle, they can also specify lots of shapes that aren't rectangular, such as trapezoids and parallelograms. Thus, if we choose four points to be the instance variables that define a rectangle, then we'll have to establish a class invariant for RECTANGLE that will forbid non-rectangular shapes. The following calculation tells us how much work we have to do to impose such a constraint.

Four points have eight degrees of freedom, but rectangles (as we've seen) can be designed to have only five. Therefore, if we choose Approach A as our internal RECTANGLE design, we'll need to write and enforce a class invariant to bring the dimensionality of the class effectively back to five. This class invariant must contain three (8 minus 5) constraints. Your subject-matter expertise about rectangles will inspire you with various ways to write this invariant.

For example, you may join the points by lines and check that three intersections are right angles. Or, you may check that one intersection is a right angle and that the lines form two pairs of equal lengths. Or, you may eliminate one of your points entirely and check that the remaining three points meet the Pythagorean condition. When you see the work needed to write the class invariant for Approach A, you might ask whether you could find a simpler core representation, one whose dimensionality would be closer to five and would therefore simplify the class invariant.

Approaches B and C: Class invariants will be simple for these internal designs, because RECTANGLE's instance variables altogether have five dimensions (degrees of freedom)—exactly the same number as we saw above for rectangles as a whole. For example, in Approach C, a **center**, **height**, **width**, and **orientation** can hardly *not* represent a legal rectangle! No matter what values you put into these variables, you'll get a rectangle. (Of course, you must ensure that **height** and **width** are nonnegative.)

Since they're independent of one another, the above four variables (**center**, **height**, **width**, and **orientation**) give the state-space of RECTANGLE five fundamental dimensions (2 plus 1 plus 1 plus 1). All other sets of instance variables representing rectangles also yield at least five fundamental dimensions. (Try some!)

So, what's really going on here? The answer is that RECTANGLE has two dimensionalities, an external one and an internal one. RECTANGLE's *external dimensionality* is its dimensionality *as a type*, and is always five.

RECTANGLE's *internal dimensionality* is its dimensionality *as a class* (an implementation of a type). This dimensionality must be at least five. The difference between the internal dimensionality and external dimensionality is the number of constraints that we must apply via the class invariant in the class's design. In Chapter 12, we return to RECTANGLE to explore both its external design and internal design further.

Finally, note that you can group fundamental dimensions into higher-complexity dimensions in several different ways, without changing dimensionality. For example, in Approach B, we saw RECTANGLE's five dimensions grouped into three: two points and an angle. Two of these three dimensions (the points) are of class POINT, which has two fundamental dimensions (both of class REAL). Forming higher-level abstractions (such as POINT, rather than merely two REALs) is usually good object-oriented design practice (as I indicated in Section 9.2.2, on encumbrance).

3. Not necessarily. If the discrepancy in **calc-bonus** is MANAGER's *only* departure from being a true subtype, then you probably wouldn't disturb the class-inheritance hierarchy. But you must document the discrepancy well—both in the overall class description and in the specific offending method. Look carefully for this type of problem in design walkthroughs; if it slips through, it will sooner or later cause a polymorphic blowup.

4. The behavior that a subclass inherits from a superclass must operate within the possibly constrained state-space of the subclass. Therefore, the subclass may need to override an inherited method with a less wide-ranging version.

However, a subclass is free to add any behavior to the inherited behavior so long as the class invariant is respected.

As an analogy, consider the tenor Luciano Pavarotti as an object of a superclass and me as an object of a subclass. I can sing too, but my volume, range, and depth of expression are all less than Signor Pavarotti's. Also, assume that I know all the songs that he knows but, unfortunately, my implementation of them is less impressive. In fact, there are some arias that I must refuse to sing at all because their range defeats me. On the other hand, I sing some of his songs with extra twiddly bits of my own invention.

Notwithstanding the above, there are several rockin' numbers that Signor Pavarotti doesn't know, but which have been very lucky for me (for example, "The Ying Tong Song" and the evergreen country favorite, "Baby, You Could Drive Me Wild, But I Can't Get Out of First Gear"). Thus, although I inherit a set of songs from Signor Pavarotti whose implementation I modify and constrain to my own talents, I also extend his repertoire with some songs that take singing into a whole new dimension.

5. Complex class invariants often have sub-expressions that can be factored out as Boolean functions. For example, the Pythagorean property of a right triangle cannot be succinctly expressed for two reasons. First, it isn't obvious which of the three sides is the hypotenuse. Second, because of real-number roundings, the Pythagorean constraint can never be expressed as an exact equality. However, you can write a Boolean function

   is-pythagorean (a, b, c: REAL) BOOL:

   which can be made part of the class invariant of, say, RIGHT-TRIANGLE and RIGHT-ISOSCELES-TRIANGLE, and which will take care of awkward complexities.

6. The problem is that we can't simply let SQUARE inherit **scale-horiz** as is. So, we have four options in the design of SQUARE:

   a. Raise an exception when a square violates its class invariant.

   b. Override **scale-horiz** so that it does nothing for squares.

   c. Override **scale-horiz** with some different behavior that preserves SQUARE's class invariant. (Perhaps invoke **scale-vert** with an equal **scale-factor** so that a square stretches equally in both dimensions.)

d. Take the more drastic approach of letting a square get stretched. Then, change its class—"migrate" it— from SQUARE to RECTANGLE.

All four of the above design options preserve the class invariant of the object's class—although admittedly the last one does so rather trickily by changing the object's class to suit its new state. The option that you choose involves looking at how SQUARE will be used in your current application as well as how it might be reused in future applications.

7. POLYGON should have two subclasses, FIXED-SIDED-POLYGON and VARIABLE-SIDED-POLYGON. TRIANGLE (and similar classes) should be a subclass of FIXED-SIDED-POLYGON. This approach allows a designer to place the **add-vertex** method in VARIABLE-SIDED-POLYGON and removes the need to override **add-vertex** in classes representing fixed-sided polygons. (If VARIABLE-SIDED-POLYGON has subclasses, then you should name them MUTABLE-TRIANGLE, MUTABLE-RECTANGLE, and so forth, if vertices could be added or removed.)

The Perils of Inheritance and Polymorphism

Inheritance and polymorphism set object orientation apart from traditional ways of building software. However, although the inheritance construct is very powerful, it's also perhaps the most overused software construct since the **go to** statement. Object-oriented debutants feel that they must design with inheritance at every possible opportunity in order to show that they've "arrived" in the world of object orientation. The result: problems being perverted to fit an "inheritance design" to the extent that some designs are utterly unimplementable.

The first section of this chapter covers four of the ways that people force inheritance into their object-oriented designs, together with my suggested alternatives to inheritance in those design situations. The second section of this chapter explores polymorphism's danger.

Polymorphism promotes conciseness in object-oriented programming, because it allows a method to be defined on more than one class and allows a variable to refer to an object of more than one class. Polymorphism thus allows the operating environment automatically to choose the correct method to be executed as a result of a message, without the need for a complicated **case** statement. This flexibility of polymorphism, which makes it so useful, unfortunately also makes it dangerous. The first danger that we'll look at is polymorphism in ordinary messages; the second danger is polymorphism within generic classes.

11.1 Abuses of Inheritance

I've taken the four examples in this section from real projects in real shops, where real people were applying object orientation, in many cases for the first time. Some of the perverse designs that I cite were secretly and gruesomely coded; others caused disputes that were lengthy, bloody, and—in one case—even team-destroying.

The aims of this section are to examine different patterns of inheritance and to prevent loss of time and morale on *your* next project by pointing out where inheritance is and isn't appropriate. The examples proceed from outrageous misuse through much more subtle, questionable uses of inheritance. By the way, I've changed the names of the classes in the four examples to protect the original perpetrators.

11.1.1 Mistaken aggregates

The top class-inheritance diagram of Fig. 11.1 shows the class AIRPLANE with its four supposed subclasses: WING, TAIL, ENGINE, and FUSELAGE. This "design" can never be expressed as code, because there's no sensible way to program the subclasses to meet the needs of the application. The designer has mixed up the concepts of class inheritance and object aggregation. If we read the diagram as it is, we would assume that a tail "is a (kind of) airplane" and also that a wing "is a (kind of) airplane."

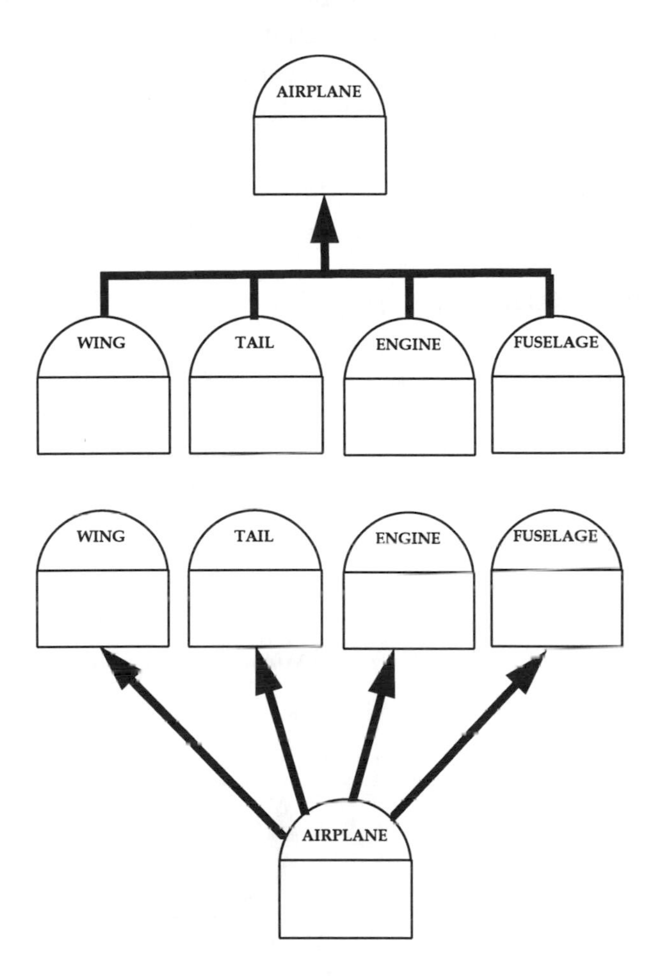

Fig. 11.1: Two "designs" for the class AIRPLANE—what's wrong with this picture?

The lower diagram shows multiple inheritance as another putative design solution to object aggregation. The designer of this second AIRPLANE read his diagram as, "An airplane is a wing, a tail, an engine, and a fuselage." That sounds almost correct. However, the true way to interpret the diagram is, "An airplane is simultaneously a kind of wing, a kind of tail, a kind of engine, and a kind of fuselage." And that certainly is wrong!

The designer was sublimely programming from this ineffable AIRPLANE "design" when I met him. He brought the design to my attention only when he began to have trouble programming the fact that an airplane has two wings.

But his problems ran deeper than this individual design: The designer was a novice to object orientation; he'd read but a single book; he'd received no training; he'd been brainwashed by a colleague that multiple inheritance was the greatest thing since multiple personality; and he worked in a shop where peer reviews were discouraged because they interfered with work. Apart from that, as they say, everything was fine!

This example is very similar to the design-notation example of Chapter 4 (GLIDER), which you may want to glance at again to review object aggregation.

11.1.2 Inverted hierarchy

The example of inheritance in Fig. 11.2 barely warrants a second glance, because its structure exactly corresponds to a normal organization chart. An employee reports to a manager and a manager reports to a board member. But there's a problem. What the diagram actually says is, "An employee is a *kind of* manager, and a manager is a *kind of* board member."

Fig. 11.2: Looks right—but is it?

I assume that the reality is the other way up, that is, "A board member is a kind of manager, and a manager is a kind of employee." (For simplicity, let's assume that board members are employees.) To depict that, we would simply invert Fig. 11.2 and put EMPLOYEE, which is the most general class, at the top.

11.1.3 Confusing class and instance

The example of multiple inheritance in Fig. 11.3 is infuriatingly subtle. When I met it in a walkthrough, I *knew* that it was wrong, but I had tremendous difficulty in explaining why. My difficulty was compounded because the actual application was an obscure, technical one that my walkthrough peers opined I was unqualified to judge.

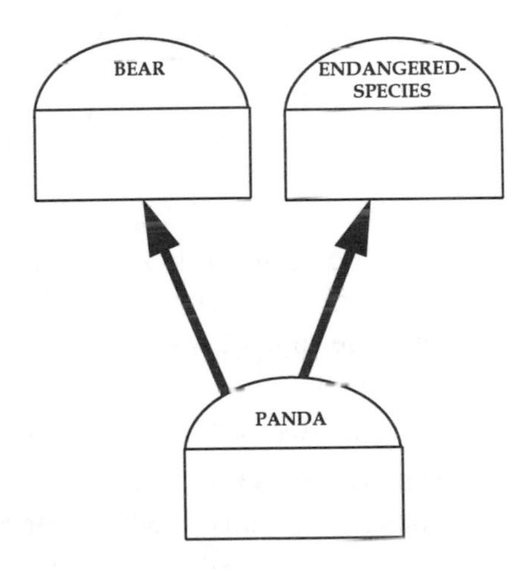

Fig. 11.3: What does "PANDA" really mean?

The path to understanding this problem is through the question, What are the instances of the three classes in Fig. 11.3? The instances of PANDA may be: An-An, Chu-Chu, Ling-Ling, Miou-Miou, Hee-Hee, and Oh-Oh. The instances of BEAR may be: Yogi, Teddy, Winnie, Paddington, and Fred. However, the instances of ENDANGERED-SPECIES are entire species: the snub-nosed muskrat, the lesser-spotted tree-gripper, the somewhat-giant rat of Sumatra, the American codhurr, the Latvian yodeling-flea, and the net-gilled nodenik, for example.

In other words, two of the classes (PANDA and BEAR) have individual animals as instances, whereas the third (ENDANGERED-SPECIES) has whole species as instances. It would be entirely reasonable to say, "Ling-Ling is a panda" or "Ling-Ling is a kind of bear." However, it's *not* correct to say, "Ling-Ling is a kind of endangered species." Thus, the class PANDA could inherit from BEAR but not from ENDANGERED-SPECIES.[1]

So, how should we design in the fact that some species are endangered? Figure 11.4 illustrates the answer.

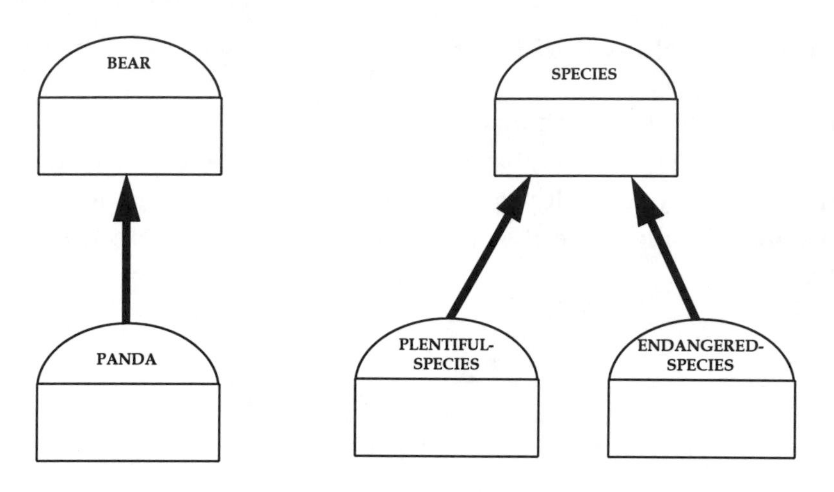

Fig. 11.4: The corrected inheritance hierarchies.

The diagram on the left shows the class PANDA inheriting from BEAR. These two classes deal with animals, while the class hierarchy on the right deals solely with species. But how do we link the two sides? How do we design in the fact that pandas and some other species are endangered?

One way is to put an instance variable, **whether-endangered**, in BEAR (or its superclass, ANIMAL). Although this would work, it's overkill, because it affords too much generality. For example, we'd be able to record that Yogi was endangered, whereas Paddington was not. I don't think that this is the goal of the application.

Instead, we should simply give every class representing a species (such as BEAR, PANDA, and TOAD) a class variable that points to the appropriate object of class SPECIES. The appropriate object is, of course, the one that represents the

[1] All right, I know that a panda is a kind of raccoon, but please bear with me.

species that the class embodies. (Actually, this class variable could be a class constant if your language allows you to declare constants.)

For example, in the class BEAR, we would have

```
class var our-species:SPECIES := bear;
```

If your language has no class variables, you could have an instance variable (or constant) that you set to **bear** whenever you instantiate Yogi, Boo-Boo, or Fred:

```
var my-species:SPECIES := bear;
```

Objects of class BEAR could look up their species—and properties of their species—at run-time with code such as

```
our-species.whether-endangered;
our-species.max-weight;
```

Or, if you use the *instance* variable approach:

```
my-species.whether-endangered;
my-species.max-weight;
```

max-weight:WEIGHT would be an *instance* variable of SPECIES. **whether-endangered:BOOL** would be an *instance* variable (or constant) in both PLENTIFUL-SPECIES and ENDANGERED-SPECIES, set to **false** and **true**, respectively.[2]

11.1.4 Misapplying is a

Our next example has this basic requirement: We need to remember the length, width, and height of rooms, which in our application are cuboids (hotel rooms, perhaps).[3] We also need to know the volume of a room. We already have the class CUBOID in our class library, so we design a class ROOM that simply inherits from CUBOID, as shown in Fig. 11.5.

[2] It could instead be made an *instance* variable of SPECIES. See Exercise 1 at the end of this chapter.

[3] A cuboid is a "cube" with three sides of different lengths. An example appears in Fig. 11.5.

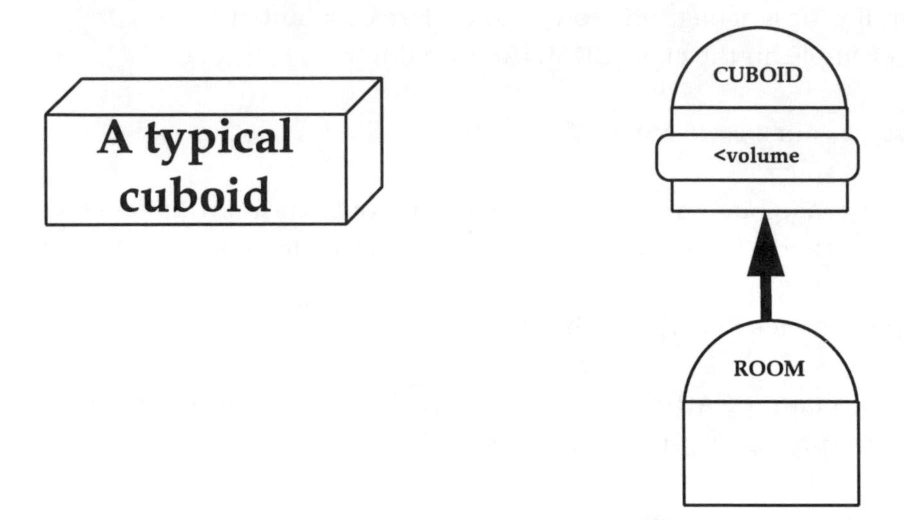

Fig. 11.5: ROOM is designed simply to inherit from CUBOID.

So far, this looks great. An object of class ROOM can return its volume simply by executing the method **volume** that ROOM inherits from CUBOID; no new code is needed. Furthermore, since a room *is a* cuboid, that requirement of valid inheritance is satisfied. However, this is where the design begins to fall apart.

The first problem is the behavior that ROOM inherits from CUBOID. This behavior comes from CUBOID's methods, such as **stretch**, **rotate**, and so on. Since it's highly unlikely that ROOM would need such behavior, we should override it—cancel it—in ROOM. On the other hand, we *could* leave in the methods as part of the official behavior of ROOM and trust that people would use them judiciously, because rotating a room in three-dimensional space would have strange effects indeed!

But bigger problems arise when we have to deal with rooms of other shapes. Let's say that some rooms are cylindrical. Inheritance, which worked so well for cuboids, should also work for cylinders. The left diagram of Fig. 11.6, therefore, shows ROOM inheriting multiply from both CUBOID and CYLINDER. (This was a particularly desperate design, because this shop's language didn't support multiple inheritance!)

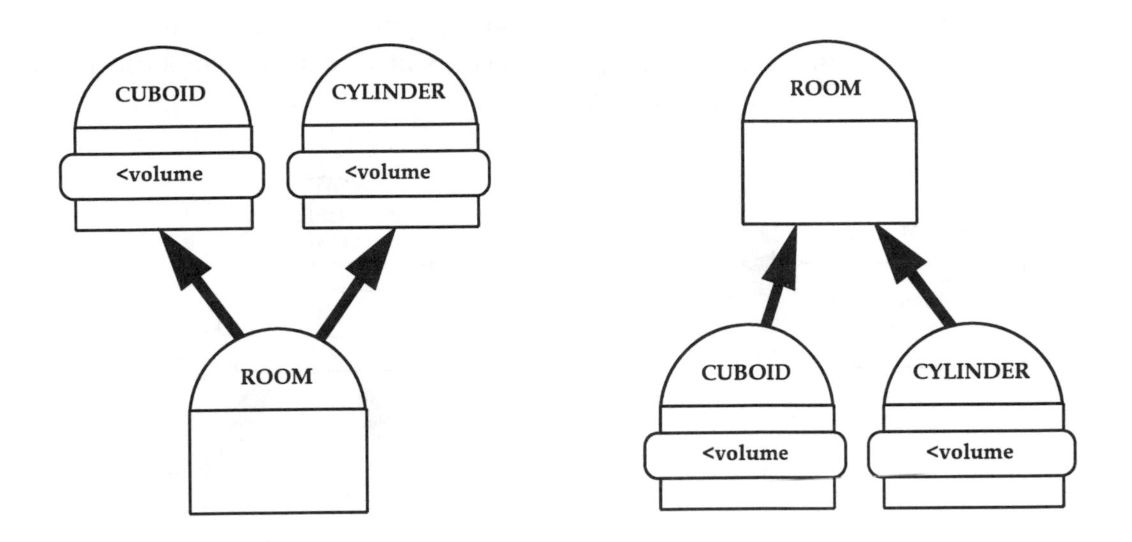

Fig. 11.6: Two attempts to introduce cylindrical rooms.

And what does this mean? The multiple inheritance implies that a given room is both a cylinder *and* a cuboid. That would yield a strangely shaped room and it certainly wasn't what the designer intended. When I asked him about this multiple inheritance, he told me that the diagram indicated that a room could be a cylinder *or* a cuboid. Another designer said, "Then you've got the diagram upside-down," and proceeded to expound the virtues of the diagram on the right of Fig. 11.6.

We're getting nowhere fast here, although the hierarchy where CUBOID and CYLINDER inherit from ROOM will at least work—after a fashion. If we instantiate an object of either CUBOID or CYLINDER, then that object will inherit all the necessary properties of ROOM. However, we still have the problem of the extraneous behavior (such as **stretch** and **rotate**), which now we have no chance to override.

But this design of Fig. 11.6 has even deeper problems. We know from Chapter 9 that we shouldn't encumber a class from a low domain (CUBOID or CYLINDER) with one from a higher domain (ROOM). If we did so, our geometry library would need the ROOM class in order to work. Also, since not all cuboids are rooms, the class CUBOID would have mixed-instance cohesion, as well as mixed-domain cohesion.

The root of the problem is in my original statement, "A room is a cuboid," which I used to justify inheritance. This was sleight of hand. A more precise statement is, "A room *has the shape of* a cuboid," which makes quite a difference. A new design for ROOM appears in Fig. 11.7.

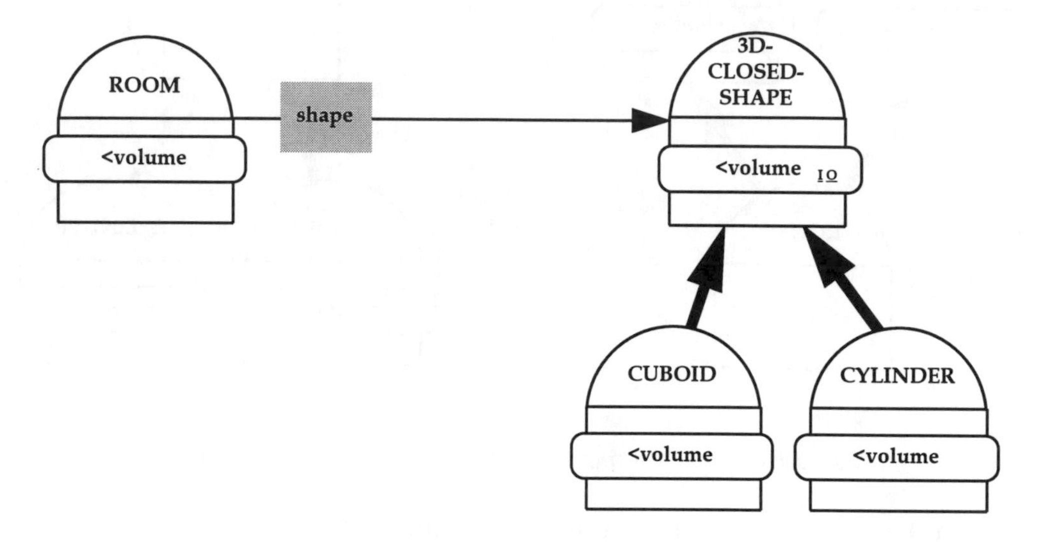

Fig. 11.7: ROOM has a variable **shape**, *of class 3D-CLOSED-SHAPE.*

This time, ROOM has an *instance* variable **shape**, which points to an object of class 3D-CLOSED-SHAPE (or of one of its subclasses, such as CUBOID, CYLINDER, or TETRAHEDRON). In other words, ROOM contains the declaration:

var shape: 3D-CLOSED-SHAPE;

At the initialization of a particular room, the variable **shape** is assigned to an object of the correct shape and size for the given room. The method **ROOM::volume** now works by asking the object pointed to by the variable **shape** to compute volume, as shown in Fig. 11.8. The algorithm actually invoked will depend on the actual shape of the room—polymorphism, again. This technique of reusing the code in another class is called *message forwarding.* An object of class ROOM has forwarded the volume message to another object of class CUBOID (or whatever).

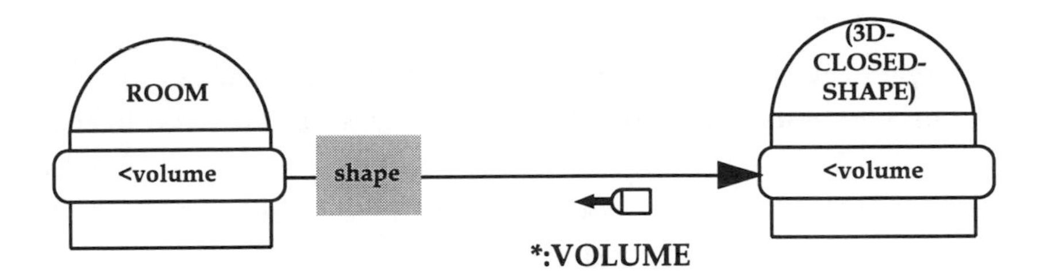

Fig. 11.8: ROOM finds its volume by asking the object referred to by **shape** *to do so.*

You may want to review the headaches that the original, inheritance-based designs caused and check that this message-forwarding design has cured them.[4]

11.2 The Danger of Polymorphism

The danger of polymorphism is that, as a result of an imperfect design, an object may receive a message that it doesn't understand (which typically causes a run-time error). Section 11.2.1 explores this design problem in terms of general messages to objects. Section 11.2.2 explores a special case, the use of polymorphism in the design of generic classes.

11.2.1 Polymorphism in messages

As we saw in Chapter 1, the term polymorphism applies both to a method (which can be defined on several different classes) and to a variable (which at various times can point to objects belonging to different classes). When these two aspects of polymorphism work in harmony, the full power of object orientation comes to the fore. However, these two aspects may also come into conflict—with unfortunate results.

In order to explain how to resolve this conflict, I need to introduce some new terms.

[4] Some authors use the term *delegation* for message forwarding. However, I've steered clear of this term, because it's more commonly used for another object-oriented concept beyond the scope of this book. (Nevertheless, I do define "delegation" in the Glossary.)

> The *scope of polymorphism* (SOP) of a method **m** is the set of classes upon which **m** is defined. A scope of polymorphism that forms a branch of the inheritance hierarchy—that is, a class A together with all of its subclasses—is termed a *cone of polymorphism* (COP) with A as the *apex of polymorphism* (AOP).

Figure 11.9 depicts a class-inheritance tree. If a method **m** is defined on each of the shaded classes, then those shaded classes form **m**'s cone of polymorphism. It's a cone because the shaded classes form a complete branch; the class A is the apex of polymorphism.[5]

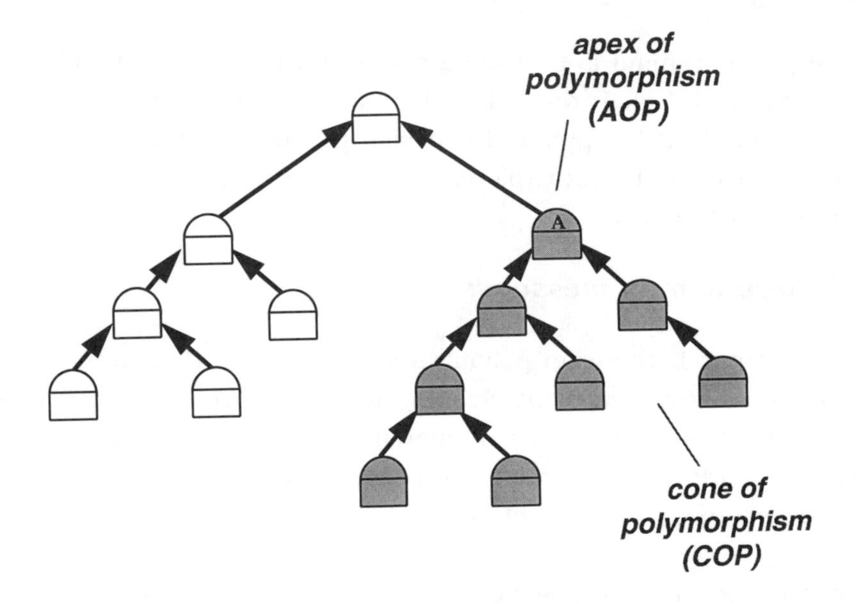

Fig. 11.9: The structure of a method's COP.

As a more concrete example, if the method **area** is defined on POLYGON and on all the subclasses of POLYGON—either locally or by inheritance—then **area**'s SOP forms a cone, with POLYGON at the apex. See Fig. 11.10.

---

[5] One of my students refers to A as the "conehead of polymorphism." Don't let me catch *you* using this term!

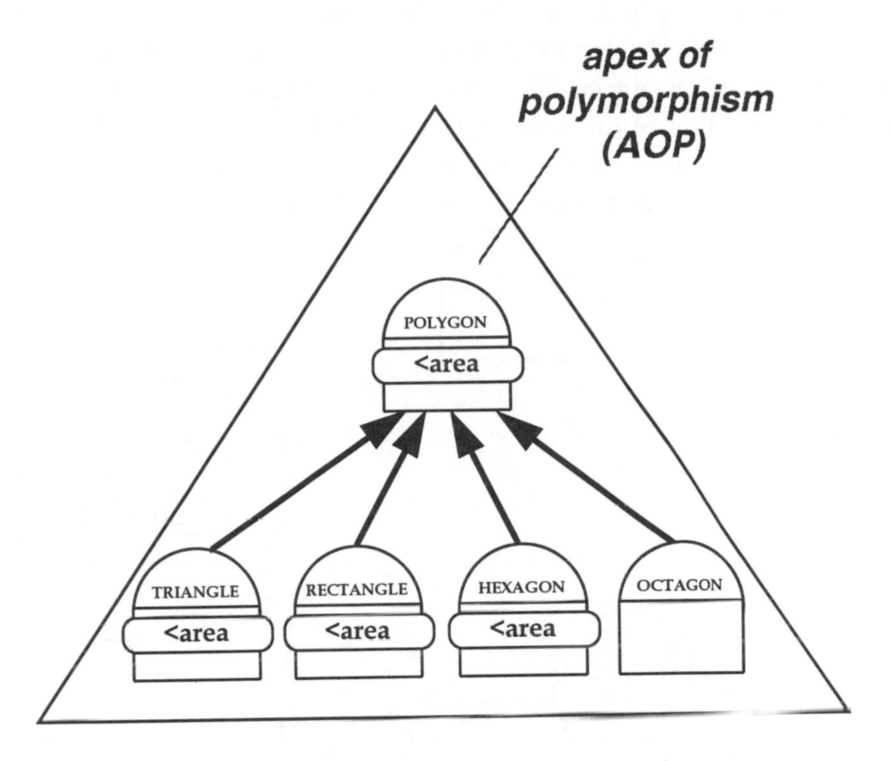

Fig. 11.10: The COP for the method **area**.

Figure 11.11 again depicts a class-inheritance tree, where the method **m** is defined on all the shaded classes. This figure shows a *ragged* SOP, because the shaded classes don't form a neat cone comprising a complete branch of the tree.

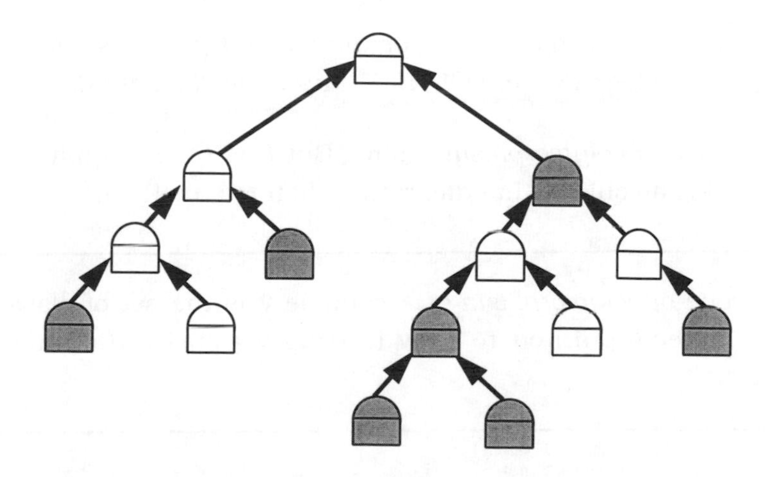

Fig. 11.11: The structure of a (ragged) SOP for a method.

A simple, concrete example of a ragged SOP for a method is a little harder to find. However, the familiar method **print** (which sends information about the target object to the printer-driver object) often has a raggle-taggle bunch of classes in its SOP. If **print** is defined on SPREADSHEET, TEXTDOC, and E-MAIL-MSG, then its SOP isn't a cone, because classes like ELEPHANT and even the "top" class, OBJECT, have no method **print** defined on them.[6] See Fig. 11.12.

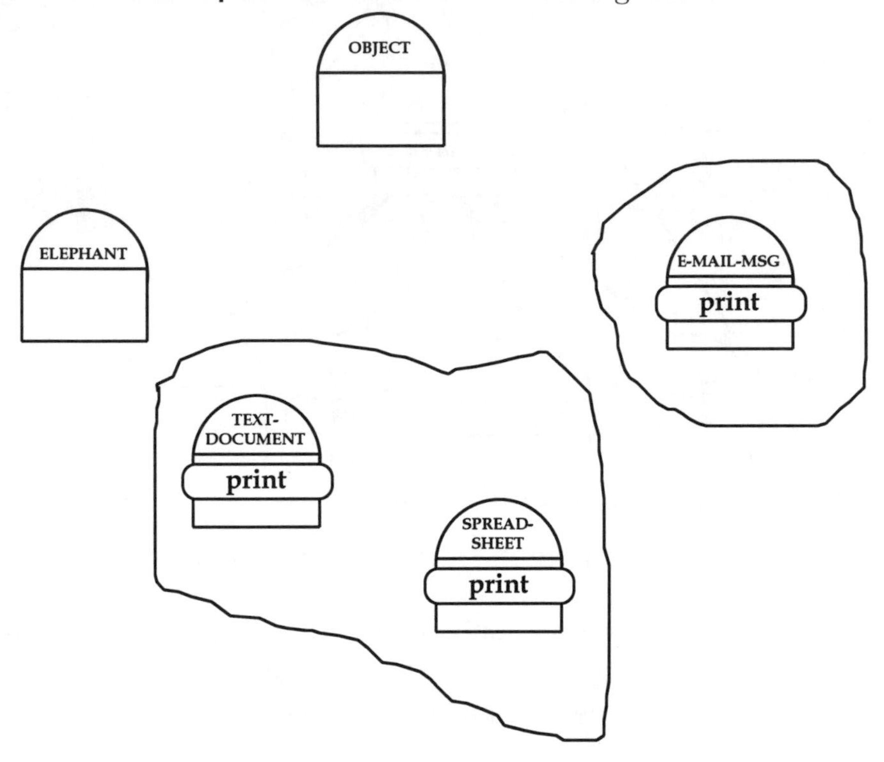

Fig. 11.12: The (ragged) SOP for the method **print** *(assuming that ELEPHANT and OBJECT have no method* **print***).*

Now I define *scope of polymorphism* again. But this time, I apply the terms to a variable that holds an object's handle, rather than to a method.

> The *scope of polymorphism* of a variable **v** is the set of classes to which objects pointed to by **v** (during **v**'s entire lifetime) may belong.

---

6 I'm assuming here that SPREADSHEET, TEXTDOC, and E-MAIL-MSG don't have a common superclass, such as PRINTABLE-DOC.

The scope of polymorphism for a variable obviously has a very similar meaning to that of scope of polymorphism for a method. The classes comprising the SOP for a variable, however, are the classes of all the objects to which the variable may refer at any time while the system is running. (Incidentally, we also use the terms *cone of polymorphism* and *apex of polymorphism* for a variable, with the same meanings as the corresponding terms for a method.)

Here are three examples to illustrate the scope of polymorphism of a variable:

1. Let's say that the declaration **var t:TRIANGLE** allows the variable **t** to point to any object of class TRIANGLE or of TRIANGLE's descendants. (This is a natural situation in Eiffel or C++, in which polymorphism of a variable is usually restricted to descendants of a given class.) In this example, therefore, the variable's SOP forms a cone, with the class TRIANGLE as the apex.

2. Let's say in this example that a variable **v** is allowed—at various times—to point to an object of class HORSE, CIRCLE, or CUSTOMER. (This may occur in Smalltalk, in which polymorphism of variables is typically unrestricted.) In this example, then, the variable's SOP isn't a cone because the classes HORSE, CIRCLE, and CUSTOMER don't have a common superclass to form an AOP.

   At least, we *presume* that they don't have a common superclass. Of course, you could introduce a nonsense class as a superclass of HORSE, CIRCLE, and CUSTOMER to provide an artificial AOP for a variable. But I know you wouldn't do that.[7]

3. In this third example, let's say that (again, as in Smalltalk) we have a declaration **var x:OBJECT**, where the class OBJECT is the top of the class hierarchy. In other words, the variable **x** may point to any object whatsoever (because all classes are descendants of OBJECT). This time, the variable's SOP does form a cone. Indeed, this cone is the largest one of all, because its apex is at the top class in the class hierarchy.

A message is composed of a variable (which points to the target object) and a method name (which states the method to be invoked). As we saw above, both the variable and the method have SOPs.

---

[7] Some object-oriented programming languages (such as Eiffel) will enforce a COP on a variable if you so instruct the compiler. No languages that I know will automatically enforce an arbitrarily ragged SOP (such as HORSE, CIRCLE, and CUSTOMER); nor, in my opinion, should they.

So, let's investigate the relationship between the SOPs of the variable and the method that make up a message. We'll see that this relationship has a significant impact on system reliability—or lack thereof. In order to keep this discussion clear, I'll assume that both the SOPs of the method and the variable are COPs, that is, they form neat cones.

I'll call the message **tobj.tm**, where **tobj** is the variable pointing to the target object and **tm** is the method to be invoked on the target object. There are two possible relationships between **tobj**'s COP and **tm**'s COP:

> *Case 1:* **tobj**'s COP lies within **tm**'s COP. In other words, the variable's COP lies within the method's COP. See Fig. 11.13.

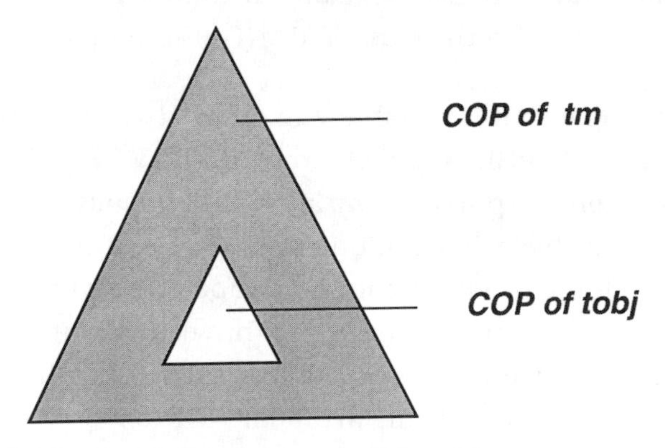

Fig. 11.13: The COP of the variable **tobj** *lies within the COP of the method* **tm**.

> *Case 2:* Part or all of **tobj**'s COP falls outside **tm**'s COP. In other words, some of the variable's COP falls outside the method's COP. See Fig. 11.14.

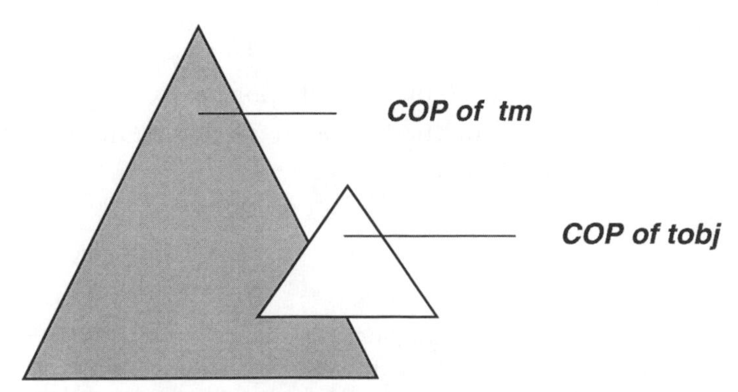

Fig. 11.14: Part of the COP of the variable **tobj** *falls outside the COP of the method* **tm**.

In the first case, all is well with the design. No matter what object **tobj** points to, that object will be of a class that "understands" the message **tm**. The second case, however, represents a miserable, non-robust design. This designer is dicing with the devil, because it's quite possible that at run-time **tobj** will point to an object upon whose class **tm** is not defined. If this happens, then the program will probably blow up with a run-time error.

For a specific example of the possible relationships between a variable's SOP and a method's SOP, consider the message **factory-component.turn-on**. As above, there are two cases:

> *Case 1:* **factory-component** always points to an object of class TAP, MOTOR, or LIGHT, all of which can turn on. Then, factory-component's SOP is within **turn-on**'s SOP and everything's fine. (However, I'd suggest changing the variable's name to **operable-component** or **switchable-component** to indicate that it refers to a component that can be operated or switched.)
>
> *Case 2:* **factory-component** refers to any piece of hardware in the factory, including objects of class TAP, MOTOR, LIGHT, PIPE, TANK, DOOR, LEVER, and so on. Not all of these kinds of components "know how to turn on." This time, therefore, much of **factory-component**'s SOP falls outside **turn-on**'s SOP and there's a significant chance of a run-time problem, when, for instance, a plain old door is told to turn on.

Whenever you indulge in the luxury of polymorphic messaging, make sure that you always check the SOP of the message's method and the SOP of the message's target variable. Then, apply this mnemonic verse about the correct relationship between a method's SOP and a variable's SOP:

> If the method's scope lies all without [the variable's SOP],
> There is not a speck of doubt.
> But if any scope should lie within,
> You have made a heinous sin.[8]

11.2.2 Polymorphism and genericity

A generic class, which I covered in Section 1.9, is a class that takes a class name

[8] Yes, I know; it's not exactly Wordsworth. But maybe it will help you to remember the correct relationship between the SOPs.

as an argument whenever objects are instantiated. (In C++, they're known as template classes.) Designers often use generic classes to construct containers such as lists, stacks, and sorted trees.

But, like the polymorphic messages that we saw in Section 11.2.1, generic classes may create run-time problems because of scope-of-polymorphism conflicts. To illustrate this, let me introduce a generic class SORTED-TREE [NODE-CLASS]. The following statement instantiates a specific tree:

```
real-num-tree := SORTED-TREE [REAL].new;
```

Executing this statement creates a new object, a sorted tree pointed to by **real-num-tree**, that will hold real numbers in its nodes. We could also write

```
cust-tree := SORTED-TREE [CUSTOMER].new;
```

which would hold objects of class CUSTOMER in its nodes. Inside the class SORTED-TREE, we would have statements such as

```
node := NODE-CLASS.new;
```

which would create a new node of class REAL (for the first tree object above) or of class CUSTOMER (for the second tree object above). Also, in the code of SORTED-TREE (say, within the method **print-tree**), we might see

```
node.print
```

which would send a message to the object pointed to by the node to "print itself." Elsewhere in the code within SORTED-TREE, we might see the following comparison:[9]

```
if new-item.less-than (curr-node; )        // new-item and curr-node each points
                                           // to a NODE-CLASS object
then ...
```

The problem with the above comparison is this: The designer of SORTED-TREE doesn't have the foggiest idea which actual class will be passed as a generic argu-

---

[9] In some languages, the syntax for this comparison would simply be **if new-item < curr-node then ....**

ment at run-time. For example, someone could write SORTED-TREE [FUSELAGE].new, SORTED-TREE [COMPLEX].new, or SORTED-TREE [ANIMAL].new.

The first of these three classes may not understand **print**; the second may not understand **less-than**; while the third may understand neither **print** nor **less-than**. Thus, there's a tremendous risk of a run-time failure when an object held in the tree, of class ANIMAL for example, is told to "print itself."

The problem occurs because the scope of NODE-CLASS is unlimited: At run-time, *any* class could be provided to SORTED-TREE to play the part of NODE-CLASS. Thus, the scope of polymorphism of **node:NODE-CLASS** is huge; indeed, it could be anything. On the other hand, the scope of polymorphism of the methods within SORTED-TREE is actually very small: It's the intersection of the SOPs of the individual methods (such as **print**, **less-than**, and so on).

Therefore, the SORTED-TREE's design violates the principle in Section 11.2.1, because the variables in SORTED-TREE have SOPs that potentially lie well outside the SOPs of the methods used in SORTED-TREE. In terms of the mnemonic rhyme, a heinous sin has been committed!

There are two solutions to this design problem: The first is for every user of a generic class to be responsible enough to ensure that the actual run-time class provided is within the SOP intersection described above. In other words, the class must be able to understand *every* message sent to its objects within the generic class's code.

So, when you program or document a generic class, you should list at the start of the class all the methods that any class provided as an actual run-time argument should possess. For example, if your generic class is SORTED-TREE, you would state that any provided classes (such as CUSTOMER, PRODUCT) should have the methods **less-than**, **greater-than**, **equal-to**, or whatever, defined on them. This will help people who use your generic class to check that they're providing an actual class with the right methods defined on it.

The second solution is to provide some kind of guard at the beginning of the generic class's code. The guard checks that the actual class supplied can understand the required messages. Unfortunately, in most mainstream object-oriented languages, this is difficult to do. Eiffel, however, has an ingenious way to form such a guard.

In Eiffel, you can insist that the actual class supplied to a generic class at run-time be within a specific cone of polymorphism. You do this by specifying the class that's the apex of polymorphism.

For example, you would write at the top of a generic class NODE-CLASS -> PRINTABLE, where PRINTABLE is the AOP. This means that the generic class will only accept the class PRINTABLE or one of its descendants as a supplied run-time class.

Next, you would design a class called PRINTABLE with a method **print** (which should be a deferred method because its implementation will be defined in descendants of PRINTABLE). Now, since everyone who supplies a class to SORTED-TREE *has to* supply a descendant class of PRINTABLE, the supplied class is guaranteed to have the method **print** defined on it.

Some shops sum up groups of methods with "-able" terms. For example, "this class must be printable" or "this class must have printable objects" mean "this class must have the method **print** defined on it." A comparable class would be one with the methods **less-than**, **greater-than**, and **equal-to** defined on it. Printability, comparability, and so on are examples of class aspects or class capabilities.

The class PRINTABLE in the above Eiffel solution is, in effect, an embodiment of the printability aspect. Incidentally, PRINTABLE is also a mix-in class, a design idea that I explain in the next chapter.

11.3 Summary

Inheritance and polymorphism bring power and conciseness to object-oriented software. They also bring dangers. The chief danger of inheritance lies in its overuse, or—more precisely—in its misapplication in situations where other object-oriented constructs would be better.

In this chapter, we look at four common abuses of inheritance. The first is the use of inheritance where aggregation is called for. This is an elementary mistake, rarely committed by experienced object-oriented designers. The second abuse is the inversion of the class-inheritance hierarchy, often caused by the lure of a misleading real-world structure.

The third misuse of inheritance is the confusion of class with instance. This tends to occur in designs that have to cope both with groups (such as species or companies) and with individuals (such as animals or employees). Since the problem is usually subtle, a designer may initially overlook it. However, when the faulty design is transformed into code, it becomes obvious that the code cannot work as intended. The fourth misuse employs inheritance where message forwarding would provide a more appropriate design construct.

The term polymorphism applies both to methods and to variables. A polymorphic method is defined on several different classes. A polymorphic variable may at various times point to objects belonging to different classes. The scope of polymorphism (SOP) of a method is the set of classes upon which the method is defined. The scope of polymorphism of a variable is the set of classes of the objects to which the variable may point. A scope of polymorphism that forms a branch of a class-inheritance hierarchy is called a cone of polymorphism (COP); the class at the top of the cone is the apex of polymorphism (AOP).

For the safe use of polymorphism in methods, the SOP of the variable pointing to the target object must lie within the SOP of the method named in the message. If a designer transgresses this guideline, then a run-time error will probably occur.

A generic class is one that takes a class name as an actual argument when its objects are instantiated at run-time. The designer of the code within a generic class cannot know what the actual class supplied to it will be. Therefore, the SOP of any variables referring to objects of the supplied class is very large. So, too, is the chance that the guideline of the previous paragraph will be violated. Some languages (such as Eiffel) enforce restrictions on the actual classes that may be supplied and thereby minimize the run-time errors caused by rampant polymorphism.

11.4 Exercises

1. In the PANDA example of Section 11.1.3, I suggested that you could make **whether-endangered:BOOL** an instance variable (or constant) of both PLENTIFUL-SPECIES and ENDANGERED-SPECIES. But are these subclasses needed? Couldn't we get by with just SPECIES, as I suggested in the footnote of Section 11.1.3?

2. As you probably know, a last-in, first-out stack is a structure that supports a collection of objects, only one of which may be accessed (read) or removed (popped) at a time. That object is said to be the head of the stack; it is the one that was most recently added to (pushed on) the stack.

   A list is a structure with almost identical properties. Comment on the design of the class STACK that inherits from LIST, as shown in Fig. 11.15. (In this example, LIST is a class that supports a singly linked list, accessible at only one end.)

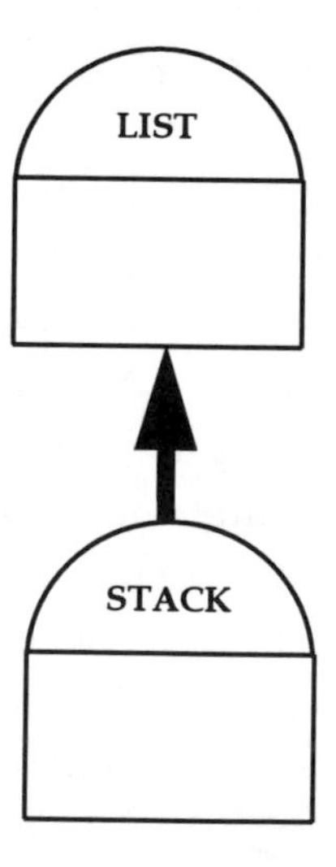

Fig. 11.15: STACK is designed to inherit its implementation from LIST.

3. Are any of the object-oriented design principles we saw in earlier chapters germane to the inheritance problems we covered in this chapter? If so, which ones?

4. In Section 11.2.1, when I defined the scope of polymorphism of a method, I implicitly dealt only with single-inheritance class hierarchies. What other

issues, if any, would arise with a method's SOP if multiple inheritance were present?

5. Assume that a method **m** is a deferred method of a class C (which is a deferred class). Assume further that **m** is defined on all subclasses of C that are not deferred. Could you consider C to be **m**'s apex of polymorphism, even though **C::m** isn't actually implemented? (To review the term "deferred class," please see Section 3.7 or the Glossary.)

6. Assume that a method **m** is defined on a class A and is inherited by all of A's descendants. Normally, this would mean that A and its descendants form a *cone* of polymorphism for **m**, with A at the apex. But, in what situation could this group of classes form a ragged SOP, rather than a complete cone?

7. Imagine that you could close your eyes and wish for an automated tool to help you evaluate your object-oriented design or program. What features might your tool provide to assess whether a variable's SOP lay within a method's SOP?

11.5 Answers

1. We could possibly remove the class PLENTIFUL-SPECIES. However, the class ENDANGERED-SPECIES is necessary if we want to record, say, **date-of-first-endangerment**, **responsible-conservation-org**, and so on. (Otherwise, if these attributes are defined only for some instances of SPECIES, then SPECIES would have mixed-instance cohesion.) If these attributes aren't relevant, we can get by with SPECIES alone. Then, we would make **whether-endangered** an *instance* variable of SPECIES.

   In fact, **whether-endangered** would have to be a variable (rather than a constant) in order to allow species to move in and out of endangerment. However, a species' moving in and out of endangerment becomes a little more difficult to design if SPECIES has the subclasses PLENTIFUL-SPECIES and ENDANGERED-SPECIES. One design approach is this: Delete an object of one subclass (say, PLENTIFUL-SPECIES) after saving its information; and then instantiate an object of the other class (ENDANGERED-SPECIES), copying across any relevant information about the species.

2. Inheritance may not be the best approach here, for the same reason that inheritance was not the best design construct to connect ROOM and CUBOID in Section 11.1.4. The reason is that LIST may have behavior that isn't appropriate for STACK—for example, a method called **insert-in-middle**, which isn't allowed for a stack. The names of methods inherited by STACK may not be quite right, either. Perhaps the method that STACK would term **push** would be termed **append** by the class LIST. (The Eiffel language allows you to rename inherited methods to avoid just this kind of problem.)

   But, for me, the biggest problem of having STACK inherit from LIST is my annoyance at seeing STACK under LIST when I browse through the class hierarchy. After all, in object orientation, implementation is supposed to be hidden from the casual observer.

   Message forwarding (from a STACK object to a LIST object) would be a better approach to designing STACK. Message forwarding tends to disturb the class hierarchy less than inheritance does (especially if, for example, you later change the design of your STACK class to use ARRAY rather than LIST).

3. Yes. The principle of type conformance, covered in Chapter 10, is especially important. Even the subtle PANDA problem, for example, could be assessed via type conformance. Informally, we could ask: Can a PANDA subtype be provided both in a context in which a BEAR type is expected and one in which a SPECIES type is expected? (The answer, as we saw in this chapter,

is, "No.") Another design criterion, valuable for assessing the problem with the room and the cuboid, is class cohesion, covered in Chapter 9.

4. An environment with multiple inheritance may have some subtle domain-of-definition problems. The most common example is so-called name clash, which occurs when two methods with the same name (but from two distinct classes) have overlapping domains of definition. See Fig. 11.16.

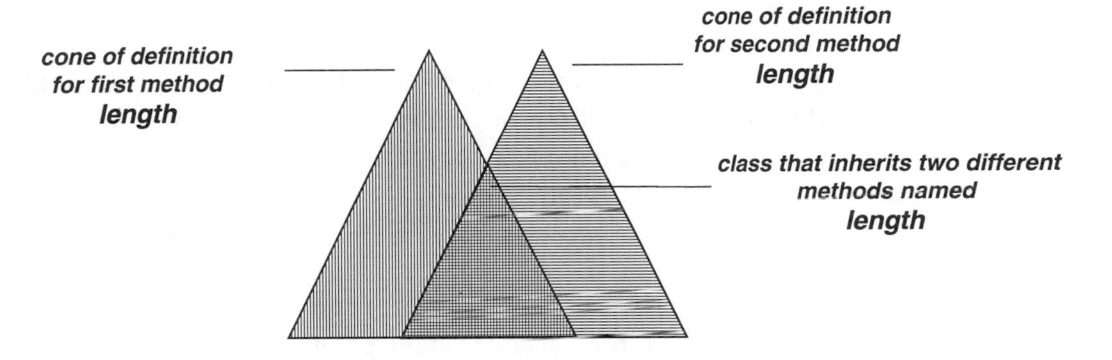

Fig. 11.16: Two methods with the same name and overlapping cones of definition.

A class inheriting both methods will be utterly confused. Language designers have come up with several solutions for determining which method gets inherited, with the best solution being to make the inheriting class rename the inherited methods unambiguously.[10]

In Section 8.2, we saw an example of multiple inheritance that caused a name clash. The class PROGRAM-RENTAL-ITEM inherits methods from both PHYSICAL-INVENTORY-ITEM and RECORDING-MEDIUM, each of which had a method named **length**. (The former means length of the cassette in inches, while the latter means playing time in minutes.) Thus, any reference to **length** in PROGRAM-RENTAL-ITEM is ambiguous.

The best solution: Rename the method **length** (the one that's inherited from RECORDING-MEDIUM) as **duration**. The method name **duration** not only removes the ambiguity of **length**, but also better captures the idea of playing time.

---

[10] [Meyer, 1992] treats this topic in detail.

5. Yes, we do consider **m**'s scope of polymorphism to form a cone, with C at the apex. It doesn't matter that **C::m** doesn't have a real implementation, since C is a deferred class and will never have any instantiated objects, anyway.

   The answer would be the same even if **m** weren't defined *at all* on C, so long as C were deferred and **m** were defined on all of C's nondeferred subclasses. For example, if the method **area** were defined on all of POLYGON's subclasses but not on POLYGON itself, then the AOP of the **area** would still be POLYGON, so long as POLYGON were a deferred class from which no objects could be instantiated.

6. The apparent COP for **m** would be a ragged SOP if some of A's descendants overrode **m**, either by canceling it out or by giving it a completely different definition from its definition as **A::m**. Overriding a method like this is therefore a risky practice: It may create the illusion that a variable's SOP lies within a method's SOP, although, because of the gaps in the method's SOP, it doesn't.

7. Such a tool might provide two lists of classes: The first list would comprise the classes to whose objects the variable might point. The second list would comprise the classes on which the method was defined. The tool might also provide an "error list," comprising the classes that appeared on the first list, but not on the second.

Class Interfaces

This final chapter is about designing a class's interface—its "outside." The quality of a class interface depends not only on its cohesion (which we looked at in Chapter 9), but also on the placement and design of its methods. This chapter completes our tour through the design factors that determine the quality of an object-oriented application and thus determine the application's robustness, reliability, extensibility, reusability, and maintainability. The exercises at the end of the chapter also tie together many of the design ideas that we've explored in previous chapters.

The chapter's opening section covers a very useful object-oriented design technique: the use of mix-in classes to add capabilities to a class without compromising the class's cohesion or the quality of its interface. Mix-in classes also enhance the reusability of classes developed for one particular application in other applications. The second section discusses organizing methods in concentric rings to create an interface within an interface and to strengthen further object orientation's central pillar of encapsulation.

The chapter's third and final section returns to the topics of state-space and behavior that we examined in Chapter 10. This time, however, I distinguish the various ways that a class's state-space and behavior may be accessed via the class's interface, and how the design of individual methods can affect the quality of a class's entire interface.

This chapter applies several design principles that we covered in previous chapters and uses a sample of object-oriented code to illuminate new design concepts.

12.1 Mix-In Classes

Figure 12.1 depicts a rectangle that's free to move and rotate so long as it remains within its enclosing frame. (I indicate the limits of its current extent on the screen with lines marked **top**, **bottom**, **left**, **right**.)

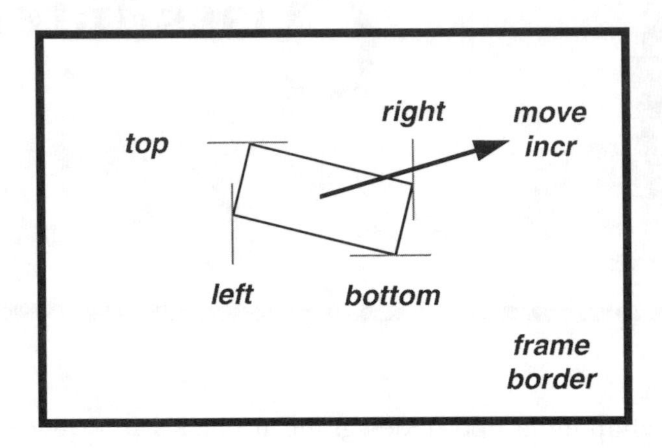

Fig. 12.1: A rectangle within a frame.

Figure 12.2 shows part of the design of RECTANGLE-IN-FRAME, which inherits from the two classes RECTANGLE and SHAPE-IN-FRAME.

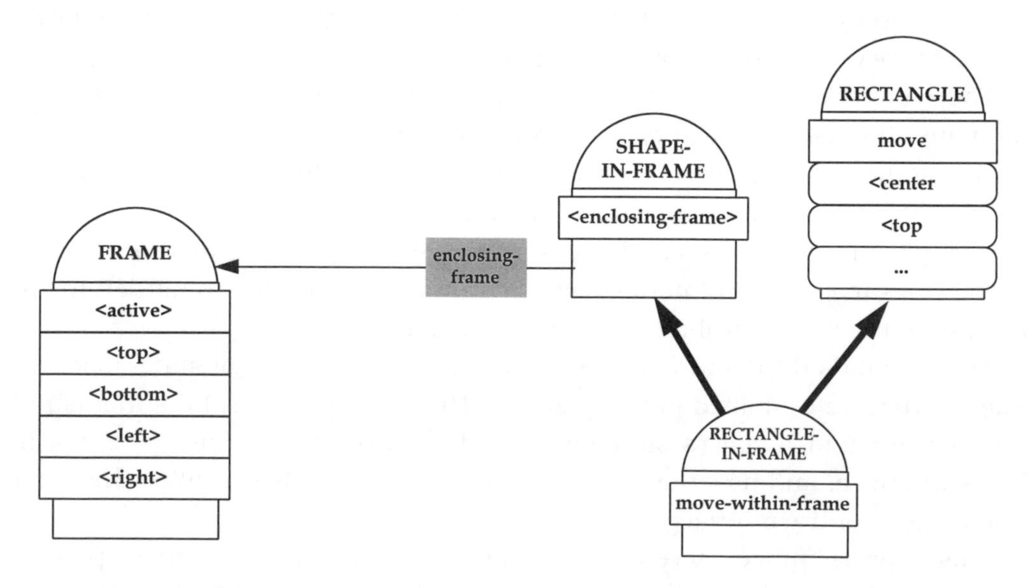

Fig. 12.2: The inheritance hierarchy for RECTANGLE-IN-FRAME.

The class RECTANGLE is the ordinary class that supports the manipulation—such as the moving, rotating, or stretching—of rectangles, a class that you may purchase as part of a class library. SHAPE-IN-FRAME is a less conventional class, which records the relationship between a rectangle and its enclosing frame. SHAPE-IN-FRAME is an example of a mix-in class.

A *mix-in class* typically supports an abstraction or mechanism that could be useful in several other classes, but which doesn't particularly belong in any one of those classes. Parceling away distinct abstractions and mechanisms into mix-in classes enhances the reusability of other classes. Normally, you don't instantiate objects from mix-in classes. Instead, other classes inherit a mix-in class's state-space and behavior. (Mix-in classes work best when your language supports multiple inheritance, as in this example.)

In the rectangle example of Fig. 12.1, a mix-in class offers a design solution to one problem presented by the rectangle and frame: our need to record the frame in which a given rectangle is enclosed. If we modify the class RECTANGLE by giving it a variable to hold this information, then we'll reduce the reusability of RECTANGLE in other applications. (To use the terms that I presented in Chapter 9, we would encumber RECTANGLE with FRAME and give it mixed-role cohesion.) Anyway, the vendor of RECTANGLE might not give us the source code to modify!

A more reasonable place to record a rectangle's relationship with its frame is the class RECTANGLE-IN-FRAME, which is all about rectangles and frames. That would be fine, except that ELLIPSE-IN-FRAME and TRIANGLE-IN-FRAME also need access to the same kind of machinery. That's why the mix-in class SHAPE-IN-FRAME is so useful. SHAPE-IN-FRAME can be mixed in with RECTANGLE to yield RECTANGLE-IN-FRAME. In another part of the system, it could be mixed in with ELLIPSE to form ELLIPSE-IN-FRAME, and so on.

Now, let's look at the code of the three classes, RECTANGLE, SHAPE-IN-FRAME, and RECTANGLE-IN-FRAME. (I've written this code in the same fictitious language that I used in Chapter 1.)

```
class RECTANGLE;

  var center:POINT;
  var height, width:LENGTH;
  var orientation:ANGLE;
  ...
  public read center, height, width, orientation;
  ...
  method v1: POINT;          // a function-style access method that returns a vertex
  begin
    var vertex:POINT := POINT.new;
    vertex.x := center.x + (height * sin (orientation) + width * cos (orientation)) / 2;
    vertex.y := center.y + (height * cos (orientation) + width * sin (orientation)) / 2;
    return (vertex);
  endmethod v1;
  ...

  method top: LENGTH;        // a function-style access method that returns the top
  begin
    return (max (v1.y, v2.y, v3.y, v4.y));
  endmethod top;
  ...

  method move (move-incr: 2D-VECTOR;); // a modifier method that
                                       // moves the rectangle
  begin
    center.x plus move-incr.x;         // the operator plus increments the
                                       // variable on the left
    center.y plus move-incr.y;
  endmethod move;
  ...
endclass RECTANGLE;
```

The internal representation of RECTANGLE objects rests on four variables: **center** records the center-point of a rectangle; **height** and **width** should be self-explanatory; and **orientation** records how much a rectangle is tilted (counterclockwise from the horizontal). These are the *core representational variables* of the class; they're the pillars that internally support the external abstraction of a rectangle. (But since the information that these variables provide is also part of the external abstraction of a rectangle, the variables are also made publicly visible.)

The class SHAPE-IN-FRAME, like many mix-ins, is simple. It contains little beyond a pointer to the frame that's to enclose the shape, and a switch recording whether the frame is active (constraining the rectangle) or not.

```
class SHAPE-IN-FRAME;

  var enclosing-frame:FRAME;                  // assume for simplicity frame
                                              // is always horizontal
  ...
  public read-update enclosing-frame;         // the frame doing the enclosing
                                              // can be changed
  ...
endclass SHAPE-IN-FRAME;
```

Notice that RECTANGLE-IN-FRAME in some sense conforms to SHAPE-IN-FRAME. That is, a rectangle in a frame *is a* shape in a frame. However, type conformance isn't usually an issue with true mix-in classes. This is because a mix-in class, say M, doesn't have instantiated objects of its own. Therefore, the question, Can I provide an object of class SUCH-AND-SUCH in the context that an object of class M is expected? doesn't arise.

Although a mix-in class rarely has objects of its own, it does represent a particular aspect of the world. Through multiple inheritance, a designer may combine aspects provided by mix-in classes into one class, from which objects will be instantiated. We saw the first example of an aspect, printability, in Section 11.2.2. In this section, we saw another example: the property of being enclosed in a frame. The final exercise of this chapter also contains an example of an aspect: the property of being a dog owner.

12.2 Rings of Methods

In this section, we investigate the structure of methods within a single class and see how to make the most of encapsulation by designing methods in inner and outer rings. As an example, I pick RECTANGLE-IN-FRAME (as shown in Fig. 12.2), the class that both creates rectangles within frames and defines the behavior that keeps a rectangle within its enclosing frame. Here's the code for one of its methods, **move-within-frame**:

```
class RECTANGLE-IN-FRAME;
  inherits from SHAPE-IN-FRAME, RECTANGLE;
  ...
  method move-within-frame (move-incr: 2D-VECTOR;);
  begin
    var  allwd-move-incr:2D-VECTOR := 2D-VECTOR.new;            // will hold the
                                                                // actual allowed move
    if   self.enclosing-frame.active                      // enclosing-frame is inherited
                                                          // from SHAPE-IN-FRAME
    then
      if     move-incr.x > 0                 // to the right in this convention
      then  allwd-move-incr.x := min (move-incr.x, self.enclosing-frame.right - self.right);
      else  allwd-move-incr.x := max (move-incr.x, self.enclosing-frame.left - self.left);
      endif;

      if     move-incr.y > 0                 // upward in this convention
      then  allwd-move-incr.y := min (move-incr.y, self.enclosing-frame.top - self.top);
      else  allwd-move-incr.y := max (move-incr.y, self.enclosing-frame.bottom - self.bottom);
      endif;
    else     allwd-move-incr := move-incr;    // there's no active frame at present
    endif;

    self.move (allwd-move-incr;);  // move is the method inherited from RECTANGLE
  endmethod move-within-frame;
  ...
endclass RECTANGLE-IN-FRAME;
```

The method **move-within-frame** is one of several methods that this class could contain. (Another would be **rotate-within-frame**.) The chief job of **move-within-frame** is to make sure that the rectangle doesn't go outside its enclosing frame when it's moved in some direction. To do this job, the method computes the allowed move for the rectangle, which is the smaller of the requested move and the distance to the frame border (in each of the **x** and **y** dimensions), and then sends a message to

self. This message invokes the method **move**, as inherited from the class RECTANGLE.

Notice how the designer uses a message to invoke **move**, rather than directly tweaking the value of the variable **center**. But why *didn't* the designer just tweak **center** directly by coding, for example,

```
center.x plus allwd-move-incr.x;
center.y plus allwd-move-incr.y;
```

instead of invoking **move**? After all, that would do exactly the same thing and would probably be more efficient. And, although the variable **center** is declared within RECTANGLE, it's also available to RECTANGLE-IN-FRAME, which is a subclass of RECTANGLE.

The answer is encapsulation—or, more specifically, implementation hiding. Invoking another method within the same object, rather than simply "grabbing" a variable directly, is beneficial for three reasons:

1. It may avoid duplication of code in the two methods.

2. It limits the knowledge of some variables' representations to fewer methods.

3. If one of the methods is in a subclass, then sending a message, rather than directly manipulating the superclass' variables, decreases the connascence between the two classes. For example, the subclass has to know fewer of the superclass' variable names.

Figure 12.3 shows how the method structure might appear when you use this approach of methods invoking methods within the same object. Methods appear in rings: inner rings, which are methods used only by other methods of the same object; and outer rings, which are methods that anybody can use. For example, in Fig. 12.3, **method-c** sends a message **self.method-f (...;...)** that invokes **method-f** on the same object. **method-c** is an outer method, because it doesn't access any variables itself. **method-f** is an inner method, invoked by **method-c** to read and update variables.

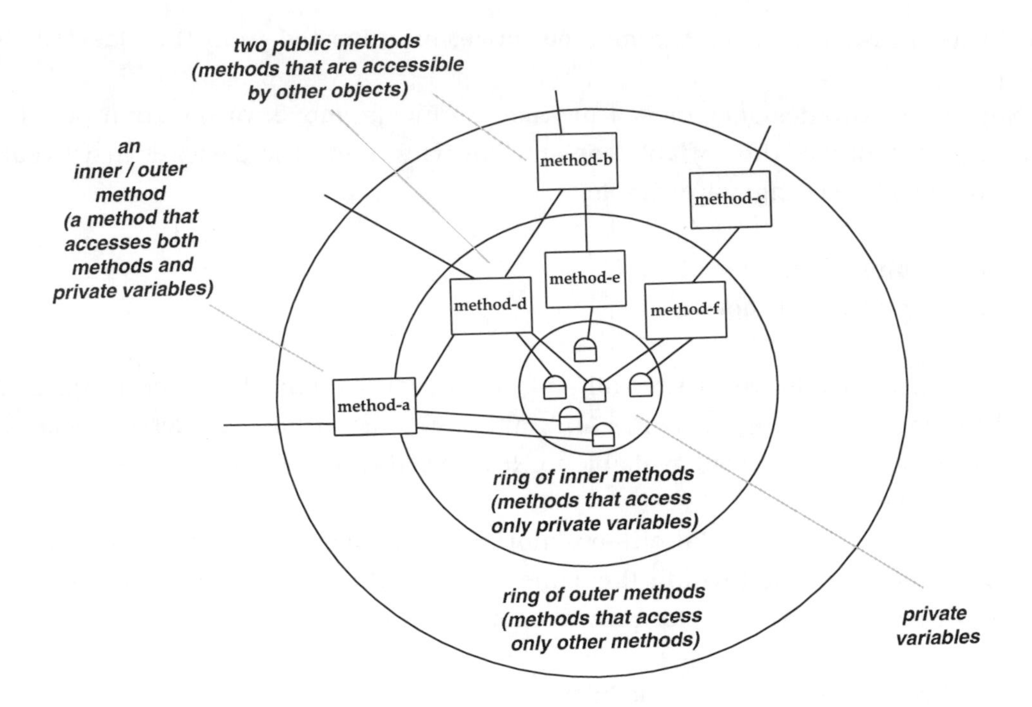

Fig. 12.3: Inner, outer, and inner/outer methods.

However, the distinction between outer and inner rings isn't as sharp as Fig. 12.3 implies. Many methods (such as **method-d**) are both outer and inner. Also, most outer methods access at least one variable directly (as does **method-a** of Fig. 12.3).

The class RECTANGLE offers an example of methods organized in rings. The method **top** invokes the methods **v1**, **v2**, **v3**, and **v4** instead of doing all its calculations directly from the core variables (**center**, **height**, **width**, and **orientation**). The designer's reasons were both to save code and to localize the knowledge of representation of variables. (These reasons were listed above as reasons 1 and 2.)

We now also have a fuller answer to the earlier question, Why didn't the designer of the method **move-within-frame** (in the class RECTANGLE-IN-FRAME) update the variable **center** directly? The reason is the danger of having methods of the subclass RECTANGLE-IN-FRAME messing around with variables of the superclass RECTANGLE. (This reason was listed above as reason 3.)

Consider what would have happened if the designer of **move-within-frame** *did* directly manipulate the center of the rectangle, and if our class vendor had then sent us a new version of the class RECTANGLE, a version that stores (rather than computes) the four vertices of the rectangle, as shown in the code below.

```
class RECTANGLE;                    // the new, improved-speed version!

   var center:POINT;
   var height, width:LENGTH;
   var orientation:ANGLE;           // these are the core representational variables
   var v1, v2, v3, v4:POINT;        // the four vertices of the rectangle, held redundantly
                                    // for efficiency
   ...
   public read center, height, width, top, bottom, left, right, v1, v2, v3, v4, orientation;
   ...
   method move (move-incr: 2D-VECTOR; );
   begin
     center.x plus move-incr.x;  center.y plus move-incr.y;
     v1.x plus move-incr.x;  v1.y plus move-incr.y;          // move the vertices with the center
     v2.x plus move-incr.x;  v2.y plus move-incr.y;
     v3.x plus move-incr.x;  v3.y plus move-incr.y;
     v4.x plus move-incr.x;  v4.y plus move-incr.y;
   endmethod move;
   ...
endclass RECTANGLE;
```

Notice that the method **move** is now more complicated, because it must maintain the redundant information held by **v1**, **v2**, **v3**, and **v4**. (The information is redundant because the four vertices can be computed from the core representational variables, **center**, **height**, **width**, and **orientation**.) If the system had simply been recompiled and relinked, then the method **move-within-frame** would exhibit a defect: It would divorce the corners of a rectangle from its center.

The fix would be to rewrite the corner-moving code. Better yet, we should reinstate the first design by invoking the method **move**, defined on RECTANGLE. In other words, we should arrange RECTANGLE's methods in rings.[1]

12.3 Quality of a Class Interface

Chapter 9 (in the section on class cohesion) discussed what you should put in the same class and what you should put in separate classes. Chapter 9 (in treating encumbrance), Chapter 10 (on the principle of type conformance), and Chapter 11

[1] I return to this example and its issue of design for efficiency in Exercise 4 at the end of this chapter.

(on inheritance) discussed how classes should relate to one another. This section of Chapter 12 covers the design of the interface to a single class. In effect, this section answers two questions: What makes a class a good implementation of an abstract data-type (ADT)? and, What causes a class to fall short of this ideal?

Section 12.3.1 discusses how an interface may support a class's state-space. Section 12.3.2 discusses how an interface may support a class's behavior. The final section, Section 12.3.3, addresses the cohesion of individual methods in an interface. Throughout Section 12.3, I use the RECTANGLE class of the previous section and a CUSTOMER-ORDER class from an order-processing system as examples.

12.3.1 State support in a class interface

As we saw in Chapter 10, during its lifetime an object moves from state to state within the state-space of its class. Messages that the object receives drive it from state to state. You'd expect that an object could be driven to only the legal states of its class's state-space. While this is true in a *good* class-interface design, I'm afraid that it's not true in *all* designs. In this section, I address four types of class interface design, and point out the deficiencies (if any) of each one in supporting a class's state-space.

1. Illegal states

A class interface that allows illegal states enables an object to reach states that violate that object's class invariant. For example, let's assume that there's a method **move-point** defined on RECTANGLE, which allows a single corner of a rectangle to be moved independently of the other corners. This is likely to allow a rectangle to become distorted into a trapezoid. In other words, a rectangle could become a non-rectangle, which would violate its class invariant.

An interface that permits an object to reach illegal states represents poor design. It's usually caused by a designer's revealing some of the class's internal implementation. (I once heard someone describe such an interface as "letting the implementation leak out.") In this example, we'd guess that RECTANGLE is implemented internally by four variables, pointing to the four corners of a rectangle. However, by exposing these corners without constraints, the designer has allowed a RECTANGLE object to fall into illegal states.

In the worst kind of design, an object may be allowed to reach *all the states possible* for the implementation, many of which could be illegal. For example, a rectangle implemented by lines for its sides, with each of these lines directly manipulable from outside the object, could wind up as four unconnected lines.

2. Incomplete states

In this kind of class-interface design, there are legal states in RECTANGLE's state-space that an object cannot reach. For example, let's imagine that, because of a poor design of RECTANGLE, no square rectangles could be created. Or, imagine another miserable design in which all rectangles with a side less than an inch in length *have to* be square. (In this second design, there could never be, say, a half-inch by quarter-inch rectangle.)

In my experience, this kind of interface-design flaw occurs less often than does the illegal states flaw. But note that an interface may have a double problem: It may support illegal states *and* incomplete states.

3. Inappropriate states

This brand of class-interface design typically offers to outside users of an object some states that are not formally part of the object's class abstraction. For example, imagine that a designer has created a STACK ("last in, first out") class. He has implemented the stack by means of an array and an array-pointer. So far, so good. But what if he now makes the array-pointer publicly visible? Then he's created an interface with inappropriate states, for an array-pointer is not part of a stack abstraction. (Users of a stack should see only the last element and whether the stack is empty or full.) As another example of this interface sin, the designer may let users of a stack look at, say, the 17th element of the stack.

(I'm assuming here that the designer doesn't let users of the stack actually *change* the array-pointer or the 17th element. If that were allowed, then the designer would have created an interface that supported illegal states. For example, a user could set the array-pointer negative or to some ridiculously large number.)

The question of inappropriate states becomes a thorny one on many projects. For example, is the *depth* of a stack appropriate information to be made public? Most people who study the concept of stacks would answer, "No; only the top of a stack is relevant." However, consider the QUEUE ("first in, first out") class. Here, many designers would consider the current length of a queue to be highly relevant to a user of a queue.

As you see from the above examples, you're probably still in for some heated discussions in your next project about what's appropriate and what's inappropriate. However, I hope that, by highlighting here the issue of inappropriate states, you can avoid some of the interface designs that I've seen recently, where random, potentially changeable pieces of classes' internal implementations were inappropriately revealed to the world.

4. Ideal states

This represents ideal design of a class interface, because an object of a class may reach any state legal for that class, but *only* states legal for the class. Obviously, knowing which states are legal and which are illegal depends on having a good understanding of the purpose of the class and a definition of its class invariant (a topic to which I return below, in the section on behavior).

12.3.2 Behavior support in a class interface

An object carries out some behavior when it moves from its current state to another state (or, sometimes, to the same state) as the result of receiving a message. The interface to a class may be badly designed so that either illegal behavior is supported or legal behavior is not supported. Below, I list and explain the seven ways in which a designer may build a class interface to support—or not support—behavior correctly. Most of these have specific deficiencies, which I also describe.

1. Illegal behavior

A class interface that supports illegal behavior has a method that allows an object to make illegal transitions from one state to another. For example, let's say that a customer order must be approved before it can be filled. If an object of class CUSTOMER-ORDER can go directly from a status of **unapproved** to **filled** by means of some method provided on the interface, then the interface supports illegal behavior.

Notice that it's the *behavior* here that's illegal—not the two states involved, each of which is a legal state for a customer order. The designer of this class has not supported the required state-transition model for CUSTOMER-ORDER, probably because he's allowed **CUSTOMER-ORDER::status** to be directly manipulated through the interface.

There are many other, often more subtle, examples of interfaces supporting illegal behavior. I recently saw a design of the class STACK in which a user of a stack object could pull out an element from the middle of the stack and then "shove together" the two disjointed stack fragments to make the stack whole again. This is decidedly *not* part of a stack abstraction.

You might be able to guess from the exercise at the end of Chapter 11 why the designer had supported such illegal behavior in his STACK interface. The answer is that he allowed STACK to inherit from LIST, which legitimately allows the removal of a middle element, and had not overridden the offending behavior in STACK. Again, as with inappropriate states, deciding which behavior is illegal and which is legal for a given class may involve some project discussion. However, you should always seek out and eliminate fortuitous cases of illegal behavior (resulting, perhaps, from the overzealous use of inheritance).

2. Dangerous behavior

When a class has an interface with dangerous behavior, multiple messages are needed to carry out a single piece of an object's behavior, and at least one of the messages takes the object to an *illegal* state. (Thus, a class interface with dangerous behavior must also permit an object to reach illegal states, which was the first poor interface design described in Section 12.3.1.)

Many of the interfaces with dangerous behavior that I've seen were bizarre. Here's an example: Let's say that a customer's order is currently approved, but it turns out that all the product lines requested on the order are out of stock. (I'm assuming they're *all* out of stock for simplicity.) Thus, we need to give the order a status of **back-ordered**.

If the interface to CUSTOMER-ORDER is designed with dangerous behavior, then changing an order's status might not be easy. For example, perhaps the only way to make the transition from **approved** to **back-ordered** is, first, to send a message to an order that sets the number of items ordered to a negative number—this is the bizarre illegal state—and, second, to send a message telling the order to fill itself. The code within **CUSTOMER-ORDER::fill** then sets the number of items ordered back to positive and sets the status to **back-ordered**. This interface therefore requires two messages to achieve one result, the first of which puts the object in an illegal state.

RECTANGLE may provide another example of this kind of interface, one that's just as gruesome as the above but not quite so weird. Let's say that we want to move a rectangle to the right. In order to do that, we have to send four messages to the rectangle object: Each message moves one corner. As the rectangle staggers to the right, it winds up in two or three intermediate illegal states. (This was also the example of an interface with illegal states that I used in Section 12.3.1.)

An interface supporting dangerous behavior breathes an evil life into an illegal-states interface because it encourages—nay, obliges—people to put an object into illegal states. Not only does it further expose an implementation that may change, but it also increases the risk of an object's being *left* in some illegal state. Notice, too, how a dangerous-behavior interface also promotes connascence of algorithm across class boundaries, because users of RECTANGLE need to know the algorithm by which a rectangle is moved (namely, one corner at a time).

3. Irrelevant behavior

Irrelevant behavior in a class interface is behavior that simply doesn't belong to that class and its objects. For example, if CUSTOMER-ORDER contained a method named **compute-loan-repayment**, then CUSTOMER-ORDER would have irrelevant behavior. The behavior isn't relevant to the class, because it has nothing to do with customer orders: It updates no CUSTOMER-ORDER object and doesn't even access any private variables of CUSTOMER-ORDER.

No, you haven't misunderstood; including irrelevant behavior in an interface is idiotic design. Fortunately for the object-oriented world, it very seldom occurs. The arch exponent of irrelevant behavior is an egregiously shoddy fellow named Genghis the Perverse, who works at a large company nowhere near yours (I hope). Genghis will happily put a method **compute-date-difference** in the interface to CUSTOMER and **determine-best-transportation-route** in PRODUCT's interface. Don't ask me why. It makes no sense to me, either. Go ask Genghis.

4. Incomplete behavior

A class interface with incomplete behavior doesn't allow all behavior needed by objects of that class to be carried out. For example, let's assume that a customer order has the status **approved**, but the customer suddenly goes bankrupt. It's entirely reasonable for the users to change the order's status back to **unapproved**. But in a system I was reviewing recently, I saw CUSTOMER-ORDER designed so that, once an order had achieved **approved** status, there was *no possible way* to return it to **unapproved** status. (The designer had ignored one of the analysis requirements.)

With incomplete behavior, we don't have a case of an interface supporting behavior awkwardly or via illegal states. An interface of this type actually *forbids* some legal behavior, because not all legal transitions among those states are supported. Notice, however, that a class with an interface that supports incomplete behavior may still support ideal states, because (in the example above) an order might somehow be able to reach an **unapproved** status; the problem is that it just can't get there from an **approved** status.

5. Awkward behavior

An object whose class has an interface with awkward behavior may require two or more messages to carry out a single piece of legal behavior. Awkward behavior resembles dangerous behavior, above, because multiple messages are needed to effect a single piece of an object's behavior. However, with awkward behavior, none of the messages takes the object to an illegal state.

For example, let's say that a customer order with a status of **approved** can become **filled** when it has stock and a shipment date assigned to it. It's perfectly reasonable that a filled order could have its shipment date changed. However, an interface may be designed so that the only way to do this is to set the status of the order back to **approved** and then reset it to **filled** with the new shipment date. You'll therefore need to send two messages in order to change a shipment date.

Notice that the object goes through a bogus, albeit legal, state. The state is bogus because it doesn't correspond to reality: The order in question is now filled and is no longer merely approved. The designer has failed to support the required behavior of changing the shipment date. Or, to be fair to the designer, he may have failed to support the required behavior because he was handed an incomplete specification for CUSTOMER-ORDER.

However, designing an interface with awkward behavior is not a capital offense. Indeed, it may not always be clear whether an object *should* be able to move from one state to another in a single step. For example, should we be able to move a rectangle to the right *and* rotate it by 30 degrees with a single message, or should that be considered two pieces of behavior? Or, if we can rescale a rectangle with its center held in the same place, should RECTANGLE's interface also support rescaling with a corner held in place? (After all, that could be done by invoking **rescale-about-center** and then **move**.)

The best way to answer these questions is to study the needs of the problem and see how the class is intended to be used. If you can predict the future infallibly, you'll always get the answers absolutely correct. (But if you can predict the future infallibly, what are you doing in the software business?) My general recommendation is: *Don't* provide a method to support a speculative piece of behavior if that behavior can already be supported by executing two or three methods. Wait until the need for the behavior actually arises before you consider adding another method to the interface. (This topic crops up again, under replicated behavior, below.)

Although I've mentioned "the needs of the problem" in this chapter, I haven't defined the term explicitly. This is deliberate, for appreciating all possible uses for a class is a matter of human judgment. It's why your experience as an object-oriented designer will always be valuable. It's also why the walkthrough (or any form of peer-group review) is vital in object-oriented design, for a solitary person can seldom appreciate all the subtleties of—and potential future changes to—a given application or class.

6. Replicated behavior

An interface to a class has replicated behavior if the same piece of behavior in an object may be carried out via the object's interface in more than one way. Class designs that I've seen contain countless examples of replicated behavior. Let me give you a representative sample to illustrate the various causes of, and reasons for, replicated behavior.

Recall the class HOMINOID of Chapter 1. This class has two methods, **turn-left** (which turns a hominoid counterclockwise by 90 degrees) and **turn-right** (which turns a hominoid clockwise by 90 degrees). Now, let's say that we need to turn a hominoid counterclockwise by, say, 60 degrees. To do so, we write another method, **turn**, which takes an argument of **turn-angle**. In adding this method, we've created replicated behavior in HOMINOID's interface because we can now turn a hominoid by 90 degrees in two distinct ways:

```
turn-left;                    // first way
turn (right-angle;);          // second way
```

This piece of replicated behavior arose for historical reasons, specifically because we generalized HOMINOID's original interface. If we'd foreseen the need for arbitrary turns originally, we might never have written **turn-left** and **turn-right**. But now that we have these two methods, what shall we do? We can't just remove them in a cavalier way, because code in dozens of other classes may be referring to them. The two solutions are these: Leave them alone and live with HOMINOID's replicated behavior and its resulting more complicated interface; or remove the two methods after, say, a year, during which time the other software can be modified to use **turn (right-angle;)** instead.

Ironically, a class may sometimes evolve in a way opposite to that in the previous paragraph, as its designer deliberately introduces replicated behavior into its interface. For example, let's say that HOMINOID currently has only the general **turn** as a method for turning. However, let's also assume that 99 percent of applications needing to turn a hominoid need to turn that hominoid by a right angle. The designer might then add **turn-left** and **turn-right** as a convenience to the many. Of course, he'll have to leave **turn** in the interface for the 1 percent, which will create the replicated behavior.

A variation on the theme of the above paragraph occurs in the following example: Imagine that we have (in a brokerage application) the class EQUITY-ACCOUNT. One of its methods is **sell-equity-position (equity, amt-to-sell; sale-ok)**, which sells a given amount of a customer's position in a given equity.

Another method is **sell-all-equity-positions (; sale-ok)**, which sells all of the customer's positions in equities (in that account). This latter method is superfluous, because the first method would achieve the same if you looped through each equity in the account, put into **amt-to-sell** the entire amount that the customer held in that equity, and then sent the message **sell-equity-position (equity, amt-to-sell; sale-ok)**.

However, that looping code, which is nontrivial, must be written wherever the application needs to sell all equity positions. This may occur in dozens of places in the applications. To avoid such duplicated effort and the accompanying connascence of algorithm, EQUITY-ACCOUNT's designer has created **sell-all-equity-positions**, which is a legitimate, though superfluous, method.

Incidentally, the method **sell-all-equity-positions** could be designed as a stand-alone function outside EQUITY-ACCOUNT. But it's so much a part of maintaining equity accounts that to separate this method from its class would introduce additional connascence in the overall design of the application.

As you can imagine from the above examples, replicated behavior often raises arguments about class design. Replicated behavior may make a class's interface more complex and more difficult to learn. Nevertheless, as we saw above, a designer may choose to postpone (or even eschew) removing replicated behavior from an interface, because of existing usage. Indeed, a designer may even *introduce* replicated behavior in order to provide a specialized method that's more useful than the general methods already in the interface.

Although there isn't always a clear-cut answer to the question of whether replicated behavior is called for, class designers must consciously address the question whenever they add a method to a class. Otherwise, unwarranted and baroque replicated behavior will grow into a class's interface by accretion, or from the whims of an argumentative designer with a forceful personality, or from arbitrary, poorly-thought-out demands from users of the class. Such a class will be more difficult than necessary to learn and to modify.

7. Ideal behavior

An interface to a class supports ideal behavior if it enforces the following three properties:

- An object in a legal state can move *only* to another legal state.
- An object can move to another state *only* in a legal way, that is, in a way that's part of the prescribed behavior for the object's class.

- There is only one way of using the interface in order to carry out a piece of behavior.

Again, knowing which behavior is legal and which is illegal depends on having a good understanding of the purpose of the class and a complete specification of its required behavior, in the sense that I discussed above.

An example of an interface with ideal behavior is provided by the class STACK [WIDGET], which is a class whose objects are stacks containing widgets. Its interface contains these methods:

```
top: WIDGET;                // returns the top element of the stack
pop;                        // removes the top element of the stack
push (new-el: WIDGET);      // places a new element on the top of the stack
is-empty: BOOL;             // returns whether the stack is empty
is-full: BOOL;              // returns whether the stack is full
```

The above interface is ideal, because its five methods encompass the entire range of behavior of a normal stack and there is only one way in which to carry out any particular operation on a stack.

12.3.3 Method cohesion in a class interface

The third way (after achieving ideal states and behavior) to spruce up your classes' interfaces is by attending to the cohesion of individual methods. For decades in structured design (SD), module cohesion has been a standard criterion for assessing a procedural module's quality. In object orientation, methods should have good cohesion in the same way that individual procedural modules in SD should have good cohesion.[2]

In SD, cohesion highlights the designer's purpose in creating a particular module—whether the designer saw a strong, application-based reason for the module or whether he just stuffed a few random lines of code into a procedure. For example, DETERMINE-INVENTORY-REORDER-POINT is likely to have high cohesion, whereas MISC-FRUNK-ROUTINES probably has low cohesion.

Functional cohesion is the ideal cohesion that you achieve by keeping distinct methods cleanly separated. Poor method cohesion results from a designer's mis-

---

[2] In structured design, Larry Constantine ranked the seven possible levels of module cohesion into an approximate order of design quality, with functional cohesion at the top and coincidental cohesion at the bottom. See [Yourdon and Constantine, 1975] or [Page-Jones, 1980], for example.

guidedly combining together methods that should have been kept apart. The two ways of forming such a combination yield alternate cohesion and multiple cohesion, respectively, which I describe next. I then conclude this section on a more positive note, by describing functional cohesion.

1. Alternate cohesion

Alternate cohesion arises when a designer combines several pieces of behavior into a single method that, on receipt of a message, applies one of these pieces of behavior to the object.[3] In other words, someone sending a message to invoke the method must supply a flag telling the method what to do—which piece of behavior to execute this time.

For example, RECTANGLE might have a method

scale-or-rotate (scale-factor:REAL, rotate-angle:ANGLE, which-to-do:BOOL)

The combination **scale-or-rotate** either changes the size of a rectangle or rotates it, depending on whether **which-to-do** is set to **true** or **false**. Notice that in each case only one of the first two arguments is used; the other one is a useless dummy. But with a little more scheming, an evil designer could make the method's interface still worse—like this:

scale or rotate (amount:REAL, which-to-do:BOOL)

Here, the **amount** argument is confusingly doing double duty: It means a **scale-factor** in one case but a **rotation-angle** in the other.

This was a mild example. I'm sure you can picture a grotesque method with 17 pieces of behavior crammed into it and 19 arguments needed in every message, over a dozen of which are usually dummies. This kind of method design makes a mockery of object orientation. Let's draw a veil over it and move on to a kinder, gentler cohesion.

2. Multiple cohesion

Multiple cohesion is similar to alternate cohesion in that a designer has stuffed several pieces of behavior into a single method. However, when a method with

[3] Alternate cohesion is equivalent to logical cohesion of SD. It could also cover SD's coincidental cohesion if part of the code of a method with alternate cohesion was completely irrelevant to the object on which the method was executing. Again, only a dedicated Genghis would commit such a crime.

multiple cohesion executes, it applies all (rather than one) of the pieces of behavior to the object.[4] For example, a method **PERSON::change-address-and-phone-num**, which changes both a person's address and telephone number, has multiple cohesion.

Often such a method yields a class interface with incomplete behavior (that is, one that lacks some legal behavior) because the method carries out several steps and may therefore skip over some legal states. In SD, this wasn't a big problem, because such a module could always be factored into two modules, **change-address** and **change-phone-num**, each of which could be called individually. In object-oriented design, you can do the same thing so long as you ensure that the two methods are publicly available in the interface. (But then, you rightly wonder, if the methods are separately available, why retain the replicated behavior that the combined **change-address-and-phone-num** introduced? The only reason is that other code may be using it, but it should be scrapped as soon as possible.)

In a PERSON class that I saw recently, the designer hadn't factored this method into two. He boasted to me that he didn't need to factor, because his **change-address-and-phone-num** "could do everything" and supported all legal behavior. He further claimed, "If a person changes address but not telephone number, then you merely invoke the method with a null phone number and the method is smart enough to avoid changing **phone-num**." Although that may be true, this design creates a cumbersome interface whereby some messages need to pass dummy arguments.

Another form of multiple cohesion occurs when a designer inserts into a method some function that makes extraneous computations that should be performed outside the class. For example, let's say that **area** is a method of RECTANGLE. Now let's introduce another method, **bigger-area-than (some-area:AREA;):BOOL**, which tells us whether the rectangle is bigger than some other area. It would be used like this:

```
our-rect-is-bigger:BOOL := rect.bigger-area-than (some-area;);
if our-rect-is-bigger
then ...
```

[4] Multiple cohesion includes both sequential and communicational cohesion of SD. Procedural and temporal cohesion of a method are rare, since all the code in a method is working on the same object. That fact boosts its cohesion level. However, I suppose that Genghis *could* create a procedurally cohesive method, part of whose code was irrelevant to the object on which the method was executing.

The method **bigger-area-than** therefore carries out two functions. The first determines the rectangle's area; the second compares it to some fixed amount that was passed to it as an input argument. However, the determination of which area is bigger should be made by the object sending the message and not by the RECTANGLE object. The code in the sender object would simply look like this:

```
if rect.area > some-area
then ...
```

The reason for moving the comparison out of the class RECTANGLE is that it isn't part of the RECTANGLE abstraction. And dedicating an entire method to each extraneous computation that should occur outside a given class is extravagant. However, you may have noticed a resemblance between the method **bigger-area-than** and the method **sell-all-equity-positions** of Section 12.3.2, which I suggested could remain part of the class interface.

The issue is this: Make sure that your class provides methods that don't engage in extra-curricular activities. This is easier said than done: What does "extra-curricular" mean for a given class? Although the answer will always be a judgment call, if you have doubt about a method, then it probably doesn't belong in the class. However, you may wish to look at whether including the method will increase or decrease connascence. Finally, if your criterion for including a method will spawn a proliferation of methods, then your method probably doesn't belong. (For example, if you allow the method **bigger-area-than**, then why not allow **smaller-area-than** and **equal-area-to** as well?)

3. Functional cohesion

Functional cohesion is a term taken directly from SD, where it represents the ideal level of cohesion for a module. A functionally cohesive method is one that is dedicated to a single piece of behavior, as defined by the needs of the problem. Functional cohesion is also known as *ideal method cohesion*.

The name of a method gives the clue to its cohesion: An "and" name implies multiple cohesion, while an "or" name implies alternate cohesion. However, a strong name with neither "and" nor "or" in it implies a method with functional cohesion.

For example, **TANK::fill**, **RECTANGLE::area**, **PRODUCT-ITEM::weight**, **CUSTOMER-ORDER::dispatch**, **CUSTOMER::set-credit-limit**, **AIRPLANE::turn**, **ACCOUNT::make-deposit**, and **CUSTOMER::telephone-num** would be functionally cohesive methods. Each method carries out a single piece of behavior that's appropriate for its class; each method has a strong name.

The part of speech in a method name depends on whether the method is intended to respond to an informative, interrogative, or imperative message (message types that I defined in Section 1.5.4). Both informative and imperative methods tend to have verb names in the imperative mood—*Object, do this!* Examples above were **make-deposit** (informative), **fill**, **dispatch**, and **turn** (all imperative). An interrogative method usually has a noun name, the name of the attribute whose value it returns. Examples above were **area**, **weight**, and **telephone-num**.

The distinction between an informative and imperative message comes, not from the method name in the message, but from the purpose of the message. The reason that **freds-account.make-deposit(deposit-amt;)** is an informative method is that (presumably) Fred has made a deposit at the bank and now it's time to update the object representing Fred's bank account. The object is catching up with what's already happened in the real world.

The reason that **water-tank.fill** is an imperative message is that right now the water tank *isn't* full; the job of the **water-tank** object is (by executing its **fill** method) to turn on various taps, wait for the tank to become full, and then turn the taps off. The object is establishing the future condition of the real world.

There is one subtle difference between informative and imperative method names. Informative method names tend to refer implicitly to the target object in the genitive (possessive) or dative (indirect object) case. For example, **fred.set-credit-limit(new-limit;)** means "set the credit limit *of* the customer Fred," whereas **freds-account.make-deposit(deposit-amt;)** means "make a deposit *to* Fred's account." Imperative method names, on the other hand, tend to refer implicitly to the target object in the accusative (direct object) case. For example, **water-tank.fill** simply means "fill the water tank."

However, I'd never enforce the above naming convention for imperative, interrogative, and informative methods as a rigid rule, because you could certainly have, for example, an interrogative method named **TANK::give-liquid-volume**. Nevertheless, I've found the above conventions to be an excellent guideline for naming methods and for checking their cohesion: You know that a method named **CUSTOMER::do-some-stuff** isn't much good!

12.4 Summary

Chapter 12 covers the external design of classes, the design of the class interface, chiefly through the placement and design of its methods. The first design approach that we looked at employs mix-in classes to free other classes of abstractions that don't belong in their interfaces. (A mix-in class is a relatively simple component that normally doesn't instantiate objects. Instead, a designer uses the abstraction or mechanism that the mix-in class embodies, via inheritance, to create a new combination class.) This new class, with its multiple avenues of inheritance, may then possess both general (say, business) abstractions and more special (say, architectural) abstractions.

By relocating restrictive abstractions from a business class into a mix-in class, a designer enhances the business class's cohesion, encumbrance, and reusability. Since the same mix-in class may be useful in several design situations, superfluous code can be eliminated from applications and class libraries.

The second design approach in this chapter addresses the organization of methods into rings to create layers of encapsulation within a single class. This approach uses information and implementation hiding in order to shield individual methods from decisions that a designer might make in choosing an internal representation for a class. For example, a method (an "inner" method) might shield other methods ("outer" methods) from knowledge of some internal variables' details. Then, if the designer should change, say, the names or classes of those variables, only one method may need to be rewritten.

The third section of the chapter covers the quality of a class's interface in terms of methods' support for the class's state-space and behavior. A class's interface may support the class's state-space in four ways: *illegal states*, in which the interface allows an object to reach states that are illegal for its class (that is, states that violate the class invariant); *incomplete states*, in which the interface does not allow an object to reach some states that are legal for its class; *inappropriate states*, in which the interface presents some states that are not germane to the class's abstraction; and *ideal states*, in which the interface allows an object to reach all states that are legal for its class and only states that are legal for its class. A class's designer should aim for a class interface that supports ideal states.

A class's interface may support the class's behavior in seven ways: *illegal behavior*, in which the interface allows an object to carry out state transitions that are illegal for its class; *dangerous behavior*, in which the interface requires an object to carry out some state transitions via multiple messages that take the object through intermediate (but illegal) states; *irrelevant behavior*, in which the class's interface supports behavior extraneous to the class; *incomplete behavior*, in which the interface does not allow an object to carry out some state transitions that are legal for its class; *awkward behavior*, in which the interface requires an object to carry out some state transitions via multiple messages that take the object through intermediate (but legal) states; *replicated behavior*, in which the interface supports the same behavior in multiple ways; and *ideal behavior*, in which the interface allows an object to carry out in one way state transitions that are legal for its class and only state transitions that are legal for its class. A class's designer should aim for a class interface that supports ideal behavior.

A single method has three possible cohesions: *alternate cohesion*, in which a designer combines in a method several pieces of behavior to be executed alternatively, depending on the value of a flag; *multiple cohesion*, in which a designer combines in a method several pieces of behavior to be executed together; and *functional (or ideal) cohesion*, in which a designer creates a method dedicated to carrying out a single piece of behavior. The strength and clarity of a method's name often reveals its likely cohesion. A class's designer should create methods with functional cohesion.

The cohesion of methods is our final criterion for class quality. The ideal class, then, has these properties: It has ideal class cohesion; its interface supports ideal states and ideal behavior; each of its methods is functionally (ideally) cohesive; it has no unnecessary encumbrance; it has an encumbrance appropriate to its domain; it has no unnecessary connascence; and it has no connascence that crosses boundaries into other classes.

A class with these exemplary design qualities is a worthy implementation of an abstract data-type. It will be as robust, reliable, extensible, reusable, and maintainable as a class can ever be. It will bring joy to all who behold it. But, more important, if you build your object-oriented systems from such well-designed classes, you'll derive the maximum value that object orientation can deliver to your organization.

12.5 Exercises

1. In the design of RECTANGLE-IN-FRAME shown in Fig. 12.2, why didn't the designer simply have RECTANGLE-IN-FRAME inherit multiply from FRAME and RECTANGLE, rather than introduce the class SHAPE-IN-FRAME?

2. Look again at the design of ROOM (Section 11.1.4), which used message forwarding and the design of RECTANGLE-IN-FRAME (Section 12.1), which used multiple inheritance. What would happen if you swapped the approaches used to design these two classes? In other words, how might you approach the design of the "room volume" problem using multiple inheritance?

3. Conversely, how would you design a solution to the "rectangles in frames" problem using message forwarding?

4. Why might the design of the class RECTANGLE (first version, in Section 12.1) lead to run-time inefficiencies? Hint: Consider the local declaration **var vertex := POINT.new;** within the method **v1**, and note that **v1** returns **vertex** as its result.

5. In Section 12.3.2, on interfaces with replicated behavior, I suggested that sometimes a designer might deliberately introduce replicated behavior to a class interface, adding specialized methods for the convenience of users. How might you use rings of methods for this purpose? How might the idea of overloading, discussed in Section 1.8, also help?

6. Many structured-design principles still apply in object-oriented design. Choose a structured-design principle and briefly explain how it might apply to object-oriented design.

7. Imagine a shipping application, in which the users ship large boxes of packages to customers. Figure 12.4 shows the aggregation structure of an object of class SHIPMENT-UNIT. It comprises a containing box holding a set of packages bearing the actual contents of the shipment.

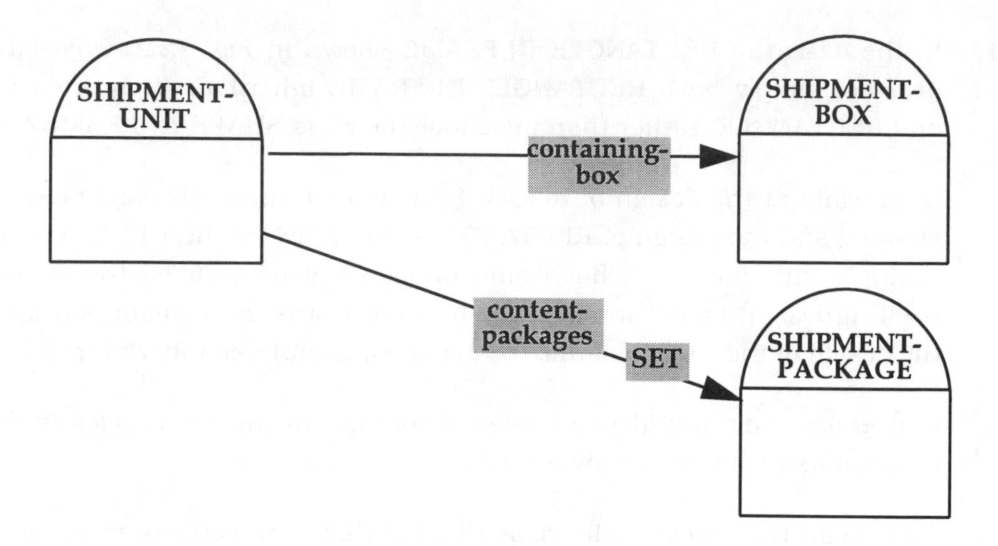

Fig. 12.4: A shipment unit is an aggregation of a containing box and a set of content packages.

The total weight of the ensemble is the sum of the weight of the containing box and the weights of all the content packages. Figure 12.5 shows one possible design of **SHIPMENT-UNIT::weight**.

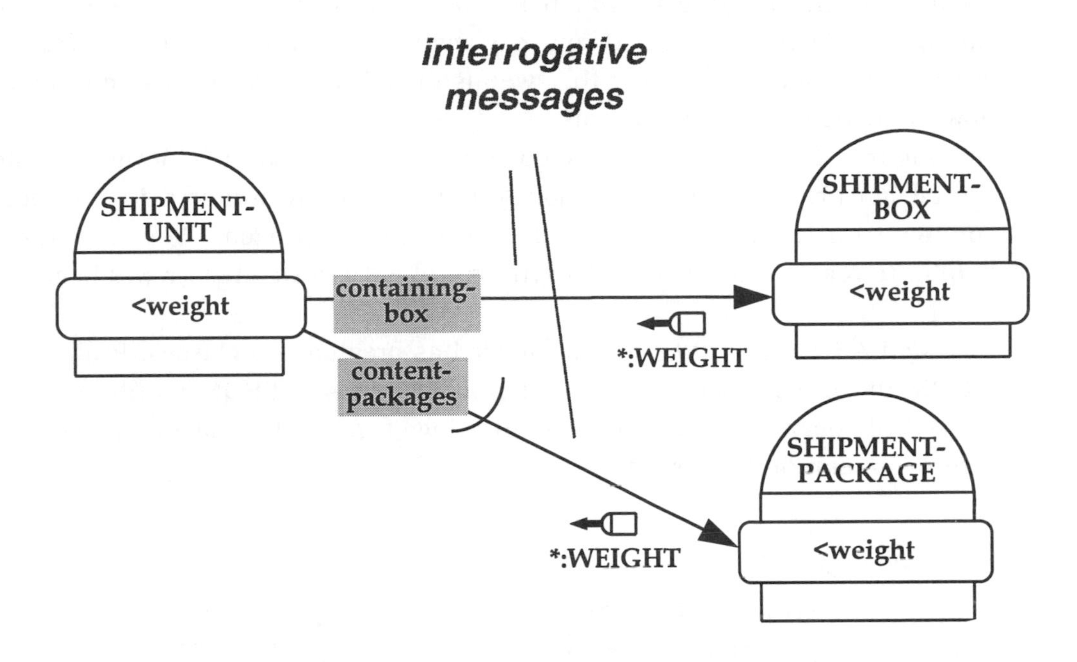

Fig. 12.5: A shipment unit finds its weight by interrogating its components.

In the design shown in Fig. 12.5, the method **SHIPMENT-UNIT::weight** sends an interrogative message first to the containing box to obtain *its* weight and then, iteratively, to all the content packages to obtain *their* weights.[5] The method adds each of the weights that it receives to a running total, which it returns as the total weight.

Is it possible to design **SHIPMENT-UNIT::weight** so that the component objects take the initiative in sending information to the aggregate object? How would that change the nature of the interface between SHIPMENT-UNIT and, say, SHIPMENT-PACKAGE? Would that design have any advantages or disadvantages?

---

[5] As you may recall from Chapter 1, an interrogative message is one that obtains information from an object. It normally does so by invoking an accessor method of the target object.

8. Imagine we have a dog-tracking application that has, as one of its requirements, the need to record which person owns which dogs. (We saw this example in Section 9.3.3, and you may wish to review some of the issues that were raised there.) Let's say that we also need to know, for a given person, how many dogs that person owns.

   Figures 12.6 through 12.9 show four (of several) possible designs. Using the design principles and terminology that you've encountered in this book, comment on the pros and cons of each design approach. You may find it helpful to read the following brief synopsis of each design before you begin.

   Design A (see Fig. 12.6): The designer has created two classes, PERSON and DOG, where we presume that the class PERSON maintains the link between a person and his dogs. A method of PERSON returns **num-of-dogs-owned**.

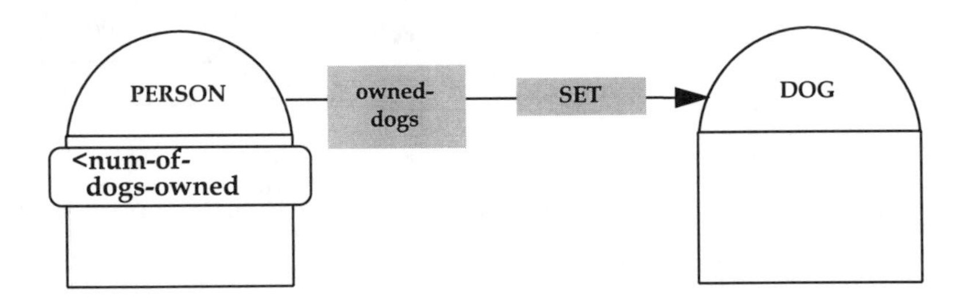

Fig. 12.6: Design A for "person owns dog."

   Design B (see Fig. 12.7): The designer has created three classes. The third one, PERSON-DOG-OWNERSHIP, is dedicated to maintaining the relationship between PERSON and DOG. Each instance of PERSON-DOG-OWNERSHIP associates one person with a set of dogs. The method **num-of-dogs-owned** will then be a class method of PERSON-DOG-OWNERSHIP, to which you would pass the appropriate person as an argument. (Figure 12.7 shows the arguments to **num-of-dogs-owned** for emphasis.) The method finds the appropriate instance of PERSON-DOG-OWNERSHIP and then returns the size of the "dog-set" for that instance.

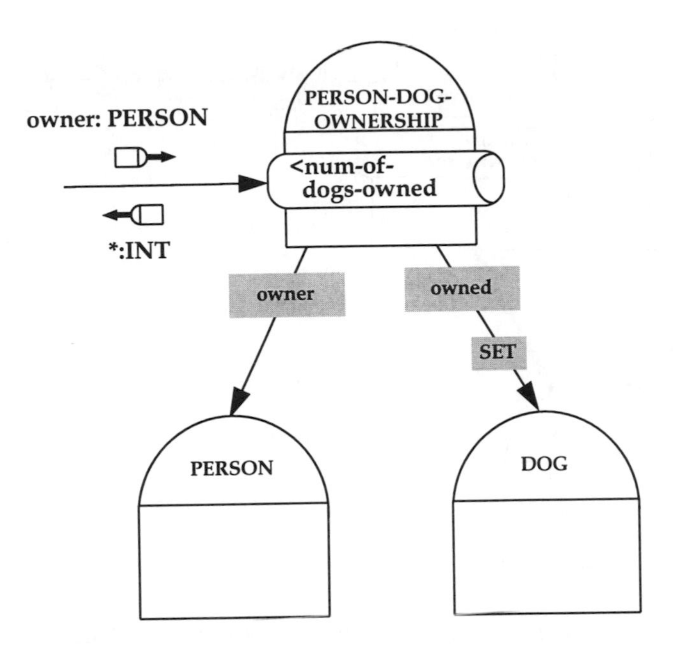

Fig. 12.7: Design B for "person owns dog."

Design C (see Fig. 12.8): The designer has created a mix-in class, DOG-OWNER, which maintains the link to dogs and returns **num-of-dogs-owned**. The class DOG-OWNING-PERSON, which inherits multiply from DOG-OWNER and PERSON, is the class from which you instantiate objects representing persons who own dogs.

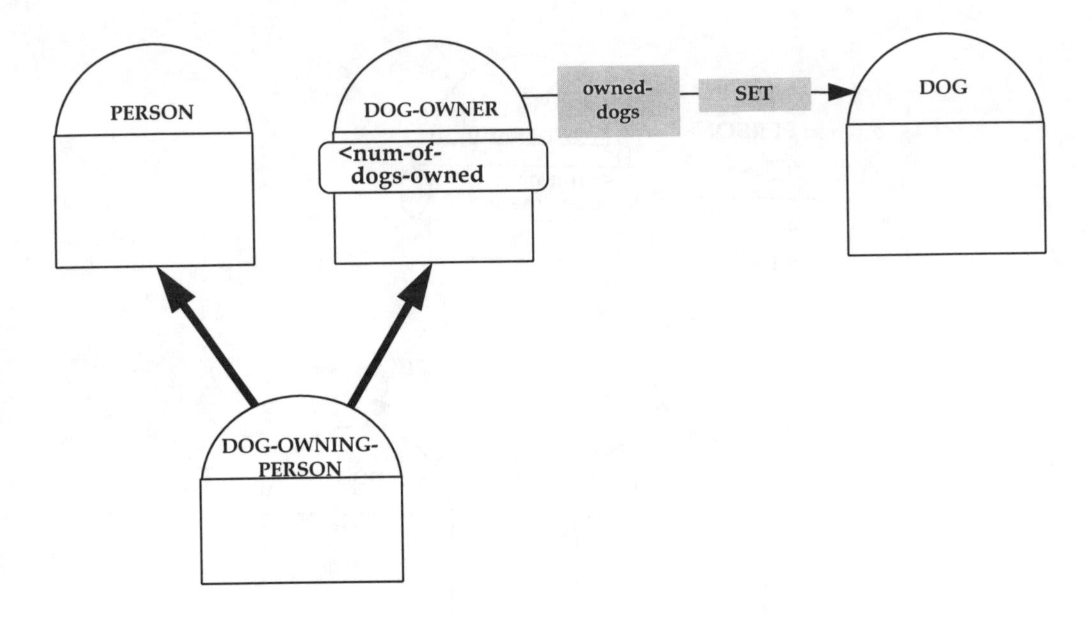

Fig. 12.8: Design C for "person owns dog."

Design D (see Fig. 12.9): As in Design C, the designer has created a class DOG-OWNING-PERSON. However, this DOG-OWNING-PERSON acquires its properties not through inheritance but by referring to two objects, the first being of class PERSON, the second being of class SET [DOG]. (Although this design resembles Design B, DOG-OWNING-PERSON lacks any class variables or class methods.)

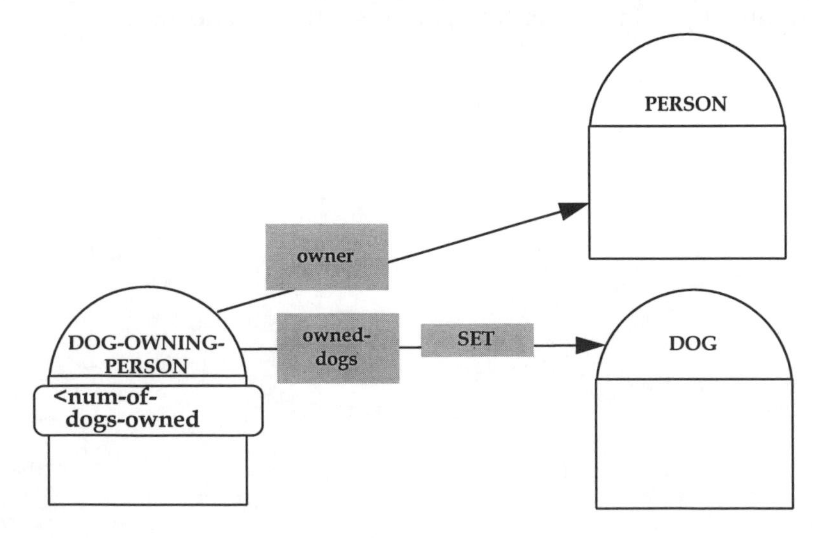

Fig. 12.9: Design D for "person owns dog."

12.6 Answers

1. The reason is straightforward: A rectangle is *not* a frame. If we were to allow RECTANGLE to inherit from FRAME, then we'd violate the principle of type conformance, covered in Chapter 10.

2. Figure 12.10 shows CUBOID-ROOM designed so that it inherits multiply from the classes CUBOID and ROOM.

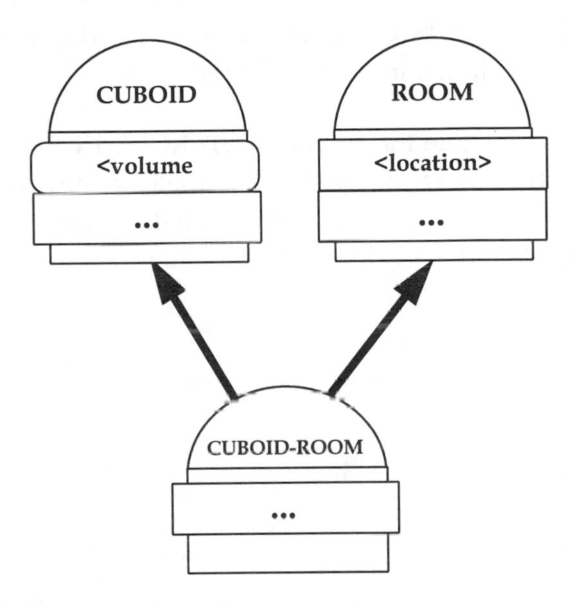

Fig. 12.10: CUBOID-ROOM inheriting multiply from CUBOID and ROOM.

This design will work in the sense that objects of class CUBOID-ROOM will understand the message **volume**. They will execute the **volume** method defined on CUBOID (where, presumably, **length**, **width**, and **height** also reside). However, as we saw in Chapter 11, such a design has the problem that CUBOID-ROOM will inherit unneeded behavior from CUBOID—for example, **rotate**. To prevent someone from using **rotate** on a cuboid room, CUBOID-ROOM's designer must override the method (and any others that aren't needed or are dangerous).

Another problem with this design is that you can't replace the class CUBOID with 3D-SHAPE, whose subclasses include CUBOID, CYLINDER, and so on. The best way to understand why not is to imagine that the designer of 3D-SHAPE had deferred the implementation of **volume** (which, in fact, is highly likely). Now, the subclass 3D-SHAPED-ROOM will inherit a **volume** method with no implementation. Not very useful! (To make this design approach work for cylindrical rooms, replicate the class-inheritance diagram of Fig. 12.10 with CYLINDER in place of CUBOID.)

Of course, the problem of having ROOM inherit from CUBOID is violation of the principle of type conformance. You could avoid all the above difficulties by having 3D-ROOM inherit from 3D-FIXED-SHAPED and ROOM. In turn, the class 3D-FIXED-SHAPED would have a variable that referred to an object of class 3D-SHAPE. This is exactly analogous to the design of RECTANGLE-IN-FRAME of Fig. 12.2, but is an overly elaborate design compared to ROOM's original design, as shown in Figs. 11.7 and 11.8.

3. Shown below is the code for one of RECTANGLE-IN-FRAME's methods, **move-within-frame**, which now moves the rectangle within the enclosing frame by means of message forwarding to a RECTANGLE object, rather than via inheritance from RECTANGLE (as in the design shown in Fig. 12.2).

```
class RECTANGLE-IN-FRAME;

  ...
  var rectangle:RECTANGLE;                        // will be initialized to point to
                                                  // the movable rectangle
  var enclosing-frame:FRAME;                      // will be initialized to point to
                                                  // the enclosing frame
  ...
  method move-within-frame (move-incr: 2D-VECTOR;);
  begin
   var allwd-move-incr:2D-VECTOR := 2D-VECTOR.new;
                                          // will hold the actual allowed move
   if        enclosing-frame.active
   then
     if     move-incr.x > 0                       // to the right in this convention
     then allwd-move-incr.x := min (move-incr.x, enclosing-frame.right - self.right);
     else   allwd-move-incr.x := max (move-incr.x, enclosing-frame.left - self.left);
     endif;

     if     move-incr.y > 0                       // upward in this convention
     then allwd-move-incr.y := min (move-incr.y, enclosing-frame.top - self.top);
     else   allwd-move-incr.y := max (move-incr.y, enclosing-frame.bottom - self.bottom);
     endif;
   else      allwd-move-incr := move-incr;     // there's no active frame at present
   endif;

   rectangle.move (allwd-move-incr;);
  endmethod move-within-frame;
  ...
endclass RECTANGLE-IN-FRAME;
```

This design has many similarities to the design of RECTANGLE-IN-FRAME shown in Fig. 12.2 (and, as code, in Section 12.1). The crucial difference, of course, is that now RECTANGLE-IN-FRAME doesn't inherit from the classes SHAPE-IN-FRAME and RECTANGLE. Instead, we have two variables (**rectangle** and **enclosing-frame**) that point to the movable rectangle and its enclosing frame, respectively.

This design retains the major advantage of the design shown in Fig. 12.2, in that the class RECTANGLE isn't encumbered with the class FRAME. However, in this design, the methods of RECTANGLE aren't automatically available to objects of class RECTANGLE-IN-FRAME. The designer of RECTANGLE-IN-FRAME must explicitly duplicate several methods of RECTANGLE (such as **rotate**) in RECTANGLE-IN-FRAME. Although the implementation of these methods will be trivial (because each one will be a single forwarded message to the **rectangle** object in the form **rectangle.rotate**, for example), this chore will be tedious. Furthermore, the design of RECTANGLE-IN-FRAME may need to be changed whenever a new method is added to RECTANGLE.

4. To answer this question in a specific way, I'll assume that local variables (that is, variables declared within a method, such as **vertex** declared within the method **v1** in the first code example in Section 12.1) are placed on the computer's stack and are removed when the method ends. This normally means that objects pointed to *only* by local variables are swept away by the garbage collector when the method ends. (Section 1.4 mentioned garbage collection of no-longer-accessible objects.) Thus, objects pointed to only within a single method don't consume memory for long; they live but an ephemeral life.

   However, in the first design of RECTANGLE (shown as code in Section 12.1), the object pointed to by **vertex** cannot simply vanish when the method **v1** terminates. Indeed, that object *must* be preserved when the method ends, because a pointer to that object is precisely what **v1** returns. Unfortunately then, if **v1** is invoked, say, 100 times, memory will fill up with, say, 60 objects. (Some objects *may* have been garbage-collected in the meantime.) This could be very inefficient of space and will be a little inefficient of time.

   The second design of RECTANGLE (shown as code at the start of Section 12.2) avoids the repeated local creation of an object within a method by keeping **v1** as an instance variable of the entire object itself. However, this design must make sure that **v1** is always up to date by obsessively updating it every time a rectangle moves. This creates quite a lot of extra code. A good compromise design would be midway between the two designs: Update **v1** only when someone asks for it and then return a pointer to **v1**, rather than a pointer to some brand-new, memory-filling object.

   Remember that since languages, compilers, and run-time environments vary quite a lot, the code in your shop's language may behave differently from my description here. However, the general point is still apt: During design, it sometimes pays to consider what will actually happen in the machine. By doing that, you may keep your design clean *and* your code efficient. That's what I aimed for in this third (compromise) design.

   Nevertheless, don't build your design efficiencies around some quirk of Version 2.3.1.2.6 of your compiler, because, when Version 2.3.1.2.7 comes out, you may be ruined. For most code, portability is more important than efficiency.

5. A designer could place the more specialized methods in the outer ring and the more general methods in the inner ring. The outer methods would then be implemented by means of messages to use the inner methods. Overloading allows different methods in the same interface to have the same name. This can be useful for implementing replicated behavior where a general method in the interface has more arguments than a similar, specialized one. However, it's often better in this situation to use different names for methods. For example, the name **sell-all-equities** is more meaningful (and safer!) than a mere **sell** with no arguments.

6. One example of a structured-design criterion is fan-out. High fan-out from an SD module often hints at a missing level in the structure-chart hierarchy. Similarly, in object-oriented design, high fan-out (say, seven or more) in a superclass/subclass hierarchy may imply classes, or even whole levels, missing from the structure. Also, if you find many messages emanating from a method, you may want to factor out a function or procedure to reduce the method's complexity. This factored-out component may also be useful to other methods in the class—or even to methods in other classes.

   Another relevant structured-design criterion is coupling. Coupling is akin to the idea of connascence of Section 8.2, but—at least as the term is usually applied—coupling refers to a less general concept than connascence does.

7. The design I showed is based on "pulling information from objects" when it is needed. This design is clean and easy to understand—but it may not execute very rapidly when you need a shipment unit's weight. A message to **SHIPMENT-UNIT::weight** may generate hundreds of messages to the objects that represent packages. To improve **weight**'s execution time, we could modify the design so that the class SHIPMENT-UNIT has a variable (say, **total-weight**) that always holds the current weight of the shipment unit. Then, **SHIPMENT-UNIT::weight** would simply return the value of that variable. The method would execute in a twinkling of the eye.

   However, to do this we must ensure that the component objects keep **total-weight** up to date: Whenever a component object is added or changes its weight, it must send a message to the shipment-unit object to inform it of the change. This would be an informative message, a message that "pushes information" into the objects that need it.

This second design, although possibly more efficient, is also more complex. Now all the component objects need to be aware of the aggregate object, which may prejudice their reusability (because they're encumbered with the machinery of another class.) Also, the aggregate object needs at least another method to capture the information passed in the informative message. Finally, if changes to package weights are frequent and messages invoking **SHIPMENT-UNIT::weight** are infrequent, then there may be little (or no) improvement in overall run-time efficiency.

Therefore, unless you have strong reasons to the contrary, design aggregate objects to obtain their information from components via interrogative ("pull") messages, rather than via informative ("push") messages emanating from the components.

8. Here are my comments on the four designs:

Design A: This design has the merit of extreme simplicity. It has the fewest classes of the four designs and is very easy to use. By this, I mean that if you have an object of class PERSON, which you refer to as **fred**, then in order to find out how many dogs Fred has, you simply write

```
freds-num-of-dogs-owned := fred.num-of-dogs-owned
```

However, the major disadvantage of this design lies in the fact that the class PERSON is encumbered with the class DOG. (As we saw in Section 9.3.3, this gives PERSON mixed-role cohesion.) In practical terms, this means that PERSON needs many "dog methods" in its interface to handle, for example, acquiring dogs and losing dogs. Imagine that we wish to place PERSON in our class library and later reuse it in a personnel application. The reusers of PERSON would be very surprised to find all the references to DOG in PERSON. Indeed, there might even be a problem getting the class PERSON to compile or link in an application that didn't also have DOG!

I would therefore recommend Design A only in situations where you have no intention of reusing PERSON in other applications.

Design B: Design B solves the mixed-role cohesion problem of PERSON in Design A by creating a class (PERSON-DOG-OWNERSHIP) to link a person and that person's dogs. Each object of that class links one PERSON object with one object of SET [DOG]. It's okay for PER-

SON-DOG-OWNERSHIP to be encumbered with PERSON and DOG, since "person-ness" and "dog-ness" are intrinsic to the notion of dog ownership. Also, intuitively speaking, **num-of-dogs-owned** is better placed as an attribute of the relationship between persons and dogs than as an attribute of person.

However, when I show Design B to a typical object-oriented programmer, his reaction is often: "This design is weird!" The reason for this response is that, to find the required number of dogs, we can no longer simply invoke an instance method on an object by writing **fred.num-of-dogs-owned**. Instead, we must invoke a class method on a class by writing **PERSON-DOG-OWNERSHIP.num-of-dogs-owned (fred)**. This method scans a table (a class variable within PERSON-DOG-OWNERSHIP that holds pointers to all the class's objects) to find the object pointed to by **fred** and the number of dogs in the associated set. For programmers only used to invoking instance methods, this approach may seem unnatural.

Another objection arises from the word "scans" in the previous paragraph: "You mean that the method has to scan an entire table. Boy, that's inefficient!" This objection may be valid; it depends on how cleverly you've designed the internals of PERSON-DOG-OWNERSHIP. (Note: You may wish to try designing this class to minimize such efficiency problems.)

Design B is a design that promotes reusability by removing unnecessary encumbrances from PERSON. However, it may suffer in efficiency. It also suffers from (what some people consider) cumbersome message syntax, the syntax of class, rather than instance, messages.

(A follow-on exercise: Could the class PERSON-DOG-OWNERSHIP be generalized so that it supports binary relationships, including many-to-many relationships, other than those between persons and dogs? If so, would the concept of genericity prove useful?)

Design C: This design, which uses the mix-in class DOG-OWNER to implement the machinery for dog ownership, has the merit of flexibility. For example, we could easily create the class DOG-OWNING-CORPORATION by having this class inherit from both DOG-OWNER and CORPORATION. This design also allows us to send a message directly to **fred** (now of class DOG-OWNING-PERSON) to find out how many dogs this person owns. (Note that the object **fred** will execute **num-of-dogs-owned** via inheritance from DOG-OWNER.) Another advantage of this design is that, since none of the classes has any mixed cohesion, the classes are likely to be easily reusable.

However, this design has a significant drawback: When we instantiate the object known as **fred**, we must instantiate it from the class DOG-OWNING-PERSON. This implies that we know that (in the real world) Fred is a dog owner and that Fred is unlikely to forsake this role. But, if Fred *does* cease to be a dog owner, then we must delete the object **fred**, making sure first that we copy the "person" information contained in **fred**. Then, we would re-instantiate **fred** as an object simply of class PERSON, using the copied information to initialize the object. The disadvantage of this, of course, is that the new "fred object" has a different handle from the old one, which could become a severe problem if there are existing references to the old object throughout the system.

A related problem occurs if Fred becomes a boat owner, a car owner, and the proud possessor of a cat. To deal with dog, cat, boat, and car ownership under this design, we may have to create up to 15 classes! (Examples would be: DOG-CAT-OWNING-PERSON, DOG-CAR-BOAT-OWNING-PERSON.)[6]

Thus, Design C is at its best in situations where roles are fixed and combinatorial explosions of classes, such as the one above, are unlikely. (A follow-on exercise: You may want to experiment with a variation on Design C, where dogs, cats, boats, and cars are subsumed under the more general term "possession," and which avoids the above explosive flaw.)

Design D: The chief distinguishing feature of this design is that a single real-world person will be represented by *two* objects in the sys-

---

[6] The basic problem here, in my opinion, is that all current mainstream object-oriented languages contain a fundamental flaw: They don't support an object's ability to acquire/lose class membership or to hold multiple class membership (apart from that implied by the inheritance hierarchy) at one time. A design approach that provides such abilities is a work-around for an object-oriented language flaw. I hope that mainstream object-oriented languages will soon provide class-migration facilities, as some object-oriented database languages are already doing. (The Iris object-oriented database has such a facility.) However, I concede that general class migration is not a trivial issue. To follow up this research topic, see, for example, [Bertino and Martino, 1993] and [Zdonik, 1990].

tem. To see this, consider again our dog owner, Fred. When Fred comes along, we'll have to instantiate an object from PERSON to hold Fred's personal information, as well as an object from DOG-OWNING-PERSON to hold **num-of-dogs-owned**, and details about Fred's dogs. The DOG-OWNING-PERSON object will refer (via an instance variable) to the PERSON object, and (via another instance variable) to a set of DOG objects.

Let's refer to one of these "Fred objects" as **fred-as-person** and to the other as **fred-as-dog-owner**. Then, to find Fred's dog count, we send the message **fred-as-dog-owner.num-of-dogs-owned**. But to find Fred's age, we send the message **fred-as-person.age**. (Note: Try embellishing the design so that **fred-as-dog-owner** forwards messages such as **fred-as-dog-owner.age** to **fred-as-person**.)

This design has a huge advantage in dynamic flexibility over Design C, by which I mean that should Fred cease to be a dog owner, then we can simply delete the object known as **fred-as-dog-owner**, while leaving the object **fred-as-person** intact. Furthermore, we can introduce cats, boats, cars, and so on without a combinatorial explosion and allow Fred to move in and out of these roles with little design or programming difficulty.

Nevertheless, this design suffers from the drawback that a single "thing" in the real world may become multiple objects in the system. Furthermore, this design lacks a reference from a PERSON object to a DOG-OWNING-PERSON object, implying that we cannot find the latter from the former.[7]

Design D works well where a real-world "thing" may have multiple roles and some roles are not permanent. However, Design D

---

[7] If we were to introduce such a reference, we would have another design, Design E, in which PERSON would again be encumbered with DOG and would lose its cohesion. However, Design E would be an excellent design approach for handling "migrating subtypes." For example, consider CUSTOMER-ORDER, an instance of which migrates from TENTATIVE-ORDER to APPROVED-ORDER, to FILLED-ORDER, and so on. The class CUSTOMER-ORDER could refer to any or all of the classes TENTATIVE-ORDER, APPROVED-ORDER, and so on, while retaining ideal class cohesion.

Jim Odell likens Design E's approach to slicing a real-world thing into a number of objects, each one capturing information about one aspect of the thing. Holding all these sliced objects together is a central "conceptual object" that points to all the slices. See [Martin and Odell, 1995].

requires senders of messages to retain handles of multiple objects, each representing a single role.

Note that the four design structures of Figs. 12.6 through 12.9 are independent of persons and dogs. In other words, they would be useful for "person owns frog," "corporation owns boat," and so on. They therefore provide examples of design patterns, set pieces that can be put to use in application after application, since they're not dependent on the specific semantics of any one application.

This exercise is typical of object-oriented design: A single analysis requirement may be designed in many legitimate ways. All four of the above designs are valid, in the sense that they can be coded, they'll run, and they'll meet the analysis requirements. Thus, your choice of which design to deploy depends on factors beyond the stark requirement itself, factors such as simplicity, flexibility, generality, or efficiency.

In object-oriented design, rarely does The One Right Answer make itself known. Instead, as a designer you must trade off the pluses and minuses of several possible designs. This book has set forth some design principles by which you can judge, and terms with which you can discuss, the merits of one design approach over another.

But, only you and your design team can ultimately decide which design is most suitable for *your* application. Have fun designing your next system!

Checklist for an Object-Oriented Design Walkthrough

This appendix contains a list of questions that will help you to hunt out common design problems during a walkthrough or inspection. You may choose to have everyone on the design team ask all the questions, or you may assign a subset of the questions to each person.

In this appendix, I haven't suggested cures for any design problems, because the purpose of the walkthrough is to *identify*, rather than to fix, problems. However, following this appendix is *The Object-Oriented Design Owner's Manual,* which suggests cures for several object-oriented design problems. If you'd like to review the basic concept of reviews (including walkthroughs and inspections), see [Freedman and Weinberg, 1990].

The questions below expose many common object-oriented design flaws. Each question addresses the design of a single class, or a group of cooperating classes, or part of a specific application. (The last six questions, in particular, address the design of an application.)

Although having a checklist will save you time in finding lurking design flaws, no checklist can be exhaustive. You should, therefore, continue to add questions to this list as you discover further recurrent design problems.

Questions

1. Should the class under review (and others like it) be built, or should it be purchased from an outside vendor? (This question is especially germane for foundation classes and many architectural classes.)

2. Does a new class really need to be built, or could an existing class in the library be modified, extended, or generalized?

3. Does the class make as much use as possible of existing classes in the library?

4. Is any connascence (including contranascence) present that's not readily apparent from the code? Where is that connascence documented?

5. Is the class so large or complicated that it's difficult to assess the connascence that exists within it?

6. Does any connascence violate the encapsulation boundaries of object orientation?

7. Does the class rely on any assumptions in order to work correctly? Do any other classes also rely on the same assumptions? How likely are those assumptions to change? Where are the assumptions documented?

8. Does the class have a degree of reusability that's appropriate to its domain?

9. Is the encumbrance of the class appropriate for its domain?

10. Is the class's context of applicability—the types of systems or situations in which it's intended to be usable—documented? Should that context be broadened by generalizing the class, or reduced by making the class more restrictive?

11. Does the class have mixed-instance, mixed-domain, or mixed-role cohesion? If so, why? If so, is any reduction in the class's reusability acceptable?

12. Is any aspect of the class's design dependent on a coding language or operating environment? If so, can that aspect be factored out? If not, is the dependence documented?

13. Is the class's invariant documented?

14. Is the class's invariant so complex that it suggests another set of core representational variables would be a better basis for the internal class design?

15. Does each of the class's methods have a documented pre- and postcondition?

16. If the class inherits from a superclass, does its type conform to the type of its superclass? That is, is its invariant at least as strong as its superclass'? For each of its methods, does the method have the same formal signature as the corresponding method in the superclass and does the method obey the principles of contravariance and covariance? If the answer to any of these questions is, "No," then why not? Is that reason documented?

17. If the class inherits from a superclass, is the principle of closed behavior followed? That is, do all methods of the superclass respect the class invariant of the subclass? If not, then what countermeasures has the designer of the subclass taken?

18. Does the class inherit any private variables or methods of a superclass? If so, why? If so, what configuration-management practices will ensure that a change to the superclass' internal design will be reflected in the subclass?

19. (This question is especially germane if the above question yielded a "Yes.") Does the subclass really capture a more specialized version of the concept that the superclass captures? In other words, does the subclass pass the *is a* test? If not, why not?

20. (This question is especially germane if the above question yielded a "No" or if the subclass cancels several inherited methods through overriding.) Is inheritance appropriate? Or would message forwarding (from the subclass to the superclass) yield a sounder class-reuse structure?

21. Is any part of the class hierarchy (superclass/subclass inheritance structure) too deep? ("Too deep" is obviously subjective, but five or more levels beneath a root class should trigger a warning.) If so, should message forwarding, rather than inheritance, be used anywhere in the hierarchy?

22. Do subclasses of a common superclass contain similar or identical features that should be moved to the superclass?

23. If the design exploits multiple inheritance, do the inherited class invariants conflict in any way in the inheriting subclass? Do any inherited names clash? Is the principle of closed behavior respected by all superclasses, or handled by the subclass? Is type conformance between superclasses and subclass obeyed (with the possible exception of deferred superclasses, such as mix-in classes)?

24. If message forwarding is used, is it appropriate? Or would inheritance yield a more efficient or maintainable class-reuse structure?

25. Does any method used by the class (or defined on the class) have a ragged SOP? If so, should other classes be extended to include that method or should the method be defined and implemented higher in the class hierarchy in order to give the method a COP?

26. For each method exploiting polymorphism, does the SOP of the variable (pointing to the target object) lie within the SOP of the method?

27. Does any message apparently need to be encased in a complicated **if**, **case**, **inspect**, or **switch** structure? If so, is this because of a poor use of object orientation (specifically, under-use of polymorphism) or because a method has a ragged SOP?

28. If the class is a generic class, is it suitably constrained (or, at least, has its constraints documented) so that, for each message within the class, the SOP of the message's variable lies within the SOP of the method?

29. If the class represents aggregate objects, are the messages between the aggregate object and its components of the correct form? In other words, have interrogative (pull) and informative (push) messages been used appropriately?

30. Do any asynchronous messages cause timing conflicts? (This question is especially important if the timing algorithm is distributed across multiple classes, or even multiple run-time objects of the same class.) Also, is the concurrency of the system so complicated that the question is difficult to answer?

31. If a broadcast message is used, is the correct subset of objects broadcast to? Is a broadcast message appropriate, or should the sender object send the message iteratively to a set of explicit objects?

32. Should the methods of the class be designed in rings in order to reduce connascence between methods and private variables?

33. Does the class's interface support illegal, incomplete, or inappropriate states? If so, why?

34. Does the class's interface support illegal, dangerous, or irrelevant behavior? If so, why?

35. Does the class's interface support incomplete behavior? If so, will that create an immediate problem, or can the incomplete behavior be tolerated for the near future?

36. Does the class's interface support awkward behavior? If so, should further behavior be added to the interface, even if that results in replicated behavior?

37. Does the class's interface support replicated behavior? If so, is that for the convenience of diverse users of the class, or has it happened by accident? If the latter, should the replicated behavior be eliminated?

38. If the class's interface *doesn't* support replicated behavior, should it? In other words, should replicated behavior (for example, restrictive methods with few arguments, as well as general methods with several arguments) be added to the interface for the convenience of users?

39. Do any methods of the class have alternate or multiple cohesion? If so, why? Should any method be replaced by two or more methods?

40. Is the class too restrictive for its current purposes, that is, the applications in which it's likely to be used?

41. Is the class too general or broad for its current purposes? In other words, does the class contain a lot of "unnecessary baggage" based on fantasy rather than firm requirements?

42. Is the design of the class difficult to generalize to meet the class's predicted purposes, that is, the applications in which it's likely to be used during the coming two years? (This question may cause long wrangles that can be resolved only by a crystal ball. Truncate such wrangles.)

43. Does the design of the class meet shop-library standards (for example, with respect to naming, sequence of arguments, and so on)?

44. Is the class documented according to shop-library standards? Does the class have (in addition to the documentation highlighted in the above questions) user documentation stating: the class's purpose and context of applicability, the use of each of its methods, the meaning of each method's argument, known inefficiencies, known defects, known oddities, and any known lack of generality?

45. Does the class have necessary auxiliary documentation, such as: the class's administration history (designer, programmer, modifiers, dates, metrics, and so on), its status (such as the fact that it's obsolete and has been replaced by another class), its physical history (location of its design, source code, compiled code, development tools used, and so on), its test history (tests carried out and results, location of test suite for current version, and so on) and the applications in which it's known to be used?

46. Consider the part of the requirements specification (produced during analysis) that the design portion under review is intended to fulfill. Does the design fulfill the spec, the whole spec, and nothing but the spec? If not, why not?

47. Are there other designs that would also fulfill the requirements specification? If so, were they considered and rejected because of maintainability, extensibility, reusability, efficiency, or some other reason? Or were they simply not considered?

48. What are the most likely changes that the users will make to the system requirements? (Again, avoid crystal-ball wrangles here.) How much impact would each one make on the design? Would it cost a great deal to carry out any of the more minor changes?

49. Does the application's human interface follow shop standards? Do the windows-navigation diagrams indicate that the system dialogue corresponds to the users' units of work? Can any changes be made to the interface to improve users' productivity?

50. If the application is distributed across processors, is the distribution appropriate? Given the system statistics (for example, rate of update, population of objects, and so on), where are the performance bottlenecks likely to arise? (This may require benchmarking to nail down precisely.) Does the design allow the partitioning to be changed after the system is deployed?

51. Finally, a couple of important questions: Can the design actually be coded? Will it work?

The Object-Oriented Design Owner's Manual

In the table that follows, I summarize the design issues that this book has covered. The first column identifies the symptom of an object-oriented design problem, and the second column covers the most likely causes of that problem. The third column identifies possible cures to eliminate each cause, while the last column points out potential dangers or ill effects that might result from the cure. Obviously, you don't want to apply a cure that's worse than the disease!

Problem symptom	Likely cause	Possible cure	Potential danger
Connascence that crosses encapsulation boundaries	Class(es) whose implementation is not properly encapsulated	Redesign class(es), paying careful attention to the classes' external interfaces	
		Avoid any reliance on a class's "accidents of implementation"	
	Use of C++ friend construct	Remove friends, replacing with connections to classes' external interfaces	
Implicit connascence	The proliferation of the same design decision across several classes	Isolate design decision into a single class, possibly creating a new class	
	Connascence that cannot easily be made explicit	Document the implicit connascence	Documentation may be inadequate or may become obsolete or lost
Large amount of potential connascence (including contranascence) that's difficult to evaluate	Class that is far too large	Break class into smaller classes	Class that no longer represents an entire abstraction
	Class hierarchy in which subclasses extensively inherit implementation details of superclasses	Use inheritance only to inherit externally visible interface of classes	May require rewriting entire library if this is a widespread problem
Poor reusability of foundation class	Design of class too restrictive	Generalize class design	Greater effort and expense of design
	Classes developed in-house	Purchase foundation-class library	May not be entirely compatible with shop's requirements, language or architecture
			Vendor reliability
Poor reusability of architectural class	Design of class too restrictive	Generalize class design	Greater effort and expense of design
	Class has mixed-instance, mixed-domain or mixed-role cohesion	Split the class into classes with ideal class cohesion	
	Shop has motley technology	Standardize shop's technology	Expense of hardware and porting software

Problem symptom	**Likely cause**	**Possible cure**	**Potential danger**
Poor reusability of business class	Design of class too restrictive	Generalize class design	Greater effort and expense of design
	Class has mixed-instance, mixed-domain or mixed-role cohesion	Split the class into classes with ideal class cohesion	
	Analysis of the class based on too-narrow segment of company	Reanalyze class in broader business context	Greater effort and expense of both analysis and design
			A class design so general that it's cumbersome to understand and maintain
			Irreconcilable business / policy differences between different segments of company
	Perception of poor reusability, because class's intended reusability unclear	Document explicitly the class's intended reusability	
Class from low domain has high encumbrance	Inappropriate method allocation, resulting in mixed-domain cohesion	Reallocate method(s) with high encumbrance to class(es) in higher domains	
	Class has mixed-domain cohesion	Split class into two (or more), each with ideal class cohesion	
	Class contains unnecessary references	Redesign class, paying attention to the Law of Demeter	
Class from high domain has low encumbrance	Class has been designed from "too fundamental" a set of classes	Use classes from library to design the class. (If such classes don't exist, design and build them too.)	Library may need to be reorganized, possibly disturbing current users of library classes
Class has mixed instance, mixed-domain or mixed-role cohesion	Class represents more than one fundamental concept	Split the class into classes with ideal class cohesion	Increase in number of classes may be deemed excessive
		Use mix-in class to create classes with ideal class cohesion	
Subclass is not true subtype of superclass	Subclass fails to obey the principle of type conformance	Redesign subclass to obey type conformance, particularly the principles of contravariance and covariance	Hierarchy of classes in the "real world" may not fully obey the principle of type conformance

Problem symptom	**Likely cause**	**Possible cure**	**Potential danger**
Behavior inherited from a superclass violates the invariant of a subclass	Subclass fails to obey the principle of closed behavior	Do not inherit violating methods in the subclass	Loss of some of the power of inheritance
		Override violating inherited methods in the subclass	
		Have senders of messages to objects of the subclass check for violations of closed behavior	Requires other classes to contain knowledge of the subclass, which creates extra code and connascence problems
		Factor superclass into two classes (CLOSED and OPEN) and have subclass inherit from CLOSED	Added complexity in class hierarchy
		Migrate an object of the subclass to another class, whose invariant will not be violated	Class migration may not be appropriate in the application
			Class migration isn't well supported in most mainstream languages
Class invariant complex and unwieldy	Core representational variables inside class allow too many degrees of freedom	Choose another internal class design with fewer degrees of freedom	May increase algorithmic complexity or preclude elegant internal class design
Subclass inheriting inappropriate methods from superclass	Inheritance used where message forwarding would be more appropriate	Forward messages from an object of the former subclass to an object of the former superclass	Design loses ability of subclass automatically to inherit new methods added later to superclass
			Possibly less efficient
Method has ragged SOP	Class hierarchy doesn't follow type hierarchy	Redesign the hierarchy following the principle of type conformance	May require rewriting entire library if this is a widespread problem
	Similar method (for example, **print**) is defined on widely different classes	(Not always a problem *per se*, but may cause mixed-domain cohesion or the problem below)	
In a message, SOP of variable denoting target object not within SOP of method	Variable of too high a class in hierarchy	Declare variable to be of lower class in hierarchy	Variable's SOP may no longer cover all the possible objects relevant to the application
	Within a generic class, the class of some objects may not be known at design time	Document at the start of a generic class the methods that a supplied class must support	Documentation alone won't *guarantee* that suitable classes will be supplied
		Constrain the supplied classes that a generic class will accept	(Eiffel is only current mainstream language that has constrained generic classes)
	Method defined too low in the class hierarchy	Define and implement method higher in hierarchy	
	SOP of method ragged	Introduce **if** statements to avoid "falling into the holes" in the method's SOP	Code may become complex and ugly and may lose power of object orientation

Problem symptom	**Likely cause**	**Possible cure**	**Potential danger**
Class interface supports illegal states	Class design reveals internal implementation	Redesign class with better encapsulation	
Class interface supports incomplete states	Poor choice of core representational variables or other poor internal design decision	Redesign class internals	
Class interface supports inappropriate states	Class designer has failed to understand the true abstraction that the class represents	Redesign the class from a solid, documented abstraction, supporting only states appropriate for that abstraction	Hackers using the class may get upset that they can no longer write tricky code exploiting the availability of inappropriate states
Class interface supports illegal or dangerous behavior	Class design reveals internal implementation	Redesign class with better encapsulation	
Class supports irrelevant behavior	Behavior that doesn't belong in the class	Move behavior to another class	
		Factor behavior into a procedural module that can be called by a method of any class	Design may be criticized for not being "object oriented enough"
Class supports incomplete behavior	Some legal behavior not supported	Generalize existing methods or add methods to support all legal behavior	
	A method has multiple cohesion	(See below)	
Class supports awkward behavior	Some legal behavior supported via multiple messages	Generalize existing methods or add methods to support all legal behavior via a single message	
Class supports replicated behavior	Some behavior supported in several different ways	Replace multiple methods, supporting replicated behavior with single, more general method	May create compatibility problems for existing users of the class
			Replicated behavior may actually be convenient, if it allows messages with fewer arguments
Large amount of connascence between methods and private variables	Implementation of core representational variables and other private variables visible to all methods	Design methods in rings	Possible slight reduction in efficiency
Method has alternate or multiple cohesion	Combined functionality within the method	Split the method into two or more methods, each with ideal (functional) cohesion	

Blitz Guide to Object-Oriented Terminology

The following table shows the approximate translations of terms that I use in this book into the terminology of some popular object-oriented languages. Since words never translate exactly across languages and since this table is necessarily concise, I don't guarantee that all cases represent an exact semantic match. Terms in parentheses are those not commonly employed by aficionados of that particular language, but which you will find in some texts on the language.

For the exact nuance of terms in a particular language, consult the manual of the language in which you're interested. Alternatively, consult [Firesmith, 1995], which provides an excellent, comprehensive list of object-oriented terms, together with their assorted definitions. In any case, please don't blame me if you go to a C++ conference and accidentally utter the object-oriented equivalent of "your father was a hamster."

This book	**C++**	**Eiffel**	**Smalltalk**
Class	Class	Class	Class
Object	Object	Object	Object
Instantiation	Construction	Creation	Instantiation
Self	This	Current	Self
Method (instance)	Member function	Feature	Method (instance)
Method (class)	Static member function	—	Method (class)
Variable (instance)	Member variable	Entity	Variable (instance)
Variable (class)	Static member variable	—	Variable (class)
Private	Private	(Private)	Private
Protected	Protected	(Restricted export)	—
Public	Public	Exported	(Public)
Message	Call	Call	Message
Sender	(Caller)	Client (simple)	Sender
Target	(Called)	Supplier (simple)	Receiver
Signature	Argument list	Signature	Argument list
Superclass	Base class	Ancestor class	Superclass
Subclass	Derived class	Descendant class	Subclass
Overloading	Overloading	—	—
Overriding	Virtual/redefinition	Redefinition	Overriding
Deferred class	Abstract class	Deferred class	Abstract class
Genericity	Template	Genericity	—

Glossary

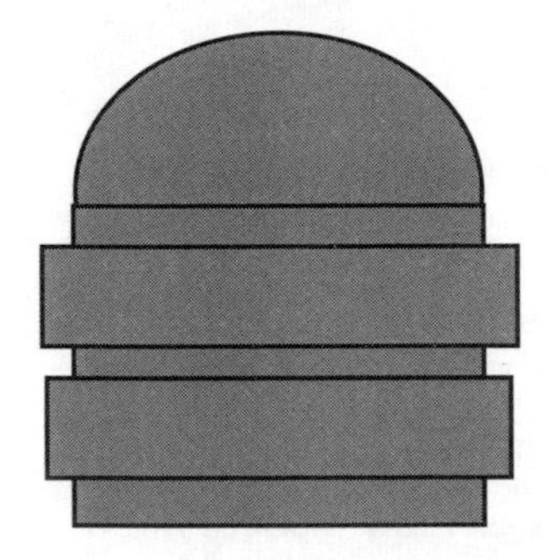

"All words are pegs to hang ideas on."

—Henry Ward Beecher
Proverbs from Plymouth Pulpit

abstract class See ***deferred class***.

abstract data-type A data-type that provides a set of values and a set of interrelated operations, and whose external definition (as seen by outside users of that data-type) is independent of their internal representation or implementation. (For example, a class is an implementation of an abstract data-type.)

accessor method A method that does not change the state of the object upon which it is executed (or, during its execution, change the state of any other object in the system).

action message An outbound message from an object resulting from the object's transition from one state to another (usually applied only to transitions represented on a state-transition diagram for that object's class).

actual argument An argument passed either to or from the target method of the message, as defined and used by the method in the sender object's class.

aggregate object An object that is composed of (pointers to) other objects. Since any realistic object may, in a sense, be considered an aggregate, this term is usually reserved for an object representing a thing in the real world that is a structure of parts.

alternate cohesion The cohesion of a method containing several pieces of behavior that are executed alternatively, depending on the value of a flag.

ancestor class Of a class C, a direct superclass of C or an ancestor of a superclass of C.

apex of polymorphism (AOP) The highest class in a cone of polymorphism.

application-class domain The group of classes (which are sometimes actually simple procedural components) whose applicability and reusability are restricted to a single application (or to a small suite of applications).

architectural-class domain The group of classes whose applicability and reusability are restricted to a single combination of hardware and software implementation technology (or to a small range of such technology).

architecture The overall hardware and software structure of a system, in particular the mapping of an essential model onto a chosen hardware and software implementation technology.

architecture model A model that represents the mapping of an essential model onto a chosen hardware and software implementation technology.

argument Information passed in a message either to or from the target method of the message. (Although the argument is usually a reference to an object, it may also be data or a reference to data.)

aspect (or ***facet*** or ***facility***) A major property of a class that allows it (or its objects) to be used in a certain context. (For example, an aspect of the class DOCUMENT is its printability.) A class may have several aspects.

asynchronous message A message whose sender object may continue to execute while the message is being processed by the target object.

attribute A term (usually) synonymous with public instance variable.

awkward behavior The property of a class interface that requires an object to carry out some state transitions via multiple messages that take the object through intermediate (but legal) states.

base class See ***superclass***.

behavior Of a class, the set of permitted transitions among states in the state-space of the class.

broadcast message A message whose sender object specifies as target objects a group of objects that fulfill a particular criterion, rather than specifying one object by means of its handle. Often, a broadcast message takes *every* object as its target.

business-class domain The group of classes whose applicability and reusability are restricted to a single business or industry. In the extreme case, this may be a single corporation or a single division within a corporation.

callback A mechanism by which the target object of a message returns the result of the message (or notification of an event occurrence) by initiating a second message, whose target object is the sender of the original message.

class A design/programming construct (a "stencil") that defines the structure (for example, methods and variables) of objects—instances of that class—that will actually be created at run-time.

class based A software environment having only object-oriented encapsulation, state retention, object identity, and classes.

class cohesion The measure of interrelatedness of the methods in the external interface of a class.

class coupling The set of connections (normally, explicit references) from one class to another class.

class-external-interface diagram A diagram that depicts a class, its methods, and the signatures of its methods.

class-inheritance diagram A diagram that depicts the inheritance relationships between subclasses and superclasses in the class-inheritance hierarchy.

class-inheritance hierarchy An organization of subclasses and superclasses that are related through inheritance.

class interface The external view of a class, specifically the following: the class's name and invariant; the name, formal signature, preconditions, and postconditions of each of the class's methods; and the externally observable state space and behavior defined by the class.

class-internal-design diagram A diagram depicting the internal design of a class, chiefly comprising the interactions among the methods and variables within the class.

class invariant Of a class C, a condition that every object of C must satisfy at all times when the object is in equilibrium.

class library A collection of classes and frameworks intended for reuse in several systems. Each class is carefully tested and is accompanied in the library by its test suite and user documentation.

class message A message that invokes a class method, rather than an instance method.

class method A method defined on a class as a whole, rather than being defined (in principle) on a single object instantiated from that class.

class migration From class A to class B by object **o**, **o**'s simultaneous loss of membership of class A and its acquisition of membership of class B. (Most object-oriented languages do not support class migration directly.)

class variable A variable defined on a class as a whole, rather than being defined (in principle) on a single object instantiated from that class.

cohesion The relatedness of elements that constitute an encapsulated unit.

component One of the objects referenced by an aggregate object.

concurrency (or ***system-level concurrency***) The ability of a system to support several loci of execution. Note that, although true concurrency requires several physical processors, concurrency may be simulated on a single processor. The latter is termed pseudo-concurrency. See also ***method-level concurrency*** and ***object-level concurrency***.

conditional [state] transition A transition on a state-transition diagram whose target state depends on the value(s) of inbound arguments, the value(s) of results of outbound message(s), the value(s) of an object's variable(s), or—sometimes—all three.

cone of polymorphism (***COP***) A scope of polymorphism that forms a complete branch in the superclass/subclass inheritance hierarchy.

confinement of behavior Of subclass S's behavior within class C's behavior, the situation where every legal transition among S's states is also a legal transition among C's states.

confinement of state-space Of subclass S's state-space within class C's state-space, the situation in which every state of S is also a state of C. (S's state-space is also said to be a subspace of C's state-space.)

connascence Between elements A and B, the property by which there is at least one change to A that would necessitate a change to B in order to preserve overall correctness.

constant A reference to an object or data value (or occasionally some other kind of element) that is fixed and therefore cannot change.

construction See ***instantiation***.

continuous variable A variable that (in principle, at least) has an infinite set of possible values, rather than a finite set of discrete values; or a variable that (in principle, at least) changes infinitely often; or both.

contranascence Between elements A and B, a form of connascence in which there is some property of A that must be held different from the corresponding aspect of B.

core representational variables Variables (usually, instance variables) used in the internal design of a class to support the class's external abstraction.

coupling The dependence of one software component upon another (or the degree thereof).

creation See ***instantiation***.

dangerous behavior The property of a class interface that requires an object to carry out some state transitions via multiple messages that take the object through intermediate (but illegal) states.

deferred class A class from which objects cannot be instantiated (normally, because the class has one or more deferred methods). A deferred class is usually used as a source for descendant classes to inherit its nondeferred methods.

deferred method A method lacking a workable implementation. Normally, a descendant class will override this inherited method with its own working method.

degrees of freedom See ***dimensionality***.

delegation A mechanism whereby an object (known as a prototype or exemplar object) permits other objects to share part or all of its state-space or behavior. Delegation is a mechanism for sharing object properties that does not require classes and inheritance. (Confusingly, some authors use "delegation" to mean message forwarding.)

derived class See ***descendant class***.

descendant class (or ***descendant*** of a class C) A direct subclass of C or a descendant of a subclass of C.

design The act of representing a chosen implementation for a set of requirements (or the resulting product thereof). Each design will possess a certain quality vector.

dimensionality (or ***degrees of freedom***) Of the state-space of a class C, the number of dimensions of the state-space of C.

dimensions Of the state-space of a class C, the set of coordinates needed to specify the state of an object of class C.

direct class-reference set Of a class C, the set of classes to which C refers directly. C refers to a class by: inheriting from it; having a variable of that class; receiving a message with an argument of that class; sending a message that returns an argument of that class; having a method with a local variable of that class; or having a friend of that class.

disnascence Between software components A and B, the absence of any connascence (or contranascence) between A and B.

domain A category determined by the range of applicability (or reusability) of a class.

dynamic binding The run-time identification of the actual component indicated by a reference. The term is normally used to describe the run-time identification of the exact method implementation that should be invoked as a result of a message.

dynamic classification The ability of an object to acquire, lose, or change its class(es) during its lifetime, without changing its handle (OID).

dynamic connascence Connascence that is defined by the execution pattern of a running system.

effective (or ***working***) ***method*** A method that is not deferred, that is, a method with a workable implementation.

encapsulation The grouping of related ideas or components into one unit, which can thenceforth be referred to by a single name. In object orientation, encapsulation usually means the grouping of methods and variables into an object or class structure, whereby the methods provide the sole facility for the access or modification of the variables. (See also ***level-0, level-1,*** and ***level-2 encapsulation.***)

encumbrance Of a class C, the size of C's indirect class-reference set. Less formally, encumbrance is the number of classes that C "needs" in order to compile, link, and run successfully.

essential event-type A predicate transition, each occurrence of which has these properties: It occurs at a finite point in time in the environment (around the system) and under the control of the environment; it is detectable by the system; and it is relevant to the charter of the system.

essential model A model of a system that depicts system requirements in a manner free of the characteristics of any particular implementation or technology. Informally, the essential model is said to assume perfect technology.

event-activity manager A (usually software) component responsible for executing the policy required on the occurrence of a given event-type.

event model An analysis model that organizes and classifies event-types and defines their associated recognizer and activity-manager components and other characteristics.

event-stimulus recognizer A (typically software) component responsible for detecting the occurrence of events of one (or sometimes more) event-types.

event thread A sequence of components responsible for dealing with the occurrence of an event. The thread begins at the event in the environment around the system and ends with the effect in the environment.

exception A serious mishap during system execution (often concerning low-level computer implementation) whose occurrence can be anticipated only in broad terms of location or time.

exception detector A component that traps an exception. (Also known as an exception thrower).

exception handler A component that prevents the system's failure or uncontrolled execution as a result of an exception. It may either recover normal execution or bring the system to a controlled halt. (Also known as an exception catcher or rescue clause).

explicit connascence Connascence that is readily apparent from a document (such as a code listing).

extensibility The property of a piece of software that allows it to be augmented or generalized by adding new software and without extensively changing the original software.

extension of behavior By a subclass S from a class C, the presence of additional behavior in S, needed to navigate the portion of S's state-space that extends from C's state-space.

extension of state-space By a subclass S from a class C, the presence of dimensions in S's state-space that are not present in C's state-space.

external dimensionality The number of dimensions (or degrees of freedom) of a class's state-space, as revealed by the class interface. It is equivalent to the dimensionality of the class, considered as an abstract data-type.

external state The ensemble of values (or, more formally, object references) that an object possesses at a given time and that are accessible outside the object (typically via accessor methods).

extrinsic B is extrinsic to A if A can be defined with no notion of B.

fan-out Of a component A, the number of references that A makes to other components. (Normally, the other components are of the same kind as one another.) Typically used in structured design for the number of modules called by a given module.

feature A term (most often employed in the Eiffel language) to encompass both a public instance method and a public instance variable.

first-order design (or ***higher-order design***) A design paradigm in which software components communicate by means of arguments with level-1 encapsulation (such as pointers to functions passed as arguments in module calls).

formal argument An argument passed either to or from the target method of the message, as defined by the method header in the target object's class.

foundation-class domain The group of classes whose applicability and reusability is unrestricted by any application, business, or technology. In other words, a foundation class has the widest possible applicability.

framework A set of collaborating classes, arranged to be able to carry out some meaningful portion of an application. (A framework is more sophisticated than a single class, but normally less sophisticated than a subsystem.) Typically, a single class in the framework has limited reusability on its own.

friend function (or ***friend class***) A C++ term for a component that, although formally defined to be external to a class C, has access to C's internals.

frozen method A method that, if inherited, cannot be overridden.

functional cohesion (or ***ideal cohesion***) The cohesion of a method dedicated to carrying out a single piece of behavior. A class's designer should aim to create methods with functional cohesion.

function-style method A method that returns an argument in its own name. It's normally (but not always) used as an accessor method.

garbage collector A component of the run-time operating environment that detects objects that are no longer referenced and removes them from memory.

genericity The construction of a class C so that one or more of the classes that C uses internally is supplied only at run-time (at the time that an object of class C is instantiated).

graphical user interface (GUI) An interface between a human and an automated system in which possible actions by the human and responses by the system are presented in the form of visual cues (such as icons).

hacking Programming without prior, formal, communicable, identifiable, or documented analysis and design.

handle An object identifier (OID) whose value (in an ideal object-oriented environment) is unique to that object in that no other object has, had, or will have a handle with that value. An object's handle is constant and is independent of the object's state.

horizontal partitioning Partitioning of a population of objects across system components (typically processors or databases) so that some objects live on one component and some on another. The term is usually applied to a population of objects belonging to the same class.

human-interface model A model defining the mapping of the essential information crossing the human-machine boundary into (typically) windows, defining also the layout of the windows, the activities carried out by the windows, the application-specific navigation among the windows, and the information passed among windows.

ideal behavior The property of a class interface that allows an object to carry out in one way state transitions that are legal for its class and only state transitions that are legal for its class. A class's designer should aim to create an interface with ideal behavior.

ideal class cohesion The property of a class that has no mixed-instance, mixed-domain, or mixed-role cohesion. A class's designer should aim to create classes with ideal cohesion.

ideal method cohesion See ***functional cohesion***.

ideal states The property of a class interface that allows an object to reach all states that are legal for its class and only states that are legal for its class. A class's designer should aim to create an interface with ideal states.

illegal behavior The property of a class interface that allows an object to carry out state transitions that are illegal for its class.

illegal states The property of a class interface that allows an object to reach states illegal for its class (that is, states that violate the class invariant).

immutable class A class whose objects are immutable objects.

immutable object An object whose state cannot change.

imperative message A message to an object that requests it to set some object (perhaps itself) or the environment to a prescribed value or state. Such a message invokes a modifier method and may also cause information to be sent to the environment to change its state. It is a future-oriented message, in that it asks the object to make some change in the immediate future.

implementation hiding An encapsulation technique whereby the encapsulated unit's externally visible interface suppresses the unit's internal details of representation, algorithm, or technology.

implicit connascence Connascence that is not readily apparent from a document (such as a code listing).

inappropriate states The property of a class interface that presents some states that are not germane to the class's abstraction.

incomplete behavior The property of a class interface that does not allow an object to carry out some state transitions that are legal for its class.

incomplete states The property of a class interface that does not allow an object to reach some states that are legal for its class.

indirect class-reference set Of a class C, the transitive closure of the direct class-reference set of C.

information hiding An encapsulation technique whereby the encapsulated unit's externally visible interface suppresses certain information available within the unit.

informative message A message to an object that informs it of the state of some object—or perhaps the environment. (Such a message invokes a modifier method.) It is a past-oriented message, in that it informs an object of what has already taken place elsewhere.

inheritance By class S from class C, the facility by which objects of class S may use a method or variable that would otherwise be available only to objects of class C, as if that method or variable had been defined upon S.

instance Of a class C, an object instantiated from C (or one that has in some other way acquired membership of C).

instance constant A constant that is (in principle) instantiated for each object of given class.

instance message A message sent to an object (as opposed to a class).

instance method A method that is instantiated (in principle) for each object of given class.

instance variable A variable that is instantiated for each object of given class.

instantiation The act (normally carried out at run-time) of creating an object.

internal dimensionality The number of dimensions (or degrees of freedom) of a class's state-space, as determined by the total dimensionality of the core representational variables in the class's internal design. It is normally reduced by class invariants to the same value as the class's external dimensionality.

internal state The ensemble of internal values that an object possesses at a given time (or, more formally, object references held by its internal variables).

interrogative message A message to an object requesting that it reveal its current state. (Such a message usually invokes an accessor method.) It is a "present-oriented" method, in that it asks an object for a current state or value.

intrinsic B is intrinsic to A if B captures some characteristic inherent to A.

irrelevant behavior The property of a class interface that supports behavior extraneous to the class.

iterated message A message that is repeatedly issued, normally to several components of an aggregate object.

iterator An operator that repeatedly issues a message, normally to several components of an aggregate object.

Law of Demeter A guiding principle for limiting the encumbrance of a class by constraining the size of its direct reference set.

level-0 encapsulation Lines of code (including data declarations) without any encapsulation.

level-1 encapsulation Encapsulation of lines of code (including data declarations) into (usually invocable) procedural modules. This is the chief level of encapsulation used in structured design.

level-2 encapsulation Encapsulation of procedural modules together with shared variables into an object module. This is the level of encapsulation used in object orientation.

literal class A class (such as INT) whose objects are literal objects. All the objects of a literal class are considered to be already instantiated and are not instantiated at run-time.

literal object A rudimentary object represented merely by its value (such as 67) and denoted by a literal (for example, "67"). It has no object handle and is invariably an immutable object.

locking See ***pessimistic concurrency control***.

logically persistent object An object able to exist after all references to its handle have been deleted.

logically volatile object An object that is deleted when no references to its handle exist.

message A request by a sender object S to a target object T that T apply one of its methods. S and T are normally distinct, although they may be the same object. (If T is a class, rather than an object, the message is termed a class message.)

message forwarding The routing of a message by the object initially receiving it to another object that is better able to process it.

message queue In a system with concurrency, a storage area for each message that an object is unable to process at the time the object receives the message.

metaclass A term, used chiefly in languages like Smalltalk, for a class whose instances are themselves classes.

method A procedural component of an object, whose procedure is executed upon the object's receipt of a message that specifies that method.

method-level concurrency Concurrency such that a single method of an object, by supporting several loci of execution, can process multiple messages simultaneously.

method postcondition A condition that must be true when a method successfully ends its execution.

method precondition A condition that must be true for a method to begin execution and to execute successfully.

method ring An informal term denoting a way to design the internals of a class so that not all methods access internal variables directly. Instead, some methods (inner methods) shield other methods (outer methods) from knowledge of some internal variables' details.

mixed-domain cohesion Of a class C, the presence of a component within C that encumbers C with an extrinsic class from a different domain.

mixed-instance cohesion Of a class C, the presence of a component within C that is undefined for at least one instance of C.

mixed-role cohesion Of a class C, the presence of a component within C that encumbers C with an extrinsic class of the same domain as C.

mix-in class A class from which objects are not normally instantiated, but which is designed to have its capabilities inherited by ("mixed in" with) other classes.

model An intentional arrangement of a portion of reality (the medium) to represent another portion of reality (the subject) such that the model represents some aspects of, and behaves in some ways like, the subject. The parts, the sets of details and the abstractions of the subject that the model encompasses, constitute the *viewpoint* of the model; the ways in which the model behaves like the subject is called the *purpose* of the model. An object-oriented design model often takes the form of a diagram, each of whose components is defined textually.

modifier method A method whose execution changes the state of at least one object in the system (normally, the object upon which the method is executed).

multiple classification The ability of an object to belong to several classes simultaneously. (The term is normally not used for properties obtained through the standard class-inheritance mechanism.)

multiple cohesion The cohesion of a method containing several pieces of behavior that are executed together.

multiple inheritance Inheritance whereby a class may have several direct superclasses.

mutable class A class, the objects instantiated from which are mutable.

mutable object An object whose state can change.

name clash A situation (typically through multiple inheritance) whereby a class or object has access to more than one component with the same name. The actual reference intended by the name must be discovered via some resolution mechanism.

navigational query A query that follows a succession of object handles (or some equivalent referents) to locate sought-after object(s).

non-inheritable method A method defined on a class C that is not available to descendants of C.

object A unit with a unique identity (separate from its state) that encapsulates procedural modules and shared variables.

object-action paradigm A term usually applied to a type of human/system interface in which the user first identifies an object and then determines which action to apply to that object.

object-aggregation diagram A diagram showing the objects to which an object of a given class refers. It is normally used to represent object structures derived from physical aggregations in the "real world."

object based A software environment having only object-oriented encapsulation, state retention, and object identity. In other words, an object-based environment lacks inheritance and the distinction between classes and objects.

object-communication diagram A diagram showing the messages passed between objects (and occasionally classes) at run-time.

object identifier (OID) See ***handle***.

object identity The property by which each object (regardless of its class or current state) can be identified and treated as a distinct software entity.

object-interaction/timing diagram A grid-like diagram that shows time on its horizontal axis, and system components on its vertical axis. Horizontal blocks within the grid represent execution times of the components (together with, optionally, components' interactions via messages, shown as vertical arrows).

object-level concurrency Concurrency such that a single object, by supporting several loci of execution, can process multiple messages simultaneously.

object module A term that refers to classes and objects indiscriminately. It is chiefly used to describe constructs in environments in which classes and objects are degenerately identical.

object oriented A software environment having "most of" the following properties: level-2 encapsulation, implementation hiding, information hiding, object identity, messages, classes, inheritance, polymorphism, and genericity (together with possible further refinements on these properties).

Object-Oriented Design Notation (OODN) A notation used to express the structure of object-oriented code. It derives from two earlier notations: Uniform Object Notation (UON) and Structured Design Notation (SDN).

object structured A software environment having only object-oriented encapsulation and state retention.

OID See ***handle***.

OODN See ***Object-Oriented Design Notation***.

operation A term (usually) synonymous with public instance method. It is also used occasionally to mean a method's external interface—name, signature, and pre- and postconditions—as opposed to the procedural code internal to the method.

optimistic concurrency control The prevention of inconsistency due to concurrency by assuming that such inconsistency will not occur and then dealing with it whenever it is discovered. (Typical techniques include time-stamping, two-phase commit, and roll-back.)

overloading The use of the same name for multiple methods (or operators) of the same class. Resolution of the ambiguity is usually by means of the signature (specifically, number and classes of arguments) of the methods.

overriding The local redefinition of the implementation of an inherited method or variable, which then takes precedence over the inherited implementation.

package A software construct that is object structured, implying that it has level-2 encapsulation but lacks both inheritance capability and any distinction between classes and objects.

parameterized class See ***genericity***.

perfect technology A hypothetical form of technology without any deficiencies or flaws, in which, for example, all processors are infinitely fast, all networks have infinite speed and bandwidth, all storage media are infinitely large, and all components are infinitely reliable.

persistent object An object that can exist for an arbitrary length of time (for example, beyond the time that all explicit references to it have ceased). The term usually implies both logical and physical persistence.

pessimistic concurrency control The prevention of inconsistency due to concurrency by assuming that such inconsistency is likely to occur and therefore taking preemptive steps to ensure that it will not. (A typical technique is locking.)

physically persistent object An object that is stored on a medium with physical permanence, such as a hard disk.

physically volatile object An object that is held in a nonpersistent medium, such as semiconductor memory.

pin-out diagram See ***class-external-interface diagram***.

pointer A variable that contains an object handle.

polymorphism Of a method, the facility by which a single method name may be defined upon more than one class and may denote different implementations in each of those classes. Of a variable, the property whereby a variable may point to (hold the handle of) objects of different classes at different times.

postcondition Of a method **m**, a condition that is true at the end of **m**'s successful execution.

precondition Of a method **m**, a condition that must be true at the beginning of **m**'s execution for **m** to execute successfully.

principle of closed behavior For a subtype S of a type T, the principle whereby the behavior of S—including that derived from T—does not violate the class invariant of any class of type S.

principle of contravariance Part of the principle of type conformance, whereby, for each method of a subtype S corresponding to a method in a type T, the precondition of **S::m** must be equal to or weaker than that of **T::m**. In particular, all the input arguments to **S::m** must either be of the same type as or be supertypes of the corresponding input arguments to **T::m**.

principle of covariance Part of the principle of type conformance, whereby, for each method of a subtype S corresponding to a method in a type T, the postcondition of **S::m** must be equal to or stronger than that of **T::m**. In particular, all the output arguments from **S::m** must either be of the same type as or be subtypes of the corresponding output arguments from **T::m**.

principle of type conformance (or ***substitutability***) For a subtype S of a type T, the situation whereby correctness is always preserved when an object of type S is provided in a context where an object of type T is expected.

private method A method that is not visible outside the class upon which it is defined.

private variable A variable that is not visible outside the class upon which it is defined.

procedure-style method A method that does not return an argument in its name. (It is often used as a modifier method.)

processor-interconnect diagram A diagram depicting the processors and their application-specific communications that result from applying computer technology to an application.

properties Of a class, the state-space and allowed behavior of the class.

protected method A method that is visible in the class on which it is defined and in descendant classes, but which is not public. (Note: The exact definition of this term tends to vary across programming languages.)

protected variable A variable that is visible in the class on which it is defined and in descendant classes, but which is not public. (Note: The exact definition of this term tends to vary across programming languages.)

public method A method that is visible outside the class upon which it is defined.

public variable A variable that is visible outside the class upon which it is defined.

qualifier (or ***scope-resolution***) ***symbol*** A symbol used to show which class a method (or, more rarely, a variable) is defined on, typically when the definition exists on more than one class. OODN uses the double colon (::) for this purpose.

quality vector A set of system qualities (such as flexibility, usability, or efficiency), each with a particular value (or priority). Each design alternative for a system (or subsystem) will possess a particular quality vector. (The chosen design is normally the one with the most appropriate quality vector for the needs of the business.)

redefinition A mechanism for carrying out overriding.

reliability The property of a piece of software that can be repeatedly depended upon to execute consistently with its specification.

repeated inheritance Inheritance in which a class may be a descendant of the same superclass by more than one route.

replicated behavior The property of a class interface that supports the same behavior in multiple ways.

rescue clause See ***exception handler***.

reusability The property of a piece of software that allows it to be deployed in more than one context (subsystem, application, organization, and so on).

ring of methods See ***method ring***.

robustness The property of a piece of software that permits it to recover without catastrophe from some modes of failure.

scanning query A query that uses a Boolean predicate to discern sought-after object(s) from other, similar objects.

***scope of polymorphism* (*SOP*)** Of a method **m**, the set of classes upon which **m** is defined (either directly or via inheritance). Of a variable **v**, the set of classes to which objects pointed to by **v** (during **v**'s entire lifetime) may belong.

scope-resolution symbol See ***qualifier symbol***.

second-order design A design paradigm in which software components communicate by means of arguments with level-2 encapsulation (such as pointers to objects passed as message arguments in object-oriented design). Object-oriented design is an example of second-order design.

self An instance constant that holds the handle of the object in which **self** is declared.

sender object An object that sends a message to another object (or to itself).

signature Of a method **m**, the name of **m**, the list of formal input-arguments to **m**, and the list of formal output-arguments from **m**. (Some authors would also include the pre- and postconditions of **m**.)

single inheritance Inheritance in which a class has at most one direct superclass.

standard method An informal term used in this book for a method that may or may not be inherited in a subclass and may or may not be overridden.

state The collection of values (or, more formally, object references) that an object possesses at a given time.

state retention The property by which an object can retain its current state indefinitely and, in particular, between activation of its methods.

state-space Of a class C, the ensemble of all the permitted states of any object of class C.

state transition (or simply ***transition***) A change by an object from one state to another state (or, possibly, to the same state).

state-transition diagram A diagram that depicts states (discrete values of some variable(s)) and the permitted transitions between those states. In object-oriented design, the state-transition diagram is often used as part of the definition of an object class. The state-transition diagram may also show inbound messages that cause transitions and outbound messages caused by transitions.

static binding The compile-time (or link-time) identification of the actual component indicated by a reference. (The term is normally used to describe the compile-time identification of the exact method implementation that should be invoked as a result of a message.)

static connascence Connascence that is defined by the lexical representation of a system (such as its source code).

Structured Design Notation (SDN) A notation (developed by Larry Constantine and others) for depicting a software design that chiefly comprises a hierarchy of procedural modules.

subclass Of a class C, a class that inherits from C.

subtype Of a type T, a type that conforms to T.

superclass Of a class C, a class from which C inherits.

supertype Of a type T, a type to which T conforms.

synchronous message A message whose sender object must suspend execution while the message is being processed by the target object.

Synthesis An approach to analyzing and designing object-oriented systems, developed and used at Wayland Systems Inc.

target method The method specified by a message.

target object An object that receives a message.

technology-interconnect diagram A diagram depicting the units of technology and their interconnections that will be used to implement an application.

trigger message An inbound message to an object that causes a transition from one state to another (usually applied only to transitions represented on a state-transition diagram for that object's class).

two-phase commit A consistency protocol especially important in systems with concurrency, in which (phase 1) an object asks each object in a group whether it's able to make some tentative change of state permanent and then (phase 2), if all objects in the group replied affirmatively, the object tells each object in the group to commit (that is, make that permanent change). If any object replied negatively, the object normally tells each object in the group to roll back (that is, forget that change of state).

type See ***abstract data-type***.

Uniform Object Notation (UON) An early forerunner of Object-Oriented Design Notation.

vertical partitioning Partitioning of a population of objects across system components (typically, processors or databases) so that some aspect(s) of each object live on one component and some aspect(s) on another. Each object is therefore physically split into parts. The term is usually applied to a population of objects belonging to the same class.

virtual function See ***deferred method***.

volatile object An object that can exist only while there are explicit references to it or while its storage medium receives electrical power. The term usually implies either logical or physical volatility.

window-layout diagram A diagram that shows the fields, buttons, and menus of a window. It is supported by a document defining the properties (such as field-validation criteria or command-button-enablement conditions) of these window components.

window-navigation diagram A diagram depicting how the users of an application may traverse from window to window through application-specific paths (usually implemented by menus and command buttons).

working method See ***effective method***.

yo-yo messaging An informal term for a design structure in which a pair of objects repeatedly exchange messages in order to accomplish some piece of an application.

zeroth-order design A design paradigm in which software components communicate by means of unencapsulated data.

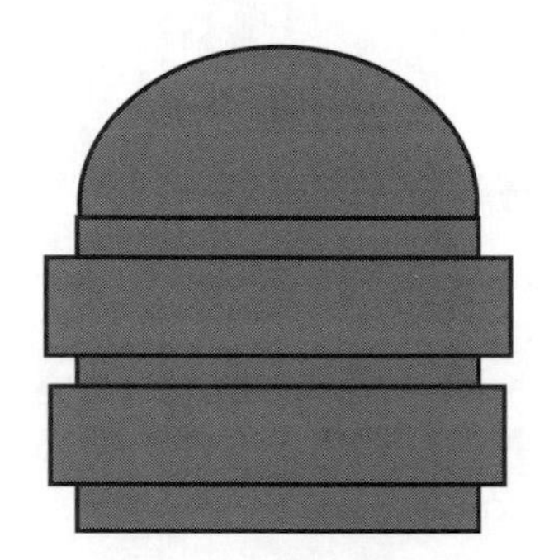

Bibliography

I refer to most of the following works in the text of the book. However, I've included other works in this Bibliography that I consider to be valuable reading on object orientation.

[Atkinson, 1991]

Atkinson, C. *Object-Oriented Reuse, Concurrency and Distribution.* Reading, Mass.: Addison-Wesley, 1991.

[Bertino and Martino, 1993]

Bertino, E., and L. Martino. *Object-Oriented Database Systems.* Reading, Mass.: Addison-Wesley, 1993.

[Booch, 1994]

Booch, G. *Object-Oriented Analysis and Design with Applications.* Reading, Mass.: Addison-Wesley, 1994.

[*Chambers'*, 1972]

Chambers' Twentieth Century Dictionary, edited by A.M. Macdonald. London: W. & R. Chambers, 1972]

[Chidamber and Kemerer, 1991]

Chidamber, S.R., and C.F. Kemerer. "Towards a Metrics Suite for Object-Oriented Design," *OOPSLA '91 Conference Proceedings*, pp. 197-211. New York: Association for Computing Machinery, 1991.

[Coleman et al., 1994]

Coleman, D., et al. *Object-Oriented Development: The Fusion Method.* Englewood Cliffs, N.J.: Prentice-Hall, 1994.

[Constantine, 1968]

Constantine, L.L. "Control of Sequence and Parallelism in Modular Programs," *AFIPS Proceedings of the 1968 Spring Joint Computer Conference*, Vol. 32 (1968), pp. 409ff.

[Cook and Daniels, 1994]

Cook, S., and J. Daniels. *Designing Object Systems.* Englewood Cliffs, N.J.: Prentice-Hall, 1994.

[Cox, 1986]

Cox, B. *Object-Oriented Programming: An Evolutionary Approach.* Reading, Mass.: Addison-Wesley, 1986.

[Dahl and Nygaard, 1966]

Dahl, O.-J., and K. Nygaard. "SIMULA—An Algol-Based Simulation Language." *Communications of the ACM*, Vol. 9, No. 9 (September 1966), pp. 23-42.

[DeMarco, 1978]

DeMarco, T. *Structured Analysis and System Specification.* Englewood Cliffs, N.J.: Prentice-Hall, 1978.

[Dijkstra, 1982]

Dijkstra, E. *Selected Writings on Computing: A Personal Perspective.* New York: Springer-Verlag, 1982.

[Embley et al., 1992]

Embley, D.W., B.D. Kurtz, and S.N. Woodfield. *Object-Oriented Systems Analysis: A Model-Driven Approach.* Englewood Cliffs, N.J.: Prentice-Hall, 1992.

[Firesmith, 1993]

Firesmith, D.G. *Object-Oriented Requirements Analysis and Logical Design.* New York: John Wiley & Sons, 1993.

[Firesmith, 1995]

_________. *The Dictionary of Object Terminology.* New York: SIGS Books, 1995.

[Freedman and Weinberg, 1990]

Freedman, D.P., and G.M. Weinberg. *Handbook of Walkthroughs, Inspections, and Technical Reviews*, 3rd ed. New York: Dorset House Publishing, 1990.

[Goldberg and Robson, 1989]

Goldberg, A., and D. Robson. *Smalltalk-80: The Language.* Reading, Mass.: Addison-Wesley, 1989.

[Graham, 1991]

Graham, I. *Object-Oriented Methods.* Wokingham, England: Addison-Wesley, 1991.

[Harel, 1987]

Harel, D. "Statecharts: A Visual Formalism for Complex Systems." *Science of Computer Programming*, Vol. 8 (1987), pp. 231-74.

[Hatley and Pirbhai, 1988]

Hatley, D.J., and I.A. Pirbhai. *Strategies for Real-Time System Specification*, 2nd ed. New York: Dorset House Publishing, 1988.

[Henderson-Sellers and Edwards, 1994]

Henderson-Sellers, B., and J. Edwards. *The Working Object.* Englewood Cliffs, N.J.: Prentice-Hall, 1994.

[Jacobson et al., 1992]

Jacobson, I., M. Christerson, P. Jonsson, and G. Overgaard. *Object-Oriented Software Engineering.* Reading, Mass.: Addison-Wesley, 1992.

[Kay, 1969]

Kay, A. *The Reactive Engine.* University of Utah, Department of Computer Science, August 1969.

[Kuhn, 1970]

Kuhn, T. *The Structure of Scientific Revolutions.* Chicago: University of Chicago Press, 1970.

[LaLonde and Pugh, 1991]

LaLonde, W., and J. Pugh. "Subclassing not= subtyping not= Is-a." *Journal of Object-Oriented Programming,* Vol. 3, No. 5 (January 1991), pp. 57-62.

[Lieberherr and Holland, 1989]

Lieberherr, K.J., and I.M. Holland. "Assuring good style for object-oriented programs." *IEEE Software,* Vol. 6, No. 9 (September 1989), pp. 38-48.

[Liskov et al., 1981]

Liskov, B., et al. *CLU Reference Manual.* New York: Springer-Verlag, 1981.

[Love, 1993]

Love, T. *Object Lessons.* New York: SIGS Books, 1993.

[Martin and Odell, 1995]

Martin, J., and J. Odell. *Object-Oriented Methods: A Foundation.* Englewood Cliffs, N.J.: Prentice-Hall, 1995.

[McConnell, 1993]

McConnell, S. *Code Complete.* Redmond, Wash.: Microsoft Press, 1993.

[Mealy, 1955]

Mealy, G.H. "A Method of Synthesizing Sequential Circuits." *Bell System Technical Journal,* Vol. 34 (1955), pp. 1045-79.

[Meyer, 1988]

Meyer, B. *Object-Oriented Software Construction.* Englewood Cliffs, N.J.: Prentice-Hall, 1988.

[Meyer, 1992]

_________. *Eiffel: The Language.* Englewood Cliffs, N.J.: Prentice-Hall, 1992.

[Moore, 1956]

Moore, E.F. "Gedanken-Experiments on Sequential Machines." *Automata Studies, Annals of Mathematical Studies,* No. 34 (1956), pp. 129-53.

[Page-Jones, 1980]

Page-Jones, M. *The Practical Guide to Structured Systems Design.* New York: Yourdon Press, 1980. Second edition: Englewood Cliffs, N.J.: Prentice-Hall, 1988.

[Page-Jones, 1991]

_________. "Object Orientation: Stop, Look and Listen!" *Hotline on Object Orientation,* Vol. 2, No. 3 (January 1991), pp. 1-7.

[Page-Jones, Constantine, Weiss, 1990]

_________, L.L. Constantine, and S. Weiss. "The Uniform Object Notation." *Computer Language,* Vol. 7, No. 10 (October 1990), pp. 69-87.

[Parnas, 1972]

Parnas, D. "Information Distributing Aspects of Design Methodology," *Proceedings of the 1971 IFIP Congress.* Booklet TA-3. Amsterdam: North-Holland, 1972.

[Porter, 1992]

Porter, H.H. "Separating the subtype hierarchy from the inheritance of implementation." *Journal of Object-Oriented Programming,* Vol. 4, No. 9 (February 1992), pp. 20-29.

[Richards and Whitby-Strevens, 1980]

Richards, M., and C. Whitby-Strevens. *BCPL—The Language and Its Compiler.* Cambridge, England: Cambridge University Press, 1980.

[Ross and Schoman, 1977]

Ross, D.T., and K.E. Schoman. "Structured Analysis for Requirements Definition." *IEEE Transactions on Software Engineering,* Vol. 3, No. 1 (January 1977), pp. 23-37.

[Sharble and Cohen, 1993]

Sharble, R.C., and S.S. Cohen. "The Object-Oriented Brewery: A Comparison of Two Object-Oriented Development Methods." *ACM Software Engineering Notes,* Vol. 18, No. 2 (April 1993), pp. 60-73.

[Shlaer and Mellor, 1992]

Shlaer, S., and S. Mellor. *Object Lifecycles: Modeling the World in States.* Englewood Cliffs, N.J.: Prentice-Hall, 1992.

[Skolnik, 1980]

Skolnik, M. *Introduction to Radar Systems.* New York: McGraw-Hill, 1980.

[Stroustrup, 1991]

Stroustrup, B. *The C++ Programming Language.* Reading, Mass.: Addison-Wesley, 1991.

[Ward and Mellor, 1985]

Ward, P., and S. Mellor. *Structured Development for Real-Time Systems.* Englewood Cliffs, N.J.: Prentice-Hall, 1985.

[*Webster's*, 1981]

Webster's Third New International Dictionary, edited by P.B. Gove. Chicago: G. & C. Merriam, 1981.

[Wegner, 1990]

Wegner, P. "Concepts and Paradigms of Object-Oriented Programming." *ACM SIGPLAN OOPS Messenger,* Vol. 1, No. 1 (August 1990), pp. 7-87.

[Wiener, 1995]

Wiener, R. *Software Development Using Eiffel.* Englewood Cliffs, N.J.: Prentice-Hall, 1995.

[Wilkes et al., 1951]

Wilkes, M.V., D.J. Wheeler, and S. Gill. *The Preparation of Programs for an Electronic Digital Computer.* Reading, Mass.: Addison-Wesley, 1951.

[Yourdon, 1989]

Yourdon, E. *Modern Structured Analysis.* Englewood Cliffs, N.J.: Prentice-Hall, 1989.

[Yourdon and Constantine, 1975]

__________, and L.L. Constantine. *Structured Design.* New York: Yourdon Press, 1975. Second edition: Englewood Cliffs, N.J.: Prentice-Hall, 1979.

[Zdonik, 1990]

Zdonik, S. "Object-oriented type evolution." *Advances in Database Programming Languages,* edited by F. Banchillon and P. Buneman. Reading, Mass.: Addison-Wesley, 1990.

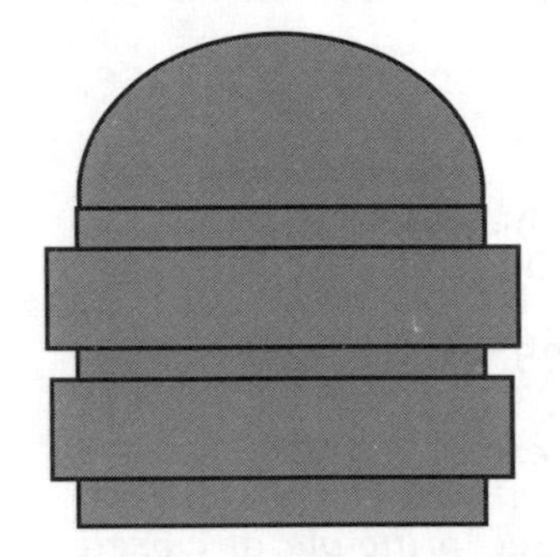

Index